THE
KNOWLEDGE
GRID Second Edition

Toward Cyber-Physical Society

THE
KNOWLEDGE
GRID Second Edition

Toward Cyber-Physical Society

Hai Zhuge

Nanjing University of Posts and Telecommunications, China
Chinese Academy of Sciences, China

World Scientific

NEW JERSEY · LONDON · SINGAPORE · BEIJING · SHANGHAI · HONG KONG · TAIPEI · CHENNAI

Published by

World Scientific Publishing Co. Pte. Ltd.

5 Toh Tuck Link, Singapore 596224

USA office: 27 Warren Street, Suite 401-402, Hackensack, NJ 07601

UK office: 57 Shelton Street, Covent Garden, London WC2H 9HE

British Library Cataloguing-in-Publication Data
A catalogue record for this book is available from the British Library.

THE KNOWLEDGE GRID
Toward Cyber-Physical Society
(2nd Edition)

Copyright © 2012 by World Scientific Publishing Co. Pte. Ltd.

ISBN 978-981-4291-77-4

Printed in Singapore by World Scientific Printers.

Foreword

The Knowledge Grid — Toward Cyber-Physical Society advances the vision of human-machine-nature symbiosis. Covering methodology as well as technologies, this innovative book aims to spur innovation.

First, the book puts forward a complex semantic space model that targets the effective management of diverse resources. This is enabled by an integration of a semantic link network model and a resource space model into a unified semantic framework that supports the fundamental concepts of generalization and specialization through multi-dimensional classifications, and also supports important aspects such as semantic self-organization, community discovery, and complex reasoning. The resulting framework offers a semantic foundation for the management of resources. Second, it advances a self-organizing, semantic environment for the sharing and management of knowledge that features a knowledge flow model, social networking methods and principles, and semantic peer-to-peer networking mechanisms.

While the first edition of this book introduced the methodology, models, and technologies, the present edition extends these within the context of the cyber-physical society, which concerns not only cyber-space, but also the physical and social spaces. The book reports on a range of disciplinary innovations that relate in different ways to semantics, knowledge, and intelligence. As a result, the book can inspire novel research in different fields, which may in turn result in new technologies that benefit humanity. I recommend the book to anybody with a deep interest in human-machine-nature symbiosis and its advancement.

Christian S. Jensen
ACM Fellow, IEEE Fellow, Aarhus University, Denmark

Preface

Exploring the source and essence of knowledge and intelligence, promoting knowledge generation and sharing, facilitating knowledge management, and extending human intelligence are the grand scientific challenges.

The Internet connects computers all around the world to support data transmission. The Web makes informative pages conveniently available to Internet users everywhere. The initial aim of the Knowledge Grid is to facilitate knowledge sharing and evolution by meaningfully linking and efficiently managing globally distributed resources.

The Knowledge Grid is an optimized human-machine environment, and will be a large-scale man-machine-nature symbiosis environment, where people, society, artifacts, minds, and nature can productively coexist and harmoniously evolve. It stands for the ideal of a live, autonomous, humanized, efficient, systematic, optimal, harmonious, and sustainable social environment.

The Knowledge Grid bases its methodology on multi-disciplinary thinking because any single disciplinary method cannot solve the issues in this complex environment. Recognizing the essence, source and principle of knowledge and mind is essential to implementing the Knowledge Grid.

The 1st edition of this book published in 2004 actually founded a specific research area. The 2nd edition completes its theory, model and method by significantly enhancing previous contents and increasing four chapters (Chapter 7, 8, 9, and 10). Applications and philosophical discussion are added to help render the ideas.

This new edition puts the Knowledge Grid research into the Cyber-Physical Society environment consisting of cyber space, physical space, socio space and mental space. The ideal goes beyond the scope of the Web, Grid computing, cloud computing, Internet/Web of Things, cyber-physical systems, social network, smart Grid, and machine intelligence.

The research work was supported by many foundations and organizations, especially the Key Discipline Fund of National 211 Project (Southwest University: NSKD11013), the Natural Science Foundation of Chongqing (cstc2012jjB40012), the Chongqing Municipal Government, the National Science Foundation of China (61075074), National Basic Research Program of China, the Nanjing University of Posts and Telecommunications, and scholar programs of Ministry of Education of China and Chinese Academy of Sciences.

I would like to thank joint and visiting professorships from the Southwest University in China, the University of New Brunswick in Canada, the University of Hong Kong, the University of Queensland in Australia, and the Kyoto University in Japan.

I sincerely thank the members of the Knowledge Grid Research Group at the Key Lab of Intelligent Information Processing, Institute of Computing Technology in Chinese Academy of Sciences for their cooperative work, especially my former students Xiaoping Sun, Xue Chen, Xiang Li, Liang Feng, Junsheng Zhang, Yunchuan Sun, Yunpeng Xing, Ruixiang Jia, Weiyu Guo, and Bei Xu.

I would like to take this opportunity to thank my parents, parents in law, and daughter. Special thank gives to my wife for her consistent support at every stage of my academic career.

Finally, I hope this book will help in promoting research of the Knowledge Grid and the Cyber-Physical Society.

Hai Zhuge
Spring in 2012

Contents

Chapter 1

The Knowledge Grid Methodology

The development of science and technology has extended human behavior and sensation, accelerated the progress of society, and enabled people to understand the physical space and themselves more profoundly. But, we still have much to find out, especially about knowledge.

What is knowledge?

How is knowledge generated?

How does knowledge evolve?

Can knowledge be inherited?

How is knowledge shared effectively?

How is knowledge stored and retrieved?

How to enable machines to obtain knowledge so that they can act intelligently?

How to create an environment to enable, facilitate, or improve knowledge creation, evolution, inheritance, sharing and service?

These are fundamental philosophic, scientific and technologic issues relevant to the Knowledge Grid methodology.

1.1 The Knowledge Space — Knowledge as a Space

Knowledge is a multi-dimensional complex space, where dimensions emerge, evolve structures (from simple to complex, or from complex to simple at higher abstraction level), and influence each other. A

1

dimension can be viewed as a space, and a space can be viewed as a dimension. The dimensions include time, the physical space, the socio space, and the mental space. Each space includes individuals, structures, rules and statuses. The mental space reflects the other spaces, builds mental semantic images, and carries out reasoning while various individuals interact with each other. A point in the space is the reflection of a set of individuals, which share one set of projections on all dimensions.

According to the new notion, knowledge is not just in the mental space, it is reflected by the cyber space, physical space and social space, and it evolves with the interaction between individuals in various spaces. Minds can reflect, discover and link knowledge in these spaces through experiencing and thinking. Machines can help discover some rules in the cyber space by statistical approaches.

The knowledge space has the following characteristics.

(1) *There are multiple origin points.* The first one is the generation of the physical space and time. The generation of mind and society is the remarkable point of the development of human beings.

(2) *A dimension can be linear or nonlinear structure of coordinates.* A coordinate can be a tree structure. A dimension can be as simple as time or as complicated as a large-scale complex system. A dimension can be regarded as a space.

(3) *Projections of points on dimensions evolve with time.* Some points do not have projections on some dimensions at certain time. For example, some rules in the physical space have no projection on the dimension of the mental space. Therefore, these rules are currently unknown.

(4) *Projection on some dimensions may concern a complex process.* For example, the projection of a point onto the dimension of the mental space involves in a complex process of perception, learning, communication, association, and reasoning.

(5) *Knowledge transition between individuals also involves in the processes in and through multiple spaces.*

Fig. 1.1.1 depicts a knowledge space, where O_0 denotes the origin of generating the universe and time, and O_h denotes the origin of generating the mental space and the social space. The generated spaces evolve with time according to different rules.

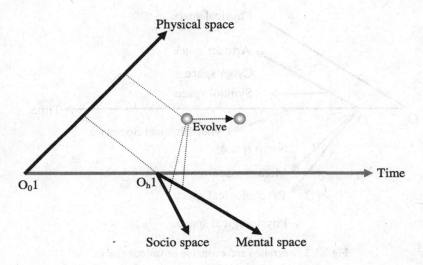

Fig. 1.1.1 A macroscopic knowledge space.

This notion of knowledge space extends the generation of knowledge not only to the origin of the mental space and the socio space but also to the origin of the physical space and time. The notion implies that knowledge is not only subjective but also objective, not only in individual mental processes but also in social processes. The links between knowledge points in and through spaces play an important role in forming and evolving the space structure.

This knowledge space notion opens new door to explore knowledge.

The generation of any space accompanies the creation of its dimensions. The evolution of spaces accompanies the expansion or shrink of dimensions. *A dimension can be viewed as a space from its coordinates. A space can be viewed as a dimension from its super-space.*

Fig.1.1.2 depicts the generation of new spaces through time. The socio space, mental space, psychological space, physiological space, and artifact space are generated largely at the same time, and then they evolve and influence each other continuously.

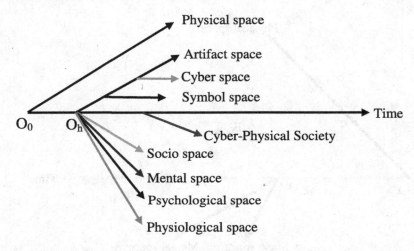

Fig.1.1.2 Generation and evolution of various spaces.

With the development of society, the artifact space keeps including new artifacts. The remarkable artifacts in the history include stone tools, iron tools, steam engines, electricity, computers, and the Internet. The cyber space is separated from the artifact space with the development of the Internet, World Wide Web and various communication devices.

The physiological space is a complex system that provides nutrition and energy for behaviors and generates the physiological motivation (e.g., generating the motivation of eating). It links self, mind and behaviors. Linking the spaces enable individuals to intelligently behave in the physical space and in the socio space. For example, it is hard for people to imagine the taste of Chinese foods without tasting them. That is, without the experience in the physical space, physiological space and psychological space, a knowledge point (a point in the knowledge space) cannot coordinate the projections into different spaces and cannot make the projection in the mental space.

These spaces can be abstracted as various networks consisting of various types of nodes and links. For example, the socio space can be abstracted as a network of human individuals and social relations, the physical space can be abstracted as a network of physical objects and relations reflecting social relations and distances or gravity in the physical space, the mental space can be abstracted as a network of concepts and semantic links (e.g., co-occur and cause-effect), and the symbol space can be abstracted as a network of symbols and the relations between symbols. There are multiple networks in the same space. Different networks obey different rules of connection. Links between individuals in different spaces (e.g., the correspondence between concepts, symbols and physical objects) connect these spaces.

The relation between mind and time was studied (B. Libet, Mind Time, Harvard University Press, 2005). Unconscious autonomous behaviors were found. From the viewpoint of cyber-physical-social intelligence, this is the effect of the physiological space. Relevant research helps understand the formation, effect and rules of knowledge and intelligence.

The physical space can contain various sub-spaces. Humans have created many artificial spaces that provide various services. One artificial space can contain the other. An artificial space belongs to both the physical space and the social space because they have both physical characteristics and social characteristics.

Some artificial spaces such as house, car, train and plane are for long-term use. Some artificial spaces such as meeting, matching and queuing are temporal for work and live. People constantly move from one space into another by making use of the functions of various spaces to fulfill various purposes in lifetime. Fig. 1.1.3 depicts the process of using some artifact spaces when traveling from home to conference hotel.

With more and more spaces being created, human behaviors are becoming more and more space-oriented, and have been extended and restricted by the capacities of various spaces.

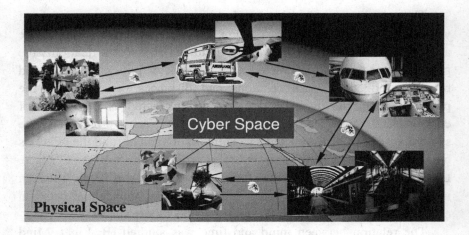

Fig. 1.1.3 The process of using various artificial spaces when traveling.

Various artificial spaces will be connected to the cyber space so that the statuses of the spaces including the statuses of physical parameters, functions, and inside individuals can be accessed and controlled under certain conditions. This is very useful for searching particular individuals with the space in some cases like security because individuals with various spaces are different from individuals or spaces. For example, person in car is different from person in plane. A hijacked plane could be remotely controlled in time through the autopilot system in the cyber space. The person who asks for help can be detected together with the space in time so that appropriate measures can be taken, because different spaces need different measures.

Newly created spaces such as new telescope and space craft could provide new means for humans to explore and reflect the physical space and therefore generating new knowledge. The process of creating spaces and using space is the process of generating and verifying knowledge.

Spaces can also be conceptual, including various mathematical theories and models as well as literature works.

The knowledge space evolves with the expansion and evolution of various artifact spaces through the interaction between the physical space and the mental space.

The cyber space will be able to reflect the temporal spaces (the status, structure and rules) for efficient retrieval. New spaces like the cyber-physical-social space will be generated with the interaction between the cyber space, physical space, psychological space, physiological space, socio space, and mental space.

Regarding knowledge *as a space implies that all knowledge operations should be on the knowledge space or a point in the space, and that the space evolves with the evolution of its dimensions and various interactions between individuals (including subjects and objects) in the space.* This raises new scientific problems for studying AI, especially in knowledge acquisition, reasoning, using, and explanation.

In contrast, information is objective, and it reflects the status or formation process of objects.

According to this notion of knowledge, any question and answer should enable the involved individuals to link to a set of relevant points in the knowledge space. Answers to a question at different times may be different due to the evolution of the knowledge space.

Traditional symbol representation of knowledge is limited in ability to represent knowledge effectively because the symbol space is just one dimension of the knowledge space. On the other hand, static representation is hard to reflect the evolution of the knowledge space.

To represent knowledge needs multiple types of links so that symbols can be linked not only to symbols but also to the individuals, behaviors, events and classes in multiple spaces (H.Zhuge, Semantic linking through spaces for cyber-physical-socio intelligence: A methodology, *Artificial Intelligence*, 175(2011)988-1019). Chapter 2 will further study this issue.

In the proposed models and methods, knowledge refers to the knowledge space or a point in the knowledge space.

1.2 The Cyber Space

To create an ideal cyber space is the common ideal of computer scientists.

Bush introduced the ideal of memex, which could browse and make notes in an extensive on-line text and graphical system, and contain a very large library, personal notes, photographs and sketches, and several screens and a facility for establishing a labeled link between any two points in the entire library (V. Bush, As We May Think, *The Atlantic Monthly*, 176(1)(1945)101-108). Since then, scientists have been pursuing an ideal cyber space.

Gray proposed the notion of personal memex and world memex. The personal memex can record everything a person sees and hears, and can quickly retrieve any item on request. The world memex can answer questions about the given text and summarize the text as precisely and quickly as a human expert in that field (J. Gray, What Next?: A Dozen Information-Technology Research Goals, *Journal of ACM*, 50(1)(2003) 41-57). He raised a challenge aim of enhancing the cyber space.

The Internet and the World Wide Web are milestones of developing the cyber space. A global cyber space is forming with continuous development and fusion of the Internet and various sensory and mobile devices. People have become increasingly reliant on it for supporting modern work and life. For example, scientists are linked one another by many Web-based systems such as email, net conversation, net forums, blogs, and facebook, share their experimental data and research results through Web 2.0 or on personal or corporate websites, and retrieve technical reports and scientific papers of interest to them from online digital libraries or from less formal websites using general-purpose search engines or vertical search engines.

Web 2.0 is an interactive information sharing platform based on the Web. Social-networking sites like facebook, video-sharing sites, wikis, blogs, mashups and folksonomies are its examples. It enables users who do not know any markup language to easily publish symbols on the Web. Wikipedia has become the largest web-based multilingual encyclopedia. Its contents are contributed and freely accessible by Web users. The other characteristic is its massive effect, which accelerates the formation of online communities. Some researchers have used the Wikipedia as a collective knowledge base to improve current approaches.

Database system research will evolve with the development of the computer architecture, software architecture, and computing model. Traditional data management in a single system may be changed to the management of semantics-rich contents and services in the cyber space. One of the research issues suggested by the Claremont report

(*Communications of the ACM*, 52(6)(2009)56-65) is to develop non-relational data models.

The exponential growth and intrinsic characteristics of the cyber space and its resources prevent people from effectively and efficiently sharing contents. Much effort has been put into solving this problem with but limited success. In any case it is hard for the cyber space to provide intelligent services because the representation of its resources does not support machine understandable semantics.

With the development of communication facilities and Web applications, computing is developing from individual to group and social behavior, from closed to open systems, from simple and centralized to complex and distributed computing, and from static computing to dynamic and mobile services of content, computing and knowledge.

1.3 Effort Toward Intelligent Interconnection Environment

Modern communication facilities such as the Internet and mobile devices provide people with unprecedented social opportunities and technical basis for promoting knowledge generation, sharing, inheritance and management. However, our increasing computing power and communication bandwidth do not of themselves improve this knowledge generation, sharing, inheritance and management. To deal with this, a new environment is needed, and the semantic ability of the facilities that project, transmit, store and evolve knowledge must be improved.

Turing described computer intelligence as a machine that can learn from experience and can alter its own instructions (A. M. Turing, Computing Machinery and Intelligence, *Mind*, 59(236)(1950)433-460). So far, machines still do not have these abilities.

Engelbart proposed a conceptual framework for the augmentation of man's intellect (D. C. Engelbart, A Conceptual Framework for the Augmentation of Man's Intellect, In Vistas in Information Handling, vol.1, Spartan Books, London, 1963). He designed the system H-LAM/T (Human using Language, Artifacts, and Methodology, in which he Trained). His aim is still significant in current artificial intelligence research.

Improving social interaction would help improve knowledge creation, evolution and sharing in our society by supporting and optimizing social activities at multiple levels (both the physical level and the mental level) and in multiple environmental spaces (cyber space, physical space, mental space, and socio space).

To overcome the deficiencies of the cyber space, scientists and developers are making great effort towards an intelligent interconnection environment. These efforts lie in the following categories:

The first is on the Web includes the *Semantic Web*, *Web Service*, *social Web*, *Web x.0* and *Web of things*, which aim to improve the current Web to different extents.

The second includes the *Grid computing* and *Cloud computing*, which aim at building a new computing platform over the Internet to provide advanced computing services from optimization and economy point of view.

The third is *Peer-to-Peer (P2P) computing*, which enables resource sharing in an egalitarian, large-scale and dynamic network.

The fourth is the *Mobile Web* and *Second Life*, which enable people to interact and share information cross geographical space through wireless and virtual roles. Time and space information is critical in these applications.

Recent developments indicate that all are indeed moving to closer targets.

The fifth is the Cyber-Physical Society, the Cyber-Physical Socio Environment, or the Cyber-Physical-Socio Intelligence (www.knowledgegrid.net/~h.zhuge/CPS.htm), which is to link the cyber space, physical space, socio space and mental space to extend human ability in these spaces.

Semantics is the basis for building intelligent applications on the Web. The *Semantic Web* is to support cooperation between Web resources by establishing ontological and logical mechanisms in standard markup languages like XML (eXtensible Markup Language, www.w3.org/XML), RDF (Resource Description Framework, wwww.w3.org/RDF), and OWL (Web Ontology Language, www.w3.org/TR/owl-features/) to replace HTML (HyperText Markup Language) and to allow Web pages to hold the descriptions of their contents. Research integrates the development of Web standards with such areas as data modeling, artificial intelligence, data mining and information retrieval. The linked data suggested by Tim Berners-Lee is a technique of exposing, sharing, and connecting data via URIs on the Web. It employs RDF and HTTP (Hypertext Transfer Protocol) to publish structured data on the Web and to connect data between data sources, allowing data in one data source to be linked to data in another data source.

The Web provides the opportunity for the development of traditional information technologies. Many applications have been done on the Web by using artificial intelligence and information processing technologies such as symbolic reasoning, logics (e.g., description logics), text mining, text summarization, information extraction, and information retrieval.

The *Web Service* is to provide an open platform for the development, deployment, interaction, and management of globally distributed e-services based on Web standards like UDDI (Universal Definition Discovery and Integration) and WSDL (Web Service Description Language, www.w3.org/TR/wsdl). It enables the integration of services residing and running in different places. Intelligent agent technique can be used to implement the active Web services. Service-oriented architecture (SOA) is to support the development of service-oriented applications. It has been widely accepted in software engineering. To systematically study service systems as a complex system, service science is introduced as a discipline cross computer science and management science.

The idea of *Internet of Things* and *Web of Things* is to integrate versatile things in the world into the Internet and Web so that things can be accessed via the standard Internet/Web protocols. The problem is that the things become digital Web resources like Web pages once they are represented by a certain language (Internet/Web languages) on certain aspect. Most physical characteristics will disappear. So, *the key should be the interaction between things rather than just representation or integration of things.*

Web 3.0 was suggested to incorporate some characteristics of the Web, Semantic Web and artificial intelligence. Web x.0 would be the trend of Web research community. Web science is introduced by summarizing relevant research works on the Web (T. Berners-Lee, et al., A Framework for Web Science, Now Publishers Inc, 2006).

The aim of the global *Grid* is to share, manage, coordinate, schedule, and control distributed computing resources, which could be machines, networks, data, and any types of devices. The ideal of the Grid is that any compatible device could be plugged in anywhere on the Grid and be guaranteed the required services regardless of their locations, just like the electrical power grid. Grid computing initially does not use Web technologies. The Grid architecture has become the service-oriented Open Grid Services Architecture (OGSA), in which some features of Web Service can be plainly seen (I.Foster, et al., Grid Services for Distributed System Integration, *Computer*, 35(6)(2002)37-46; I. Foster and C.Kesselman, The grid2: blueprint for a new computing infrastructure, Elsevier, 2008).

The *Peer-to-Peer* networking should work not only at the computing level but also at the semantic level. How to automatically map a semantic space into a peer-to-peer network is an important research problem that must be solved before the gap between the peer-to-peer network and high-level intelligent applications can be bridged (D. Schoder and K. Fischbach, Peer-to-Peer Prospects, *Communications of the ACM*, 46(2)(2003)27-29; H.Zhuge and X.Li, Peer-to-Peer in Metric Space and Semantic Space, *IEEE Transactions on Knowledge and Data Engineering*, 19 (6) (2007) 759-771; H.Zhuge and X.Sun, A Virtual Ring Method for Building Small-World Structured P2P Overlays, *IEEE Transactions on Knowledge and Data Engineering*, 20 (12) (2008) 1712-1725).

The *Semantic Grid* (H.Zhuge, Semantic Grid: Scientific Issues, Infrastructure, and Methodology, *Communications of the ACM*, 48(4)(2005)117-119) attempts to incorporate the advantages of the Grid, Semantic Web and Web Service approaches. By defining standard mechanisms for creating, naming, and locating services, the Semantic Grid can incorporate peer-to-peer technology under Open Grid Service Architecture OGSA, and so it enables autonomous computing objects to cooperate in a network of equals and with scalability.

The *Cloud computing* is becoming hot in recent years. There are several different views. According to IBM's report, cloud computing is user-oriented and offers highly efficient acquisition and delivery of IT and information services. It is characterized by massive scalability, superior user experience, and Internet-driven economics. Some views refer it to both the applications delivered as services over the Internet and the hardware and system software in the data centers that provide those services. Cloud computing views infrastructure, platform and software as a service (SaaS). An obvious benefit is the reduction of cost for users. Different from Grid computing, cloud computing obtains the support from industry sector. In 2009, several UC Berkeley professors proposed their visions on cloud computing "Above the Clouds: A Berkeley View of Cloud Computing". Cloud computing can be seen as the development of client/server architecture and the implementation of McCarthy's ideal that computation may someday be organized as a public utility, which was pointed out in 1960. It would be interesting to integrate Cloud computing, Grid computing, and P2P computing to benefit from all of their advantages.

The *Mobile Web* enables users to access Web contents by mobile devices. The number of mobile Web users surpassed the number of PC-based Internet users for the first time in 2008. Besides the reliability and accessibility issues, how to map the data formats of content providers onto the specifications of mobile devices is an implementation issue. The approaches to index moving objects have been studied (D.P.Foser, C.S. Jensen, and Y.Theodoridis, Novel Approaches to the Indexing of Moving Object Trajectories, VLDB2000, pp.395-406). The mobile Web changes the information sharing paradigm. A changing physical location and the context become important factors of mobile information services. A context includes computing environment, social environment, and physical environment. Capturing context in real time and representing context is critical for context-aware applications, but machines are limited in ability to make sense on context as they only behave according to human instructions.

The *Second Life* is to establish an online interactive 3D virtual space mixing the real-world objects and virtual objects. Objects and events in the virtual world may be captured from the physical world by various sensors and mobile devices. Interaction in the mixed space may influence both the virtual world and the real world. A key technical issue is how to manage large amount of events and communications among concurrent users. The Second Life will play an important role in training and entertainment. It may form a virtual society mirroring the real society. So far, it is still at the level of man-machine interaction.

The National Science Foundation CPS Summit defines Cyber-Physical Systems as *physical and engineered systems whose operations are monitored, coordinated, controlled and integrated by a computing and communication core.* Researchers from multiple disciplines such as embedded systems and sensor networks have been actively involved in this emerging area. In the future, infrastructure will be regarded as a service (IaaS).

Different from the Cyber-Physical Systems, the Cyber-Physical Society focuses more on human and society. The integration of the physical space, cyber space and mental space was early envisaged in the *future interconnection environment* (H.Zhuge, The Future Interconnection Environment, *Computer*, 38(4)(2005)27-33) as follows: *"The physical, virtual, and mental worlds will interact and evolve cooperatively"*. The physical world was defined as *nature, natural and artificial materials, physical devices, and networks.* The virtual digital world was defined as *the perceptual environment constructed mainly through vision (text, images, color, graphs, and so on) and hearing, and to some extent touch, smell, and taste.* The mental world was defined as *ideals, religions, morals, culture, arts, wisdom, and scientific knowledge, which all spring from thought, emotion, creativity, and imagination.*

The physical space provides the material basis for the generation and evolution of human beings and civilization. The progress of human society created the cyber space, which is linking the physical space and the other spaces to form a complex space. Human abilities will be extended in the complex space.

1.4   Challenge and Opportunity

The development of operating systems, advanced languages, and database systems were crucial events in computing history, and were also very important to the success of personal computing. The Internet and its applications are moving towards a scalable computing. But, the current Internet application platform is still far from an ideal intelligent interconnection environment.

Demanding application requirements provide researchers with many challenges and opportunities. Complex, mobile, intelligent and personalized applications require the support of completely new data models (e.g., the model based on multi-dimensional classifications H.Zhuge and Y.Xing, Probabilistic Resource Space Model for Managing Resources in Cyber-Physical Society, *IEEE Trans. on Service Computing*, http://doi.ieeecomputersociety.org/10.1109/TSC.2011.12), programming languages, operating systems and computing platform to support massively distributed sharing, coordination, deployment, parallel execution and management of dynamic services and resources, and the implementation of applications that are beyond the ability of the current Internet.

Fig. 1.4.1 depicts the evolutionary trend of computing, where WoT/IoT (Web of Things or Internet of Things), Web x.0, and Cyber Physical Systems (CPS) would extend to the phase of Cyber-Physical-Socio-Mental Environment CPSME, which contains the cyber space, physical space, socio space and mental space.

The intelligent interconnection environment (Cyber-Physical-Socio-Mental Environment) can exhibit its potential if it can be based on an advanced computing platform, which supports new resource organization models, new computing models, and new networks incorporating the Internet with information capturing, mobile, and wireless devices.

A key component of the new computing environment is the *interactive semantics* that enables interaction among services, humans, and platforms (H.Zhuge, Interactive Semantics, *Artificial Intelligence*, 174(2010)190-204). The improvement of computing architecture can improve the approach to efficiently obtain information, but it does not help understand information, neither the interaction among various resources. *The interactive semantics regards interaction as the foundation of generating semantics in society.* This proposition was then partially explained by social scientists (L.G.Dean, R.L.Kenda, S.J.Schapiro, B.Thierry, and K.N.Laland, Identification of the Social and Cognitive Processes Underlying Human Cumulative Culture, *Science*, 335(6072)(2012)1114-1118).

The future computing environment will evolve in a multi-dimensional space as shown in Fig.1.4.1.

A computing environment can have mappings at different dimensions. Mapping a computing environment into the physical dimension can obtain the physical characteristics, relations and measures. Mapping a computing environment into the social dimension can get the social characteristics, relations and measures.

This model puts the evolution of the computing environment into the multi-dimensional space for the first time, therefore opens a new door to studying the future computing environment.

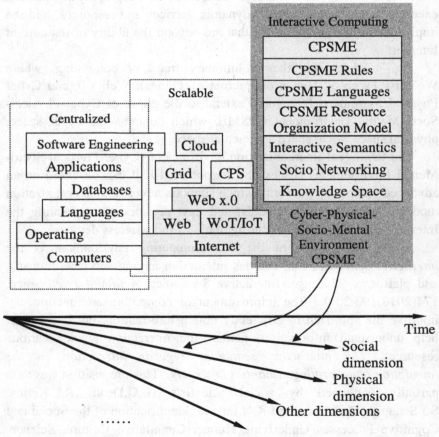

Fig.1.4.1 Evolution of computing environments in a multi-dimensional space.

The *Cyber-Physical Society* is defined as a *multi-dimensional complex space that generates and evolves diverse subspaces to contain different types of individuals interacting with, reflecting or influencing each other directly or through the cyber, physical, socio and mental subspaces. Versatile individuals and socio roles coexist harmoniously yet evolve, provide appropriate on-demand information, knowledge and services for each other, transform from one form into another, interact with each other through various links, and self-organize according to socio value chains. It ensures healthy and meaningful life of individuals, and maintains a reasonable rate of expansion of individuals in light of overall capacity and the material, knowledge, and service flow cycles* (H.Zhuge, Semantic linking through spaces for cyber-physical-socio intelligence: A methodology, *Artificial Intelligence*, 175(2011)988-1019; H.Zhuge, Cyber Physical Society, 1st *International Workshop on Cyber-Physical Society*, in conjunction with the 6th *International Conference on Semantics, Knowledge and Grids*, 2010, China).

The *cyber space* consists of various devices and digital resources, mechanisms for transforming digital resources through the devices, and various structures and algorithms for efficiently providing rich services for humans. The Web has become the largest cyber space in the world containing rich contents in various languages.

The *physical space* contains physical resources (or objects) evolving, moving and transforming from one form into another according to physical laws. Resources can be linked through such relations as distance and gravity or classified from physical structures or features.

The *socio space* includes individuals (human, agent, behaviour, event, etc), structures, and rules. Individuals are self-organized into classes according to economic, politic, or cultural statuses. Social networks can be a complex network with complex flows through complex nodes.

The *mental space* reflects various individuals in different spaces as semantic images, and operates the semantic images. The basic semantic image is concept. Concepts can be composed to form commonsense, rules, methods and theories. Chapter 2 will further discuss this issue.

The cyber space, physical space, socio space, and mental space will cooperate with each other in the cyber-physical society. Different spaces can explain specifically on what, where, why, when, and how.

1.5   The Knowledge Grid Environment

1.5.1 *The notion*

The ideal of the Knowledge Grid is to foster knowledge creation, evolution, inheritance, and sharing in a sustainable environment of humans, events, physical objects, cyber resources, machines and roles (H. Zhuge, China's e-Science Knowledge Grid Environment, *IEEE Intelligent Systems*, 19(1)(2004)13-17; H.Zhuge, The Future Interconnection Environment, *Computer*, 38 (4)(2005)27-33).

The Knowledge Grid is an environment consisting of autonomous individuals in multiple spaces, self-organized semantic communities, adaptive networking mechanisms, and evolving semantic networking mechanisms. It maintains meaningful connections between individuals, various flows for dynamic resource sharing, mechanisms for managing resources effectively, and appropriate knowledge services for problem solving and innovation. It supports innovation and harmonious development of science, technology and culture. (H. Zhuge, The Knowledge Grid Environment, *IEEE Intelligent Systems*, 23(6)(2008) 63-71).

The *Knowledge Grid methodology* is a multi-disciplinary system methodology for developing various Knowledge Grids that obeys cyber, physical and social principles, rules and laws.

Since the publication of the first edition of The Knowledge Grid in 2004, great progress has been made in the computing area. The progress will benefit Knowledge Grid research greatly. Implementation of the Knowledge Grid ideal will speed up the development of human civilization.

The following is a brief history of Knowledge Grid development.

An initial Knowledge Grid system was developed for sharing and managing various resources (documents, comments, questions, and answers) on the Web (H. Zhuge, A knowledge grid model and platform for global knowledge sharing, *Expert Systems with Applications*, 22(4)(2002)313-320). Resources are classified by multi-dimensional resource space, where a knowledge dimension classifies knowledge into the following classes: *concept, axiom, rules* and *method*. Users can accurately put resources into categories and get resources from a category according to the categories in mind. Users are responsible for determining and maintaining the categories of resources. The idea of multi-dimensional classifications was then developed into a systematic Resource Space Model for managing various resources (H.Zhuge, The Web Resource Space Model, *Springer*, 2008; H.Zhuge, Y.Xing and P.Shi, Resource Space Model, OWL and Database: Mapping and Integration, *ACM Transactions on Internet Technology*, 8/4, 2008). One distinguished characteristics of the multi-dimensional space is the ability of specialization and generations on multiple dimensions.

Then, the Knowledge Grid idea was developed to include dynamic knowledge management due to the following motivation: *knowledge is generated, shared and evolved in a flowing process rather than static symbol representation* (H. Zhuge, A knowledge flow model for peer-to-peer team knowledge sharing and management, *Expert Systems with Applications*, 23(1)(2002)23-30; H.Zhuge, Discovery of Knowledge Flow in Science, *Communications of the ACM*, 49(5)(2006)101-107). In contrast, traditional knowledge-based systems focus on the codification of knowledge, management of the statically codified knowledge in knowledge base, and provision of knowledge based on symbol reasoning.

The implementation of Knowledge Grid needs a scalable, self-organized, high-performance and decentralized semantic computing, and communication platform for supporting decentralized knowledge sharing (H.Zhuge, et al, A Scalable P2P Platform for the Knowledge Grid, *IEEE Transactions on Knowledge and Data Engineering*, 17(12)(2005)1721-1736; H.Zhuge, Communities and Emerging Semantics in Semantic Link Network: Discovery and Learning, *IEEE Transactions on Knowledge and Data Engineering*, 21(6)(2009)785-799).

The following statements help distinguish the ideal of Knowledge Grid from others.

Knowledge Grid environment ≠ Knowledge discovery + Grid computing.
Knowledge Grid environment ≠ Knowledge base + Grid computing.
Knowledge Grid environment ≠ Distributed data mining.
Knowledge Grid environment ≠ Distributed knowledge base.

The above notion of the Knowledge Grid is essentially different from other notions of applying AI techniques (e.g., knowledge extraction, mining, and synthesis) to large data sets. Berman's idea has no essential difference from traditional AI problems (*Communications of the ACM*, 44(11)(2001)27-28). Cannataro and Talia's idea (*Communications of the ACM*, 46(1)(2003) 89–93) is similar to the distributed data mining (C.Clifton, et al., Tools for Privacy Preserving Distributed Data Mining, *ACM SKGKDD Explorations Newsletter*, 4(2)(2002)28-34).

The Knowledge Grid environment has the following distinguished characteristics.

1.5.2 *Virtual characteristic*

Many computer scientists are exploring ideal computing and resource organization models for the future interconnection environment. The editorial of the first special issue on Semantic Grid and Knowledge Grid for the *Future Generation Computer Systems* journal (20(1)(2004)1-5) described the following scenario: The future interconnection environment will be a platform-irrelevant *Virtual Grid* consisting of requirements, roles and resources. The Knowledge Grid will be such a virtual Grid, which concerns knowledge, knowledge sharing, and principle of knowledge sharing.

Humans can effectively share knowledge no matter whether computers are used or not. Actually, various human-level knowledge grids work in our society no matter whether people are aware of this or not. So, Knowledge Grid research should go beyond the scope of traditional computing area.

With machine-understandable semantics, resources in the cyber space can actively and dynamically form clusters to provide on-demand services by understanding requirements and functions. Versatile resources can be encapsulated to provide services by way of a *single semantic image*. The cyber space could intelligently assist people to accomplish complex tasks and solve problems by organizing versatile resource flow cycles through virtual roles to use appropriate cyber, physical and socio resources.

With the development of society and science, people have more profound understanding of the nature, society, and themselves than ever. So, appropriate rules and principles of the nature, society and economics should be adopted when we develop the Knowledge Grid as an intelligent interconnection environment.

1.5.3 *Social characteristic*

The Knowledge Grid has social characteristics. In the real world, people live and work in a *Socio Grid* obeying social and economic rules. The Knowledge Grid is a *socio grid environment*, where people enjoy and provide services through versatile flow cycles like control flows, material flows, energy flows, information flows and knowledge flows. People can communicate with and gain knowledge from each other through mutually understandable interactive semantics.

An artificial interconnection environment can only be effective when it works harmoniously with the physical space and the socio grids. For example, an effective e-business environment requires harmonious cooperation between information flows, knowledge flows, material flows, e-services, and social services. The e-services belong to e-business platforms. The material flows and social services belong to the physical space and social space. The information flows and knowledge flows belong to both the social space and the cyber space. Interactions between individuals in the socio grid and the cyber space are based on an interactive semantics.

In future, different artificial interconnection environments will co-exist and compete with each other for survival, rights and reputation, and will harmoniously evolve with the *cyber-physical-socio grid* (H.Zhuge and X.Shi, Eco-grid: A Harmoniously Evolved Interconnection Environment, *Communications of the ACM*, 47(9)(2004)79-83).

Social networking is regarded as one of top 11 technologies of the decade (IEEE Spectrum, Jan, 2011). Some researchers even regard social networking and relevant research as a science, which can help leverage the ability to collect and analyze data at a scale that may reveal patterns of individual and group behaviors (D. Lazer, et al. Computational social science, *Science*, 323(5915)(2009)721-723). At the current stage, the study of social networking in the cyber space can inspire research on cyber-physical-socio networking.

The ideal of the Cyber-Physical Society extends the research ground of the Knowledge Grid environment.

1.5.4 *Adaptive characteristic*

"On-demand services" is a fashionable catchphrase in the context of the future interconnection environment. But there is no limit to human demand. So, it is impossible and unreasonable to provide all participants with services on demand as long as service generation and service provision carry a significant cost and services themselves differ in quality.

Economics is concerned with three kinds of entity: *participants*, *markets* and *economic systems*. The market is an important mechanism for automatically and reasonably adjusting the decisions and behaviors of market participants, for example, agents and soft-devices (H.Zhuge, Clustering Soft-Devices in Semantic Grid, *IEEE Computing in Science and Engineering*, 4(6)(2002)60-63).

Besides the influence of the market, participants' behaviors and decisions can be adjusted by negotiation. Governments, organizations and socio rights also play important roles in influencing market participants' behaviors and decision making. Market participants, producers and consumers, look for satisfactory rather than optimal exchanges through agreement (the evaluation of "satisfactory" involves social and psychological factors). Being based on simple principles, the market mechanism adapts the interests of participants by avoiding complex computation.

The natural ecological system establishes a balance among natural species through *energy flow*, *material flow* and *information flow*. These flows in their turn influence the socio system (H. Zhuge and X. Shi, Fighting Epidemics in the Information and Knowledge Age, *Computer*, 36(10)(2003)114-116). Different species evolve together as parts of the entire ecological system.

The Knowledge Grid also supports three major roles: *producers*, *consumers* and *a market mechanism* for adapting to the behavior of different participants. It should adopt economic and ecological principles to balance the interests of knowledge producers and knowledge consumers, and adapt to knowledge evolution and expansion (H. Zhuge and W.Guo, Virtual knowledge service market for effective knowledge flow within knowledge grid, *Journal of Systems and Software*, 80(11)(2007)1833-1842).

1.5.5 *Semantic characteristic*

Semantics is the basis for people to interact with each other and with machines, and for machines to correctly understand and process various resources in the cyber space. It is generated for interaction, and evolves with complex psychological and cognitive processes. The exploitation of psychological, cognitive and philosophical issues will help study semantics.

Research on semantic information processing has a long history in the computing field (M.L. Minsky, ed., *Semantic Information Processing*, MIT Press, 1968). Knowledge representation approaches such as frame theory (Minsky, 1975), the Knowledge Representation Language KRL (D.G. Bobrow, 1979), and the Semantic Network (M.R. Quillian; H.A. Simon, 1970) are attempts to expressing semantics. Before the emergence of the Internet interchange standard XML and the Resource Description Framework RDF (www.w3.org/RDF/), the Knowledge Interchange Format KIF (www.logic.stanford.edu/kif) and Open Knowledge Base Connectivity OKBC (www.ai.sri.com/~okbc) were two standards for sharing codified knowledge.

Knowledge acquisition was the bottleneck of traditional knowledge engineering. Data mining approaches help a bit by automatically discovering some association rules in large-scale databases. These approaches can also be used to discover some links within and between texts (H.Zhuge and J.Zhang, Automatically Constructing Semantic Link Network on Documents, *Concurrency and Computation: Practice and Experience*, 61(9)(2010)1824-1841).

Why were the symbolic approaches, especially the KIF and OKBC of AI, and ODBC in the database area, not widely adopted in the Internet age? Thinking this question would implicate the right research method.

One cause is the success of HTML, which is easy to use both for a writer and, in cooperation with a browser, for a reader. Its main advantage is that *"anything can link to anything"* (T. Berners-Lee, J. Hendler and O. Lassila, Semantic Web, *Scientific American*, 284(5)(2001)34-43).

A second cause is that traditional AI's knowledge representation approaches try to explicate human knowledge, while the Web focuses on structuring Web contents and the links between contents, that is, it is easy to use and verify.

A third cause is that cooperation between machines (applications) has become the dominant aim in realizing intelligent Web applications, while traditional knowledge engineering focuses on cooperation between human and machine.

A fourth cause is the cross-platform requirement. Consequently, XML has been adopted as the information exchange standard of the World Wide Web.

A fifth cause is the tree structure of XML. Humans have used the same structure to organize the main contents of texts like book when large-scale symbols cannot be efficiently organized by sequential order. Users tend to adopt the way of interaction that is in line with habit. *So far, we still do not know the best form that is suitable for humans to understand.* This concerns the study of semantics.

What are the problems of semantics in the Knowledge Grid environment?

The first is the representation problem — to formally represent semantics is the basis of machine processing. Prior research into representing semantics should be a helpful reference, but in-depth understanding of semantics concerns cognitive processes. The first step of research should focus on understanding the rich semantic links between resources (some are explicit while others are implicit), on establishing an appropriate semantic computing model to efficiently operate semantic link networks, on the understanding of the process of forming and using semantics, and on seeking an approach that synthesizes the semantics expressed in different semantic spaces.

The second is the acquisition problem — to enable machines to automatically acquire semantics (reflection from various spaces).

Chapter 1 The Knowledge Grid Methodology *Chapter 1 The Knowledge Grid Methodology* 25

Resources in different spaces may have different forms. The first step of research should focus on the approaches to discover various classes, semantic links, and communities. The second step should look into various interactions in different spaces or through spaces.

The third is the normal organization problem — to properly organize semantics under a certain normal forms and the integrity constraints so that the correctness and efficiency of semantic operations is guaranteed. If we can solve this problem, resources in the environment can be correctly organized and used in light of their semantic images.

The fourth is the problem of processing semantics — to refine, abstract and synthesize large-scale semantic images to provide appropriate and succinct semantic images. An example is to obtain the topological patterns and networking rules from social networks.

The fifth is the maintenance problem — to maintain consistency and reasonability between semantic images in the large-scale and dynamic semantic environment.

The sixth is the interaction problem — to trace, record and use the semantic images in the interaction processes is the way to get semantics as semantics evolves with interaction. This issue was discussed in detail in (H.Zhuge, Interactive semantics, *Artificial Intelligence*, 174(2010)190-204).

The seventh is the emerging semantics problem — to find the rules of emerging semantics. Some semantics can only emerge during interaction or during the evolution of semantic images rather than pre-defined. To find the emerging rules is a challenge issue.

The eighth is the generation and evolution of semantics — to find the rules of generating and evolving semantics. The semantic representations in previous researches are actually *forms* (semantic indicators) rather than *semantics. Semantics can be only emerged through the closed loop of experiencing in multiple spaces* (H.Zhuge, Semantic linking through spaces for cyber-physical-socio intelligence: A methodology, *Artificial Intelligence*, 175(2011)988-1019).

Current research on the Semantic Web is less than ideal because they do not fully address the above problems.

At a high level, the Knowledge Grid is a space of requirements, roles and services. Services are provided according to resources that are implemented on the basis of a uniform resource model. Services can actively find and advertise requirements. People can play the roles of services, and enjoy services provided by others. Requirements and services are organized into conglomerations that belong to different communities. Some services can play the broker role and be responsible for dynamically integrating services to meet varying requirements.

At a low level, a semantic space organizes and uses resources by way of a *single semantic image*, that is, various resources are mapped into a single semantic space to expose their commonality. Humans behave intelligently according to single semantic images of the environment. Although many ways based on logics and algebra tried to represent semantics, the single semantic image should be based on the most basic semantics that humans can easily understand and often use in daily life.

What is the most basic semantics?

(1) *Classification*. Classification is the basic intelligent mechanism of humans. Infants have the ability to classify things into two classes: *self* and *external things*. The nature of resources determines their categories. Humans have invented various tools such as bookshelf and drawer to manage physical resources, used taxonomy to manage knowledge in the mental space, and used file systems to manage digital files in the cyber space. Further, different classification methods can be used to classify a set of resources.

(2) *Link*. Various links connect individuals in the physical space, cyber space, and socio space to indicate certain semantics. For example, food web organizes living creatures where links represent material (food) flow, family relations and cooperation relations help organize individuals in society where links represent blood relation or friendship, and hyperlink connects Web pages to form the World Wide Web.

(3) *Reasoning*. Rules in cyber, physical, social and mental spaces regulate classifications and links. Various reasoning can carry out on classifications and links according to the rules. General reasoning also includes the influence on the statuses of nodes and links according to the rules.

The single semantic image could be based on the above basic semantics to uniformly reflect various resources, behaviors and events. As the basis of interaction, an interactive semantic base is introduced in (H.Zhuge, Interactive semantics, *Artificial Intelligence*, 174(2010)190-204).

Normalizing the classification space and relational network can guarantee the correctness and effectiveness of resource operations. The semantic space requires a semantic browser that enables not only people but also services to exploit the semantics of a resource being browsed, to extract from the resource and reason from the extract, to explain the display, and to anticipate subsequent browsing.

A huge semantic gap exists between low-level semantics used in the cyber space and high-level semantics (or socio semantics) used by humans as shown in Fig. 1.5.5.1 Various ontology mechanisms and semantic computing models are ways to reduce the gap.

The Knowledge Grid will enable knowledge generation, evolution and service based on multi-level semantics and semantic computing models.

Current Web technologies and software tools only use some simple semantic indicators such as keywords (tags) and surface attributes (texture, color, and so on). Users have to search an enormous name space to find what they need within huge and expanding Web resources.

Complex cognitive and psychological processes are involved in this huge gap. Some computer scientists seek to obtain semantics by establishing domain ontology mechanisms for explaining semantics. Building tools and finding methods for creating ontology mechanisms are becoming popular in the Semantic Web area. Ontology can reflect people's consensus on semantics in the name spaces of the symbolic space to a certain extent. But it is hard to cope with the complexity of human cognitive processes.

A *semantic computing model* that could at least partly bridge this huge gap must be found. The model should go beyond the scope of traditional formal semantics, which has been extensively investigated in computer science in the past with success that is significant in theory but limited in practice. The model should balance the formal and informal and reflect human cognitive characteristics.

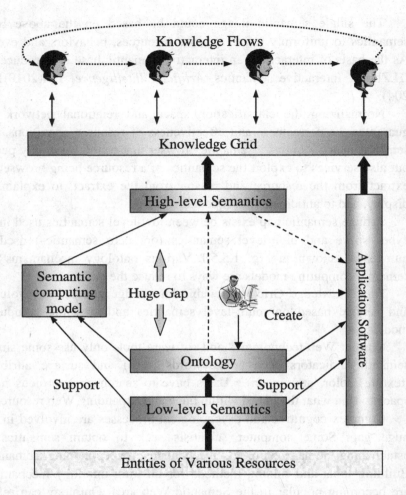

Fig. 1.5.5.1 Gap between low-level semantics and high-level semantics.

Semantics evolution has been accompanying socio interaction, but humans do not have profound understanding on it. Peoples in different areas have different understandings as they have been building different ontology mechanisms. Humans have created many symbol systems to represent semantics, and are pursing better semantics representation approaches to realize machine intelligence.

A key problem is: Can semantics be correctly represented?

Turing machines are specialized in processing symbols according to algorithms designed by humans, but they are limited in ability to understand and process socio semantics when carrying out socio interaction. This is because they do not have a semantic worldview and cannot reflect themselves.

The future intelligent interconnection environment will enable individuals to reflect themselves, effectively interact, and know socio situation through time and spaces. As it is hard to accurately represent socio semantics in a rigid, isolated and static form, the integration of a dynamic semantic link network and an evolving multi-dimensional classification space can be used as a semantic image to reflect the socio semantics (H.Zhuge, Interactive Semantics, *Artificial Intelligence*, 174(2010)190-204).

Epistemology, which has been neglected in previous efforts towards the future computing environment, plays the key role in human cognitive processes.

1.6 Epistemology and Knowledge

Epistemology is a branch of philosophy. It concerns the nature, scope and source of knowledge. Computer scientists could improve their understanding of computing by studying the history and variety of epistemology.

Empiricism sees knowledge as the product of sensory perception. Knowledge results from a kind of mapping or reflection of external objects, from our sensory organs, possibly assisted by instruments, into our brain to be used by our minds. Aristotle, Bacon, Locke and Hume are representative philosophers.

Rationalism considers knowledge to be the product of rational reflection and reasoning. Knowledge results from the organization of perceptual data on the basis of cognitive structures called *categories*. Categories include *space*, *time*, *objects* and *causality*. Rationalism is relevant to the development of mathematics. Leibniz and Kant are representative philosophers.

Pragmatism emphasizes that theory is abstracted from practice and applied to practice. It holds that knowledge consists of mental models that simplify our perception of the real world. It is assumed that a model only reflects the main characteristics of the real world. Otherwise, it would be too complicated to be of any practical use. Thus, different or even seemingly contradictory models for solving the same problem could co-exist. Problem solving is a process of developing and selecting useful models. Mathematical modeling plays an important role in scientific problem solving. Peirce is the representative philosopher.

Individual constructivism sees individual as trying to build coherence between different pieces of knowledge. In the mental construction process, knowledge that succeeded in integrating previously incoherent pieces of knowledge will be kept, and knowledge that is inconsistent with the bulk of other knowledge that the individual has will tend to be rejected.

Social constructivism regards consensus on different subjects as the ultimate criterion for judging knowledge. Truth or reality will be accorded only to those constructions on which most people of a social group agree. Karl Marx's theory of ideology can be regarded as a type of social epistemology. An ideology is a set of beliefs, a worldview, or a form of consciousness that is in some fashion false or delusive. The cause of these beliefs and their delusiveness is the social situation and interests of the believers. The theory of ideology is concerned with the truth and falsity of beliefs, so it is a kind of *classical social epistemology*. *Feminist epistemology and philosophy of science* studies the ways in which gender influences, and ought to influence, our conceptions of knowledge, the knowing subject, and practices of inquiry and justification.

Evolutionary epistemology assumes that knowledge is constructed by a subject or a group of subjects in order to adapt to their environment in the broad sense. That construction is a process going on at different levels — at biological as well as psychological or social levels. Construction happens through blind variation of existing pieces of knowledge, and the selective retention of those new combinations that somehow contribute more to the survival and reproduction of the subjects within their given environment. Knowledge is regarded as an instrument questing for survival. Evolutionary epistemology emphasizes the importance of natural selection. Selection is the generator and maintainer of the reliability of our sensory and cognitive mechanisms, as well as of the *fit* between those mechanisms and the world. Trial and error learning and the development of scientific theories can be explained as evolutionary selection processes.

An active evolutionary view is that *knowledge can actively pursue goals of its own.* It notes that knowledge can be transmitted from one individual to another, and thereby lose its dependence on any particular individual. A piece of knowledge may be successful even though its predictions may be totally wrong, as long as it is sufficiently convincing to new carriers. In this theory, the individual having knowledge has lost his primacy, and knowledge becomes a force in its own right with proper goals and ways of developing itself. This emphasizes communication and social processes in the development of knowledge, but instead of regarding knowledge as the object constructed by the social system, it rather *views social systems as constructed by knowledge processes.* Indeed, a social group can be seen as organized by members sharing the same types of knowledge. *To keep evolution sustainable, knowledge should have the characteristic of diversity.* Research on knowledge flow network is somewhat like this point of view (H.Zhuge, Discovery of Knowledge Flow in Science, *Communications of the ACM*, 49 (5) (2006) 101-107).

The following references can help readers know more about epistemology:

(1) F. Heylighen (1993), Epistemology Introduction, in: F. Heylighen, C. Joslyn and V. Turchin (editors): *Principia Cybernetica Web*, http://pespmc1.vub.ac.be/epistemology.html.
(2) P.D. Klein, (1998). Epistemology. In E. Craig (ed.), *Routledge Encyclopedia of Philosophy*. London: Routledge. http://www.rep.routledge.com/article/P059.
(3) E. Anderson, Feminist Epistemology and Philosophy of Science, *Stanford Encyclopedia of Philosophy*, http://plato.stanford.edu/entries/feminism-epistemology/.
(4) M. Brady and W. Harms, Evolutionary Epistemology, *Stanford Encyclopedia of Philosophy*, http://plato.stanford.edu/entries/epistemology-evolutionary/.

(5) R. Feldman, *Stanford Encyclopedia of Philosophy* article, Naturalized Epistemology.
(6) A. Goldman, Social Epistemology, *Stanford Encyclopedia of Philosophy*, http://plato.stanford.edu/entries/epistemology-social/.

1.7 Ontology

Ontology — another branch of philosophy — is the science of what is, and of the kinds and structures of the objects, properties and relations in every area of reality. Ontology in this sense is often used in such a way as to be synonymous with metaphysics. In simple terms, it seeks to classify entities. A scientific field has its own preferred ontology, defined by the field's vocabulary and by the canonical formulations of its theories.

Traditional ontologists tend to model scientific ontologies by producing theories, organizing them, and clarifying their foundations. Ontologists are concerned not only with the world as studied by sciences, but also with the domains of practical activities such as law, medicine, engineering, and commerce. They seek to apply the tools of ontology to solving problems that arise in these domains.

In the field of information processing, different groups of data-gatherers have their own idiosyncratic terms and concepts that guide how they represent the information they receive. When an attempt is made to put information together from different groups, methods must be found to resolve terminological and conceptual incompatibilities. At first, such incompatibilities were resolved case by case. Then, people gradually came to realize that providing once and for all common backbone taxonomy of entities relevant to an application domain would have significant advantages over resolving incompatibilities case by case. This common backbone taxonomy is called an *ontology mechanism* by information scientists.

In the context of knowledge sharing and reuse, an ontology mechanism establishes a terminology for members of a community of interest. These members can be humans, application software, or automated agents. Ontology can be represented as a formal vocabulary organized in taxonomic hierarchies of classes, whose semantics is independent of both user and context.

1.8 System Methodology

Previous efforts toward the future interconnection environment have not yet made use of the principles and methods of system methodology.

Darwin's theory of evolution holds time to be an "arrow" of evolution. The subjects of the evolutionary process evolve as time progresses, so the overall process is irreversible, just like time. Life evolves from simple to complex, from a single-celled ameba to a multi-celled human being.

The second law of thermodynamics (R.J.E. Clausius and L. Boltzmann) tells us of a degenerate arrow: all processes manifest a tendency toward decay and disintegration, with a net increase in what is called the *entropy*, or state of randomness or disorder, of the overall system.

The theory of dissipative structure was created against the background of the collision between the two arrows.

1.8.1 *The theory of dissipative structure*

A system with dissipative structure is an open system that exists far from thermodynamic equilibrium, efficiently dissipates the heat generated to sustain it, and has the capacity to change to higher levels of orderliness.

According to Prigogine's theory, systems contain subsystems that continually fluctuate. At times a single fluctuation or a combination of them may become so magnified by positive feedback that it shatters the existing organization. At such revolutionary moments, it is impossible to determine in advance whether the system will disintegrate into chaos or leap to a new, more differentiated, higher level of order. The latter case is called a dissipative structure, so termed because it needs more energy to sustain itself than the simpler structure it replaces and is limited in growth by the amount of heat it is able to dissipate.

According to the theory of dissipative structure, the exponential growth of Web resources tends to disorder. The current efforts towards the future Web are trying to establish a new kind of order — *the order of diverse resources*. But how such an order can be prevented from becoming disordered again is a critical issue that needs to be considered as we work towards the future interconnection environment.

Here is an interesting question: *Can we design a dissipative structure for the future interconnection environment or the Cyber-Physical Society?*

1.8.2 *Synergetic theory*

Synergetics is a theory of pattern formation in complex systems. It tries to explain structures that develop spontaneously in nature. Readers can obtain more information from H. Haken's works (*Synergetics, An Introduction: Nonequilibrium Phase-Transitions and Self-Organization in Physics, Chemistry and Biology*, Springer, 1977; *Synergetics of Cognition*, Springer-Verlag, 1990 (with M.Stadler); *Principles of Brain Functioning: A Synergetic Approach to Brain Activity, Behavior, and Cognition*, Springer-Verlag, 1995).

The purpose of introducing the relevant concepts here is to provoke constructive thought about their possible influence on the future interconnection environment.

How order emerges out of chaos is not well defined, so synergetics employs the ideas of probability (to describe uncertainty) and information (to describe approximation). Entropy is a central concept relating physics to information theory. Synergetics concerns the following three key concepts: compression of the degrees of freedom of a complex system into dynamic patterns that can be expressed as a collective variable; behavioral attractors of changing stabilities; and the appearance of new forms as nonequilibrium phase transitions.

Systems at instability points are driven by a *slaving principle*: *long-lasting quantities can enslave short-lasting quantities* (that is, they can act as order parameters). Close to instability, stable motions (or "modes") are enslaved by unstable modes and can be ignored, thereby reducing the degrees of freedom of the system. The macroscopic behavior of the system is determined by the unstable modes. The dynamic equations of the system reflect the interplay between stochastic forces ("chance") and deterministic forces ("necessity").

Synergetics deals with self-organization, how collections of parts can produce structures. Synergetics applies to systems driven far from equilibrium, where the classic concepts of thermodynamics are no longer adequate. Order can arise from chaos and can be maintained by flows of energy or matter.

Synergetics has wide applications in physics, chemistry, sociology and biology (population dynamics, evolution, and morphogenesis). Completely different systems exhibit surprising analogies as they pass through instability. Biological systems are unique in that they exhibit interplay between structure and function that is embodied in structure and latent in form.

The ideas introduced above imply that synergetics can help us explore the intrinsic self-organization principle of the future interconnection environment and its resources (for example, how can the components such as services form a well behaved structure to provide an appropriate service, and how can individuals in social networks appropriately cooperate to achieve ideal performance), and find better approaches to solve existing problems in processing information and knowledge.

1.8.3 *The hypercycle — a principle of natural self-organization*

A living system has three features: *self-reproduction*, *metabolism*, and *evolution*.

A *hypercycle* is a system that consists of self-reproducing macro-molecular species that are linked cyclically by catalysis. It is interesting to investigate pre-biotic evolution since it might explain how molecular species having a small number of molecules could evolve into entities with a great amount of genetic information.

The idea of the hypercycle, introduced by Eigen in 1971, has been experimentally and theoretically verified by Gebinoga in 1995. The purpose of introducing here the concept of the hypercycle is to provoke some rethinking about work towards the future intelligent interconnection environment.

The following example explains the concept of the hypercycle. Living cells contain both nucleic acids and proteins, and molecules of the two classes interact. Genetic information controls the production of polypeptide chains, that is, proteins. Data encoded in nucleic acids ensure that certain proteins can be produced. Information about proteins helps the replication of nucleic acids and enables information transmission. A system of nucleic acids and proteins helping to replicate each other is an important basis for evolution as evolution can occur only when the state information can be obtained, maintained and extended.

M. Eigen and P. Schuster consider hypercycles to be predecessors of protocells (primitive unicellular biological organisms). As quasispecies, hypercycles have also been mathematically analyzed in detail.

The self-reproducing automaton was investigated early on by John von Neumann.

A similar system of catalytically interacting macromolecules called a *syser* is comprised of a polynucleotide matrix and several proteins. There are two obligatory proteins: the replication enzyme and the translation enzyme. A *syser* can also include some structural proteins and additional enzymes. The polynucleotide matrix encodes the composition of proteins, and the replication enzyme controls the matrix replication process. The translation enzyme controls the protein synthesis according to the data encoded in the matrix. Structural proteins and additional enzymes can provide optional functions. Different *sysers* should be inserted into different organisms for effective competition.

Compared to hypercycles, *sysers* are more like simple biological organisms. The concept of *sysers* makes it possible to analyze evolutionary stages starting from a mini-*syser*, which contains only a matrix and replication and translation enzymes. An adaptive *syser* includes a simple molecular control system, which "turns on" and "turns off" synthesis by some enzyme in response to change in the external medium.

Readers can know more about the hypercycle from M. Eigen and P. Schuster' work (*The Hypercycle: A principle of natural self-organization*, Springer, Berlin, 1979).

The notion of a *soft-device*, an uniform resource model of the future interconnection environment, is introduced in "Clustering Soft-Devices in Semantic Grid" (H.Zhuge, *IEEE Computing in Science and Engineering*, 4(6)(2002)60-63) and envisions that the future interconnection environment will be a world of versatile soft-devices and roles. Ideal soft-devices have the same function as *sysers*.

Hypercycle theory will give us some useful notions for when we explore the organization mode of the future intelligent interconnection environment. For example, the future intelligent interconnection environment can be imagined as a living system or environment, which consists of resource species in the form of soft-devices (or active services) and versatile flow cycles. Resources could be dynamically organized into diverse flows such as knowledge flows, information flows, and service flows to provide users or applications with on-demand services. Once a requirement is confirmed, all relevant flows could be formed automatically (H.Zhuge and X.Shi, Eco-Grid: A Harmoniously Evolved Interconnection Environment, *Communications of the ACM*, 47(9)(2004)79-83).

The future intelligent interconnection environment can be imagined as a quasihuman body, which has knowledge and intelligence and operates with special hypercycles. It can cooperate with people in a humanized way and provide appropriate, up-to-date, on-demand and just-in-time services.

1.8.4 *General principles and strategies*

The Knowledge Grid methodology should adopt the principles and rules of social science, economics, psychology, physiology, biology, ecology and physics, and inherit the fundamental ideas, views, rules and principles of system science.

General Principles

(1) *Integrity and uniformity principle* — The idea of integrity requires us to resolve the issue of correctness (for example, the correctness of operations). The idea of uniformity requires us to resolve the issue of simplicity, that is, to simplify a system. The integrity theory of the relational database model is a good example of integrity and it could give us useful ideas for developing the theory and system of a Knowledge Grid, especially in managing its resources.

(2) *The hierarchical principle* — H.A. Simon unveils the hierarchical principle of artificial systems in his book (*The Sciences of the Artificial*, Cambridge, MA: The MIT Press, 1969). The construction of a Knowledge Grid' should follow this principle. Furthermore, different levels of a system could work in different spaces. Consistency and harmony should be maintained between multiple spaces.

(3) *The open principle* — This principle would keep the Knowledge Grid away from the equilibrium state. Standards are a critical criterion for open systems. The Knowledge Grid could make use of the standards generated with the development of the current platforms such as the Internet, Web, Grid, and Cloud.

(4) *The self-organization principle* — Resources including systems themselves can actively collaborate with each other according to some principles (for example, the economic principles) and common regulations.

(5) *The principle of competition and cooperation* — Resources including systems (multiple systems or environments could coexist) evolve through competition and cooperation so that competitive resources or systems could play a more important role.

(6) *The optimization principle* — Optimization means making a system more effective. Material flow, information flow, knowledge flow and service flow can be optimized to achieve efficiency in logistic processes.

(7) *The principle of sustainable development* — Sustainable development requires individuals and communities, the interconnection environment and its human-machine interfaces, the human-machine society, and even the natural environment to harmoniously coexist and co-evolve.

(8) *Symmetry and self-similarity.* Symmetry is an important concept in science, for example, symmetry refers to the invariance under any transformation in physics. Self-similarity means that the whole is similar to its part. Knowing symmetry and self-similarity can help raise the effectiveness of operations such as control and navigation.

General Strategies

The following strategies could help develop the Knowledge Grid as an intelligent interconnection environment.

The fusion of inheritance and innovation — the Knowledge Grid environment should absorb the advantages of the current efforts such as Web x.0, Grid, Cloud, Semantic Web, and Web Services. The Web applications should be able to work in the new environment. Smooth development would enable the environment to exploit research on the Web.

The fusion *of centralization and decentralization* — Advantage should be taken of both centralization and decentralization. On the one hand, an ideal system should be able to dynamically cluster and fuse relevant resources to provide complete and on-demand services for applications. On the other hand, it should be able to deploy the appropriate resources onto the appropriate locations to achieve optimized computing.

The fusion of abstraction and specialization — On the one hand, we need to abstract a variety of resources to investigate common rules, and on the other hand, to investigate the special rules of different resources to properly integrate and couple resources.

The fusion of mobility and correctness — On the one hand, the Knowledge Grid should support mobile applications to meet the needs of ubiquitous applications. On the other hand, we should guarantee the quality of services and the means of verification.

The fusion of symbolic and non-symbolic approaches — Current ontology only uses the symbolic approach, which is very similar to traditional knowledge base construction. The combination of the symbolic approach and the non-symbolic approach like the connectionist approach would help find better solutions for intelligent applications.

The incremental strategy — As a worldwide interconnection environment, the Knowledge Grid will undergo a development process similar to that of the World Wide Web — from simple to complex, from immature to mature, from a small community to a large-scale human-machine-nature environment with an exponential expansion of developers, users, services, and demands. So, the Knowledge Grid development methodology should support an incremental strategy.

Adoption of new computing models — The functions of new computing models will go beyond the abilities of the Turing machines. It is hard for any single model to yield an ideal solution. An ideal computing model should incorporate the advantages of various models or be a set of collaborative models. The new computing model should support massive interactions in the future interconnection environment and the computing processes that are not predesigned. (H.Zhuge, Semantic linking through spaces for cyber-physical-socio intelligence: A methodology, *Artificial Intelligence*, 175(2011) 988-1019).

Cross-disciplinary research — Compared to the physical, mental and social spaces, the artificial interconnection environment is at a very primitive stage. The principles and rules of physical, mental and social spaces will inspire us to establish the principles and rules of the ideal Knowledge Grid environment.

1.9 Dynamic Knowledge Management

Early in 1880, the American engineer F.W. Taylor investigated workers' efficiency, and formulated a scientific management method for raising productivity by standardizing operations and work. He published his authoritative book *The Principles of Scientific Management* in 1911. With increasing industrial productivity and social development, scientific management methods nowadays pay increasing attention to production processes and even social changes, psychological factors, environmental impact, and so on.

With the development of information technology, enterprises more and more become knowledge organizations, which lead to great changes in decision processes, management methods and working conditions. P.F. Drucker pointed out that the existing knowledge organizations, such as the symphony orchestra, can inspire us to develop new management approaches to knowledge organizations (*Harvard Business Review on Knowledge Management*, Boston, MA: Harvard Business School Press, 1998). However, much team work has become decentralized with the development of Internet and mobile communication devices.

After all, a large-scale orchestra can perform very well with just one conductor. Organizational learning and knowledge innovation become the key competitive abilities of a knowledge organization (I. Nonaka, A dynamic theory of organizational knowledge creation, *Organization Science*, 5(1)(1994)14-37). Nowadays, how to establish a high-performance self-organized knowledge innovation team becomes a key research issue.

Knowledge flow was studied from management point of view (A.K. Gupta and V.Govindarajan, Knowledge flows and the structure of control within multinational corporations, *Academy of management review*, 1991; M.E. Nissen, An extended model for knowledge-flow dynamics, *Communications of the Association for Information Systems*, 8(2002)251-266). An epistemological dimension is used to classify knowledge into explicit knowledge and tacit knowledge. An ontological dimension is used to describe knowledge that is shared between members of an organization. Knowledge flow within dimensions is of four types: 1) social flow, in which knowledge moves from creation by an individual to acceptance by the organization; 2) externalization flow, in which knowledge moves from tacit form to explicit; 3) combination flow, in which the knowledge of small teams is combined and coordinated to generate the knowledge of a large team; and 4) internalization flow, in which explicit knowledge of the organization becomes tacit.

Traditional knowledge engineering requires knowledge engineers to acquire knowledge from domain experts, codify knowledge and then store knowledge in knowledge base so as to support knowledge sharing and question-answering based on possible reasoning. This kind of knowledge is statically stored like digital resource in library.

Knowledge sharing in society is dynamic. People may get different answers when asking one question at different times. This is because knowledge evolves in the sharing process. Knowledge sharing has diverse forms, for example, in broadcasting or peer-to-peer.

The knowledge flow notion in computing area was stated firstly as follows:

Knowledge *flow is invisible, but it works with any cooperative team no matter whether people intentionally make use of it or not. Team members are linked with various types of "knowledge transmission belts" like the production line. Any team member can put knowledge onto a proper belt, which then automatically conveys the knowledge to the team member who requires it. Any team member can get the required knowledge from the belt linked to him/her when performing his/her task. These belts together with the team members constitute a knowledge flow network. People can raise the effectiveness of teamwork by properly designing the network and controlling its execution process* (H. Zhuge, A knowledge flow model for peer-to-peer team knowledge sharing and management, *Expert Systems with Applications*, 23(1)(2002)23-30).

This knowledge transmission belt can be regarded as a kind of super link that can pass through knowledge flow (H.Zhuge, Semantic linking through spaces for cyber-physical-socio intelligence: A methodology, *Artificial Intelligence*, 175(2011)988-1019).

A peer-to-peer knowledge flow refers to the propagation of external and explicit knowledge that can be formalized, transmitted via communication media, and stored in computing machinery. The planning of a knowledge flow network seeks to formalize and optimize knowledge flows (H.Zhuge, Knowledge flow network planning and simulation, *Decision Support Systems*, 42(2) (2006)571-592).

Knowledge flows will pass through socio networks like the citation networks of scientific publications to form communities and reputations (H.Zhuge, Discovering Knowledge Flows in Science, *Communications of the ACM*, 49(5)(2006)101-107).

A knowledge flow network is in itself a kind of organizational knowledge that is more relevant to the roles of the organization and less focused on individuals. It is more concerned with the content of knowledge and with effective knowledge sharing in distributed cooperative teams especially the geographically distributed virtual organization.

Knowledge sharing in the Knowledge Grid environment needs a kind of mechanism to reflect human cognition. Different people may see a different epistemology in the same object or event. Epistemological mechanisms help humans and agents understand, generate and describe new knowledge when they share resources. An easy way to implement an epistemological mechanism would be to develop an epistemological appendage, generated and used in conjunction with the original resources.

Some researchers are interested in mining Web usage logs. These logs record data about the Web's users. The researchers are striving to use the results of mining Web usage logs to support personalized Web services. However, the Web logs only reflect a small portion of users' behavior, and they are unable to capture users' actual intentions, thinking or understanding, even if the lifetime logs could be recorded.

A personalized epistemological appendage together with domain ontology could improve the current Web's keyword-based approaches and ontology-only approaches. The appendage could be in form of a complex semantic space integrating classification, semantic link, and reasoning (H.Zhuge, Complex Semantic Space, Keynote at *the 20th IEEE International Conference on Collaboration Technologies and Infrastructures*, Paris, France, June 27th-29th, 2011).

Determining the dimensions of knowledge within an organization is important for managing knowledge in the organization. The dimensions of abstract knowledge can include the following three dimensions: the *knowledge category* dimension (e.g., disciplines), the *knowledge level* dimension (e.g., concept, rule, method, and theory), and the *knowledge host* dimension (knowledge may be specific to individual and community).

10. The Knowledge Grid as a Research Area

1.10.1 *Research scope*

It is helpful to know what are *not* the major concerns of the Knowledge Grid research. Traditional natural language processing, information retrieval, recognition of human speech and handwriting, and formal semantics are not the major concern of the Knowledge Grid. Security and scientific computing are not its key issues. The Knowledge Grid will go beyond the traditional Web, Grid, cloud, information retrieval, filtering, mining and question answering (H. Zhuge, China's e-Science Knowledge Grid Environment, *IEEE Intelligent Systems*, 19(1)(2004)13-17).

Efforts towards the future interconnection environment supply the Knowledge Grid with several candidate techniques and implementation platforms.

The Grid computing is not the only platform for realizing the Knowledge Grid, but the ideal, method and techniques of the Grid computing could be helpful references.

The meaning of the term *grid* in the Knowledge Grid is broader than it is in Grid computing. Actually, people have a long history of using the word "grid" in drawing and mapping, geodetic surveying, and mathematics. The word was borrowed from the power grid to refer to clustered computing power when the concept of Grid computing appeared in 1995.

As depicted in Fig. 1.10.1.1, the Knowledge Grid emerges and evolves with the interaction between different spaces (dimensions), which also evolve.

Humans use knowledge to design the power Grid, which makes use of natural resources to generate and transmit electricity for society. The principle of the power Grid inspires the Grid computing. The development of Grid computing accelerates the emergence of the smart Grid. A cyber-physical-socio innovation closed loop will be formed if the Knowledge Grid can be integrated with the smart grid to extend the ideal of the Grid and to enrich human knowledge.

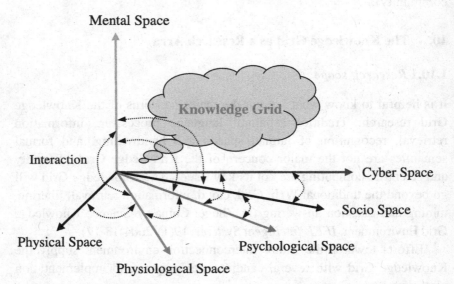

Fig.1.10.1.1 Dimensions of the Knowledge Grid and interactions between dimensions.

In the long run, a Knowledge Grid environment should be a large-scale, autonomous, living, sustainable and intelligent network where the mental space, psychological space, social space, and physical space can develop together, functioning and evolving cooperatively. It would collect useful resources from the environment, transform and organize them into semantically rich forms that could be used easily by both machine and human. Geographically dispersed people and resources could work together to accomplish tasks and solve problems by using the network to actively promote the flow of material, energy, technique, information, knowledge and service through roles and machines, improving both the natural and the artificial environments.

Intelligence, Grid, peer-to-peer and environment represent humanity's four aspirations for the future working and living environment. The intelligence reflects humanity's pursuit of recognizing themselves, society and the nature. The Grid reflects humanity's pursuit of optimization and systemization. The peer-to-peer reflects humanity's pursuit of freedom and equality. The environment reflects humanity's pursuit of understanding the nature and its harmony.

1.10.2 *Parameters*

As a large-scale dynamic human-machine-nature system, a Knowledge Grid environment will be a complex space characterized by the following five parameters:

(1) *Space* — the capacity to hold a great variety of versatile individuals.
(2) *Time* — the arrow of evolution, which generates and evolves with the space.
(3) *Structure* — the construction of the environment and individuals in the environment.
(4) *Relation* — the abstract structure, distance, interaction or influence among parameters and among individuals in different spaces.
(5) *Measurement* — the evaluation of the status of, and the prospects for, individuals, processes and their relations.

Einstein's general theory of relativity reveals the relations between space and time in the physical space: space and time are malleable entities. On the largest scales, space is naturally dynamic, expanding or contracting over time.

A Knowledge Grid environment will foster the growth of knowledge by supporting behaviors in different spaces. As a product of complex space, knowledge evolves and endures throughout the life of the race and the life of individuals to wave and evolve social networks in various spaces.

Human social activities generate and develop the semantics of natural languages. Cyber-physical-socio-mental behaviors will need to be based on a kind of cyber-physical-socio semantics, and need to establish an "understanding" between inanimate resources and humans. Such semantics will be needed so that resources, services and knowledge in the Knowledge Grid can be beneficially used and protectively regulated by humans.

1.10.3 *Distinctive characteristics of the knowledge grid*

The Knowledge Grid has the following distinctive characteristics in knowledge generation, sharing, evolution and service.

(1) *Reflecting knowledge.* It will record individuals' behaviors, detect events in the cyber, physical, and social spaces, and make summarization, abstraction and reasoning. Intelligent individuals are responsible for transforming knowledge from one form into the other and developing individuals' knowledge.

(2) *Intelligently clustering and fusing distributed knowledge.* In the Knowledge Grid environment, related knowledge distributed around the world could intelligently cluster together and fuse to provide appropriate on-demand knowledge services with underlying reasoning and explanation. So, knowledge providers should include some meta-knowledge (knowledge about knowledge), and could use a kind of uniform model to encapsulate the provided knowledge and meta-knowledge to realize active and clustered knowledge services.

(3) *Single semantic entry point access to worldwide knowledge.* In the Knowledge Grid environment, people could access knowledge distributed around the world from a single semantic access entry point without needing to know where the required knowledge is.

(4) *Single semantic image.* The Knowledge Grid environment could enable people to share knowledge and to enjoy reasoning services in a single semantic space where there are no barriers to mutual understanding and pervasive knowledge sharing.

(5) *Worldwide complete knowledge service.* The Knowledge Grid could gather knowledge from all regions of the world and provide succinct and complete knowledge relevant to the solution of particular problems. To achieve this goal, we need to create new knowledge organization and service models.

(6) *Dynamic evolution of knowledge.* In the Knowledge Grid environment, knowledge would not be just statically stored, but would evolve to keep up-to-date with sharing and innovation. The Knowledge Grid can show how knowledge evolves from macroscopic to microscopic and how behaviors influence the evolution.

1.10.4 *The knowledge grid's general research issues*

The Knowledge Grid has the following general research issues:

(1) *Effective organization of various resources. Self-organization and autonomy will be the major feature of this resource organization.* The structure of a Knowledge Grid system is very important just like a child's learning ability is based on its innate mental structure (J.McCarthy, The Well-Designed Child, *Artificial Intelligence*, 172(2008)2003-2014). The first edition of this book introduced a Semantic Link Network and Resource Space Model as the basic structure for managing resources in the Knowledge Grid. This edition will enhance the two models and integrate them into a single semantic image.

(2) *Theories, models, methods and mechanisms for supporting knowledge reflection and representation.* The Knowledge Grid

should be able to help people or virtual roles effectively reflect, and conveniently share knowledge in a machine-processable form that could directly, or after transformation, be understood by humans. An open set of semantic primitives should be built to help knowledge representation. These primitives should be able to represent multi-granular knowledge. Reflecting knowledge has two meanings: one is when people learn from each other directly, or from the resources published by others, and then publish new knowledge on the Knowledge Grid; and, the other is when the Knowledge Grid gets knowledge from numeric, textual or image resources by discovery, induction, analogy, deduction, synthesis, and so on.

(3) *Knowledge display and creation.* These come mainly through an intelligent user interface (for example, a semantic browser) that enables people to share knowledge with each other in a visual way. The interface should implement the distinctive characteristics of the Knowledge Grid and be able to inspire people's discovery of knowledge through analogy and induction. The development of interface accompanies all development stage of computing systems.

(4) *Propagation and management of knowledge within virtual organizations.* This could eliminate redundant communication between team members to achieve effective knowledge management in a cooperative virtual team in the cyber-physical society. Knowledge flow management is a way to achieve knowledge sharing in a virtual team.

(5) *Knowledge organization, evaluation, refinement and derivation.* Knowledge should be linked and organized according to certain normal forms to obtain high retrieval efficiency and ensure the correctness of operations. The Knowledge Grid should be able to eliminate redundant knowledge and refine knowledge so that useful knowledge can be increased. It can also derive new knowledge from existing well-represented knowledge, from case histories, and from raw knowledge.

(6) *Knowledge integration.* Integrating knowledge at different levels and in different domains could support cross-domain analogies, problem solving, and scientific discovery.

(7) *Abstraction*. It is a challenge to automatically capture semantics from a variety of resources, to make abstractions, and to reason and explain in a semantic space. The semantic constraints and rules of abstraction ensure the validity of resource usage at the semantic level.

(8) *Scalable network platform*. The Knowledge Grid should enable a user, a machine or a local network to freely join in and leave without affecting its performance and services. It is a challenging task to organize and integrate knowledge within a dynamic network platform.

(9) *Interactive semantics*. Semantics is the fundamental issue of computer science and information science. How to enable machines to have the ability to process semantics is a challenge issue. Semantics can be classified into two categories: *social semantics* and *natural semantics*. Social semantics is hard to be accurately represented and the correctness cannot be proved, but it can be explained and indicated. Natural language processing, text analysis and statistical method do not attack the core of semantics study as socio interaction is more fundamental then symbol language. Humans can effectively interact with each other before the emerging of symbol language. Animals can effectively interact with each other without using symbol language. The new notions such as *interactive semantics*, *semantic worldview*, *semantic images*, *semantic lens* and *the process of explaining semantic image* were proposed (H.Zhuge, Interactive Semantics, *Artificial Intelligence*, 174(2010)190-204). Interactive semantics consists of interactive system and the semantic images of individuals, communities and the system rather than the static representation. Semantic images evolve with the evolution of the system such that systems, communities, and individuals can have *selfness*. The semantic lens can help individuals to observe semantics from different facets, scales and abstraction levels across time. Individuals can understand and interact with each other based on the semantic worldview, semantic base and semantic image. The study of interactive semantics will be a new direction of studying semantics.

1.10.5 *Differences between the web and the knowledge grid*

Here we use examples to make a brief comparison between the Web and the Knowledge Grid. With the Web, people with an illness can use search engines to retrieve relevant medical information, and browse hospital or health websites to find suitable hospitals and doctors, depending on what URLs they can remember. As there are more than a thousand million health websites, people are often annoyed by the large amount of useless content in a search result and by the time consumed in browsing through many websites. They may be further confused by the various opinions of different doctors. They may also worry about whether the result of their searching is based on up-to-date knowledge. Entering related symptoms, they can usually only obtain results for separate symptoms. Further, the whole searching process may overlook some experts, especially those who specialize in uncommon diseases.

Such searches will be improved by the Knowledge Grid, which can accurately and completely locate all relevant knowledge, cluster and synthesize the search result and then actively present it to users according to their illness profiles and the locations of hospitals and doctors. The users can get an explanation of the search result with underlying reasoning based on the clustered knowledge. The relationship between the symptoms of a disease will be considered during reasoning. The search results can adapt to change in illness profiles. Knowledge provided by different doctors worldwide will be refined, checked, fused and evaluated as to usefulness, consistency and time-effectiveness.

In the Knowledge Grid, new knowledge can be derived from: existing knowledge, patients' feedback, and mining in medical textbooks, papers, online contents, and other related sources such as contents captured from patients' daily life through smart homes. Ill people can also choose to provide symptoms of their disease through a single semantic entry point when accessing the Knowledge Grid to obtain instant consulting services. The result may include several candidate treatments selected by considering such factors as cost, waiting time, skill level, real-time transportation, and so on. In emergent case, the appropriate hospital, the route and vehicle from home to hospital will be recommended according to the real-time hospital situation (about patients, doctors, equipments, et. al.) and traffic situation. Family members are able to know the real-time status of the patient through mobile devices and sensors.

Similar advantages of the Knowledge Grid also exist in scientific research, business, education and other application domains.

1.10.6 *The technological basis of the knowledge grid*

The Knowledge Grid is not pie in the sky. It is based on existing methods and technologies such as the Web, Cloud, Grid, Semantic Web, Web Services, Sensor Network, mobile communications, Peer-to-Peer, AI, modeling, information processing technologies (for example, data and text mining, information filtering, extraction, fusion and retrieval), and system methodology as shown in Fig. 1.10.6.1.

The adoption of a new system methodology, a new resource organization model, a new computing model, and the principles of relevant disciplines will further challenge the current software

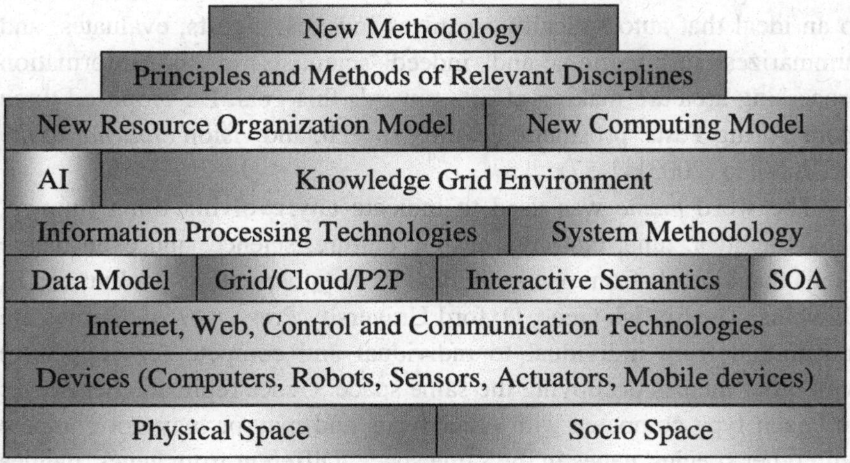

New Methodology		
Principles and Methods of Relevant Disciplines		
New Resource Organization Model	New Computing Model	
AI	Knowledge Grid Environment	
Information Processing Technologies	System Methodology	
Data Model	Grid/Cloud/P2P	Interactive Semantics	SOA
Internet, Web, Control and Communication Technologies		
Devices (Computers, Robots, Sensors, Actuators, Mobile devices)		
Physical Space	Socio Space	

Fig. 1.10.6.1 The methods and technologies of the Knowledge Grid environment.

methodology. The implementation of the ideal Knowledge Grid requires a new methodology that can cope with resources in different spaces through cyber-physical-socio processes, and support competition and sustainable development according to the cyber, physical, socio principles and rules.

1.10.7 A new dream

Gray summed up computing history in his 1999 Turing Award Lecture: the dream of Charles Babbage (1791-1871, the father of the computer) has been largely realized, and the dream of Vannevar Bush has almost become reality, but it is still difficult for computer systems to pass the Turing Test — computing systems still do not have human intelligence although significant progress has been made. Gray extended Babbage's dream to the following: *computers should be highly secure and available, and they should be able to program, manage, and replicate themselves.*

Scientists have made significant progress towards establishing highly secure and available systems — the major goal of the Grid and cloud computing. But so far, we are still far from the goal of self-programming, self-managing and self-replicating. Gray extended Bush's Memex vision to an ideal that automatically organizes indexes, digests, evaluates, and summarizes information, and indeed scientists in the information processing area are making efforts towards this goal. He proposed three more Turing Tests: prosthetic hearing, speech, and vision (*Journal of the ACM*, 50(1) (2003)41-57).

The word *meme* was used to indicate any evolving thing (human, behavior, idea, tune, clothing, design, culture, science, and even meme itself) that spreads from one individual to the other within a culture in (R. Dawkins, The Selfish Gene, Oxford University Press, 1976). Memes are transmitted from individual to individual and compete (or cooperate) with other memes occupying the same space. Genes replicate themselves, and each type competes with other types and may or may not compete with other species' genes in the same space. Different from genes, memes do not necessarily need a concrete medium to transfer.

Carrying out experimental research on finding various memes in cultures and sciences will be very interesting.

What modern society needs from the future computing environment has gone far beyond the scope of the Turing Test and other automatic machine intelligence problems such as self-programming. Computing has evolved from mainframe computers to personal computers, to locally networked computers, to the Internet, and to the Cyber-Physical Society (or Cyber-Physical-Socio-Mental Environment when the mental space is considered). People now primarily use computers interactively on a large scale, so that the *dynamics*, *evolution*, *cooperation*, *fusion*, *sustainability*, and *socio effects* of computer use have become major concerns.

Fig. 1.10.7.1 shows the evolution of the man-machine environment, where interaction evolves from machine semantics to social semantics and to multiple semantic spaces. The Knowledge Grid is the platform that supports the large-scale knowledge sharing and management in the Cyber-Physical-Socio-Mental Environment.

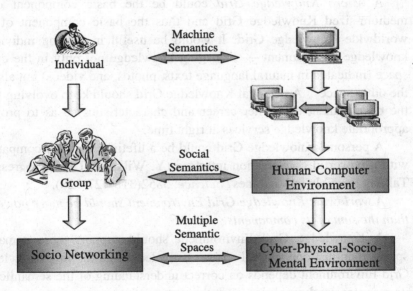

Fig. 1.10.7.1 The evolution of the man-machine environment.

Communication in human society is carried out in multiple semantic spaces, such as the emotional, cultural, artistic, scientific, and that of daily life, which establish the basis for mutual understanding. Loosely or tightly coupled rules could be used to coordinate between these semantic spaces. Traditional research on natural language processing only focuses on one space — the text space, where some information has inevitably been lost in the reading and writing processes. This is one reason why different people have different understandings of the same text. So, it is impossible to realize the dream of automatically processing natural language if only text analysis is used.

We need an incremental strategy to develop the Knowledge Grid. A worldwide Knowledge Grid is a long-term target. A preliminary stage developing a medium-sized Knowledge Grid based on an institution's intranet would be an appropriate step in the long march towards the long-term target. It could support more effective knowledge management within institutions of various kinds. Institutional Knowledge Grids could then become components of the worldwide Knowledge Grid.

A *Micro Knowledge Grid* could be the basic component of a medium-sized Knowledge Grid and thus the basic component of the worldwide Knowledge Grid. It would be useful in helping individual knowledge management — managing knowledge not only in the cyber space (indicated in natural language texts, photos, and videos) but also in the other spaces. A personal Knowledge Grid should keep evolving with the development of his/her career and characteristics so as to provide appropriate knowledge services at right time.

A personal Knowledge Grid could be a lifetime artificial companion with a powerful conversation interface (Y. Wilks, Is There Progress on Talking Sensibly to Machines? *Science*, 5852(318)927-928).

A worldwide Knowledge Grid Environment should be more powerful than the sum of its components.

A Knowledge Grid Environment should support more semantic spaces than just one symbol space. Knowledge sharing in a Knowledge Grid Environment depends on correct understanding of the semantics of its resources and processes. But these semantics are not the same as the traditional formal semantics. These should be a kind of interactive semantics, which supports sensing, fusion, mapping, reasoning, abstraction, and transformation between semantic spaces. The semantics of the Knowledge Grid should be easily understood by humans and readily processed by machines.

The internal structures of resources that indicate the same semantics could be completely different. So, finding effective ways (for example, markup languages) to express the internal structure will be much more complex than finding ways to express the external semantics — the semantic links between resources. Since no object in the world exists in isolation, the semantics of a resource could be determined or roughly reflected by the semantics of the resources related to it and the links between them. This is one cause of studying the semantic link network.

A Knowledge Grid can also cooperate and harmoniously co-evolve with other systems like the society. The research aims are to understand ourselves and the law of the society as well as to support decision, wellness, and teamwork. Any effort violating this aim will be insignificance.

Symbolic systems are elegant computing models. Artificial intelligence was regarded as evidenced by the behavior of working symbolic systems. However, symbolic systems have their own particular scope of ability. Non-symbolic systems also have their particular scope of ability. The Knowledge Grid environment should combine the approach of symbolic systems with the approach of non-symbolic systems (this still needs much work).

Billions of years of natural evolution have created a natural environment and an intelligent species that has evolved into human society.

If we draw an analogy between the future interconnection environment and the world of nature, a challenging question arises: what is the field theory of the Knowledge Grid environment? As its basic material, the various resources in the interconnection environment exist in a special field, where resources flow from higher intensity nodes to lower intensity nodes. Social energy is introduced to measure the potential and motion energy in social network (H.Zhuge, Semantic linking through spaces for cyber-physical-socio intelligence: A methodology, *Artificial Intelligence*, 175(2011)988-1019). But the duplication and generation of resources does not cause the loss of any other resource, and the flow of resources also does not mean the loss of any resource. This means that the law of energy conservation in the physical space does not hold in the abstract knowledge space. The laws and principles in this special field will become the basic theory of the future Knowledge Grid environment.

If we draw an analogy between the Knowledge Grid environment and human society, challenging questions arises:

What is the economics of the future intelligent interconnection environment? Economics is an artificial virtual system that helps raise the efficiency of society and realize human aspirations. Continually, we can ask the following questions: *What is the market? What are the prices of services in the Knowledge Grid environment?*

If we draw an analogy between the Knowledge Grid environment and the human physiological system, some further challenging questions arise:

(1) *What is the circulatory system of the future intelligent interconnection environment?* This question impels us to investigate and establish models for material, information, knowledge and service flows.

(2) *What is the immune system of the future intelligent interconnection environment?* This question impels us to investigate the principles of resource clustering and security.

(3) *What is the digestive system?* This question impels us to investigate the principles of generation and understanding of various resources.

(4) *What is the nervous system?* This question impels us to investigate the principles of the control flow within the Knowledge Grid environment.

(5) *What is the ecology? What are the rules of evolution? Will the environment degrade and its species diversity decrease?* To answer these questions requires us to carry out research relating ecology to a cyber-physical-socio-mental ecosystem.

(6) *What are the sustainable development principles and the rules of the future interconnection environment that could evolve harmoniously with human society?* This question impels us to explore the relationship among society, economy, culture and the Knowledge Grid environment.

So far, we can assert that both the notion and the ideal of the Knowledge Grid Environment are understandable, useful and challenging. The methodology of the Knowledge Grid Environment should also include the testable and incremental aspects that Gray mentioned in his Turing Award Lecture.

The incremental aspect would make our short-term target modest. The major characteristics of the Knowledge Grid will be realized by a medium-sized Knowledge Grid in some application area, such as e-science and e-learning, based on the Web x.0, Web of Things, P2P, Cloud, and Grid technologies.

As for the testable aspect, we can use the following basic criteria to evaluate whether it is a Knowledge Grid environment or a knowledge based system within the prior art:

(1) *The cost of knowledge*, including acquisition, reasoning, provision, and maintenance.
(2) *The effectiveness of knowledge services*, for example, the response time.
(3) *The quality of knowledge services*, for example, users' degree of satisfaction with the services.
(4) *The improvement of knowledge services*, for example, whether the services can be improved during use. The improvement means two aspects: the way of service and the development of knowledge.
(5) *The involvement of multiple spaces*. The Knowledge Grid can link symbols to multiple spaces when interacting with humans, while traditional knowledge base systems are only in the cyber space.

On average, a Knowledge Grid should perform better than other systems in 70% of tests.

1.10.8 *Beyond the vision of turing and bush*

Turing described computer intelligence as a machine that can learn from experience and can alter its own instructions. Bush not only envisioned the multi-media but also the information system, Internet and Web. It seems that almost all previous research works in the computing area are to realize their dreams. To go beyond their vision is a grand challenge.

The Cyber-Physical-Socio-Mental Environment is a vision that goes beyond the vision of Turing and Bush.

It is a multi-dimensional complex space that generates and evolves diverse spaces to contain different types of individuals interacting with, reflecting, or influencing each other directly or through the cyber, physical, socio and mental spaces. Versatile individuals and socio roles coexist harmoniously yet evolve, provide appropriate on-demand information, knowledge and services to each other, transform from one form to another, interact through various links, and self-organize according to socio value chains. Change of individual, community or relation in one space can influence those in the other spaces. It ensures healthy and meaningful life of individuals, and maintains a reasonable rate of expansion of individuals according to overall capacity and the material, knowledge, thought and service flow cycles.

The cyber space, physical space, socio space, and mental space will evolve and cooperate with each other in the complex space. Scientific issues will go beyond the cyber space.

Fundamental research concerns the origin and essence of material, life, intelligence and society. These issues obviously go beyond the visions of Turing and Bush.

Different spaces can explain specifically on *what, where, why, when,* and *how* (H.Zhuge, Semantic linking through spaces for cyber-physical-socio intelligence: A methodology, *Artificial Intelligence*, 175(2011)988-1019).

(1) *The socio space can explain*: How do individuals effectively cooperate? What are relevant socio rules? What are the socio effects and socio value?

(2) *The physical space can explain*: How is it related to physical phenomena and laws? Where and when does it happen? What are its physical effects?

(3) *The mental space can explain*: Which category does it belong to? What is the cause? What does it imply? What are the similar cases? What is the appropriate method to solve a problem? What is the probable effect of the method?

(4) *The cyber space can explain*: What is the cyber effect? What services it can provide with?

Sciences and technologies specific to a single space will converge to a general theory and methodology for studying and developing the new environment. The following are some revolution aspects:

(1) *Science*. Scientists will be able to access research objects and thoughts as well as their formation processes on demand through times. This means that they can not only communicate with peers but also access important thoughts through time. They can not only use languages to express ideas but also link language representations to reasons in multiple spaces, to relevant research, and to applications. Scientific thoughts will efficiently influence society through the links between spaces.

(2) *Education*. Students can learn natural and socio laws not only from linguistic and mathematical description in textbooks but also from the linked physical and socio phenomena through times. Learning resources can be self-organized according to students' real-time interest and psychological statuses. Knowledge is created, enhanced, and rebuilt through interaction between coherent motions in different spaces.

(3) *Engineering*. Artifacts can be linked to the ideas, to the design, to the manufacturers, and to the manufacturing processes. The statuses of engineering can also be monitored in lifetime so that necessary maintenance can be carried out on time to ensure healthy status. Function, structure, designer, owner, developer, and even ecological and socio effects will be accessible. All spaces will cooperatively reflect the formation processes of artifacts when they are required, designed, built, sold, used, and recycled.

(4) *History and culture*. Individuals, family trees, thoughts, and socio events will be sensed and preserved as cyber semantic images that can be accessed through times. Recommendation or evaluation will be explained from historical and cultural point of view.

(5) *Society and life.* Society will be safer and life quality will be higher as health of individuals can be detected and evaluated on time, and evaluation results can be linked to measures. Evaluation result will be linked to socio influence through time.

(6) *Intercultural collaboration.* It will help people with different cultural backgrounds collaborate effectively by transforming symbols, linking symbols to different spaces, and establishing peers' semantic images in their mental spaces. As the consequence of collaboration, the collaborators' mental spaces evolve toward more commonalities.

The Cyber-Physical-Socio-Mental Environment has dual nature: the real space containing real individuals, and a virtual space containing the structure, rules, reasons and status of individuals. The virtual space will change when the real space significantly changes.

A simple Knowledge Grid framework consists of the following three levels to support self-organization and normalization in organizing decentralized resources:

(1) High level — the knowledge flows, which work in minds and pass through minds and socio networks for creating and sharing knowledge with the help of the cyber space.

(2) Middle level — the complex semantic space integrating diverse models, including the Semantic Link Network and the Resource Space Model, which will be introduced in the following chapters.

(3) Low level — the decentralized sense, link, organization, synthesis, and storage of knowledge in the cyber space.

The methodology of the Knowledge Grid environment is for guiding human individuals to carry out continuous research and development. It does not follow any single methodology. It incorporates diverse methodologies, including *empiricism*, *rationalism*, *pragmatism*, *individual constructivism*, *social constructivism* and *evolutionism*:

(1) *From empiricism point of view.* The Knowledge Grid methodology argues that knowledge as a complex space evolves and it is enriched in structure and individuals through human

behaviors in multiple spaces, and that the cyber space can reflect and extend human behaviors and experience, e.g., in remote sensing and discovering rules in large-scale data set. Experimental science belongs to empiricism as scientists' judgments rely on experiment results.

(2) *From rationalism point of view.* The Knowledge Grid methodology emphasizes rational thinking, reasoning, and the development of systematic theory during research. The categories of space, time, objects and causality are used in constructing knowledge space in research process.

(3) *From pragmatism point of view.* The Knowledge Grid methodology emphasizes human requirements, well-being and harmonious development of individual, society and nature. It emphasizes both formal models and informal models when developing models. It emphasizes the relation between theory and practice while respecting the differences between them and the independent development.

(4) *From individual constructivism point of view.* The Knowledge Grid methodology argues that individuals contribute and influence knowledge evolution and indication. Symbols and models are created, evaluated, and used by individuals. It also emphasizes that individuals are not isolated, and they interact with each other to evolve knowledge in the social space.

(5) *From social constructivism point of view.* The Knowledge Grid methodology argues that social space is one dimension of knowledge. Social semantic link networks are waved along time and semantics emerges and evolves with the evolution of the network. The social space provides the resources, regulations, cooperation, recognition and culture for individuals.

(6) *From evolutionism point of view.* The Knowledge Grid methodology argues that individuals (humans and resources), spaces, environments, theories, models, and methods co-evolve with time.

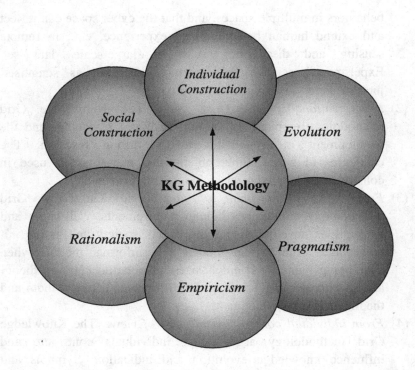

Fig. 1.10.8.1 The Knowledge Grid Methodology.

The Knowledge Grid (KG) Methodology adopts previous knowledge theories and methodologies as its dimensions when developing its multi-dimensional methodology as shown in Fig. 1.10.8.1.

A point in the space has a projection on each dimension. Thought can transfer between dimensions.

A semantic link network of this book's chapters is depicted in Fig. 1.10.8.2.

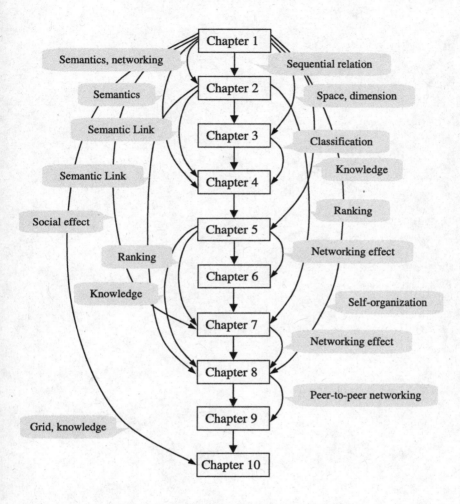

Fig. 1.10.8.2 A semantic link network of chapters.

The following chapters present detailed research and practice — some attempts to fulfill the ideal of the Knowledge Grid environment.

Chapter 2

The Semantic Link Network

Humans live with networks of versatile relations. What are the essential characteristics of relational networking? What are the laws, methods and models for relational networking? How do the relational networks emerge semantics? How to make use of the relational networks to support basic intelligence? One of the major tasks of science is to unveil various relations.

2.1 The Idea of Mapping

The idea of geographical mapping helps in exploring the Knowledge Grid environment. A geographical map is a pictorial abstraction of a region's physical or social properties. People can use certain features of such a map to accurately and efficiently locate or identify places or regions.

(1) *Coordinate location.* Lines are drawn on maps to link points of equal latitude (distance from the equator) and points of equal longitude (angle from a standard straight line joining the two poles, usually the Greenwich meridian). These enable people to locate a surface feature on a map if they know its coordinates—the latitude and longitude.

(2) *Referential location.* People can locate a surface feature on a map even if they don't know its coordinates, provided they know its distance and direction from a known point or feature on the map. For example, a town about twenty kilometers to the west of the center of Beijing can be found indirectly on a map by referring to the location of the center of Beijing.

65

(3) *Regional partition.* Maps often have lines drawn on them to mark the boundaries of different social or climatic regions. Where there is a hierarchy of regions, different kinds of lines are used to mark the boundaries at different levels of the hierarchy. Knowing what region, such as country or district, a surface feature is in can make it easier to find on a map.

(4) *Color.* When regions are marked on a map, neighboring regions are usually filled in with contrasting colors. This makes it much easier to see the extent of any particular region of search.

(5) *Overlays.* To map information of different kinds, such as traffic, climate, and ecological data, onto the same area, transparent overlays with boundary markings are sometimes used. The distribution of properties such as traffic and population density, rainfall and temperature, and cropping, can then be conveniently compared.

(6) *Legends.* A legend is used to explain aspects of a map, such as the name, scale, and meaning of the symbols and labeling.

If we can create a *semantic map for the Web*, users will be able to use the map to effectively browse its contents. If we can create a *semantic map for the society and a knowledge map for thoughts*, it would bring us much closer to the ideal Knowledge Grid.

Location by coordinates, the most important aid in geographical mapping, can be adapted to Web mapping by using classification. This approach requires Web page providers to encode categories when adding resources. A well-defined classification scheme will help both providers and users.

Referential location of a kind has been the purpose of Web hyperlinks from their beginning, as they enable users to browse from page to page. However, they do not entail semantic relationships, and we cannot accurately locate a resource by just referring to a known resource and giving the semantic relationship.

Regional partition of the Web is provided by the names in the URL (Uniform Resource Locator) of each of its pages. Each URL identifies exactly where in the Web a resource is stored, much like a postal address.

Color can help distinguish classifications. So far, the use of color on the Web is quite arbitrary. There are no regulations for using color to convey semantic properties although national preference in selecting color has been studied. Building a semantic image as a map for the Web is a way to smart Web applications.

A map provides people the context and tool for efficiently finding a location relevant to people. Multi-layer and multi-facet information embedded in a location enable on-demand information services through the cyber space with mobile devices.

The initial motivation of creating the semantic link network model and method (in short SLN) is to reflect the complex systems as a semantic image like the map, to analyze the basic nature of the systems, and to support some basic intelligence.

The idea of map implicates an approach to modeling the functions in the cyber space, physical space, social space, and mental space.

2.2 Basic Concepts and Characteristics

Humans wave semantic link networks consciously and subconsciously in life-time and through generations, and act intelligently with knowing a part of the network.

Fig.2.2.1 depicts a semantic link network formed by the following scientific activities: reading, writing, citing, discussing, submitting, publishing, conferencing, and collaborating.

Semantic Link Network has the following characteristics:

(1) *Dynamicity*. It keeps evolving with continuous interactions and reasoning. It cannot be simply regarded as a static graph.
(2) *Rules*. It contains social rules for regulating the evolution of the network and the reasoning rules for deriving links. For example, students could not be the supervisor of student, and professor could not be the supervisor of professor.
(3) *Openness*. An individual can link to the network according to the rules. This is different from the Web, which enables any page to link to any other page.

(4) *Self-organization.* There is generally no central control on the organization and evolution of the network except the consensus of the rules.

(5) *Complex reasoning.* New semantic links may be derived from the existing network and rules through various reasoning, including relational, deductive, inductive, and analogical reasoning.

(6) *Order sensitive.* The effects of different orders of operations may be different.

(7) *Support basic intelligence.* Individuals can behave intelligently with knowing a part of the network, even though only a very small part of the network.

(8) *Locality and global influence.* The influence of operation is local in short-term, but influence may be global in long-term.

(9) *Multiple spaces.* While experiencing in the physical space and the cyber space, humans wave semantic link networks in the social space, cyber space, and their mental spaces. So, semantic links pass through the cyber space, physical space, social space, and mental space.

Previous research on complex networks and social networks neglect the networking semantics (R. Albert, H. Jeong, A.-L. Barabási, Diameter of the world wide web, *Nature*, 401 (1999) 130-131; M. E. J. Newman, Coauthorship networks and patterns of scientific collaboration, *PNAS*, 101 (2004) 5200–5205; M. E. J. Newman and J. Park, Why social networks are different from other types of networks, *Phys. Rev. E*, 68(2003)036122; J. Balthrop, et al., Technological networks and the spread of computer viruses, *Science*, 304(2004)527–529; B. Karrer and M. E. J. Newman, Competing epidemics on complex networks, *Phys. Rev. E*, 84(2011)036106).

Relationship is a key component of the semantic link network.

The following issues come from the semantic link network:

(1) How to model the dynamic network?
(2) What are its motion principles?
(3) How to discover the implicit relations?
(4) What are its networking effects?

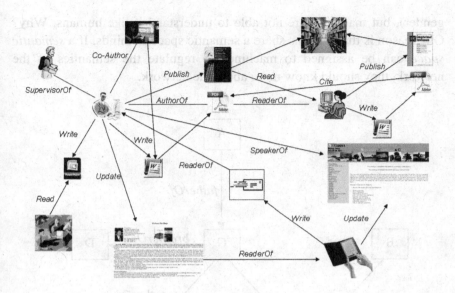

Fig. 2.2.1 Humans have been waving Semantic Link Networks in life-time and through generations.

(5) What is the semantics emerging with the motion of the network?
(6) How does knowledge flow through the network?
(7) What are the principles and methods for effectively sharing knowledge through the network?

Symbiosis is a relation between two individuals or species that benefit each other. It is a basic relation for organizing individuals or species in the biological world.

Blood relation links one person to another by birth rather than by marriage. It is a basic relation of forming a society.

Kinship is a relationship between persons that share a genealogical origin. In anthropology, it includes persons related both by descent and marriage. The kinship relation through marriage is commonly called *affinity* in contrast to *descent*. Kinship is one of the most basic relations for organizing individuals.

From the network shown in Fig.2.2.2, humans know that it is about family relationships and can infer some characteristics of nodes (e.g., gender), but machines are not able to understand it like humans. Why? One reason is that humans share a semantic space in minds. If a *semantic space* can be assigned to machines to regulate the semantics of the network, they should know more about the network.

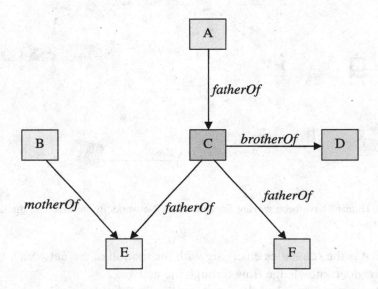

Fig. 2.2.2 A simple network of family relationship.

Definition 2.2.1 A *semantic link network* (SLN) is a relational network consisting of the following main parts: a set of *semantic nodes*, a set of *semantic links* between the nodes, and a *semantic space*. Semantic nodes can be anything. The semantic link between nodes is regulated by the attributes of nodes or generated by interactions between nodes. The semantic space includes a classification hierarchy of concepts and a set of *rules* for reasoning and inferring semantic links, for influence nodes and links, for networking, and for evolving the network.

A semantic link network can be denoted as $SLN=<N, L, \Im, f>$, where $\Im$ *is the semantic space* consisting of a concept hierarchy $\wp$ and a rule set $\Re$, and f is a mapping from $\{N, L\}$ into $\Im$. Sometimes, we simply use $SLN=<N, L, \Re>$ to denote a semantic link network in a given domain.

The following are further explanations:

(1) A semantic node can be anything, for example, text and image, individual (human or agent), event, concept, class, or even an SLN. A semantic node has attributes that reflect features in one or more spaces (e.g., the physical space and physiological space). The attributes of a node render its class.

(2) A semantic link indicates the relation between semantic nodes. It can be indicated by a relation indicator (a certain form of symbol) or a combination of relational indicator according to predefined *lightweight grammar*. The semantics of the indicator is regulated by the semantic space. Some semantic links are determined by the attributes of semantic nodes, while others are determined by direct or indirect interaction between semantic nodes.

(3) The rules regulate semantic nodes and semantic links. Implicit semantic links may be derived from the rules and semantic links. For example, *brotherOf* relation between nodes E and F can be derived from the *fatherOf* relation between nodes C and E and the *fatherOf* relation between nodes C and F. Semantic nodes may also influence each other through the rules.

(4) The classification hierarchy describes the subclass and super-class relations between concepts. For example, *fatherOf*, *brotherOf* and *motherOf* are subclases of *family relationship*.

The type and number of semantic nodes, semantic links and rules vary with applications. With the rule set varies between small and large, reasoning changes between light and heavy. The rule set can be deteriorated to some restricts on network, e.g., the influence between nodes' attributes.

The co-occurrence relationship is the most basic relationship of social events. In many cases, the relations between two co-occur events are unknown, we say that they are linked by co-occurrence relation. The co-occurrence relation can be specialized into many relations with deepening the understanding of the two events.

The hyperlink Web can be regarded as the degradation of the SLN as hyperlinks are only connections between Web pages to allow for Web browsing. The hyperlink can also be regarded as a co-occurrence relation because the two linked pages are often browsed one after another.

Adding semantic space and semantic indicators to the hyperlink network may gain the following advantages:

(1) *Semantics-based resource organization and retrieval.* Simple hyperlinking as in the current Web basically supports ad hoc retrieval, and provide the ranking basis for various search engines. Neither approach is well suited to semantic retrieval. By adding semantic qualification, the SLN can make retrieval more effective.

(2) *Semantics-based reasoning and browsing.* The semantic relationships encoded in the links of SLNs support coarse relational reasoning, which enables intelligent browsing and retrieval.

(3) *Semantic overlaying.* An SLN can be a semantic overlay for the Web, which provides the context for intelligent applications.

Fig. 2.2.3 is an example of using semantic links to cluster images. Tags are words attached to images by Web users. An image can have multiple tags given by different users. The semantics of tags can be indicated by clustering tags and statistic analysis on the usages of tags (P.A. Chirita, et al., P-TAG: large scale automatic generation of personalized annotation tags for the web, *WWW07*).

Images can be clustered according to the relations between the tags. One way to find the relations between tags is to find the co-occurrence relations between the words in commonly interested Web pages. A distance between words can be defined according to some criteria. For example, the distance between two words occurred in one sentence can be defined as shorter than the distance between the words occurred in different sentences. If two words often co-occur in the same sentence, a co-occurrence link is possibly between them. For example, a co-occurrence link is possibly between "boat" and "river". To reflect the uncertainty, a probabilistic semantic link is necessary.

Arbitrarily annotating semantic relations will make the network hard to be understood, but formal computational semantics is usually unacceptable by users and actually not computational (Y. Wilks, Computational Semantics Requires Computation, *FLAIRS Conference*

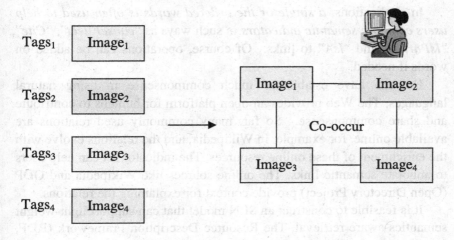

Fig. 2.2.3 Using semantic links to cluster online images.

2011). Statistical approaches are suitable for machine processing, but abstraction plays a more important role in forming and understanding semantics (J.B. Tenenbaum, et al., How to grow a mind: Statistics, structure, and abstraction, *Science*, 331 (6022)(2001) 1279-1285; J. Heinz and W. Idsardi, Sentence and Word Complexity, *Science*, 15(2011)295-297).

One factor of the success of the Web is its simplicity in linkage and usage mode.

How to appropriately indicate the semantics of relations?

Because of the domination of natural language used in communication, humans have to rely on words as semantic indicators because the semantics of words have been regulated in commonsense. For machine understanding, a light-weight language is needed to compose the indicators.

The light-weight language consists of a set of keywords, a simple grammar regulating the relations between keywords, and the relations between keywords, instances and classes. As an abstract concept, a class includes attributes and functions.

In applications, *a single or the ordered words is often used to help users compose semantic indicators* in such ways as *"causeEffect"*, *"Cite"*, *"IsPartOf"* and *"IsA"* to links. Of course, operations can be added on words if needed.

Humans have established much commonsense in using natural languages. The Web provides an open platform for humans to contribute and share commonsense. So far, many commonly used relations are available online, for example, in Wikipedia, and the relations evolve with the enrichment of these online resources. The indicator set can help users to annotate semantic links. The online sources like Wikipedia and ODP (Open Directory Project) provide context for explaining the relations.

It is feasible to construct an SLN model that can support light-weight semantics-aware retrieval. The Resource Description Framework (RDF, www.w3.org/RDF/) plays the similar role in technique. RDF can be one implementation solution of applying SLN to Web applications. But, SLN research concerns dynamicity and generality, and it is at more abstraction level and methodology level.

Why are SLNs relevant to the Knowledge Grid ?

Semantics is the basis of understanding and sharing knowledge. An SLN embodies a kind of coarse semantics and it has some of the characteristics of the Web. Given a formal structure and a well developed method and theory, an SLN can be used as a semantic interconnection overlay of the Knowledge Grid. However, the Knowledge Grid should have multiple semantic overlays for different semantic scales.

With the development of society and information technology, humans become increasingly relying on various explicit or implicit relationships to live and work. The key issue of many applications, from general Web search to specific domain applications like geographical information retrieval, is how to accurately locate the necessary resources and relationships in large and complex SLNs.

A semantic link can be represented as $X \text{---} \alpha \rightarrow Y$ in simple, and a relation "$\text{---} \alpha \rightarrow$" is called an α-link or semantic link. The co-occurrence can be denoted as $X \text{------} Y$ in simple.

The following are some concepts on semantic links:

(1) If there is a semantic link chain from X to Y, we say that Y is *semantically reachable* from X.

(2) If X—α→Y $\Rightarrow$ X—β→Y, then we say that α implies β, denoted by $f(\alpha) \subseteq f(\beta)$, or $\alpha \subseteq \beta$ in simple, i.e., the semantic image of α is semantically included by (or, is a subclass of) the semantic image of β. For example, X—*SonOf*→Y $\Rightarrow$ X—*OffspringOf*→Y if *SonOf* is the subclass of *OffspringOf* in a class hierarchy.

(3) If we have X—α→Y, Y—α→Z $\Rightarrow$ X—α→Z (where $\Rightarrow$ stands for implication), we say that α or the α-link is transitive.

(4) We say that X is semantically equivalent to Y, denoted by X—*equal*—Y, or $X = Y$, if they can substitute for each other wherever they occur.

The following is a set of general semantic links:

(1) The *cause-effect link*, denoted by *ce* as in r—*ce*→r', for which the predecessor is a cause of its successor, and the successor is an effect of its predecessor. The cause-effect link is transitive, that is, r—*ce*→r', r'—*ce*→r'' $\Rightarrow$ r—*ce*→r''. Cause-effect reasoning can chain along cause-effect links because of this transitivity.

(2) The *implication link*, denoted by *imp* as in r—*imp*→r', for which the semantics of the predecessor implies that of its successor. The implication link is transitive, that is, r—*imp*→r', r'—*imp*→r'' $\Rightarrow$ r—*imp*→r''. Implication links can help a reasoning process find the relationships between documents.

(3) The *subtype link*, denoted by *stOf* as in r—*stOf*→r', for which the successor reserves all the features of its predecessor. The subtype link is transitive, like set inclusion, that is, r—*stOf*→r', r'—*stOf*→r'' $\Rightarrow$ r—*stOf*→r''.

(4) The *similar link*, denoted by *(sim, sd)* as in r—*(sim, sd)*→r', for which the semantics of the successor is similar to that of its predecessor, and where *sd* is the degree of the similarity between r and r'. Like the partial-inheritance relationship (H. Zhuge, Inheritance rules for flexible model retrieval, *Decision Support Systems*, 22(4)(1998)379-390), the similar link is intransitive.

(5) The *instance link*, denoted by *insOf* as in r—*insOf*→r', for which the successor is an instance of the predecessor.

(6) The *sequential link*, denoted by *seq* as in r—*seq*→r', which requires that r be browsed before r'. In other words, the content of r' is a successor of the content of r. The sequential link is transitive, that is, r—*seq*→r', r'—*seq*→$r'' \Rightarrow r$—*seq*→r''. The transitivity enables relevant links to be connected in a sequential chain.

(7) The *reference link*, denoted by *ref* as in r—*ref*→r', for which r' is a further explanation of r. The reference link is transitive, that is, r—*ref*→r', r'—*ref*→$r'' \Rightarrow r$—*ref*→r''. However, partial reference like the citation link is intransitive.

(8) The *equal link*, denoted by *e* as in r—*e*→r', for which r and r' are identical in meaning. Clearly, any resource is equal to itself.

(9) The *empty link*, denoted by ϕ as in r—ϕ→r', for which r and r' are completely irrelevant to each other.

(10) The *null or unknown link*, denoted by *Null* or *N* as in r—*N*→r', for which the relation between two resources is unknown or uncertain. The *Null* relation means that there might be a relationship, but we do not yet know what it is. A null link can be replaced by a provider or by a reasoning process.

(11) The *non-α relation*, denoted by *Non* (α) or α^N as in r—α^N→r', for which there is no α relationship between r and r'. It is sometimes useful in the reasoning process to know that a particular relationship between two resources is absent.

(12) The *reverse relation operation*, denoted by *Reverse* (α) or α^R as in r—α^R→r'. If there is a semantic relation α from r to r', then there is a reverse relation from r' to r, that is, r'—α→$r \Rightarrow r$—α^R→r'. A semantic relation and its reverse declare the same thing, but the reverse relation is useful in reasoning sometimes.

Is there any primitive set of semantic indicators?

It is ideal that there exists a set of semantic indicators (properties or factors) Ω in a given domain, such that any semantic relationship between two resources can be described by an indicator or combination of indicators in Ω.

For example, *overlap*, *include*, *disjoin*, *neighbor*, and *equal* are semantic indicators for geographical relations. The *overlap* and *disjoin* are not primitive indicators in describing geographical relations since *overlap* and *disjoin* relations can be defined by the *include* relation.

Different domains have different semantic link primitives. In some domains, primitives are small and simple. In social network, *spouseOf* and *childOf* are primitives in family relations as other relations can be derived from the primitives and the attributes of semantic nodes.

For semantic relations α, β and $\gamma \in \Omega$, we have: $\alpha \subseteq \beta \subseteq \gamma \Rightarrow \alpha \subseteq \gamma$.

Let X, Y and Z be different semantic nodes, and α and β be two semantic indicators. We say that α is semantically orthogonal to β, denoted by $\alpha \perp \beta$, if and only if X—α→Z and Y—β→Z can uniquely determine Z, that is, if there exists Z' such that X—α→Z' and Y—β→Z', then Z is semantically equivalent to Z'.

If two semantic link chains X_1—α_1→X_2—α_2→ ... X_{n-1}—α_{n-1}→X_n and Y_1—β_1→Y_2—β_2→ ... Y_{m-1}—β_{m-1}→Y_m are both transitive, and $X_n = Y_m$ can be uniquely determined, the two chains are orthogonal in SLN.

Orthogonal semantic relationships play an important role in some applications especially those that are relevant to layout or geographical positioning.

Like latitudes and longitudes, orthogonal semantic links help people accurately locate a node. For example, if we want to find the destination X and know that A—*SouthOf*→X and B—*EastOf*→X, then X can be largely located at the meeting point of the two links.

Let SLN_1 and SLN_2 be two SLNs sharing the same rule set. If there is a sub-graph of SLN_2 that is semantically equivalent to SLN_1, we say that SLN_1 is semantically included by SLN_2, denoted by $SLN_1 \subseteq SLN_2$.

The semantic inclusion relationship is transitive, that is, $SLN_1 \subseteq SLN_2$, $SLN_2 \subseteq SLN_3 \Rightarrow SLN_1 \subseteq SLN_3$.

SLN_1 implies SLN_2 if there is a mapping φ. $SLN_1 \to SLN_2$ such that:

(1) *for any node n in SLN_1, we have $n = \varphi(n)$ or the semantic image of n is included by the semantic image of $\varphi(n)$*;

(2) *for any semantic link l in SLN_1, we have $l = \varphi(l)$ or the semantic image of l is included by the semantic image of $\varphi(l)$; and,*

(3) *for any rule in SLN$_1$, we have rule = φ (rule) or the semantic image of rule is included by the semantic image of φ (rule).*

Two SLNs are *semantically equivalent* to each other if there is an isomorphism between them such that corresponding nodes are the same or semantically equivalent to each other, the semantic indicators of the corresponding links imply each other, and the corresponding rule sets are the same.

The notion of the *minimal cover* of an SLN introduced in section 2.4 provides an effective approach for determining the relationship between SLNs. Section 2.8 will discuss the implementation of the operations on SLNs.

2.3 Relational Reasoning and the Semantic Space

Relational reasoning rules are rules for chaining related semantic links to obtain a reasoned result. Reasoning acts through rules, as for example r—ce→r', r'—ce→$r'' \Rightarrow r$—ce→r''. A rule for reasoning can also be represented as $\alpha \cdot \beta \Rightarrow \gamma$, where α, β and γ are semantic indicators, and the above rule can be represented as $ce \cdot ce \Rightarrow ce$.

A simple case of reasoning is where all the semantic links have the same type, that is, single-type reasoning. For transitive semantic links, we have the following reasoning rule: r_1—α→r_2, r_2—α→r_3, ..., r_{n-1} —α→$r_n \Rightarrow r_1$—α→r_n. In general, *ce, imp, st, ref, and e* are transitive in many fields.

Some semantic links are general, while others are specific to domain. Some rules in one domain may not be valid in the other domains. Some general heuristic reasoning rules are given in (H.Zhuge, Communities and Emerging Semantics in Semantic Link Network: Discovery and Learning, *IEEE Transactions on Knowledge and Data Engineering*, 21(6)(2009)785-799; H.Zhuge, Retrieve Images by Understanding Semantic Links and Clustering Image Fragments, *Journal of Systems and Software*, 73(3)(2004)455-466).

In some applications, an order relationship "≤" could be defined on the semantic link set. To obtain a well reasoned result, the reasoning mechanism should find the strongest link among its candidates.

Semantic links can also be inexact. An inexact semantic link represents an uncertainty for its relationship, and is denoted by r—(α, cd)→r', where α is a semantic indicator and cd is the degree of certainty. Inexact single-type reasoning is of the following form:

$$r_1$$—(α, cd_1)→r_2, r_2—(α, cd_2)→r_3, ..., r_n—(α, cd_n)→r_{n+1}
$$\Rightarrow r_1$$—(α, cd)→r_{n+1}, where $cd = min\ (cd_1, ..., cd_n)$.

Different types of inexact semantic links can be also chained according to the rules, for example:

$$r$$—(ce, cd_1)→r', r'—(imp, cd_2)→$r'' \Rightarrow r$—$(ce, min\ (cd_1, cd_2))$→r''.

Another kind of inexactness is associated with the similar link. For example, connecting the *cause-effect* link to the similar link can give the following inexact reasoning rules:

$$r$$—ce→r', r'—(sim, sd)→$r'' \Rightarrow r$—(ce, cd)→r'',

where cd is derived from sd ($cd = sd$ is a simple choice).

With relational reasoning rules, some implicit semantic links can be derived out as indicated by the dotted lines in Fig.2.3.1. Only with a *semantic space* (e.g., constructed by rules and classification hierarchy), a labeled network can be called a semantic link network.

The *semantic link network* will be enhanced in the cyber-physical society:

(1) *The cyber space*, which mainly consists of classification hierarchy and rules. It can be centralized or distributed in the cyber space, social space, and mental space. The rules include not only the reasoning rules but also the rules in the cyber space, physical space and social space.

(2) *The physical space*, which provides the Euclidean space and resources for individuals to live, work, study and interaction. The local spaces where the individuals reside and the distances between individuals indicate local semantics around individuals in the physical space. For example, home, office, and airplane are local spaces that offer space-specific semantics.

(3) *The social space*, which provides commonsense, social rules and economic principles for indicating and understanding semantics.

(4) *The global semantic link network*, which provides the context for the local semantic link networks. Individuals usually know a small part

of the network, but they have the ability to emerge appropriate local semantic link network, and to use it as the context to render the meaning through interaction, although indication may be incomplete. For example, individuals can emerge appropriate local semantic link networks in mind during conversation. This is why incomplete sentences (even incorrect in grammar) do not disturb understanding in conversation.

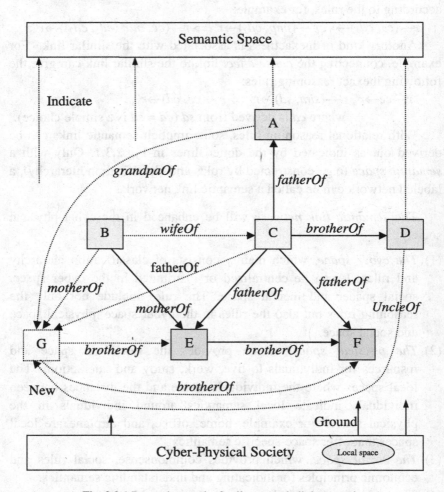

Fig. 2.3.1 Reasoning on the family semantic link network.

(5) *Language*, which provides the ground for semantic indicators. It has evolved a symbol space that obeys specific rules that are different from the physical space and social space.

The cyber-physical society provides rich semantics for semantic link network. The semantic link X—α→Y or X—α—Y will be mapped from the representation in the symbol space into the enriched semantic space $\mathfrak{S}$:

$$f: \{X—\alpha→Y\} → \mathfrak{S}.$$

Where f is a mapping from the symbol space representing X, Y and α into the semantic space, or from one symbol space into another well-defined symbol space, in which all symbol expressions are commonsense.

The semantics of the indicators $f(\alpha)$ is explained by a semantic space defined by a hierarchy of classes and rules. Fig.2.3.2 shows the relations among the physical space, map, concept hierarchy, and indicator space.

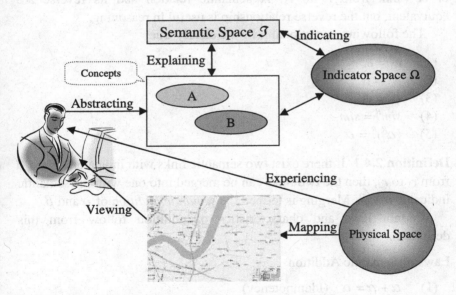

Fig. 2.3.2 The relations among the physical space, map, semantic space, and indicator space.

Section 2.19 will further discuss the issues of semantics.

2.4 An Algebraic Model of the SLN

Operations such as reversal, addition and multiplication can be defined for transforming and composing semantic links. These operations take one or two semantic indicators in and put one semantic indicator out.

Semantic indicators and the operations on them constitute an algebraic system. This section investigates such an algebraic system and its characteristics, assuming that there are no contradict semantic links in the same SLN.

By representing an SLN as a matrix of semantic indicators, reasoning can be carried out by the self-multiplication of the matrix.

If there is a semantic link with indicator α from node r_1 to node r_2, there is a reverse semantic link from r_2 to r_1 called the reversal semantic link, denoted by *Reverse* (α) or α^R.

For example, a cause-effect link from r_1 to r_2 signifies that r_1 is a cause of r_2 and that r_2 is an effect of r_1, that is, it implies a *Reverse* (*ce*) or ce^R link from r_2 to r_1. A semantic relation and its reverse are equivalent, but the reverse relationship is useful in reasoning.

The following operational laws are clearly true:

(1) $e^R = e$.
(2) $N^R = N$.
(3) $\phi^R = \phi$.
(4) $sim^R = sim$.
(5) $(\alpha^R)^R = \alpha$.

Definition 2.4.1 If there exist two semantic links with indicators α and β from r_1 to r_2, then the two links can be merged into one with the semantic indicator $\alpha + \beta$. Merging is termed the *semantic addition* of α and β.

Certain laws and characteristics of addition follow from this definition.

Laws of Semantic Addition

(1) $\alpha + \alpha = \alpha$ (Idempotency).
(2) $\alpha + \beta = \beta + \alpha$ (Commutativity).
(3) $(\alpha + \beta) + \gamma = \alpha + (\beta + \gamma)$ (Associative Addition).
(4) $\alpha + Null = \alpha = Null + \alpha$.

(5) If $\alpha' \leqslant \alpha$, then $\alpha + \alpha' = \alpha$. In particular, $e + \alpha = e$, where α is a semantic indicator that is compatible with e.

(6) $(\alpha + \beta)^R = \alpha^R + \beta^R$.

Characteristic 2.4.1 For any two semantic indicators α and β in an SLN, we have $\alpha \leqslant \alpha + \beta$ and $\beta \leqslant \alpha + \beta$.

Characteristic 2.4.2 For any three semantic indicators α, $\cdot$ β and γ in an SLN, if $\alpha \geqslant \beta$ and $\alpha \geqslant \gamma$, then $\alpha \geqslant \beta + \gamma$.

Definition 2.4.2 If there are two relations, α from r_1 to r_2, and β from r_2 to r_3, in an SLN, and if we can get the semantic indicators γ_1, γ_2, ..., and γ_k from r_1 to r_3 by reasoning, then we call the reasoning process *semantic multiplication*, denoted as $\alpha \times \beta = \gamma$ where $\gamma = \gamma_1 + \gamma_2 + \ldots + \gamma_k$.

Laws of semantic multiplication

(1) $\alpha \times e = \alpha = e \times \alpha$

(2) $\alpha \times N = N = N \times \alpha$

(3) $\alpha \times \phi = N = \phi \times \alpha$ (note that $\phi \times \phi = N$)

(4) $(\alpha + \beta) \times \gamma = \alpha \times \gamma + \beta \times \gamma$, and $\alpha \times (\beta + \gamma) = \alpha \times \beta + \alpha \times \gamma$

(5) $(\alpha \times \beta)^R = \beta^R \times \alpha^R$

Lemma 2.4.1 For any semantic links $r_1 \!\!-\!\alpha\!\rightarrow\! r_2$, $r_1 \!\!-\!\beta\!\rightarrow\! r_2$, and $r_2 \!\!-\!\gamma\!\rightarrow\! r_3$ in an SLN, if $\alpha \geqslant \beta$, then the semantic relation from r_1 to r_3 is $\alpha \times \gamma$ ($\alpha \times \gamma \geqslant \beta \times \gamma$).

Within a certain time period, semantic link network is stable, especially, the semantic space is stable. We can define the concept of semantic closure.

Definition 2.4.3 The *semantic closure* of an SLN $S = <N, L, Rules>$ is $S^+ = <N, L', Rules>$ such that:

(1) $L \subseteq L'$; and,

(2) A semantic link is added to L' if it is available via rule reasoning on L.

The closure has the following characteristics:

Characteristics:

(1) $S \subseteq S^+$.

(2) *An SLN is equivalent to its closure.*
(3) *Two SLNs are equivalent if and only if their closures are the same or equivalent.*
(4) *The equivalence between closures is a reflexive, symmetric and transitive relation.*

Lemma 2.4.2 For two SLNs S and T, S is equivalent to T if and only if $T \subseteq S^+$ and $S \subseteq T^+$.

The *minimal semantic cover* is obtained by removing all redundant semantic links from a semantic cover.

Definition 2.4.4 An SLN M is the *minimal semantic cover* of another SLN S, if M and S satisfy the following conditions.

(1) $M^+ = S^+$; and,
(2) no semantic link l exists in M such that $(M - l)^+ = M^+$.

The minimal semantic cover of an SLN involves in the fewest possible semantic links while its semantics indication is unchanged. Although the minimal cover of an SLN is unique in most cases, exception can be found in a circular network (B. Xu and H. Zhuge, Basic operations, completeness and dynamicity of cyber physical socio semantic link network CPSocio-SLN. *Concurrency and Computation: Practice and Experience*, 23(9)(2011) 924-939).

Matrix representation. An SLN can be represented by an adjacency matrix called the Semantic Relationship Matrix (SRM). An SLN with n nodes $r_1, r_2, ..., r_n$ can be represented by an SRM as follows, where α_{ij} represents the semantic indicator from r_i to r_j, $\alpha_{ii} = e$, and $\alpha_{ij} = \alpha_{ji}^R$:

$$\begin{bmatrix} \alpha_{11} & \alpha_{12} & \cdots & \alpha_{1n} \\ \alpha_{21} & \alpha_{22} & \cdots & \alpha_{2n} \\ \cdots & \cdots & \cdots & \cdots \\ \alpha_{n1} & \alpha_{n2} & \cdots & \alpha_{nn} \end{bmatrix}$$

If there are no semantic links between r_i and r_j, then $\alpha_{ij} = \alpha_{ji} = Null$. The SRM of any SLN is unique if the allocation of nodes is fixed.

Generally, an element in SRM should be a set of semantic indicators as there may have multiple semantic links between the same pair of nodes. A three dimensional tensor can be used to represent a semantic link network (T. Franz, et al. TripleRank: Ranking Semantic Web Data by Tensor Decomposition. *In Proceedings of the International Semantic Web Conference*, 2009, pp.213-228).

A large-scale complex SLN can be separated into several networks with simpler semantic links, and block matrix can be used to decrease the scale (H. Zhuge, et al., Algebra model and experiment for semantic link network. *IJHPCN*, 3(4)(2005) 227-238).

Reasoning on an SLN derives implicit semantic links between nodes by semantic link reasoning. Suppose an SLN has n nodes: $r_1, r_2, ..., r_n$, and its SRM is *mat*. Can we reliably derive the semantic relations of any two nodes from the SRM?

Clearly, we can get α_{ij} as the semantic link between r_i and r_j if the link is in the matrix. However, α_{ij} is sometimes *Null* even though there may in fact be a semantic link that can be computed. In such cases the reliable semantic link, denoted by $\alpha_{ij}^{\#}$, is derived by reasoning.

Theorem 2.4.1 In an SLN, a reliable semantic link can be computed as $\alpha_{ij}^{\#} = mat_{i*} \times mat^{n-2} \times mat_{*j}$, where mat_{i*} is the ith row vector and mat_{*j} is the jth column vector.

Corollary 2.4.1 In an SLN, we have $\alpha_{ij}^{\#} \geqslant \alpha_{ij}$.

If we compute the semantic links of all pairs of nodes in an SLN, then we can get a new SRM, called the full SRM (FSRM), denoted by mat_f. An FSRM is the SLN matrix of the closure of the original SLN. We can get the reliable semantic link between any two nodes in the SLN from the FSRM. Of course, some of these semantic links are in the original SLN, and some are derived. Any semantic reasoning can be done by self-multiplication of the SLN matrix.

The FSRM is an efficient tool for semantic reasoning because there is a reliable semantic link between every pair of nodes.

Corollary 2.4.2 For a semantic link matrix *mat* and its FSRM mat_f, we have:

(1) $mat_f = mat^{n-1}$.
(2) $mat_f \times mat = mat_f$.

This corollary suggests a useful way to compute the FSRM.

The following are some characteristics.

Characteristics 2.4.

(1) *A semantic link may have several minimum spanning graphs.*
(2) *Different semantic links may exist between the same pair of semantic nodes.*
(3) *The spanning graph of a semantic link l is a subgraph of the minimum semantic cover such that this subgraph's closure includes l.*
(4) *The minimum spanning graph of semantic link l is a subgraph of the minimum semantic cover such that this subgraph's closure includes l, and there is no other subgraph, whose closure also includes l.*
(5) *Removing a semantic link outside the minimum semantic cover does not influence the semantics of SLN.*
(6) *Adding a semantic link belonging to the closure of the SLN and then removing it do not influence the semantics of SLN.*
(7) *Adding a set of semantic links to SLN may change the minimum semantic cover and the closure of SLN.*

2.5   SLN Normalization

2.5.1 *The normal forms of an SLN*

SLN normal forms are used to ensure the correctness and effectiveness of an SLN's semantic indication and operations. The following definitions help in removing redundancy and inconsistency.

Two semantic nodes are equivalent in indicating semantics if they have the same attributes and belong to the same class.

Definition 2.5.1 If there is no semantically equivalent node in an SLN, then we say that the SLN is in first normal form, or 1NF.

1NF regulates the SLN by excluding redundant semantic nodes.

Definition 2.5.2 If an SLN is in 1NF and there is no inconsistent and implication semantic link between the same pair of nodes, then we say the SLN is in second normal form, or 2NF.

2NF regulates the SLN by excluding redundant and inconsistent semantic links.

Definition 2.5.3 If an SLN is in 2NF and there is no isolated node or part, then we say that the SLN is in third normal form, or 3NF.

The 3NF guarantees that we can reach all the nodes in SLN starting from any of its nodes.

Definition 2.5.4 If an SLN is in 3NF and it cannot be simplified into semantically equivalent one by removing semantic links, then we say that the SLN is in fourth normal form, or 4NF.

2.5.2 *Operations on SLNs*

Applications or user interfaces that manage the resources of, or need services such as browsing for, a large-scale SLN need operations applied to that SLN.

There are six basic operations:

(1) Add a semantic node to the SLN.
(2) Remove a semantic node from the SLN.
(3) Add a semantic link to the SLN.
(4) Remove a semantic link from the SLN.
(5) Add a rule to the SLN.
(6) Remove a rule from the SLN.

Graph-like operations can be defined as follows. Let $SLN_1 = <N_1, L_1,$ $Rules_1>$ and $SLN_2 = <N_2, L_2, Rules_2>$ where N_1 and N_2 are node sets, and L_1 and L_2 are semantic link sets.

(1) *Intersection*: $SLN_1 \cap SLN_2 = <N_1 \cap N_2, L_1 \cap L_2, Rule_3>$, where $Rule_3$ is generated by removing the rules relevant to the semantic links in $L_1 \cup L_2 - L_1 \cap L_2$ from $Rule_1 \cup Rule_2$.
(2) *Union*: $SLN_1 \cup SLN_2 = <N_1 \cup N_2, L_1 \cup L_2, Rule_1 \cup Rule_2>$.

(3) *Inclusion*: returns *true* if $SLN_1 \subseteq SLN_2$, otherwise returns *false*.

Where $L_1 \cap L_2 = \{n—\alpha{\rightarrow}n' \mid \alpha = min\ (\alpha_1, \alpha_2),\ n—\alpha_1{\rightarrow}n' \in SLN_1,$
$n—\alpha_2{\rightarrow}n' \in SLN_2\}$, if α_2 is equal to or implies α_1, $min\ (\alpha_1, \alpha_2) = \alpha_1$ else
$min\ (\alpha_1, \alpha_2) = Null$. $L_1 \cup L_2 = \{n—(\alpha_1+\alpha_2){\rightarrow}n' \mid n—\alpha_1{\rightarrow}n' \in SLN_1,$
$n—\alpha_2{\rightarrow}n' \in SLN_2\}$.

In the following, we focus on three operations *join*, *split*, and *view*.

Definition 2.5.5 Two SLNs can be joined in one of the following three ways.

(1) If they have one common node, then the join operation (called *join by node*) merges the common node.
(2) If they have one common semantic link or chain, then the join operation (called *join by semantic link*) merges the common chain.
(3) If at least one semantically distinct link can be added between two SLNs, then the join operation (called *join by link addition*) adds such a link.

Lemma 2.5.1 The join operation conserves 1NF, 2NF, and 3NF characteristics.

Proof. The join operation (either *by node* or *by link addition*) does not add any semantically equivalent node or link, so join conserves 1NF and 2NF. For the case of 3NF, we consider the following two aspects:

1) *Join by node or by a chain (of semantic links)*. Let SLN_1 and SLN_2 be two SLNs, and let SLN be the join of SLN_1 and SLN_2 by merging the common node n (or chain C) of SLN_1 and SLN_2. If both SLN_1 and SLN_2 are 3NF, then any node in SLN_1 is accessible from any node in SLN_2 through n (or any node of C or chain C), and vice versa. So SLN is 3NF.
2) *Join by link addition*. Let l be the semantic link added between node n in SLN_1 and node n' in SLN_2. If both SLN_1 and SLN_2 are 3NF, then any node in SLN_1 is accessible from n and any node in SLN_2 is accessible from n', so any node in SLN_1 is accessible from any node in SLN_2 through l, vice versa. Hence SLN is 3NF.

Thus, we conclude that the join operation conserves 1NF, 2NF and 3NF characteristics.

By duplicating nodes or links, or by deleting nodes and links, a single SLN can be split into two SLNs.

The split operation does not increase semantically equivalent nodes and links in either of the split SLNs, so it conserves 1NF and 2NF. The split operation may break accessibility within either of the split SLNs, so it does not necessarily conserve 3NF. But, we can add some conditions to enable it to conserve both 3NF and 4NF characteristics. Fig. 2.5.2.1 shows different split operations.

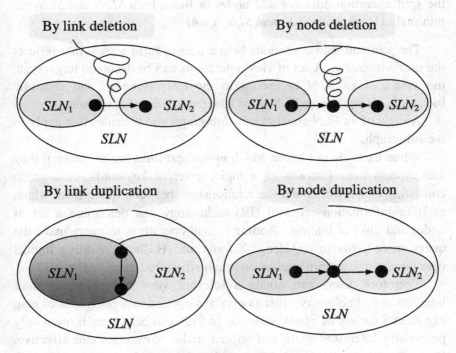

Fig.2.5.2.1 Split operations.

Lemma 2.5.2 The split operation conserves 1NF and 2NF.

Lemma 2.5.3 Let *SLN* be 3NF and let it be split into SLN_1 and SLN_2. If $SLN_1 \cup SLN_2 = SLN$, then both SLN_1 and SLN_2 are 3NF.

Proof. The condition $SLN_1 \cup SLN_2 = SLN$ ensures that the split operation does not remove links or nodes, that is, it allows only splitting by duplication. Hence the connectivity of both SLN_1 and SLN_2 is the same as that of SLN. Otherwise, we assume that node n in SLN_i ($i = 1, 2$) is not accessible from p in SLN. Consequently, n is also not accessible from p because no nodes or links are lost during the split operation. Hence both SLN_1 and SLN_2 are 3NF.

Lemma 2.5.4 Let SLN be 4NF and let it be split into SLN_1 and SLN_2. If $SLN_1 \cup SLN_2 = SLN$, then both SLN_1 and SLN_2 are 4NF.

Proof. From the previous lemma, both SLN_1 and SLN_2 are 3NF. Since the split operation does not add nodes or links, both SLN_1 and SLN_2 are minimal. Hence, both SLN_1 and SLN_2 are 4NF.

The join and split operations help a user to form a view that reflects the user's interests. A set of view operations can be designed to generate the views of an SLN according to the interest nodes and semantic indicators. It enables an SLN to be adapted to the needs of users.

A view of an SLN consists of a sub-graph and the rules that apply to the sub-graph.

When users do not know which nodes and links are of interest, they can express their interests as a topic, a set of keywords, or a graph consisting of keywords and the relationships between them, from which existing information retrieval (IR) technology can determine a set of nodes and links of interest. Adding logical operations to query make the query more powerful (Q.Zeng, X.Jiang and H.Zhuge, Adding logical operators to tree pattern queries on graph-structured data, *VLDB* 2012).

Therefore, users can obtain a relevant view by specifying their interests in a simple way. Just as overlays applied to a geographical map can meet a variety of needs, views of an SLN can help users browse only potentially interested parts and so can make browsing more effective. Since the view operation does not add nodes or links, it conserves 1NF and 2NF characteristics.

Lemma 2.5.5 SLN views conserve 1NF and 2NF characteristics.

Lemma 2.5.6 If two views have the same normal forms, then their join produces a view that conserves these normal forms.

2.6 Constraints and Displaying

The normal forms provide guidance towards precise SLNs. The following criteria are for building an appropriate SLN.

(1) Any semantic node or semantic link of an SLN should have mapping image (semantic image) in the semantic space.
(2) Any operation of adding a node to an SLN should accompany an operation of adding a link to connect that node to an existing node. This criterion ensures that no node of an SLN is isolated.
(3) Use of the resource represented by any node in an SLN should obey all restrictions and protocols for its use or execution environment laid down when the node was created.

An SLN can be used for the purposes such as browsing, reasoning, reusing and controlling. In some applications, constraints are needed to guarantee appropriate operations. The SLN maker can apply constraints of the following kinds:

(1) A constraint on nodes' attributes.
(2) A constraint on the relationships between attributes for coordinating nodes.
(3) A constraint between a node and its links, specifying a relationship between the links (such as *and*, *or*, *and-split*, *or-split* in the workflow model) and the conditions on links involved.
(4) A meta-constraint, that is, a constraint on constraints. The application of a given SLN is a particular form of explanation, reasoning or execution of the network under these constraints.

SLN can be displayed at the entity resource (e.g., document) level or the abstract semantic level, and can shift between these two levels.

An execution engine and monitor engine can be designed as in the workflow management systems (www.wfmc.org). The execution view should show an SLN satisfying at least the 3NF. Constraints can be set from application requirements when establishing the SLN and can be verified during execution. SLN reasoning can be carried out starting from a user's view of interest, and can be of the following two kinds:

(1) *View reasoning*. Reasoning between views of an SLN is carried out according to the transitivity of inclusion ($\subseteq$) and implication ($\rightarrow$) between views. For example:

$view_1 \subseteq view_2$, $view_2 \subseteq view_3 \Rightarrow view_1 \subseteq view_3$;

$view_1 \rightarrow view_2$, $view_2 \rightarrow view_3 \Rightarrow view_1 \rightarrow view_3$; and,

$view_1 \rightarrow view_2$, $view_3 \subseteq view_2 \Rightarrow view_1 \rightarrow view_3$.

(2) *Link reasoning* of the following five types:

- *Transitive*: reasoning about transitive semantic links: X_1—α→X_2, X_2—α→X_3, ..., X_{n-1}—α→$X_n \Rightarrow X_1$—α→X_n.

- *Implication*: α→β, X—α→Y, Y—β→$Z \Rightarrow X$—β→Z.

- *Abstraction*: if X is an abstraction of Z, Z—α→$Y \Rightarrow X$—α→Y. For example, if *Professor* is an abstraction of the person named *Zhuge*, we have: *Zhuge*—*supervise*→*Zhang* $\Rightarrow$ *Professor*—*supervise*→*Zhang*.

- *By analogy*: X—α→Y, $X \sim X'$, $Y \sim Y' \Rightarrow X'$—α→Y', where $\sim$ represents a similar relationship. The result can be given a certainty degree *cd*, which can be determined from the similarity degrees of $X \sim X'$ and $Y \sim Y'$.

- *Hybrid*: any combination of the above types.

SLN reasoning is to derive implicit semantic links, which is likely to help people to act intelligently.

2.7 SLN Ranking

Nodes in an SLN have ranks differentiating their importance in the network.

2.7.1 *Hyperlink network ranking*

To rank and refine Web search results, search engines analyze hyperlink structure (M.R. Henzinger, Hyperlink Analysis for the Web, *IEEE Internet Computing*, 5(1)(2001)45-50). The HITS algorithm

(J.M. Kleinberg, Authoritative sources in a hyperlinked environment, *Journal of the ACM*, 46(5)(1999)604-632) and the PageRank algorithm (L. Page, et al., The pagerank citation ranking: bringing order to the web, *Technical report*, Stanford, Santa Barbara, CA 93106, January, 1998) are typical of the algorithms used to rank Web pages using hyperlink analysis.

Both algorithms calculate the scores for each page of the entire Web by taking link structure into account. A Web graph consists of Web pages as nodes and hyperlinks as edges.

The HITS algorithm measures the importance of a single Web page from two aspects: *authority* and *hub*. A page with high authority has many pages pointing to it, which implies its authority; a page with a high hub points to many other pages, which implies its richness in material. The authority of a page is computed by summing up the hub scores of all pages pointing to it, while the hub score is the summation of the authority of all pages pointing to it.

PageRank reduces the importance of a page to a single parameter — rank. It simply recognizes that a page with many other pages pointing to it is important because it is frequently cited by others. The rank of a page is evenly distributed among all pages it points to. A page gets a small donation from the rank of each page pointing to it. Then, its rank is calculated by summing up all the donations it gets.

HITS uses both in-links and out-links of a page, whereas PageRank only uses the in-links.

2.7.2 *SLN ranking*

A semantic link can be assigned a *certainty degree* (denoted by cd) to reflect the likelihood of a particular semantic relationship between its nodes or components (i.e., community). An inexact link can be shown as $C_1 \!\!-\!\!(l, cd) \rightarrow C_2$, where C_1 and C_2 are components, l indicates a relation, and $cd \in (0, 1)$.

The certainty degree is valuable for ranking components according to their semantic importance when using an SLN. Semantic link structure reflects the relationships between components, just as hyperlink structure reflects the relationships between Web pages.

Naturally, we can adopt hyperlink analysis to rank nodes or components of an SLN, though in the PageRank algorithm every Web page has only one rank. But for an SLN we must take into account different semantic links, as *different semantic links may play different roles in structuring and evolving the network*.

For a semantic component C, we can devise an overall rank, called the *T*-rank, and a set of individual *l*-ranks for different *l*-links.

2.7.3 *A ranking algorithm*

Let C and D be components of an SLN, l be a semantic link in semantic link set L, F_C^l be the set of components of the SLN l-linked from C, and B_C^l be the set of components of the SLN l-linked to C. The sum of the certainty degrees of all l-links from C can be denoted by

$$N_C^l = \sum_{v \in B_C^L} cd_l^{v \to C},$$

where $cd_l^{v \to C}$ is the certainty degree of an l-link from v to C. The rank of a component C can be defined as follows:

$$R(C) = \beta \sum_{l \in L} R_l(C),$$

where $R_l(C) = \beta_l \times \sum_{D \in B_C^l} \frac{R_l(D) \times R(l)}{N_D^l},$

and

$$R(l) = w_l \times cd_l^{D \to C}.$$

$R(C)$ is the *T*-rank of C. $R_l(C)$ is the *l*-rank of C, derived from all the *l*-links pointing to C. β_l and β are normalization factors such that the total *l*-rank (or *T*-rank) of all components is constant. $R(l)$ is the rank of an *l*-link, being the product of the weight of the link type (w_l) and the certainty degree of the link ($cd_l^{D \to C}$).

A vector of ranks of different semantic links on a semantic node $(R_l(C) | l \in L)$ is useful as applications may concern the roles of different semantic links. So both $R(C)$ and $R_l(C)$ should be known for a semantic link network application.

The *l*-rank of a component is shared among its outward *l*-links to contribute to the *l*-ranks of the components pointed to. As far as the inexactness of semantic links is concerned, the certainty degree is attached to the corresponding *l*-link.

The above formulas show that the rank of a component C depends recursively on the ranks of the semantic links pointing to it. Individual *l*-ranks $R_l(C)$ can be calculated by using an iterative algorithm similar to that of PageRank.

The ranking algorithm

Let A^l be an $n \times n$ matrix with rows and columns corresponding to semantic components, where N is the total number of components of the SLN under consideration.

Assume $A^l_{i,j} = cd_l^{C_i \rightarrow C_j} / N^l_{C_i}$ when there is an *l*-link from C_i to C_j with certainty degree $cd_l^{C_i \rightarrow C_j}$, otherwise $A^l_{i,j} = 0$. A^l is called the *l*-link adjacency matrix.

If we treat R_l as a vector over semantic components, then we have $R_l = \beta_l (A^l)^T R_l$. So R_l is an eigenvector of $(A^l)^T$ with eigenvalue β_l. We want the dominant eigenvector of $(A^l)^T$.

The algorithm for computing *T*-rank is described as follows:

Function *T*-rank (S, A^l)

where A^l is the *l*-link adjacency matrix and S is an initial vector of *l*-ranks. S can be almost any vector over the semantic components, so we can simply set S to an *n*-dimensional vector with every element s_i equals to $1/n$.

{

For each l in Ω

{

$R_l^0 \leftarrow S$

Do

$R_l^{i+1} \leftarrow (A^l)^T R_l^i$

$\delta \leftarrow \left\| R_l^{i+1} - R_l^i \right\|_1$

// note: $\left\| R \right\|_1$ is the l_1 norm of vector R

>   While $\delta > \varepsilon$
>   }
> $R \leftarrow O$ // note: O is a zero vector
>   For each l in Ω
> $R \leftarrow R + w_l \times R_l$
>   Return R
> }

Relevant experiments have been described in (H. Zhuge and L. Zheng, Ranking Semantic-linked Network, *Proceedings of WWW2003*, Budapest, May, 2003, available at www2003.org/cdrom /papers/poster/p148/P148-Zhuge/P148-Zhuge.htm).

It is an interesting topic to infer additional semantics from users' behavior (including interactions between users) when they browse an SLN.

Chapter7 will present a new approach to ranking.

2.8   Implementation of SLN Operations

2.8.1 *Matching between SLNs*

The SLNs discussed here contain no isolated nodes. Matching between two structures of SLN, expressed as graphs $G = (V, E)$ and $G' = (V', E')$, needs to distinguish the following five types of relationship:

(1) *Intersection*. There exists at least one edge that is contained in both E and E'. An edge expressed as $e = \alpha(x, y)$ comprises two vertices x and y and a semantic indicator α.
(2) *Null*. The intersection of E and E' is an empty set.
(3) *Equal*. Every edge in E is also in E', and every edge in E' is also in E.
(4) *Inclusion*. Every edge in E is also in E'.
(5) *Inverse inclusion*. Every edge in E' is also in E.

Let G be a 2NF SLN with at least two vertices and one edge, and *mat* (G) be the SRM of G, with the nodes of rows and columns in the same sequence. Every element of *mat* (*G*) is a possibly empty set of semantic indicators.

Let SLN $G' = (V', E')$ be a subgraph of $G = (V, E)$. For every edge $e = \alpha(x, y) \in E$, if $x \in V'$ and $y \in V'$, and $e \in E'$, we call $G' = (V', E')$ a *fully induced sub-semantic-graph* of G with vertex set V', denoted by $G_V(V')$.

For two SLNs $G = (V, E)$ and $G' = (V', E')$, if $V = V'$, let $R(G)$ be the result of a subtraction, $R(G) = mat(G) - mat(G')$.

$$R(G_{ij}) = mat(G_{ij}) - mat(G'_{ij}) = \bigcup_{i=1}^{3} W_i^k, \, k = 0, 1;$$

where $W_i^k = \{0\}$ if $<i = 1, k = 1>$; $W_i^k =$ null if $<i = 1, k = 0>$, $<i = 2, k = 0>$, and $<i = 3, k = 0>$; $W_i^k = \{+\}$ if $<i = 2, k = 1>$; and, $W_i^k = \{-\}$ if $<i = 3, k = 1>$.

$R_{ij}(G) = \{0\}$ means that there is at least one element that is contained in both $mat_{ij}(G)$ and $mat_{ij}(G')$. $R_{ij}(G) = \{+\}$ means that there is at least one element that is contained in $mat_{ij}(G)$ but not in $mat_{ij}(G')$. $R_{ij}(G) = \{-\}$ means that there is at least one element that is contained in $mat_{ij}(G')$ but not in $mat_{ij}(G)$.

The relationship between G and G' can be determined by the following steps.

(1) Let $V_{int} = V \cap V'$, and G_1 and G_2 be their fully induced sub-graphs with vertex set V_{int}. $G_1 = (V_{int}, E_1) = G_V(V_{int})$ and $G_2 = (V_{int}, E_2) = G'_{V'}(V_{int})$. The relationship between G_1 and G_2 can be determined by the algorithm *Rel_SLN_Vertex* described below, which is also suitable for determining the relationship between any two networks that have the same vertex set.

(2) From the relationship between G_1 and G_2, algorithm *Rel_SLN* determines the relationship between G and G'.

Algorithm 2.8.1 Let $G_1 = (V, E_1)$ and $G_2 = (V, E_2)$ be two structures of SLN, and let *mat* (G_1) and *mat* (G_2) be $n \times n$ SLN matrices. The following algorithm sets up a correspondence between the vertices of each SLN and the rows and columns of its matrix, and also a mapping between rows and columns of the two matrices. It is then used to determine the relationship between the structures of SLN.

Rel_SLN_Vertex (SLN G_1, SLN G_2)
{   *Pre_Process* (*mat* (G_1), *mat* (G_2)); // establishes the node
                                         correspondence between G_1 and
                                         G_2.
    Subtract (*mat*(G_1), *mat*(G_2), *R*(G)); // $R(G) = mat(G_1) - mat(G_2)$
    RtnStr = *Result* (*R* (*G*));
    Return *RtnStr*;
}

The algorithm *Rel_SLN* determines the relationship between any two structures of SLN $G_1 = (V_1, E_1)$ and $G_2 = (V_2, E_2)$ and returns a value in {"intersection", "empty", "equal", "inclusion", "inverse inclusion"}.

Algorithm 2.8.2

Rel_SLN (SLN G_1, SLN G_2)
{   If ($V_1 == V_2$) Return *Rel_SLN_Vertex* (G_1, G_2);
    If ($V_1 \subset V_2$)
    {   Let $G_3 = (V_1, E_3) = G_2 {}_{V2} (V_1)$;
        rtn = *Rel_SLN_Vertex*(G_1, G_3);
        If (*rtn* == "empty" || *rtn* = "inclusion") Return *rtn*;
        If(*rtn* == "equal") Return "inclusion";
        If ((*rtn* == "intersection") || (*rtn* == "inverse inclusion")) Return
           "intersection";
    }
    If ($V_1 \supset V_2$)
    {   Let $G_3 = (V_2, E_3) = G_1 {}_{V1} (V_2)$;
        rtn = *Rel_SLN_Vertex* (G_2, G_3);
        If (*rtn* == "empty") Return *rtn*;
        If ((*rtn* == "inclusion") || (*rtn* == "equal"))
           Return "inverse inclusion";
        If ((*rtn* == "intersection") || (*rtn* == "inverse inclusion")) Return
           "intersection";
    }

Let $V_{int} = V_1 \cap V_2$;   // let V_{int} be the intersection of set V_1 and V_2.

If $V_{int} == \Phi$ Return "empty";

If $(V_{int} != \Phi)$

{   Let $G_3 = (V_{int}, E_3) = G_1 {}_{V1} (V_{int})$ and

    $G_4 = (V_{int}, E_4) = G_2 {}_{V2} (V_{int})$;

    $rtn = Rel\_SLN\_Vertex(G_3, G_4)$;

    If $rtn ==$ "empty" Return "empty";

    If $(rtn !=$ "empty"$)$ Return "intersection";

}

}

From the relationship returned by algorithm *Rel_SLN*, we can find which SLN contains richer semantics. For example, if the returned value is "inclusion", then G_2 has richer semantics; if the returned value is "inverse inclusion", then G_1 contains richer semantics.

Algorithm *Rel_SLN* can only be applied to a simple SLN — one containing only atomic nodes.

A complex SLN is one containing a complex node — a node that is itself an SLN. Algorithms for determining the relationship between complex SLNs can be designed by viewing the complex nodes as atomic nodes, and then determining the relationship between corresponding complex nodes.

2.8.2 *The union operation*

The union operation is a kind of *semantic integration* of SLNs, which can combine semantic components. The union operation is useful for forming a complete semantic image (*single semantic image*) during browsing and reasoning.

The union of two structures of SLN $G_1 = (V_1, E_1)$ and $G_2 = (V_2, E_2)$, $G_3 = (V_3, E_3) = G_1 \cup G_2$, can be constructed as follows:

(1) View all the nodes in G_1 and G_2 as atomic nodes, $V_3 = V_1 \cup V_2$ and $E_3 = E_1 \cup E_2$.

(2) If a node $V_{1c} \in V_1$ is a complex node, and $V_{1c} \notin V_1 \cap V_2$, then the SLN expanded by V_{1c} yields the SLN expanded by the node V_{3c} (corresponding to V_{1c}) of G_3.

(3) If a node $V_{2c} \in V_2$ is a complex node, and $V_{2c} \notin V_1 \cap V_2$, then the SLN expanded by V_{2c} yields the SLN expanded by the node V_{3c} (corresponding to V_{2c}) of G_3.

(4) If the node $V_c \in V_1 \cap V_2$ is a complex node (let G_{1Vc} and G_{2Vc} be the SLNs expanded by V_c in V_1 and V_2 respectively, $V_{3c} \in V_3$ be the complex node corresponding to V_c, and G_{3V3c} be the SLN expanded by V_{3c}), then we have $G_{3\,V3c} = G_{1Vc} \cup G_{2Vc}$.

Algorithm 2.8.3 The algorithm *Union_SLN* for uniting two structures of SLN.

Union_SLN (SLN G_1, SLN G_2, SLN G_3)
{ $V_{int} = V_1 \cap V_2$;
    $d = |V_1| + |V_2| - |V_{int}|$;
    $V_3 = V_1 \cup V_2$;
    Let L_1, L_2 and L_3 be arrays with one dimension;
    Set all the nodes in V_1, V_2, and V_3 to arrays L_1, L_2, and L_3
        respectively and ensure each location of L_i only contains one
        node;
    Initialize (*mat*(G_3));
    // *mat*(G_3) is a $d \times d$ SLN-matrix, every $mat_{i,j}(G_3)$ is set to *null*
    For every $mat_{i,j}(G_3)$ $(1 \le i \le d,\ 1 \le j \le d)$
    {   Let $node_i = L_3[i]$ and $node_j = L_3[j]$;
        If (both $node_i$ and $node_j$ belong to V_{int})
        {   Let v_{1_i}, v_{1_j}, v_{2_i}, v_{2_j} satisfy the following equations:
            $node_i = L_1[v_{1\_i}]$, $node_j = L_1[v_{1\_j}]$,
            $node_i = L_2[v_{2\_i}]$, $node_j = L_2[v_{2\_j}]$;
            $mat_{i,j}(G_3) = mat_{v1\_i,\,v1\_j}(G_1) \cup mat_{v2\_i,\,v2\_j}(G_2)$;
            // the union of two sets.
        }
        If (only one node belongs to V_{int})
        {   Suppose that another node belongs to V_k;
            // k belongs to $\{1, 2\}$
            Let v_{k_i} and v_{k_j} satisfy the following equations:
            $node_i = L_k[v_{k\_i}]$, $node_j = L_k[v_{k\_j}]$;
            $mat_{i,j}(G) = mat_{vk\_i,\,vk\_j}(G_k)$;

    }

    If (neither $node_i$ nor $node_j$ belongs to V_{int})

    {   if (both $node_i$ and $node_j$ belong to V_k)

        // k belongs to $\{1, 2\}$

        {   Let v_{k_i} and v_{k_j} satisfy the following equations:

           $node_i = L_k[v_{k\_i}]$, $node_j = L_k[v_{k\_j}]$;

           $mat_{i,j}(G) = mat_{vk\_i,\ vk\_j}(G_k)$;

        }

        If ($node_i$ and $node_j$ are not in the same SLN)

        $mat_{i,j}(G_3) = null$;

    }

    }//End for

}

The algorithm *Union_SLN* only applies to simple SLNs. For complex SLNs, the algorithm *Rel_HyperSLN* needs two more steps:

(1) View the complex nodes in two networks as atomic nodes, and then use *Union_SLN* to unite them.

(2) Use *Rel_HyperSLN* to decide how to unite complex nodes.

2.8.3 *SLN-level reasoning*

For a given set of SLNs $S = \{G_1, G_2, \ldots, G_n\}$, the algorithm *Rel_SLN* can yield a set of SLNs that have *inclusion* or *inverse inclusion* relationships. Suppose that $\{G_{s1}, G_{s2}, \ldots, G_{sm}\}$ $(1 \leq si \leq n, 1 \leq i \leq m)$ is the result that satisfies $G_{s1} \subseteq G_{s2} \subseteq \ldots \subseteq G_{sm}$. So, when users want to know something from G_{si} $(i = 1, 2, \ldots, m{-}1)$ in applications, G_{sm} can be used to replace G_{si}.

The detailed implementation of SLN reasoning and its role in implementing an intelligent browser are described in "Semantic Link Network Builder and Intelligent Semantic Browser" (H. Zhuge and R. Jia, *Concurrency and Computation: Practice and Experience*, 16(13)(2004)1453-1476).

The SLN inclusion relationship can be extended to an *implication-inclusion relationship* $\leq$: $G_1 = <N_1, L_1, Rule_1> \leq G_2 = <N_2, L_2, Rule_2>$ if and only if (1) $N_1 \subseteq N_2$; (2) for any $e \in L_1$, there exists $e' \in L_2$ or

e' can be derived from $Rule_2$ such that e' is equal to or implies e; and, (3) $Rule_1 \subseteq Rule_2$. Such an implication-inclusion relationship extends SLN reasoning.

To extend SLN applications, the following problems are worth thinking about:

(1) How might the semantic relationship between SLNs be determined? An SLN provides the semantic context for its nodes. There are also semantic relationships between SLNs. Algorithms for finding such semantic relationships would help advance use of the SLNs.

(2) How might a closely related subset of a large SLN be found that satisfies a user's query? Especially for a dynamic SLN.

(3) How might semantic links in a given set of resources be automatically found or established? An approach to solving this problem by extending data mining algorithms with analogical and deductive reasoning was early suggested (H. Zhuge, et al., An Automatic Semantic Relationships Discovery Approach, *WWW2004*, www2004.org/proceedings/docs/2p278.pdf).

2.9   SLN Analogical Reasoning

Analogical reasoning is an important way of thinking. It is non-deductive, that is, the conclusion does not deductively follow from the premises. Its use can uncover semantic relationships that are not available to deduction.

Analogical reasoning was investigated in AI and cognitive science (R.E. Kling, A Paradigm for Reasoning by Analogy, *Artificial Intelligence*, 10(1978)147-178; D. Genter, Structure Mapping: A Theoretical Framework for Analogy, *Cognitive Science*, 7(1983)155-170). Structural analogical reasoning works by structure mapping between related objects. However, research progress has been limited in recent years due to a bottleneck in capturing the structure of objects. *By its very nature, an SLN yields structural and semantic data that can be used to support analogical reasoning.*

2.9.1 *Analogical reasoning modes*

In many cases, only one component of a large SLN is necessary for reasoning. A semantic component consists of semantic nodes and semantic links on the same topic (under the same direct super-class in classification hierarchy). Sharing concept hierarchy with other components, a semantic component can be represented as $SC = <C, L, Rules>$. C is a set of fine-grained semantic components or nodes. L is the set of semantic links between members of C. $L = \{<c_i, l, cd, c_j>\ |\ c_i, c_j \in C\}$. $<c_i, l, cd, c_j>$ denotes c_i—$<l, cd>\rightarrow c_j$. *Rules* are about L and C. Let U be the set of all semantic components in an SLN.

The following three relations between semantic components in U can be defined:

(1) *Inclusion.* The relationship between a semantic component SC' and its fine-grained components SC. Such a relationship can be denoted by $SC \subseteq SC'$. SC is called a sub-component of SC'. The inclusion degree *IncD* (SC, SC') denotes the proportion of SC' taken up by SC.
(2) *Similarity.* Two semantic components SC and SC' are similar if their graph structures are isomorphic, that is, if there exists a one-to-one correspondence between their nodes and edges. We denote such a relationship by $SC \cong SC'$.
(3) *Partial similarity.* Two semantic components SC and SC' are partially similar if they have similar sub-components. We denote such a relationship as $SC \approx SC'$. $SimD(SC, SC')$ denotes the degree of similarity between SC and SC'. The inclusion degree reflects the degree of similarity between a semantic component and its sub-component. If $SC \subseteq SC'$, then $SimD(SC, SC') = IncD(SC, SC')$.

A structural mapping can be established from the *illustrative problem-solution pair* to the *target problem-solution pair* as shown in Fig. 2.9.1.1, where the dashed arrow from the solution S' to the problem P' means that S' is the solution to P' discovered by structural analogy.

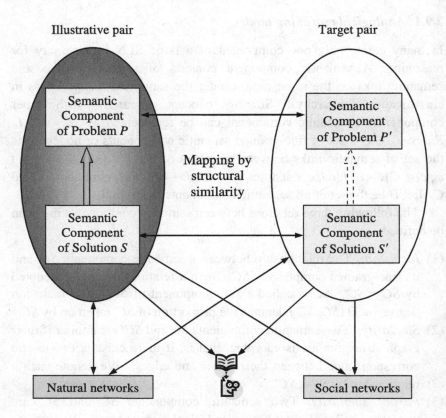

Fig. 2.9.1.1 Structural analogy in different networks.

The set of SLN analogical rules, *RULES*, is a subset of $U \times U$. A rule $r \in RULES$, denoted by $SC_1 —<l, cd> \rightarrow SC_2 (SC_1, SC_2 \in U)$, means that there is an *l*-type semantic link with certainty degree *cd* from SC_1 to SC_2 established manually, or computed by deduction or analogy.

The following are some propositions:

(1) In solutions to *l*-type problems, for SC_1, $SC_1—<l, cd> \rightarrow SC_2 \Rightarrow SC_2$, means that SC_2 includes all resources (components) that have an *l*-relationship with a resource of SC_1.

(2) If $SC_1—<l, cd> \rightarrow SC_2$ and $SC_1 \subseteq SC_1'$, then $SC_1'—<l, cd'> \rightarrow SC_2$, where $cd' < cd$.

(3) If $SC_1 \!-\!\!<l, cd\!> \to SC_2$ and $SC_2' \subseteq SC_2$, then $SC_1 \!-\!\!<l, cd'\!> \to SC_2'$, where $cd' < cd$.

SLN analogical rules for two semantic components are stronger than rules for their sub-components. Analogical reasoning should use the strongest rules possible.

For *rule*: $SC_1 \!-\!\!<l, cd\!> \to SC_2$ and *rule'*: $SC_1' \!-\!\!<l, cd'\!> \to SC_2'$, if $SC_1 \subseteq SC_1'$ and $SC_2 \subseteq SC_2'$ then *rule'* is semantically stronger than *rule*, denoted by *rule* < *rule'* or *rule'* > *rule*. The degree to which *rule'* is stronger than *rule* can be measured by $PD = 1/(IncD\,(SC_1, SC_1') \times IncD\,(SC_2, SC_2'))$.

Analogical reasoning goes from premises to conjecture. The premise portion includes existing SLN analogical rules and some relations (e.g., *inclusion*, *similarity* and *partial similarity*) between semantic components. The conjecture is the rule reasoned from the premises. The certainty degree of the conjecture depends on various degrees in the premises, the certainty degrees of the rules, the inclusion degrees, and the similarity degrees. Because of the uncertainty inherent in analogical reasoning, the certainty degree of the concluding rule takes the uncertain type $\sim cd$.

Based on the above propositions, we offer the following analogical reasoning modes of SLN.

(1) *Fidelity enforcement mode*

Premises: $SC_1 \!-\!\!<l, cd\!> \to SC_2,\ SC_1' \cong SC_1,\ SC_2' \cong SC_2$.
Conjecture: $SC_1' \!-\!\!<l, \sim cd\!> \to SC_2'$.

Since a semantic component could be a hierarchy, in some cases it is difficult to determine if $SC_1' \cong SC_1$. Sometimes, a transformation function φ (for example, semantic reconstruction by adding, deleting, splitting and merging sub-components) can help. So, we have:

Premises: $SC_1 \!-\!\!<l, cd\!> \to SC_2$.
$\varphi(SC_1') \cong SC_1,\ SC_2' = \varphi'(SC_2''),\ SC_2'' \cong SC_2$.
Conjecture: $SC_1' \!-\!\!<l, \sim cd\!> \to SC_2'$

where φ and φ' reflect a kind of invariance between components.

(2) *General mode*

Premises: SC_1—$<l, cd>$→SC_2, $SC_1' \approx SC_1$, $SC_2' \approx SC_2$.
Conjecture: SC_1'—$<l, \sim cd'>$→SC_2'

where $\sim cd' = cd \times min$ $(SimD$ $(SC_1, SC_1'), SimD$ $(SC_2, SC_2'))$.

As in fidelity enforcement mode, we have:

Premises: SC_1—$<l, cd>$→SC_2,
             $\varphi(SC_1') \approx SC_1$, $SC_2' = \varphi'(SC_2''), SC_2'' \approx SC_2$.
Conjecture: SC_1'—$<l, \sim cd'>$→SC_2'

where $\sim cd' = cd \times min$ $((SimD$ $(SC_1, \varphi(SC_1')), SimD$ $(SC_2, SC_2''))$.

(3) *Multiple analogy modes*

For two semantic components $SC = <C, L>$ and $SC' = <C', L'>$, the union of SC and SC' is $SC \cup SC' = <C \cup C', L \triangle L'>$, where $L \triangle L'$ is the result of eliminating redundant links from $L \cup L'$.

Given $SC_{1i} \subseteq SC_1$, $SC_{2i} \subseteq SC_2$, $SC_{1i}' \subseteq SC_1'$, and $SC_{2i}' \subseteq SC_2'$, if the following fidelity enforcement reasoning is true for $i = 1, 2, ...,$ and k.

Premise: SC_{1i}—$<l, cd>$→SC_{2i}, $SC_{1i}' \cong SC_{1i}$, $SC_{2i}' \cong SC_{2i}$.
Conjecture: SC_{1i}'—$<l, \sim cd>$→SC_{2i}'

Then, we have:

Premise: SC_1—$<l, cd>$→SC_2
Conjecture: SC_1'—$<l, \sim cd'>$→SC_2'

where
$$\sim cd' = cd \times Min\ ((|\bigcup_{i=1}^{k} C_{1i}|/|C_1|) \times (|\triangle_{i=1}^{k} L_{1i}|/|L_1|),\ (|\bigcup_{i=1}^{k} C_{2i}|/$$
$$|C_2|) \times (|\triangle_{i=1}^{k} L_{2i}|/|L_2|),\ (|\bigcup_{i=1}^{k} C_{1i}'|/|C_1'|) \times (|\triangle_{i=1}^{k} L_{1i}'|/|L_1'|),\ (|\bigcup_{i=1}^{k} C_{2i}'|$$
$$/|C_2|) \times (|\triangle_{i=1}^{k} L_{2i}'|/|L_2'|)\ ).$$

Multiple analogy employs inductive reasoning.

(4) *Inexact analogy mode*

Premise: $SC_1 \!—\! <l, cd> \!\to\! SC_2,$

$$SC_1' \subseteq SC_1, \; IncD \, (SC_1', SC_1) > \sigma, \; SC_2' \subseteq SC_2$$

Conjecture: $SC_1' \!—\! <l, \sim cd'> \!\to\! SC_2'$

where $\sim cd' = cd \times min \, (IncD \, (SC_1', SC_1), IncD \, (SC_2', SC_2))$ and σ is the lower bound of the inclusion degree.

Correspondingly, we have:

Premise: $SC_1 \!—\! <l, cd> \!\to\! SC_2, \; \varphi(SC_1') \subseteq SC_1, \; IncD \, (\varphi \, (SC_1'), SC_1) > \sigma,$

$$SC_2' = \varphi' \, (SC_2''), \; SC_2'' \subseteq SC_2$$

Conjecture: $SC_1' \!—\! <l, \sim cd'> \!\to\! SC_2'$

where $\sim cd' = cd \times min \, (IncD \, (\varphi(SC_1'), SC_1), IncD \, (SC_2'', SC_2))$.

The proposed analogical modes still hold if we replace "semantic component" with "SLN".

2.9.2 *Process of analogical reasoning*

Suppose that developers construct some semantic components and store them in a *semantic components base* (*SCB*). Then, they store the (problem-solution) component pairs with an *l*-type relationship in an *l*-*type illustrative pairs base* (*l_IPB*) in a three-tuple form (IDB_{SB}, IDB_{PB}, cd), where *l* is a semantic relation, IDB_{SB} is the solution component, IDB_{PB} is the problem component, and cd is the certainty degree of the *l*-link from IDB_{SB} to IDB_{PB}.

The general procedure of the fidelity enforcement analogical mode is as follows.

(1) *Discover similar components in the SLN*. The analogical agent analyses the *SCB* and computes the similarity degree of pairs of components. Pairs (cB_{iB}, cB_{jB}) with similarity degree greater than a certain lower bound are regarded as similar and are stored in the *similar components base* (*simB*) in a form such as $(IDcB_{iB}, IDcB_{jB}, SimD \, (cB_{iB}, cB_{jB}))$.

(2) *Prepare a new problem*. When a user presents a new problem *r* with the *l*-type relationship, a human or virtual agent checks if it matches

an existing component p in the *SCB*. If it does not exist, an attempt is made to derive a semantic component p from r. If p exists, it is added to the *SCB* and step (3) is skipped. Otherwise, if there are items like (IDB_{SB}, IDB_{PB}, cd) in the *l_IPB*, the best of these is used to select sB_{bestB} from the *SCB*, sB_{bestB} is returned to the user as the best solution to r, and the process ends.

(3) *Find components similar to the new problem.* The analogical agent computes the degree of similarity between the new p and other components in the *SCB*. Any similar component pairs are stored in the *simB* as (IDB_{PB}, IDB_{PsimB}, $SimD$ (pB_{simB}, p)). If no similar pairs are discovered, the process ends without a result.

(4) *Analogy by similarity.* The matching agent selects the component pB_{maxB} with the highest degree of similarity to p from all components in the *simB*. If there are solutions to pB_{maxB} in the *l_IPB* then the agent finds the best solution sB_{bestB}' as in step (3), selects the component sB_{maxB} with the highest degree of similarity to sB_{bestB}' from the *simB*, adds it to the *l_IPB* as a newly discovered problem-solution pair

($IDsB_{maxB}$, IDB_{pB}, ~($cd_{s_{best}'-<l,cd>\rightarrow p_{max}}$ $\times min$ ($SimD$ ($IDsB_{bestB}'$, $IDsB_{maxB}$), $SimD$ (p, pB_{maxB})))), and returns sB_{maxB} from the *SCB* to the user as the solution to r. If there is no sB_{maxB}, then the pair (IDp, $IDpB_{maxB}$, $SimD(pB_{maxB}$, p)) is taken from the *simB* and step (4) is repeated until all pB_{simB} have been considered. If there is no sB_{maxB} for any pB_{simB}, the process ends without a result.

The processes for other analogical modes can be obtained by appropriately modifying the process for the fidelity enforcement mode. To ensure the reliability of conjectures, the validity of any computed solution should be verified manually, so that only valid solutions are added to the *l_IPB*.

Useful conjectures can be drawn when we look into the relationship between reasoning and rank. Reasoning can affect a semantic component's rank since semantic links added by reasoning will change components' ranks. In reasoning on an SLN, the rank of its components can be different before and after the computation.

Problem-solving applications usually work on multiple candidate semantic components. So, the candidate solution (semantic component) link with the strongest semantic link ($l_{strongest}$, if there is any semantic priority order) and the greatest certain degree for the problem (semantic component) should be taken as the best solution. Now we take the component's rank into account. The component's rank provides an overall view of the SLN to help in choosing the best candidate solution, especially in analogical reasoning. Since analogical reasoning is uncertain in nature, semantic link deduction is in general more reliable than analogical reasoning.

In analogical reasoning, using rank to select the best solutions is more rational than using semantic priority or certainty degree. The candidate solution component with the highest T-rank or with the highest $l_{strongest}$-rank should be selected as the best solution. Thus, we need to introduce component rank to modify the definitions of inclusion and similarity degrees.

For $SC \subseteq SC'$, the inclusion degree can also be measured as follows:

$$IncD_r(SC, SC') = \left(\frac{\sum\limits_{sc \in \{C\}} R(sc)}{\sum\limits_{sc \in \{C'\}} R(sc)} \right) \times \left(\frac{\sum\limits_{l \in \{L\}} w_l}{\sum\limits_{l \in \{L'\}} w_l} \right).$$

Characteristic 2.9.1 Let $SC_1 = <C_1, L_1>$ and $SC_2 = <C_2, L_2>$ be two semantic components. The symbol $\propto$ denotes: $>$, $=$ or $<$. If $SC_1 \subseteq SC$, $SC_2 \subseteq SC$, $SC_1' \subseteq SC'$, $SC_2' \subseteq SC'$, $SC_1 \cong SC_1'$, $SC_2 \cong SC_2'$, and $IncD_r(SC_1, SC) \propto IncD_r(SC_2, SC)$, we do not always have $IncD_r(SC_1, SC) \propto IncD_r(SC_2, SC)$.

The similarity degree is based on the inclusion degree, as follows:

$$SimD_r(SC, SC') = IncD_r(SC_k, SC) \times IncD_r(SC_k', SC'),$$

where $1 \leq k \leq n$ and
$IncD_r(SC_k, SC) \times IncD_r(SC_k', SC') = max\,(IncD_r(SC_1, SC) \times IncD_r(SC_1', SC'),\ IncD_r(SC_2, SC) \times IncD_r(SC_2', SC'),\ \dots,\ IncD_r(SC_n, SC) \times IncD_r(SC_n', SC'))$.

A strategy of raising the effectiveness of analogical reasoning is to *make use of the minimum semantic cover for analogy.*

Analogical reasoning is an important reasoning mode of SLN, which can help establish an autonomous semantic link network model (H. Zhuge, Autonomous semantic link networking model for the Knowledge Grid, *Concurrency and Computation: Practice and Experience,* 19(7)(2007) 1065-1085), recommend useful information, discover knowledge, and promote imagination in many applications such as e-learning and e-science. With the evolution of an SLN, the semantic components may change, so the results of analogical reasoning may be different.

Study of analogical reasoning in psychology provides some evidence for developing the right computing model (R.J. Sternberg and B.Rifkin, The development of analogical reasoning processes. *Journal of Experimental Child Psychology,* 27(2)(1979) 195-232; D.E.Rumelhart and A.A.Abrahamson, A model for analogical reasoning, *Cognitive Psychology.* 5(1)(1973)1-28).

Analogy can be extended in the Cyber-Physical Society as it can carry out in and through the cyber space, physical space, socio space and mental space rather than just in the cyber space.

2.10 Dynamicity of SLN

A dynamic SLN reflects dynamic semantic relationships between its resources. Here presents the notion and principles of dynamic SLNs, and describes the functions of a browser.

In a dynamic SLN, the semantic relationships between resources can be changed at any time. A semantic link can carry a temporal relationship between its nodes, which can be either a document or another dynamic SLN.

Such a dynamic semantic link can change its nature under different conditions and at different times. The condition can be given by an event name or a Boolean expression. The time duration can be in one of the following three forms: $[-, t]$ (effective up to time t), $[t, t+\Delta t]$ (effective between time t and $t+\Delta t$), or $[t, -]$ (effective from time t on). If there is no condition, then the link is static during the given time duration. If there is no time duration, then the link depends only on its condition.

A single dynamic semantic link consists of the link definition and a dynamic semantic description.

$r_A \rightarrow r_B < [l_1 (condition_1, presence\text{-}time, duration_1), ...,$
$l_n (condition_n, presence\text{-}time, duration_n)]$

By changing the condition, presence time, and duration, we can dynamically adapt a link to reflect change.

A dynamic SLN can be given a life cycle, during which its content can be changed by dynamic semantic links or by adding new content. The presence time also records the order of adding semantic links to SLN.

Using SLN to organize the resources of the future Web, users may obtain different contents when inputting the same request at different times. This would enable people to get up-to-date contents and to put the contents to new uses.

Relationships between semantic links impose constraints on dynamic change if change of one semantic link would create incompatibility with another semantic link, and so affect the whole or a portion of an SLN. If change does not conflict with the transitive and implicative relationships between existing semantic links, then it is a compatible change.

Fig. 2.10.1 shows an example of semantic link change. The change of the semantic link between *A* and *C* does not conflict with the semantic link between *B* and *C*, and the link between *A* and *B*. We can still derive $B—ce \rightarrow C$ from $B—ce \rightarrow A$ and $A—st \rightarrow C$. So, the change is compatible.

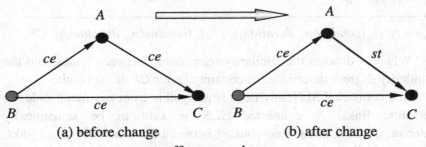

(a) before change   (b) after change

ce: cause-effect;   *st*: subtype

Fig. 2.10.1 Compatible change of semantic link.

The following measures ensure the compatibility of semantic link change:

(1) Limiting change within the semantic scope determined by the transitive and implicative relationships between all types of semantic links. Change can also be carried out smoothly by adjusting the certainty factors of links.

(2) Limiting link change towards lower abstraction level.

(3) Limiting the condition and duration change of a link according to the conditions and durations of its neighbors and of the SLN at the next higher level.

(4) Changing all affected semantic links to maintain overall semantic compatibility when incompatible change is otherwise inevitable.

A dynamic SLN can use the following reasoning paradigms.

Forward dynamic semantic link chaining under a single condition:

$r_A \rightarrow r_B [l.(condition_1, presence\text{-}time_{\ 1}, duration_1)]$
$r_B \rightarrow r_C [l.(condition_2, presence\text{-}time_{\ 2}, duration_2)]$

$r_A \rightarrow r_C [l.(condition_3, presence\text{-}time_3, duration_3)]$, and $duration_3 = duration_1 \cap duration_2$.

Analogical reasoning:

$r_A \rightarrow r_B [l_1 (condition_1, presence\text{-}time_{\ 1}, duration_1), ...,$
$l_n.(condition_n, presence\text{-}time_{\ n}, duration_n)]$
$r_A \sim r_{A'},\ r_B \sim r_{B'}.$

$r_{A'} \rightarrow r_{B'} [l_1 (condition_1, duration_1), ..., l_n.(condition_n, duration_n)]$, CF

Where $\sim$ denotes the similarity relationship between nodes, and the similarity degrees determine the certainty factor CF of the result.

In a connected SLN, any node is accessible from any other node via semantic links. A connected SLN is said to be semantically interconnected if there is no conflict between the semantics of its links. A semantic link will disappear when its conditions and timings do not satisfy its dynamic description. Disappearance of semantic links may destroy the connectivity.

Dynamic change of semantic links may cause an SLN to be continually changing between connected and disconnected states. A connected network may even break into several isolated semantic fragments, some of which may reconnect after changes to their semantic links.

Two criteria — *disruption* and *focus* — can be used to measure the connectivity of an SLN.

Computation of these involves *fragments* (the number of fragments), *nodes* (the number of nodes), and *topics* (the number of topics, the corresponding concepts at higher abstraction level). The smaller the degree of disruption and the larger the degree of focus, the better the connectivity.

The *degree of disruption* of an SLN depends on the number of fragments and the number of nodes. The degree of disruption for a particular topic depends only on the number of fragments and nodes relevant to the topic.

The *degree of focus* for a topic depends only on the number of fragments relevant to the topic. The degree of focus of the overall network depends on the sum of the degrees of focus of all topics and the total number of topics. The minimum number of fragments is one, so the degree of focus on a topic is equal to or less than one.

$$disruption\ (time) = \ fragments\ (time)\ /\ nodes\ (time)$$
$$disruption\ (time, topic) = fragments\ (time, topic)\ /\ nodes\ (time, topic)$$
$$focus\ (time, topic) = 1\ /\ fragments\ (time, topic)$$
$$focus\ (time) = \sum_{topic} Focus(time, topic)\ /\ topics$$

A well-behaved dynamic SLN should evolve to increase the focus, and decrease the disruption, of its topics.

What are the advantages if we build an SLN browser?

The Web browser retrieves Web pages from their Web locations as provided by the user or through hyperlinks. The browser displays Web pages only in human readable not in "machine" (software mechanism) understandable forms. On the other hand, the contents of Web pages and their hyperlinks are not easily adapted to new content or new uses.

Unlike the Web browser, the semantic browser is a retrieval mechanism that can generate and display a view of a large SLN. The view can be displayed either as a network or as a page of text. The SLN browser will have the following key features.

(1) *Real-time update*. While they are being browsed, semantic links may change as events happen or as conditions are satisfied. The browser updates the view on display in real-time.

(2) *Change tracing*. Each node (or link) will record semantic link (or node) changes so that the nature of the evolution of the SLN can be studied.

(3) *Dynamic semantic link reasoning*. Semantic link reasoning is carried out to provide hints to help users anticipate results. The hints may vary as the semantic links vary.

(4) *Explanation*. The browser can explain a result, and any changes in it, from the reasoning rules and the record of changes.

(5) *Accessibility checking*. Since semantic links between resources change dynamically, accessible resources may become inaccessible. The browser will check the accessibility of the views on display whenever its links change. A resource becoming inaccessible may fragment the view of a topic. The browser will retrieve and display the fragments.

(6) *Evaluation*. The browser will evaluate the degrees of focus and disruption of the SLN for the topic of interest and display these with the content being browsed.

(7) *Emerging semantics*. The browser will display different structures with the evolution of SLN. In each display, the nodes and links in the tightly connected components are about the same topic.

The dynamic SLN reflects dynamic semantic relationships between various resources. This enables users to browse up-to-date content and to easily put that content to new uses. The dynamic semantic browser can intelligently steer the browsing of any view of the network using various semantic link reasoning paradigms, trace content change and evaluate the degrees of focus and disruption.

An SLN can be regarded as a dynamic process of sequentially adding semantic links to the current SLN.

The following characteristic reflects the dynamicity of SLN evolution.

Defintion 2.10.1 Removing semantic links l and a from the minimum semantic cover of SLN constructs SLN'. If the closure of SLN' does not include a while the closure of SLN'$\cup\{l\}$ includes a, we say that l *determines* a (or a is determined by l). All semantic links determined by l forms a *determining set* of l.

Characteristics

(1) *The determining set of two semantic links may have intersection.*

(2) *Semantic links are only determined by the semantic links in the minimum semantic cover.*

(3) *If the semantic link to be deleted is not in the minimum semantic cover, the SLN equals to the original SLN after deletion.*

(4) *If the semantic link to be added is in the closure of the SLN, the SLN equals to the original SLN after addition.*

(5) *Deleting a semantic link and no other accompany operations and then adding the same semantic link between the same pair of nodes does not change the SLN.*

(6) *Adding a semantic link and then deleting it may change the minimum semantic cover of the SLN, therefore the SLN is changed.*

(7) *If a semantic link l in the minimum semantic cover can be derived out by relational reasoning $l_1 \times l_2 \rightarrow l$, and l's determining set does not include l_1 or l_2, l should not be in the minimum semantic cover.*

(8) *Any removed semantic link in the minimum spanning graph cannot be derived out from the graph any more.*

The following are some concepts and characteristics on the spanning graph of SLN.

Definition 2.10.2. The *spanning graph of a semantic link l* is a subgraph of the minimum semantic cover and its closure includes *l*.

Definition 2.10.3. The *minimum spanning graph of a semantic link M* is a subgraph of the minimum semantic cover such that its closure includes *M*, and there is no smaller subgraph whose closure includes *M*.

A semantic link may have several minimum spanning graphs, and these minimum spanning graphs may have intersection.

No more semantic links can be derived from the minimum spanning graph of SLN.

2.11 SLN Abstraction

Abstraction plays an important role in the transition from the perceptual image of objects to rational thinking about them. Different individuals may come to different conclusions when abstracting from the same perceptions. Such differences can produce diversity of knowledge, and promote healthy evolution from the viewpoint of ecology.

Abstraction on concepts carries out in the classification hierarchy of the semantic space of SLN. Abstraction on semantic nodes and abstraction on semantic links are based on abstraction on concepts. Therefore, abstraction between SLNs is based on the abstraction on concepts.

Definition 2.11.1 The structure of a semantic link network $SLN'=<N', L'>$ is called an abstraction of $SLN=<N, L>$ if and only if there exists an onto mapping $A: <N, L> \rightarrow <N', L'>$ such that for any semantic link $n_i\text{---}l \rightarrow n_j$ of *SLN*, there exists a corresponding link $A(n_i)\text{---}A(l) \rightarrow A(n_j)$ of *SLN'*, $A(n_i)$ and $A(n_j)$ are the abstraction of n_i and n_j respectively in the classification hierarchy, and, $A(l)$ is the same as *l* or the super-class of *l*.

The abstraction of $A(n)$ from *n* concerns the following three cases:

(1) Both *n* and $A(n)$ are atomic concepts. In this case, node $A(n)$ is the abstraction of *n* if and only if $A(n)$ is the parent of *n* in a conceptual abstraction hierarchy.

(2) Node *n* is an SLN and *A(n)* is an atomic concept. In this case, node *A(n)* is the abstraction of the SLN.

(3) Both *n* and *A(n)* are SLNs. In this case, the abstraction between the nodes becomes the abstraction between SLNs (definition 2.11.1).

From the above definition, we can define an abstraction operation $\cap_A$ that generates an abstract SLN from *n* SLNs: $\cap_A (SLN_1, SLN_2, ..., SLN_n) = SLN$, where *A* stands for the topic area of the abstraction. The algorithm for realizing this operation is based on the intersection operation of SLNs but using abstraction as outlined above to replace equivalence.

For a given set of SLNs as the original source of abstraction, repeating the following steps can generate an abstraction tree as shown in Fig.2.11.1:

(1) Generate a set of abstract SLNs by abstracting any combination of source SLNs.

(2) Generate the source set at a new level by clustering the abstract SLNs that are similar to each other.

(3) If the result has more than one abstract SLN, repeat from step 2.

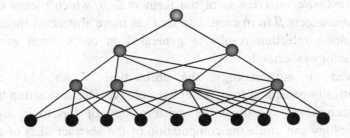

Fig. 2.11.1 An abstraction tree.

Abstraction usually works with analogy (H. Zhuge et al, Analogy and Abstract in Cognitive Space: A Software Process Model, *Information and Software Technology*, 39(1997)463-468). Fig. 2.11.2 shows the relationship between analogy and abstraction. While abstractions are carried out on sets of objective existence, analogy can provides links and references between abstractions.

The abstraction process is a process of semantic selection. The abstraction tree reflects the epistemology of the topic area. If the abstraction tree is derived from many diverse SLNs, and adding new SLN abstractions doesn't change the tree, then the epistemology of the topic area is completed. Once completed, the abstraction tree can be independent of the SLNs and evolve during use.

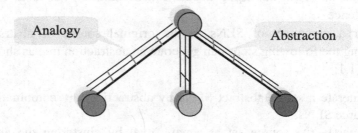

Fig.2.11.2 Abstraction with analogy.

A *semantic selection* is of the form $\alpha \leq_C \beta$, which means that the topic area selects β from candidate set C as more abstract than α. A set of semantic selection results is generated in one's mind as his/her epistemology is formed.

Given an epistemology, the abstraction of an SLN can be automatically generated from the epistemology. The abstraction tree and the selection set constitute the epistemology of the topic area. An epistemology can guide the computation of the abstract SLN of a given SLN. The formation of a community's epistemologies from their common SLNs reflects a kind of social selection process based on shared values.

A society consisting of resources, resource producers and consumers can build a mutual understanding between individuals from knowledge of each others' epistemologies. If the epistemologies can be processed by machine, mutual understanding will thereby be easier to attain.

Now, we can view a scenario of resource management in the Knowledge Grid environment: The resources' providers (humans or machines) need to attach their epistemologies to the resources. The resource consumers (humans or machines) can use and understand the resources by using the attached epistemologies. Each consumer is also a provider. Therefore, the environment needs to manage the epistemological attachments in addition to resources. With the attachment, service providers like search engine will be able to provide not only the links and documents but also multi-facet navigation and explanations.

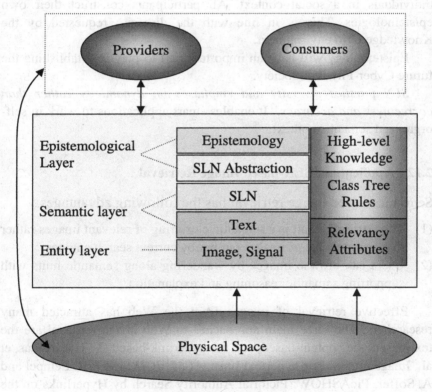

Fig.2.11.3 Interaction through multi-layer abstractions.

Fig. 2.11.3 depicts interaction between providers and consumers through multi-layer abstractions. Images are the direct reflection of the physical space. Texts are a kind of abstraction, which indicate certain semantics. Attributes can be extracted from entities or sensed directly from the physical space. Hyperlinks and semantic links establish the relevancy between entities. High-level knowledge includes models and methods.

Current research into ontology seeks to establish consensus between different understandings in domains. The effectiveness of this effort is questionable if we look at the nature of the World Wide Web and the background of the evolution of culture and emerging new domains.

Epistemology as described here respects differences between individuals in a social context. All participants construct their own epistemologies. This is in line with the diversity requested by the Knowledge Grid environment.

Epistemology will have an important part to play in establishing the future Cyber-Physical Society.

SLN pursues diversity and emphases on dynamicity rather than correctness and accuracy. It enables smart applications to work in self-organized semantic context.

2.12 Application: SLN-based Image Retrieval

Semantics-based image retrieval has the following advantages:

(1) The retrieval result is a semantic clustering of relevant images rather than a simple list of images put out by current search engines.
(2) Users can browse images by wandering along semantic hints with supporting semantic reasoning and explanation.

Effective retrieval of images from the Web has attracted many researchers. The three main approaches to Web image retrieval are the text-based, the content-based, and the hyperlink-based (V. Harmandas, et. al., Image retrieval by hypertext links, *ACM SIGIR*, 1997; R. Lempel and A. Soffer, PicASHOW: Pictorial Authority Search by Hyperlinks on the Web, *WWW Conference*, 2001).

The text-based approach applies text-based Information Retrieval (IR) algorithms to keywords in annotations of images, captions of images, text near images, the entire text of pages containing an image and filenames. These approaches support a specific natural language for queries.

The content-based approach applies image analysis techniques to extract visual features from images. The features are extracted in a preprocessing stage and stored in the retrieval system's database. The extracted features are usually of high dimensionality, and need fewer dimensions to allow scalability.

The hyperlink-based approach makes use of the link structure to retrieve relevant images. The common basic premise is that a page displays or links to an image when its author considers the image to be of value to the viewers (H.Zhuge, Retrieve Images by Understanding Semantic Links and Clustering Image Fragments, *Journal of Systems and Software*, 73(3)(2004)455-466).

These approaches are almost independent of the semantics of the image itself. The main obstacle to semantics-based image retrieval is that it is hard to describe an image semantically. But the semantics of an image can be implied by related images and their semantic relationships. Thus, semantic links can help realize semantic image retrieval.

The following three sets of semantic links list position relationships:

(1) *X is-above Y*; *X is-below Y*; *X is-left-of Y*; and, *X is-right-of Y*
(2) *X is-north-of Y*; *X is-south-of Y*; *X is-east-of Y*; and, *X is-west-of Y*.
(3) *X is-ahead-of Y*; and, *X is-behind Y*.

The positional links can be described in a *simple grammar* as X *is-β-of Y*, where $\beta \in$ {*above, below, left, right, north, south, east, west, ahead, behind*} is called a semantic indicator. The pairs *above/below, left/right, south/north, east/west, ahead/behind* are each symmetric.

Other positional links can be composed from two different semantic indicators, depending on their meaning. For example, *X is-north-west-of Y*; *X is-south-east-of Y*; *X is-south-west-of Y*; and, *X is-north-east-of Y* are meaningful semantic links, but *X is-north-south-of Y* isn't. In general, the composite links can be described as: X *is-α-β-of Y*.

Rules can be derived from the positional links as shown in Table 2.2. From the rules in the table, we can derive two generalization rules and one transitivity rule.

Generalization Rule 1. X *is-*α_1*-*α_2*-of* $Y \Rightarrow Y$ *is-*β_1*-*β_2*-of* X if and only if
(1) *is-*α_1*-*α_2*-of* and *is-*β_1*-*β_2*-of* are both meaningful;
(2) X *is-*α_1*-of* $Y \Rightarrow Y$ *is-*β_1*-of* X; and,
(3) X *is-*α_2*-of* $Y \Rightarrow Y$ *is-*β_2*-of* X.

A relation is meaningful if it has a corresponding concept in the mental space.

Generalization Rule 2. If α and β are mutually symmetric, then X *is-*α*-of* $Y \Rightarrow Y$ *is-*β*-of* X.

Transitive Rule. X *is-*α*-of* Y and Y *is-*α*-of* $Z \Rightarrow X$ *is-*α*-of* Z.

Table 2.2 Rules for positional links.

No	Rule	Category
1	X *is-above* $Y \Rightarrow Y$ *is-below* X	X *is-*α*-of* $Y \Rightarrow Y$ *is-*β*-of* X
2	X *is-below* $Y \Rightarrow Y$ *is-above* X	ditto
3	X *is-left-of* $Y \Rightarrow Y$ *is-right-of* X	ditto
4	X *is-right-of* $Y \Rightarrow Y$ *is-left-of* X	ditto
5	X *is-north-of* $Y \Rightarrow Y$ *is-south-of* X	ditto
6	X *is-south-of* $Y \Rightarrow Y$ *is-north-of* X	ditto
7	X *is-east-of* $Y \Rightarrow Y$ *is-west-of* X	ditto
8	X *is-west-of* $Y \Rightarrow Y$ *is-east-of* X	ditto
9	X *is-ahead-of* $Y \Rightarrow Y$ *is-behind* X	ditto
10	X *is-behind* $Y \Rightarrow Y$ *is-ahead-of* X	ditto
11	X *is-north-west-of* $Y \Rightarrow Y$ *is-south-east-of* X	X *is-*α_1*-*α_2*-of* $Y \Rightarrow$ Y *is-*β_1*-*β_2*-of* X
12	X *is-south-east-of* $Y \Rightarrow Y$ *is-north-west-of* X	ditto
13	X *is-south-west-of* $Y \Rightarrow Y$ *is-north-east-of* X	ditto
14	X *is-north-east-of* $Y \Rightarrow Y$ *is-south-west-of* X	ditto

Orthogonal semantic relations exist between positional indicators. We use $\alpha_1 \perp \alpha_2$ to denote that relation α_1 is orthogonal to relation α_2.

Such orthogonal relationships indicate the characteristics of concepts that help image retrieval and assist high-level applications on images.

The following are six sets of orthogonal relationships determined by the spatial concepts in mind:

(1) *below* ⊥ *left, below* ⊥ *right, above* ⊥ *left,* and *above* ⊥ *right*;
(2) *south* ⊥ *west, south* ⊥ *east, north* ⊥ *west,* and *north* ⊥ *east*;
(3) *behind* ⊥ *left, behind* ⊥ *right, behind* ⊥ *above, behind* ⊥ *below*;
(4) *behind* ⊥ *south, behind* ⊥ *east, behind* ⊥ *west, behind* ⊥ *north*;
(5) *ahead* ⊥ *south, ahead* ⊥ *east, ahead* ⊥ *west, ahead* ⊥ *north*; and,
(6) *ahead* ⊥ *left, ahead* ⊥ *right, ahead* ⊥ *above, ahead* ⊥ *below*.

Two more rules follow from these orthogonalities.

Symmetry Rule. If $\alpha_1 \perp \alpha_2$, then we have $\alpha_2 \perp \alpha_1$.

Orthogonal Rule. In a two-dimensional space, if $\alpha_1 \perp \alpha_2$, $\alpha_3 \perp \alpha_1$ and $\alpha_4 \perp \alpha_2$, then $\alpha_3 \perp \alpha_4$.

The position of an image can be determined by using the following rule.

Position Determination Rule. The position of image X can be determined by two positional links X *is-α_1-of* A and X *is-α_2-of* B if and only if α_1 and α_2 are positionally orthogonal.

Besides the semantic and positional links discussed so far, the following *existence semantic* links also help cluster images.

(1) X *is-coincident-with* Y;
(2) X *is-not-coincident-with* Y;
(3) X *is-compatible-with* Y;
(4) X *is-not-compatible-with* Y; and
(5) X *is-complementary-to* Y.

Further, experience with layout, hierarchy, importance and relevance also help image retrieval. Capturing such experience for computation is a challenge.

The semantic link network approach can be used for coordinating and fusing various contents by incorporating specific rules, because the contents of resources are not isolated. The key is to find the semantic links between the contents. Semantics-based content fusion is an important intelligent mechanism.

Actually, semantics was often lost, distorted, or hidden in texts when they were made. So, discovering hidden semantics, correcting distortion, and inferring semantics is also a challenge.

2.13   Application: Active Document Framework (ADF)

Humans create symbol languages and rely on them to indicate semantics — *the mapping between the symbol space, the physical space, and the social space (including the mental space)*. An active semantic link network of concepts can simulate some functions of minds. Readers rebuild the semantics of authors by reading the symbols in passive documents.

People need to learn languages to build the ability of using symbols. But symbols do not uniquely indicate physical objects and concepts. Although grammars and sentences can be used to raise the accuracy of indication, readers often misunderstand authors.

Current e-documents are as passive as hardcopy documents. People need to use a search engine to retrieve documents of possible interest and to browse document(s) page by page in the same way as reading the hardcopy documents. Passive documents have two shortcomings: first, the user will feel it is difficult to efficiently get appropriate content when browsing a large document (especially large-scale documents); second, the search engine does not have any context about the document, which prevents it from providing an ideal content service.

An active document (AD) is a mechanism that can help humans to efficiently construct, maintain, read and interact with the active documents, which are based on semantic link networks of language components (words, sentences, and paragraphs). It includes interactive interfaces for constructing, maintaining, and browsing the semantic link networks of language components and a set of engines for implementing intelligent behaviors. It can interact with each other and with humans through diverse roles. The interactions wave semantic link networks of active documents, which provides the ground for active documents.

As compared in Fig. 2.13.1, active documents can better reflect semantics as they represent various relations in document and can uncover more semantics and interact with author and reader.

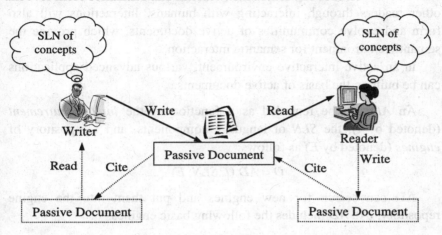

A library of passive documents

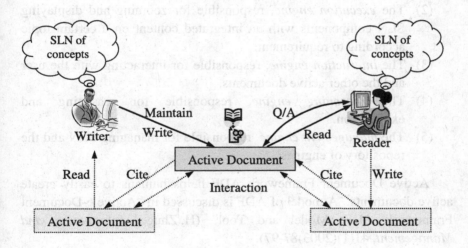

An interactive environment of active documents

Fig. 2.13.1 Comparison between passive document and active document.

Interactions between active documents enable an active document to accurately provide contents for readers, from itself SLN, from other active documents through interacting with them, and from the authors or other readers through interacting with humans. Interactions will also form and evolve communities of active documents, which provide the semantic environment for semantic interaction.

In an active interactive environment, various advanced applications can be built on the basis of active documents.

An *AD* can be regarded as a function of the *input requirement* (denoted by *I*), the *SLN* of language components, and a repository of *engines* (denoted by *E*) as follows:

$$O = AD \ (I, SLN, E).$$

AD can search for new engines and put them into the engine repository. An *AD* includes the following basic engines.

(1) The *search engine*, responsible for searching and analyzing documents, extracting the components, and adding them to SLN.
(2) The *execution engine*, responsible for zooming and displaying SLN components with an integrated content on a certain topic according to requirement.
(3) The *interaction engine*, responsible for interacting with the user and the other active documents.
(4) The *reasoning engine*, responsible for reasoning and explanation.
(5) The *management engine*, responsible for managing SLN and the repository of engines.

Active Document Framework ADF helps humans to easily create active documents. A model of ADF is discussed in "Active e-Document Framework ADF: Model and Tool" (H. Zhuge, *Information and Management*, 41(1)(2003)87-97).

To implement the idea of ADF, designing the engines for easily establishing and maintaining the semantic link network and the Interactive Semantic Base are the key (H.Zhuge, Interactive Semantics, *Artificial Intelligence*, 174(2010)190-204).

We can foresee the scenario of ADFs in the Knowledge Grid environment through the following behaviors (H.Zhuge, Clustering Soft-devices in the Semantic Grid, *Computing in Science and Engineering*, 4(6)(2002)60-62):

(1) Designers create and maintain active documents.
(2) Users publish requirements through an human-machine interface.
(3) Active documents find requirements.
(4) Users interact with active documents to learn content by browsing through semantic links, add semantic links on documents under constraints, or express further requirements.
(5) Active documents interact with each other.

2.14 Application: e-Learning

An e-learning system using the semantic link network to organize learning resources has the following advantages:

(1) Learner's profile can be described in a semantic link network of concepts. A concept is a basic semantic image of behaviors, events, or resources, or an abstraction of a class of semantic images. The ranks of concepts evolve with the operations on the interested learning resources and the network. The ranks of the concepts corresponding to the often operated resources will become higher.
(2) Learners can be provided with a semantic map of learning resources while operating the system, not only at the instance level but also at multiple abstraction levels (regard nodes as classes). Reasoning mechanisms can help users to know implicit links and foresee the result of operations.
(3) Learners can be provided with not only the required learning resources but also the reference resources.
(4) The system can explain a learning resource through diverse reasoning.
(5) The relational, inductive, and analogical reasoning can help understand implicit semantic links, and can inspire creative thinking and broaden knowledge of learners.

(6) Learners can know the formation process of a semantic link network of learning resources by recording the evolution history of the network.

(7) The learning processes can be analyzed by retrieving the formation processes of the learners' individual semantic link networks. The learning processes can be improved by discovering the influence of operating the semantic link networks (e.g., adding or deleting a semantic link). It is useful for learners to know which semantic links or nodes are influenced by operations.

Semantic links can help learners to know learning contents from multiple aspects and at different levels, for example: the *causeEffect* link can help learners to know the effect when they know the cause, and know the cause when they know the effect.

Semantic links can be chained and compared for relational reasoning and analogical reasoning. The *similar* link can help learners to know similar contents when learning. The *sequential* link can help arrange learning contents sequentially step by step. The *reference* link can help learners get appropriate references about the learning contents. The implication link can help learners to know the underlying content about the current learning resources (H.Zhuge, Communities and Emerging Semantics in Semantic Link Network: Discovery and Learning, *IEEE Transactions on Knowledge and Data Engineering*, 21(6)(2009)785-799).

Discovering semantic communities and implicit links in the semantic link network of learning resources can provide an e-learning system with the following functions:

(1) Enable learners to focus on learning relevant contents within a semantic community that matches interests, which are rendered by the often indicated concepts.

(2) Explain or indicate a concept through diverse semantic links.

(3) Explain a semantic link network of learning resources by its community hierarchy.

(4) Explain a semantic community by its minimum semantic cover and maximum spanning tree.

(5) Filter out the special SLN with the links of definite types to match learning interest.
(6) Expand the given concept to the linked concepts through given semantic links.
(7) Automatically generate learning paths and find the shortest path.
(8) Automatically cluster and recommend learning resources according to the emerging semantic communities and links.
(9) Discover local emerging semantic communities, and reflect the law of forming and evolving semantic communities.

As depicted in Fig.2.14.1, extending the learning system from the cyber space to the cyber-physical society can obtain more advantages.

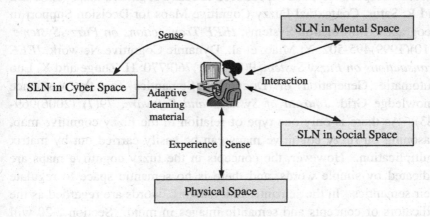

Fig. 2.14.1 Panoramic learning in cyber-physical society.

For example, the e-learning system can search and organize learning resources not only in the cyber space but also in the social space and the physical space, and provide the learning resources in rich forms according to the characteristics of the learner. The system can sense the expression, location and performance of the learner through sensors so that it can adapt to change and provide appropriate learning resources for the learners at appropriate time, at appropriate location, and in appropriate space.

A learner can interact with people to obtain indirect experience through social network. As the consequence, his/her profile will be updated, and the cyber space will also be updated. He/She can also experience in the wider scope in the physical space through sensors. His/her mental space reflects the learning resources and fuses them with the active SLN in the mental space. So, learners can obtain maps of contents rather than isolated learning resources, and can learn in a panoramic learning environment.

2.15 Potential Applications, Relevant Work and Q&A

There is great scope for the SLN to develop.

When nodes and links only represent concepts and cause-effect relations respectively, SLN is reduced to fuzzy cognitive maps (Z.Q. Liu and R. Satur, Contextual Fuzzy Cognitive Maps for Decision Support in Geographic Information Systems, *IEEE Transactions on Fuzzy Systems*, 7(10)(1999)495-502; Y. Miao, et al., Dynamic Cognitive Network, *IEEE Transactions on Fuzzy System*, 9(5)(2001)760-770; H. Zhuge and X. Luo, Automatic Generation of Document Semantics for the e-science Knowledge Grid. *Journal of Systems and Software*, 79(7) (2006)969-983). As there is only one type of relation in the fuzzy cognitive map, reasoning on fuzzy cognitive maps can be easily carried out by matrix multiplication. However, the concepts in the fuzzy cognitive maps are indicated by simple words, and there is no semantic space to regulate their semantics. In the semantic link network, words are regarded as the indicators of concepts and semantic images in mind. Section 2.20 will discuss the mental concept in detail.

SLN can also be reduced to other models. As an abstraction model and method, the study of SLNs can help the study of other models.

SLN is also an approach to realizing a semantics-rich Web. It is significant in method and theory, but its real application relies on the transition to SLNs from current standards (www.w3c.org) as well as on industry efforts to establish standards for semantic grounds.

More applications of SLN are worth mentioning:

(1) Use of SLN to organize useful resources and support cooperative research and learning. Applications have shown that it is feasible to

use SLN to organize teaching materials to support interactive and adaptive learning.

(2) Use of SLN to organize resources in a semantics-rich network to realize semantic peer-to-peer resource management (H. Zhuge, et al., Query Routing in a Peer-to-Peer Semantic Link Network, *Computational Intelligence*, 21(2)(2005)197–216).

(3) Use of SLN to organize resources to support relational query (H. Zhuge, Autonomous Semantic Link Networking Model for the Knowledge Grid, *Concurrency and Computation: Practice and Experience*, 19(7)(2007)1065-1085).

(4) Prediction of the missing semantic links in some semantic link networks similar to the work of predicting missing links (A. Clauset et al., Hierarchical Structure and the Prediction of Missing Links in Networks, *Nature*, 453(2008)98-101).

In general, SLN is a self-organized and evolving space of semantic links.

As a knowledge representation approach, a semantic net is a network that represents semantic relations between concepts. It is first invented by R. H. Richens in 1956, developed by R. F. Simmons, A.M. Collins and colleagues in 1960s (A. M. Collins and M.R. Quillian, Retrieval Time from Semantic Memory. *Journal of Verbal Learning and Verbal Behavior*, 8 (2) (1969) 240–248; A. M. Collins and E. F. Loftus, A Spreading-Activation Theory of Semantic Processing. *Psychological Review*, 82 (6) (1975) 407–428). It was proposed as a human associative memory model and applied to natural language processing in the early 1970s. Some expert systems adopted semantic net as their knowledge representation mechanism. Reasoning on semantic network/net is based on the matching between semantic nets.

From the basic expression, the subject-predicate-object triple expressions of the Resource Description Framework (RDF, www.w3.org/RDF/) is similar to the semantic net and the classic conceptual modeling approaches such as Entity-Relationship (ER model) or class diagrams. The subject denotes the resource, and the predicate expresses a relationship between the subject and the object. The representation of RDF is based on the Extensible Markup Language

(XML, www.w3.org/XML/), which facilitates the exchange of data cross platform. RDF can be regarded as the development of the semantic network in Web platform. RDF syntax was recommended by W3C in 2004.

The Web Ontology Language OWL is for use by applications that need to process the content instead of just presenting text to humans. It provides additional vocabulary along with a formal semantics. It has three increasingly-expressive sublanguages: OWL Lite, OWL DL, and OWL Full (www.w3.org/TR/owl-features/).

Standardized in 1999, the topic map that organizes information by using the concepts of *topics*, *occurrence* and *association* (www.topicmaps.net/pmtm4.htm; P. Auillans, et al., A Formal Model for Topic Maps, *Proc. 1ˢᵗ International Semantic Web Conference*, LNCS 2342(2002)69-83).

In database area, the foreign key establishes reference relation between tables. A foreign key is a field in one table that matches a candidate key of another table. It actually links tables to provide wider access scope of data.

Linked Data is a technique proposed by Tim Berners-Lee for exposing, sharing, and connecting pieces of data on the Semantic Web using URIs and RDF. There are many projects on this topic. Linked Data can be regarded as the extension of the foreign key in database on the Web.

The following are some questions and answers about SLN.

Question 1: It is difficult to determine the exact semantic link between resources sometimes.

Answer: The first cause is that people do not really recognize the resources, e.g., the meaning of paintings. The second cause is that using a simple word to indicate a relation is difficult sometimes. To overcome this difficulty, we can use a set of words to indicate one relation just like people use a set of words to search web pages. Words could be restricted by simple program. Different people could use different sets of words to indicate the same link to support the diversity of viewpoint and culture. The third cause is that the explanation of a semantic link sometimes is difficult. Chapter 8 will introduce a decentralized networking system making use of implicit semantic links.

Question 2: People consciously or subconsciously use versatile semantic links, but people usually are not specialized in determining the semantic links between resources.

Answer: The first cause is that there may exist many semantic links on multiple facets between two objects, people may not know or cannot decide immediately the exact relation in certain situation. The second cause is that different people may use different words to indicate the same relation.

Question 3: It is not easy to determine the general reasoning rules on semantic links.

Answer: Most semantic links and rules are domain specific, so only those who are familiar with the domain can establish the SLN schema. If different users define different rules, the consistency between the rules should be checked.

Question 4: There are several approaches such as semantic net and RDF, do we still need the Semantic Link Network?

Answer: First, scientific exploration is endless, new models will emerge with the development of IT technology. Second, *developing a single dominant model is not the right development trend of technology*. The Knowledge Grid in the Cyber-Physical Society will allow diverse technologies co-exist and co-evolve. SLN is a promising semantic model that could co-exist with other semantic models. Third, SLN is not only a technique but also a methodology of modeling the self-organized social space.

Question 5: What technologies can be used to study and develop the Semantic Link Network?

Answer: As a theoretical framework and method, SLN will develop with the evolution of the Web and the major advanced networking systems. Research on real social networks will significantly influence the development of the SLN. Research on culture in the Cyber-Physical Society will influence the evolution of the SLN.

Question 6: *How to establish a semantic link network on the Web?*

Answer: The Web is designed for humans to read. Before clicking the link, people can guess the meaning from the words (anchor's content) on the link in the displayed text, but the links in the linked page is unknown. It will be very helpful if a semantic map (an abstract semantic link network) of the linked page can be seen when people point to the link. Furthermore, an automatic navigation system can be designed to guide people to browse the interested contents.

A more advanced system can self-organize the interested contents through semantic links and display the contents in a meaningful order. Developing a new Web browser based on this idea can fundamentally improve the current approaches (browse and search) to accessing the Web and completely change user experience.

The following steps constitute one solution to implement a semantic link network on the Web:

(1) Discovering the semantic links between Web pages within the selected Web site.
(2) Adding rules to the semantic link network, and using standard rule representation like RuleML (http://ruleml.org/) to facilitate rule exchange on the Web.
(3) Building classification, manually or by online extraction, for example, from Wikipedia (www.wikipedia.org) and ODP (www.dmoz.org).
(4) Linking semantic indicators to classes.
(5) Carrying out reasoning to derive implicit semantic links.
(6) Discovering communities.
(7) Displaying Web pages according to the communities and the semantic links.

2.16 SLN 2.0: Autonomous Semantic Data Model

A semantic data model is an abstraction of the real world by defining the relations between data. The types of data and the types of relations between data are predefined and regarded as commonsense. It is an important research topic in database and software engineering (M.Hammer and D.McLeod, The Semantic Data Model: A Modeling Mechanism for Database Applications, *SIGMOD*78).

Usually, a semantic data model like the ER model (P.Chen, The Entity-Relationship Model: Toward a Unified View of Data, *ACM Transactions on Database Systems*, 1(1)(1976)9-36) is established at the analysis stage. It should be fixed before the design stage as it will be transformed into the data structure of the information system, and it should not be changed at the system development stage and execution stage. A certain change of domain business will lead to the failure of the system. This is the main cause of low success rate of information system development. Traditional static semantic data models are for closed systems, which cannot reflect the dynamic nature of society.

A graph database uses graph structures with nodes, edges, and properties to represent and store information. It is often faster for associative data sets, and it is more directly relevant to the object-oriented data model (M.Gyssens, et al., A graph-oriented object database model, *IEEE Transactions on Knowledge and Data Engineering*, 6(4)(1994)572-586). It can scale more naturally to large data sets as they do not require expensive join operations. Avoiding rigid schema, they are more suitable to manage ad-hoc and changing data with evolving schemas. Relational databases are good at performing repeat operations on large numbers of data elements. Graph database supports graph queries such as sub-graph, reachability, and the shortest path between two nodes.

Graph data model research can trace to the early network data model, i.e., Data Structure Diagram (C.Bachman, The Evolution of Storage Structures, *Communications of the ACM*, 15(7)(1972)628-634; C.Bachman, The Programmer as Navigator. ACM Turing Award Lecture. *Communications of the ACM*, 16(11)(1973)653-658).

Social network research provides more graph features for graph data models to support advanced queries, for example, about the degree distribution, diameter, and community (S.Wasserman and K. Faust, Social Network Analysis: Methods and Applications, Cambridge University Press, 1994).

However, database based on graph models has the following major limitations:

(1) *It neglects the semantics in graph. Although it can query the features of the graph, it knows little semantics of the graph. Therefore, it is limited in ability in supporting queries on semantics of the graph.*
(2) *It does not support query on implicit relations.*
(3) *It does not know the effect of operating graph.*
(4) *It does not support abstraction on graph.*
(5) *It does not support relational and analogical reasoning on graph.*

A social SLN is dynamic and open. Any semantic node and semantic link can be added to and removed from the network. Users are diverse, and there is no obvious difference between users and designers — *they are all explorers in essence.* Users can maintain the semantic link network. The temporal links reflect the control flows through semantic links. Open domain applications usually do not need global central control.

The semantics of the SLN evolves with the evolution of the network structure. In the meanwhile, the mental spaces of users, designers and programmers change. The users' interests and the content of queries will be also changed. Therefore, the application system including the interface needs to be adaptive.

Fig. 2.16.1 compares the static semantic data model and the dynamic semantic data model. The static data model usually needs to be transformed into a data structure like relational table. The dynamic semantic data model allows systems to directly operate on the data model. The self-organized model allows users to define and maintain individual SLNs. Queries will be routed in a peer-to-peer network when individual SLN is not able to answer.

The following discussions support the implementation of an autonomous semantic data model.

Semantic Distance and Extensible Concept Hierarchy. The semantic distance between two classes (concepts) in a classification tree can be defined as the sum of their distances to the nearest common ancestor. From the root, the first-level of the classification tree regulates commonsense, and the second-level regulates domain commonsense. Users are encouraged to use commonsense to indicate semantics. They can use their own keywords to indicate the semantics of the semantic nodes and semantic links by extending the classification. Individual indicators should be given individual classes or instances, which can be up-graded to commonsense in terms of its popularity during using or confirmation from authorities.

Metric Space. It values the semantic nodes and semantic links as well as the possibly attached attributes. The value of a semantic link is in positive proportion to the following three factors: (a) the values of its two ending nodes; (b) the times of its occurrence in SLN; and, (c) the times it participates in reasoning. The value of a semantic node is in positive proportion to the values of its neighbor nodes. The metric space is also responsible for measuring the probability over the SLN.

Abstract SLN. An abstract SLN reserves the abstract semantic nodes, abstract semantic links, and the rules defined in the semantic space.

Instances. An instance SLN consists of instances of semantic node types and instances of semantic link types. An abstract SLN can generate several SLN instances by instantiating its semantic nodes and semantic links.

The schema of relational database defines the structure of database, which consists of a set of relations with attributes and the dependencies between attributes. The relational schema can be normalized to ensure consistency, non-redundancy and efficiency. A form of SLN schema is defined in (H. Zhuge, Communities and Emerging Semantics in Semantic Link Network: Discovery and Learning, *IEEE Transactions on Knowledge and Data Engineering*, 21(6)(2009)785-799).

SLN Schema is a triple denoted as *SLN-Schema* = *<NodeTypes, LinkTypes, Rules>* under the given *concept hierarchy* in the domain. *NodeTypes* is a set of resource types, each of which is represented as *NodeType* = [*name*: *field*] | [*name*: *field*, ..., *name*: *field*]. *LinkTypes*

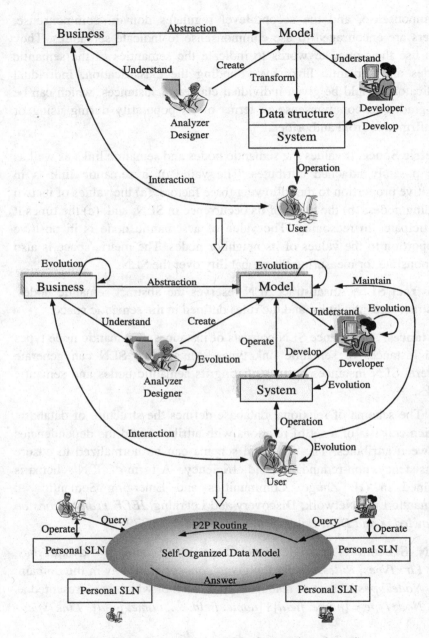

Fig. 2.16.1 Semantic data models: from static to dynamic

is a set of semantic link types belonging to *NodeTypes×NodeTypes*, each of which is represented as *name* (*linkType*)(*NodeType*, *NodeType*). *Rules* is a set of reasoning rules on *LinkTypes*, denoted as *Rules*={ $\alpha\beta\Rightarrow\gamma | \alpha, \beta, \gamma \in LinkTypes$ }. The field can be defined by the basic data type, classification trees, or rules in the semantic space.

A schema view is a subset of the node type, the link type, and the rules of the schema.

Maintenance operation of schema includes appending or deleting node type or link type. Deleting a link type and node type in the schema should check whether there are corresponding instances exist, or whether there is corresponding node type and link type in the schema view.

A domain SLN schema reflects consensus on the basic semantics of a domain. Users can append SLN instances to the system by instantiating the schema or a schema view. Reasoning on instances is based on the reasoning rules defined in the schema or schema view.

Another form of schema was defined in (H. Zhuge and Y. Sun, The Schema Theory for Semantic Link Network, *Future Generation Computer Systems*, 26(3)(2009)408-420). The algorithms for SLN schema extension and reduction and reasoning algorithms for deriving more semantic links were introduced.

A decentralized, easily extensible data management architecture in which any user can contribute new data, schema information, and mappings between other peers' schemas was proposed (A.Y. Halevy, et al., Schema Mediation in Peer Data Management Systems, *ICDE 2003*, USA).

The following are two strategies to construct an SLN as a data model.

Schema-based Strategy. Create SLN schema first and then instantiate it by giving the names and values of semantic nodes and semantic links. This strategy requires users to contribute to and share the same schema. This also implies that users have consensus on the primitive semantic space.

Appending a new node (e.g., "XiaopingSun") to or deleting a node in the SLN is implemented by determining the type of the node (e.g., "pers4on"), selecting a semantic link type from the schema and linking the new node to the existing node (e.g., "Hai Zhuge"). If there is no corresponding link type or node type, the user should create a *personal schema view*, and append the new link type or the new node type to the schema first. Then, the user can publish the new link type, node type, or rules. If most users can use them, they can become the elements of public schema.

SLN schema is useful in defining SLN for closed domain applications. But, it is not appropriate to define a rigid schema in open domain, especially, for self-organized and frequently changing applications.

Self-Organized Strategy. Users create their individual schemas, and then define SLN instances. Users can only maintain their own schemas. There are two ways to realize cooperation between individual schemas: (1) Individual schemas work in peer-to-peer paradigm. (2) Creating a global schema by unifying individual schemas. The global schema needs to be maintained when any individual schema is changed.

No-Schema Strategy. Users freely link nodes one another. Semantic communities can be discovered to limited operations. Change is limited bottom-up from the semantic community hierarchy. Change is firstly limited within semantic communities. If an operation leads to the damage of a community, the change will be limited within the corresponding up-level community. New communities will be linked to an up-level community. Abstract SLNs can be created by making abstraction on semantic nodes and semantic links according to the semantic space. This strategy can adapt to the change of domains. Semantic links such as *equal*, *specialization*, and *generalization* can be established between nodes in different individual SLNs.

Semantic distance can be used to discover and measure communities. Semantic distance between nodes within community should be shorter than those between communities. The semantic link within the same semantic community takes higher priority to route queries than the semantic link through communities.

Abstraction and community are two dimensions to recognize a network as depicted in Fig. 2.16.2. Each concept can consist of a hierarchy of concepts representing abstraction at different levels. Each community can be a hierarchy of communities representing communities of different scales.

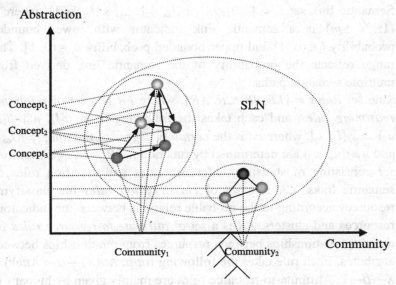

Fig. 2.16.2 Abstraction and community as dimensions of SLN.

2.17 Probabilistic Semantic Link Network

Semantic links sometimes are uncertain due to the following causes:

(1) Multiple semantic links may exist between two resources (things or nodes) and between clusters of resources. These links may play different roles in the network.
(2) Semantic links may be assigned by the users who are not sure.
(3) Semantic links may be predicted by inference rules, derived by relational, statistical or analogical reasoning.

So, SLN needs to reflect the uncertainty.

A probabilistic Semantic Link Network takes the following form: $<\{R, C, T\}, L, Rules>$, where

(1) Resource set $R = \{r_1, ..., r_x\}$, a resource cluster set $C = \{c_1, ..., c_n\}$, and an indicator set $T=\{t_1, t_2, ..., t_q\}$. An indicator t_i is a word or a set of words under a light-weight grammar for indicating the semantics of a resource or cluster.

(2) Semantic link set $L = \{s_1[l_1, u_1], s_2[l_2, u_2], ..., s_y[l_m, u_m]\}$, where s_i $(1\leq i \leq m)$ is a semantic link indicator with lower bounded probability $l_i \in (0, 1]$ and upper bounded probability $u_i \in (0, 1]$. This range reflects the probability of the semantic link derived from multiple semantic paths.

(3) Rule set *Rules* = $\{LR, IR, CR, AR\}$, where *LR* is a set of *relational reasoning rules*, and each takes the following form $\alpha[l_\alpha, u_\alpha]\times\beta[l_\beta, u_\beta] \xrightarrow{cd} \gamma[l_\gamma, u_\gamma]$, where *cd* is the *certainty degree* of the rule, $l_\gamma=f(l_\alpha, l_\beta)$ and $u_\gamma=f(u_\alpha, u_\beta)$ are determined by function f. *IR* is an *inference rule set* consisting of statistical inference rules and assertion rules on semantic links. *CR* is a set of *classification rules* for classifying resources according to the probable relations between the indicators, resources and clusters. *AR* is a set of *attribute-to-resource rules* for deriving relationships between resources from relationships between attributes. Each rule takes the following form: $Att(X) \xrightarrow{\alpha} Att(Y) \Rightarrow X \xrightarrow{\beta} Y$. Attribute-to-resource rules are mainly given by humans or interactions between humans and machines through statistics.

Classification rules can be obtained from the cluster networks and the indicator–resource networks.

Inference rules predict semantic links between resources according to the semantic links between existing clusters. This type of rules is usually acquired by statistical method from existing SLN.

Reasoning rules reflect the relations between semantic links. A general reasoning rule can be specialized in different domains by specializing semantic links, for example, the *equal* link can be specialized as the *sameTopic* link, and the *partOf* link can be specialized as the *subSite* link. SLN supports the following relational reasoning: $R_1 \xrightarrow{\alpha[l_\alpha, u_\alpha]} R_2, R_2 \xrightarrow{\beta[l_\beta, u_\beta]} R_3 \Rightarrow_{cd} R_1 \xrightarrow{\gamma[l_\gamma, u_\gamma]} R_3$, where R_1, R_2 and R_3 are resources, α, β and γ indicate the semantics of the semantic links, and $[l_\gamma, u_\gamma]=f([l_\alpha,u_\alpha], [l_\beta, u_\beta], cd)$, e.g., $f([l_\alpha,u_\alpha], [l_\beta, u_\beta], p)= [cd \cdot l_\alpha \cdot l_\beta, cd \cdot u_\alpha \cdot u_\beta]$.

The *attribute-to-resource rules* can be given by users or learned from a set of samples for some purposes. A resource has attributes of multiple facets.

P-SLN concerns the following types of semantic link networks:

(1) *Cluster–resource network* consists of resource clusters, resource entities, the *instanceOf* link between resource and cluster, the *equal*, *similar*, and *subCluster/partOf* links between clusters and between resources.
(2) *Citation network* mainly consists of *reference* links. The generalization of *cocite*, *cocited*, *sequential* and *similar* links.

Table 2.16 Comparison between SLN and P-SLN.

Components	SLN	P-SLN	Explanation
semantic links	$X—\alpha\rightarrow Y$	$X—\alpha[l_\alpha, u_\alpha]\rightarrow Y$	l_α and u_α are the lower bounded and upper bounded probabilities of semantic indicator α.
reasoning rules	$\alpha\times\beta\rightarrow\gamma$	$\alpha[l_\alpha, u_\alpha] \times\beta[l_\beta, u_\beta]$ $\xrightarrow{cd} \gamma[l_\alpha l_\beta, u_\alpha u_\beta]$	l_α and l_β are the lower bounded probabilities of semantic indicators α and β; u_α and u_β are the upper bounded probabilities of α and β; cd is the *certainty degree* of the rule.
classification rules		$p(c \mid t_i)$	The probability of an indicator t_i in a resource belongs to cluster c.
inference rules		$src—r[l_r, u_r]\rightarrow tgt$	l_r and u_r are the lower bounded and upper bounded probabilities of semantic link r between clusters *srt* and *tgt*.
Attribute-to-resource rules	$Att(X)—\alpha\rightarrow$ $Att(Y) \Rightarrow$ $X—\beta\rightarrow Y$	$Att(X)—\alpha\rightarrow Att(Y)$ $\Rightarrow X—\beta\rightarrow Y$	$Att(X)$ is an attribute of resource X

(3) *Attribute network* consists of such links as *sequential* and *equal* between attributes of resources. Different types of attribute may be measured by different functions.

(4) *Indicator–resource network* consists of the *indicate* links between indicators and resources. Its probability is the weight of the indicator. The *co-occur* link exists between a pair of indicators if they are used to indicate the same resource.

Table 2.16 shows the difference between the SLN and the P-SLN.

The probabilistic values of semantic links take part in reasoning. When new resources are added to the P-SLN, semantic links between the new resource and the existing nodes are inferred by the inference rules and the reasoning rules.

As the consequence, the statistical inference rules of semantic links are updated, the indicators of resource clusters are updated, and the resource classification rules are also updated.

2.18 Discovering Semantic Link Network

2.18.1 *The general process*

Human civilization helps individuals establish worldview through lifetime learning. Humans can learn rules to discover various relationships. Machines do not have any worldview, so a semantic worldview is needed to help automatically discover semantic links (H.Zhuge, Interactive Semantics, *Artificial Intelligence*, 174(2010)190-204).

Fig. 2.18.1.1 shows the process of automatically discovering semantic links between resources. A general discovery mechanism should separate the rules from the mechanism.

If users only want to discover the interested links, the following information is helpful:

(1) The superclass of the interested links, which enables the discovery mechanism to find all of the subclasses by searching the multi-disciplinary classification top-down.

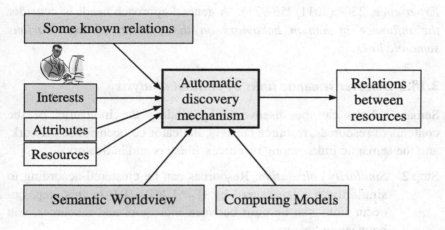

Fig. 2.18.1.1 The process of automatically discovering relations.

(2) A class C and its ancestor C', which enables the discovery mechanism to search classes top-down from C' and bottom-up from C.

(3) A pair of interested relations (e.g., *coauthor* and *cite* are commonly interested links in e-science applications), which enables the discovery mechanism to find the closely relevant relations by searching the multi-disciplinary classification bottom-up until reaching a common concept, then top-down from the relation pairs to the leaves.

(4) A semantic link instance (including the semantic link, the semantic nodes and their attributes), which enables the discovery mechanism to find the relations that are influenced by the given semantic link.

Discovering the interested semantic links among a set of resources can be regarded as the extension or enhancement of the communities in the individual semantic link networks waved during lifetime. As the consequence, the individual semantic images are extended and enhanced.

Some semantic links can also be discovered by content analysis. The approach to discovering semantic links among documents was suggested (H. Zhuge and J. Zhang, Automatically constructing semantic link network on documents. *Concurrency and Computation: Practice and*

Experience, 23(9)(2011)956-971). A general approach needs to consider *the influence of human behaviors on the contents through various semantic links*.

2.18.2 *Discover semantic links by content analysis*

Semantic links can be discovered by finding the indicators of the contents of resources, resource clusters, indicator co-occurrence network, and the semantic links among resources, clusters and indicators.

Step 2. *Similarity calculation.* Resources can be clustered according to similarity, e.g., measured by $|T_1 \cap T_2|/|T_1 \cup T_2|$. In this step, co-occur links can be built between indicators and resources, and between indicators.

Step 3. *Hierarchical clustering.* A hierarchical SLN can be constructed according to the similarity between resources and the similarity between clusters. *InstanceOf* and *subCluster* are two major semantic links in the hierarchical structure of resource networks. The *subCluster* links may exist between the clusters of different levels. Clusters at the same level are similar to each other. Resources are clustered iteratively until all of the resources are in the same cluster or the times of iteration exceeds the predefined maximum value. Each resource cluster has a representative indicator set. Similar to the global indicator co-occurrence network, each resource cluster has a local indicator co-occurrence network recording the co-occurrence of indicators of the resources in the same cluster.

Step 4. *Estimating semantic links according to representative indicators.* Semantic links between resources or clusters x_1 and x_2 such as *similar*, *partOf* and *equal* can be estimated according to the following rules, where T_1 and T_2 are indicator sets.

(1) If $|T_1 \cap T_2|=0$, then x_1—*irrelevant*—x_2.

(2) If $0 < |T_1 \cap T_2| < min(|T_1|,|T_2|)$, then x_1—*similar*—x_2.

(3) If $|T_1 \cap T_2| = min(|T_1|,|T_2|) < max(|T_1|,|T_2|)$, then x_1—*partOf*→x_2.

(4) If $T_1 = T_2$, then x_1— *equal*—x_2.

(5) If $T_1 \subset T_2$, then x_1 is the *subCluster* of x_2, denoted as x_1—*subCluster*→ x_2.

(6) Besides, a resource r can be regarded as an instance of a cluster c (denoted as r—*instanceOf*→c) if r belongs to c.

Step 4. *Reasoning*. More semantic links can be derived from applying the reasoning rules to the semantic link network. If some semantic links exist between two nodes in the SLN, there would be one or more semantic link paths between them. The probability of a derived semantic link is the function of all probabilities of the semantic links in the path, which ensures that the probability of the derived semantic links reduces with the increase of the length of the semantic link path. The relations and the probability of the semantic links evolve with the semantic link reasoning.

Table 2.18 shows some relational reasoning rules on the indicator sets, which enable the semantic link network to carry out relational reasoning.

If there are semantic links between two resources, the two resources should share some indicators that imply the semantic links. The larger are the number and weights of the connecting indicators, the higher the probability of the semantic links between them.

Table 2.18 Some relational reasoning rules.

Relational reasoning rules	Characteristics
subCluster×*subCluster*⇒ *subCluster*	$T(c_1) \subset T(c_2)$, $T(c_2) \subset T(c_3) \Rightarrow T(c_1) \subset T(c_3)$
partOf× *irrelevant*⇒ *irrelevant*	$T(c_1) \subset T(c_2)$, $T(c_2) \subset T(c_3) \Rightarrow T(c_1) \subset T(c_3)$
partOf×*partOf*⇒ *partOf*	$T(r_1) \subset T(r_2)$, $T(r_2) \subset T(r_3) \Rightarrow T(r_1) \subset T(d_3)$
instanceOf×*subCluster*⇒ *instanceOf*	$T(r_1) \subset T(r_2)$, $T(r_2) \subset T(r_3) \Rightarrow T(r_1) \subset T(d_3)$
instanceOf×*subCluster*⇒ *instanceOf*	$r_1 \in c_1$, $c_1 \subset c_2 \Rightarrow r_1 \in c_2$
partOf×*instanceOf*⇒ *instanceOf*	$T(r_1) \subset T(r_2)$, $r_2 \in c \Rightarrow r_1 \in c$

The initial inference rules depend on the initial resource set. After initialization, the semantic links between resources can be discovered.

2.18.3 *Enrich semantic links through evolution*

The P-SLN evolves with the changes of nodes and semantic links. New resources may change existing clusters. The indicators of new resources activate the changes of the cluster's indicator sets.

When a new resource comes, its category can be determined according to the relations between its indicators and those of existing clusters.

A resource may belong to several clusters, so the indicator-cluster association rules can be used to infer the resource classifications. Then, new resources can be inserted into the resource cluster networks. New resources will change the cluster networks and the indicator networks, and the resource-cluster-indicator networks will influence the resource classification rules.

The evolution of cluster networks carries out with the following operations:

(1) *Addition of new resources.* Semantic links between a new resource and its clusters and those between the new resource and other resources can be established according to the indicators of the new resource, the existing resources, and the clusters. New resources may cause the change of the indicator set. The cluster's indicators evolve with the changes of the resource's indicators.
(2) *New resource clusters occurrence.* Semantic association degrees between the new cluster and the old clusters need to be calculated. If new clusters are clustered into the clusters at the higher level, the depth of the cluster networks may increase due to re-clustering.

An inference rule is influenced by the following factors:

(1) *Change of the source or target clusters of semantic links.* Addition of new resources will lead to the change of the clusters or the occurrence of new clusters.
(2) *Occurrence of new semantic link types.* When new resources are

added, semantic link types may be increased. The change of the number of semantic links leads to the change of inference rules.

(3) *Change of classification rules.* The association rules between indicators, resources and clusters will evolve with the changes of the cluster's representative indicators. The classification rules change with the certainty degree of the semantic links between resources and clusters.

Since inference rules evolve with the changes of the probabilistic semantic link network, the semantic link types and the probability values are related to the insertion order. Semantic links and their certainty degrees may be different if resources are inserted into the semantic link network in different orders. When duplicate resources are added to the semantic link network, inconsistency may occur. But, this reflects the uncertainty of the network. Different inference results are caused by different initial resource sets. Newly added resources will influence the classification and the semantic link inference on the new resources. With the evolution of the network, the diversity of semantic links increases, and the intervals of the certainty degrees evolve.

The following are *major steps of discovering semantic links*:

Step 1. *Creating classification rules*

Resources can be clustered according to the representative indicators and their weights. The inference rules between indicators and classes can be obtained by the following statistic method.

The association between indicator t and cluster c_1 can be calculated by the following formula:

$$P(c_1 \mid t) = \sum_{i=1}^{n} P(c_1 \mid r_i) P(r_i \mid t),$$

where $P(c_1 \mid r_i)$ is the probability that resource r_i belongs to class c_1, and $P(r_i \mid t)$ is the probability that t is used as one of the indicators to represent resource r_i. $P(c_1 \mid r_i)$ is calculated by the cluster algorithms while $P(r_i \mid t)$ are calculated by the following Bayes formula:

$$P(r_i \mid t) = \frac{P(t \mid r_i) p(r_i)}{\sum_{t \in r} P(t \mid r) p(r)},$$

where $P(t|r_i)$ means the probability that t is used as one of the indicators to represent resource r_i.

Step 2. *Building semantic link inference rules*

One resource may belong to several clusters. The probability of α can be calculated as follows, where l and u are the lower bounded and the upper bounded certainty degrees of α, and *src* and *tgt* are the source and target clusters, $cd(l(\alpha), src, tgt)$ and $cd(u(\alpha), src, tgt)$ are respectively the lower bounded and the upper bounded certainty degrees of α between *src* and *tgt*, and A is a semantic link between *src* and *tgt*.

$$\text{Min-cd}(\alpha, src, tgt) = \frac{\sum cd(l(\alpha), src, tgt)}{\sum cd(u(A), src, tgt)}$$

$$\text{Max-cd}(\alpha, src, tgt) = \min(\frac{\sum cd(u(\alpha), src, tgt)}{\sum cd(l(A), src, tgt)}, 1)$$

If resources r_1 and r_2 are given, their classifications can be found by using the classification rules, and the certainty degree of semantic link β between r_1 and r_2 can be inferred if r_1 belongs to class *src* and r_2 belongs to class *tgt*. The following is the general semantic link inference rule.

$$src—\beta[\text{Min-cd}(\alpha, src, tgt), \text{Max-cd}(\alpha, src, tgt)]\rightarrow tgt.$$

Step 3. *Discovering semantic links*

Semantic links between the newly added resources and the existing resources can be inferred. Given resources r_1 and r_2, semantic links between them can be inferred as follows.

(1) Obtain the indicator sets T_1 and T_2 of r_1 and r_2.
(2) Find resource clusters for resources r_1 and r_2 according to the similarity between the indicator sets or the cluster's indicator sets, and the indicator–cluster association rules among resources, indicators and clusters.
(3) If r_1 and r_2 are in the same cluster, find the semantic links according to the indicator sets. Semantic links such as *irrelevant, similar, partOf* or *equal* can be discovered.

New semantic links can be derived from the evolving probabilistic semantic link network.

The resource classification rules, inference rules and cluster association networks automatically evolve with the evolution of the network.

After specialization, the proposed approach can be used to automatically construct a semantic overlay on any resource set to support advanced applications such as recommendation and relational query.

2.19   SLN 3.0: Cyber-Physical-Socio-Mental Network

Things are related not only in the cyber space but also in and through the physical space, social space and mental space. Some relations are objective, some are subjective, some are explicit, and some are implicit. Some networks are natural like the food web, while some are artificial like the World Wide Web. Consciously and subconsciously networking, maintaining and making use of versatile relations, humans act intelligently to evolve the social space and influence the other spaces.

The cyber-physical society operates with various self-organized semantic link networks and the method that can record, discover, understand, predict, indicate, maintain, and evolve various explicit and implicit semantic links.

2.19.1 *Origin of semantics*

Lived in the space where objects are interrelated explicitly or implicitly, humans recognize and learn the relations through cognitive processes, and use the relations to link external objects to internal concepts and link concepts to concepts to construct and maintain a semantic link network through spaces to support intelligent activities.

Human senses such as sight, hearing, touch, smell, taste, time, pain and temperature are the origin of human semantics. Categorizing the values of senses into classes, naming these classes, mapping them into the mental space as concepts, and abstracting classes into class hierarchies.

Human recognition on classification and set leads to the establishment of some basic relations such as *subclassOf, instanceOf* and *memberOf. These basic semantic links can be discovered by the equivalence relations between senses, between attributes, and between classes.*

The recognition of symbiosis, blood, and kinship relations also start from senses and classifying senses.

Interaction plays an important role in establishing consensus on classifications, naming, and mapping objects and relations in the physical space and social space into the mental space.

Natural languages are generated from indicating physical objects and concepts and further used to indicate complex meaning for effective interactions. They have evolved into a rich symbol space with diverse grammars. The symbol space evolves with the development of the cyber space, social space and mental space. Language has become an important function of these spaces for interaction. The study of language evolution concerns formal method, learning method, and evolutionary dynamics (M.A. Nowak, et al., Computational and Evolutionary Aspects of Language, Nature, 417(2002)611-617).

SLN can be regarded as a language on relations with various rules.

Taxonomies are established and evolved with the development of various domains. Human understanding is based on the internal structure and through multiple channels. The symbols used to indicate the basic relations should be explained by the scenes in the real world and the abstract characteristics on classification, set and number.

Localization of social behaviors in human history determines the diversity of languages. People can use their own words to indicate objects by extending the classification hierarchy. The frequently used words will be gradually accepted as commonsense and linked to the existing classes (concepts).

Individuals have freedom to use symbols to indicate physical objects, concepts and relations. It takes time to establish consensus on using symbols within community, especially in a multi-cultural community. Different indicators may be used to indicate the same relation, and one indicator may be used to indicate multiple objects or relations, so mappings between indicators are needed to establish uniformity on the diversity. Therefore, a relation may be indicated by a set of symbols. Relations on relations enable humans to derive new relations based on existing relations.

A semantic link network in the social space is waved through various social interactions. These interactions are the driven force to evolve the society. The relations keep evolving with the development of human recognition of the physical space and social space. Mapping the social semantic link networks in minds while interacting with each other, humans evolve the mental semantic link networks.

Fig.2.19.1.1 shows the structure of the interactive semantic base that facilitates understanding during interaction between individuals through machines (H. Zhuge, Interactive Semantics, *Artificial Intelligence*, 174(2010)190-204).

Classification Method	Rules
Structure and Relations	
Primitives	
Commonsense: Number and Set	

Fig. 2.19.1.1 The interactive semantic base.

A semantic link network also bridges human semantics and machine semantics through the cyber space as shown in Fig. 2.19.1.2. Various interactions enrich the diversity of semantic nodes and semantic links.

In the above discussion, both relation and semantic link are used. What is the difference between relation and semantic link?

Relation is general and static, while semantic links can be specific or general, explicit or implicit, and can be changed from time to time.

Various semantic link networks keep evolving with the development of society and culture.

Semantic link network's social and dynamic features make it different from traditional semantic net.

The semantic link network in the cyber-physical-social-mental complex space provides the semantic context for humans or machines to act meaningfully through sense.

A relevant phenomenon is that children's writing ability does not significantly rely on the amount of reading materials.

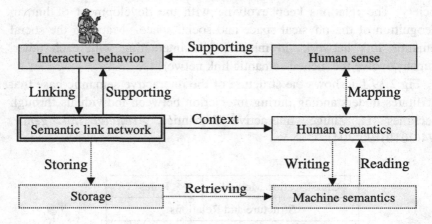

Fig. 2.19.1.2 Semantics of the semantic link network.

Establishing rich links between reading materials and between reading materials and the sense of writing plays an important role in the development of writing ability.

In macrocosm, semantic links go through the physical space, cyber space and mental space to enable these spaces to interact effectively and co-evolve harmoniously. Various closed-loop flows through the links are the basis of forming the ability.

Different people have different abilities of semantic networking and appropriately connecting to the existing networks of different types. Different people may involve in different levels of a semantic link network due to the difference of cognitive ability and social status.

To discover some unknown relations and rules in society and nature needs scientific research. Some intrinsic relations need long-term in-depth research.

2.19.2 *Characteristics*

Since SLN 3.0 will pass through not only the cyber space but also the physical space, socio space and mental space, semantic nodes represent physical objects, social individuals, and mental concepts, which obey socio rules. The following are its characteristics.

(1) *Autonomous*. Semantic nodes can actively connect to the appropriate nodes according to socio rules. Generally, there is no central control during semantic networking.
(2) *Self-evolution*. The structure and semantics of a semantic link network evolve with operating, networking and interacting behaviors.
(3) *Semantic community discovery*. Semantic communities emerge and evolve with the motion of the network. Community discovery is at a certain coordinate of the time dimension.
(4) *Reflecting uncertainty*. Uncertain semantic links reflect uncertain physical phenomena and relations.
(5) *Complex and temporal link*. Some semantic links reflect the complex relation that cannot be explained in a single concept. Some semantic links can pass through various flows such as material flow, information flow, and service flow. Some semantic links exist only within a period of time.
(6) *Relation prediction*. Potential and future relations can be derived or predicted according to relational and statistic reference rules and various reasoning mechanisms.

In addition to the basic maintenance operations, advanced operations on the semantic link network include the following:

(1) *Recommendation*. SLN 3.0 can recommend appropriate resources, links and communities to relevant individuals.
(2) *Complex reasoning*. SLN 3.0 supports relational reasoning, analogical reasoning and inductive reasoning as well as complex reasoning.
(3) *Influence aware*. Influence of operations will be aware when operating SLN 3.0.

(4) *Explanation.* SLN 3.0 can explain the semantics of a semantic link, path or a community according to the semantic space, complex reasoning and influence analysis.

(5) *Query answering.* SLN 3.0 can answer queries on various relations between semantic nodes, and can quickly locate specific community that includes some semantic nodes or links.

Research on SLN 3.0 mainly concerns the following issues:

(1) The method for discovering, predicting, establishing, and maintaining complex semantic link networks.

(2) The intrinsic characteristics and rules of semantic link network motion.

(3) The emerging semantics with the evolution of the network.

(4) Diverse models for reasoning (e.g., relational reasoning, analogical reasoning, inductive reasoning, and complex reasoning), prediction and influence.

(5) Various influences in the semantic link network, and the method of making use of influence.

(6) Various flows through semantic link networks and relevant rules.

2.19.3 *Intension and extension*

Some semantic models represent physical systems by specifying the *intensions* of objects: attributes and relations between attributes (e.g., function dependence in the relational data model) or relations between functions.

Some objects like ancient artifacts are hard to be directly indicated by symbols (because only some experts can know the real meaning, e.g., in some Chinese ancient cave paintings as shown in Fig.2.19.3.1), but they can be largely indicated by the known relations between artifacts. How to indicate the relations between paintings? What are the rules of linking one painting to the other?

A certain range of semantic link network represents the *extension* of a semantic node as shown in Fig. 2.19.3.2.

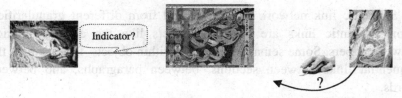

Fig. 2.19.3.1 Semantically linking ancient paintings.

The *minimum extension* of a semantic node (e.g., X in the figure) is determined by the directly connected semantic links (e.g., α, β, η and γ), and the directly linked semantic nodes (e.g., A, B, C and D).

The semantic community of a semantic node can be seen as the *maximum extension* of a semantic node in a large complex semantic link network. A definition of the semantic community is given in (H.Zhuge, Communities and Emerging Semantics in Semantic Link Network: Discovery and Learning, *IEEE Transactions on Knowledge and Data Engineering*, 21(6)(2009)785-799).

Analogical reasoning, inductive reasoning and relational reasoning are approaches to infer the intension and extension of a semantic node.

For example, the intensions of X and Y could be regarded as similar to each other if the extensions of X and Y are similar to each other (there exists a kind of structural mapping between the two extensions).

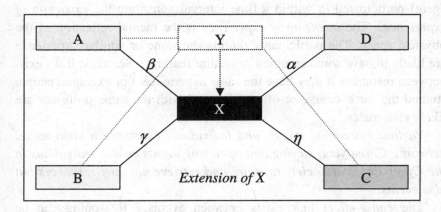

Fig. 2.19.3.2 The intensions of the neighbor semantic nodes and the directly connected semantic links determine the minimum extension of a concept.

Semantic link network can be viewed from different granularities. Some semantic links are between objects like the citation relation between papers. Some semantic links are within objects, for example, the sequential links between sections, between paragraphs, and between words.

2.19.4 *Semantic Link Network of events SLN-E*

Besides resources, the social space consists of versatile intangible and temporal events. An event is an interaction between resources R and individuals I at particular *time* and *venue*.

Event (*time, venue, R, I*).

The *time* is an interval consisting of the start time and the end time of the event. The *concurrent, overlap, inclusion*, and *sequential* links between events can be determined according to the time intervals of the events.

The *venue* can be a region or a space, according to which, the geographical links between events can be determined. The links may be about distance and direction. So, the *inclusion, overlap* and *disjoint* links can be referred according to the distance between regions.

The sequential events that a resource or an individual (human or agent) participated in within a time interval constitute the *extension of experience*. The *intension of experience* is the mental reflection of the physical space. The participants sharing the same or similar experience are likely to have some common or similar features. Semantic links exist between resources if they have the same experience. For example, people studied the same course or often discussed with the same professor are likely classmates.

Various resources, events, and individuals constitute a vivid social network. Classifying, storing and retrieving events enable individuals in the Cyber-Physical Society to share and retrieve not only resources but also events.

The *cause-effect* link exists between events. Reasoning can be carried out through the semantic link chain of the cause-effect links. Through the link or chain, the causes of an event can be found.

Events can be clustered into categories according to the types of participants and interactions. Categories can also be clustered into higher-level categories to form a class hierarchy. An event is an instance of a category. Two events *Event=(time, venue, R, I)* and *Event'=(time', venue', R', I')* can be united into one as follows if there are semantic links between *time* and *time'* and between *venue* and *venue'*: *Event∪Event' = (time—α→time', venue—β→venue', R∪R', I∪I')*.

As depicted in Fig.2.19.4.1, connecting the semantic link network of resources to the semantic link network of events enriches the semantic link network. The connection can be made since a resource can participate in one or multiple events. Events would enable some isolated resources to be linked. The semantic link network of events also supports relational reasoning.

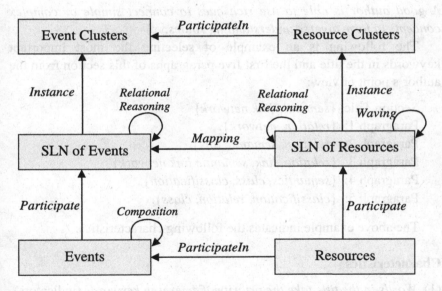

Fig. 2.19.4.1 Connecting the semantic link network of resources to the semantic link network of events enables applications to freely access the clusters of events or resources, the SLNs of events or resources, and the events and resources.

In human history, only very important events are recorded. Previous information systems only store and manage static resources like data and texts. Most events are lost during social development, so *it is important to explore the future with knowing a little story about the past.*

The semantic link network of events and resources provide applications with rich semantic links between events, between resources, and between events and resources, as well as various reasoning paradigms. Discovering rules in the semantic link networks of events and resources is important to support intelligent applications.

In the near future, a movie could be automatically generated by searching relevant resources (music, text, image, and video) and events and coordinating them for displaying sequentially. Reasonable coordination between resources and events is the key issue.

2.19.5 *Through minds via words*

A good author is able to use rich cues to connect simple or complex concepts to form diverse understanding routes.

The following is an example of selecting the most important keywords in the title and the first five paragraphs of this section from the author's point of view:

Section Title: {*semantic link network*}.
Paragraph 1: {*relation, network*}.
Paragraph 2: {*relation, semantic link*}.
Paragraph 3: {*relation, link, semantic link network*}.
Paragraph 4: {*semantics, class, classification*}.
Paragraph 5: {*classification, relation, class*}.

The above example indicates the following characteristics:

Characteristics

(1) *Words in the title take the priority of emerging keywords* (indicators).
(2) *Previously emerged keywords take the priority of emerging keywords.*
(3) *Words relevant to previously emerged keywords take the priority of emerging keywords.*
(4) *Sequential relation constructs the backbone structure.*

Characteristic (1) holds because authors carefully select the appropriate title words to represent the core idea of an article. Characteristics (2) and (3) hold because of the *relevance emerging principles* discussed in (H.Zhuge, Interactive Semantics, *Artificial Intelligence*, 174(2010)190-204).

Characteristic 4 indicates the following method:

The sequential relation is the main evidence to collect and link the text pieces distributed on the Web into a meaningful text.

Besides the explicit sequential relations, the following cues can be found:

The title links paragraph 1, 2, and 3 through the keywords *network* and *semantic link network*.

Paragraph 1 links paragraph 2, 3, and 5 through the keywords *relation* and *network*.

Paragraph 2 links paragraph 3 and 5 through the keywords *relation* and *semantic link*.

Paragraph 3 links paragraph 5 through the keyword *relation*.

Paragraph 4 links paragraph 5 through the keywords *classification* and *class*.

If the sequential relation is unknown, the five paragraphs can be retrieved according to the keywords in the title of this section, and then can be re-organized according to the implicit links. These links help readers understand the meaning of the paragraphs.

Fig.2.19.5.1 shows some links through the title and the five paragraphs. The sequential link between paragraphs indicated by P_1—seq→P_2 reflects the sequential browsing order.

The Vector Space Model and its improvement represent the general content of text (G. Salton, et. al., A Vector Space Model for Automatic Indexing, *Communications of the ACM*, 18(11)(1975)613-620), based on which, only the similarity between texts can be measured according to the angle between vectors. It is hard to reflect rich semantic links within text.

Readers need to scan the text to pick out the keywords and find the cues between paragraphs. To better understand the content, readers need to traverse the implicit semantic link network several times by different routes. If the implicit semantic link networks can be known by information service systems, an intelligent navigation system can be built to help readers to quickly understand the author's meaning. One way is to build a convenient authoring tool to help authors to describe the semantic link networks (H. Zhuge, et al., Semantic Link Network Builder and Intelligent Semantic Browser, *Concurrency and Computation: Practice and Experience*, 16(14) (2004)1453-1476). The other way is to automatically discover semantic link networks.

Let's look into how do writing and reading pass through semantic link networks.

A writer organizes the words in the symbol space to indicate the corresponding concepts in the mental space and control hand to write the words sequentially according to the following localization principle:

The distance between two words in one sentence is closer than that in two sentences, and the distance of two words in one paragraph is closer than that in two paragraphs. The concepts corresponding to the closer words take higher priority to emerge in reader's mind.

While forming the text, the author selects words from his/her memory to compose a text, and all of the selected words have certain probability of being changed during revision. This also fits human reading scope. The probabilities of some words are higher than others if some *related* words have higher probabilities. For example, if the word "semantic" occurs, the probability of selecting the word "link" as the following word is high since they often co-occur in the sequential order. Therefore, the two words are probably two semantic nodes of the same probabilistic semantic link in the text.

Reading is a process of constructing semantic link networks of concepts in reader's mind by discovering and browsing the semantic link networks of words waved by the author.

During browsing the text, multiple words can be probably selected within the range of reader's view. The new semantic link network can be the shrink, expansion or revision of the original network.

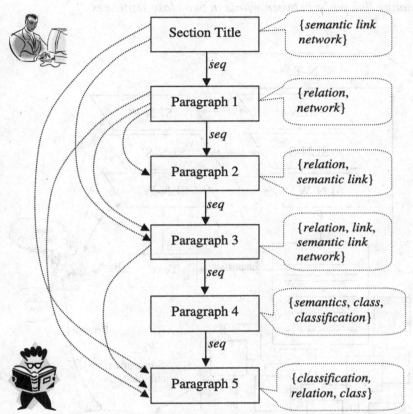

Fig.2.19.5.1 Semantic links through the first five paragraphs of section 2.19.

Semantic link network can be used to improve the quality of text summarization. Previous text summarization approaches need quality criteria (R. Barzilay, K. R. McKeown and M. Elhadad, Information fusion in the context of multi-document summarization, *ACL '99*).

Usually, a summarization can be made by extracting the important sentences from the original text. An advanced summarization may reorganize sentences or even reorganize words. Cues interpret the core idea of authors, so important cues should be maintained in the generated texts. People read a text sentence by sentence, so we have the following principle:

An understandable text should ensure that there are semantic links or semantic link paths between words in two close sentences.

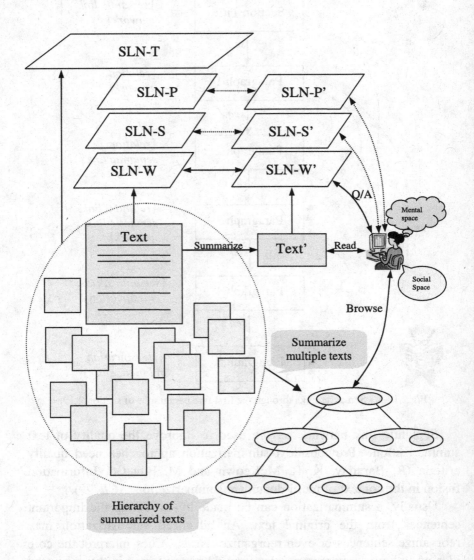

Fig. 2.19.5.2 SLN-based text summarization.

We can build semantic link networks of different levels from the given text: word level (SLN-W), sentence level (SLN-S), paragraph level (SLN-P), and text level (SLN-T) as shown in Fig. 2.19.5.2. The word order is the basis of interpreting meaning.

The following is the basic principles of SLN-based text summarization.

(1) *The important words and the semantic links between the words in SLN-W should be in the semantic link network of words SLN-W' in the summary.*

(2) *The important sentences and the semantic links between sentences in SLN-S should be in the semantic link network of sentences SLN-S' in the summary.*

(3) *The important paragraphs and the semantic links between paragraphs in SLN-P should be in the semantic link network of sentences SLN-P' in summary.*

The importance can be measured by various centralities.

One way to summarize multiple texts is based on the single text summarization approach: Summarizing each text first, and merging the summarized texts into one text, and then summarizing the merged text.

A semantic link network of texts (SLN-T) can provide a context for summarizing either multiple texts or single text. Since a semantic community in SLN-T includes closely related contents, the following is the SLN-based approach to summarizing multiple texts:

(1) Discover communities in SLN-T. As the result, a community hierarchy is formed.

(2) Summarize texts in the bottom-level (smallest) communities.

(3) Summarize each community according to the semantic links between the summarized texts.

(4) Replace the bottom communities with the summarized texts.

(5) Repeat from (2) until the top-level communities have been replaced.

The SLN-based summarization approach can output hierarchies of the semantic link networks of the summarized texts for readers to browse.

The generated SLNs and the community hierarchies in SLNs can also provide a kind of knowledge in texts for answering questions. The answers will be based on the semantic links, the structure of the community hierarchies, and the rules that can derive out implicit links.

So, the SLN-based text summarization approach provides the following three ways for users to efficiently link the author's mind and the reader's mind through texts:

(1) Read the summarized text to establish the general concepts and semantic links in mind.

(2) Browse the community hierarchies to know the contents top-down or bottom-up.

(3) Ask questions and get answers according to SLN reasoning and the hierarchies.

The above three ways can be either used separately or integrated into a single interface.

As shown in Fig. 2.19.7, a mental space and a social space accompany, evolve with, and influence the interaction process. The semantic images of words also evolve with the process and experience in the physical space and social space. Text summarization should be put into the interaction process so as to better know the real interest of the user.

2.19.6 *Through society, culture and thought*

Diverse types of semantic link networks need to be coordinated to provide semantic grounds for various socio behaviors as depicted in Fig.2.19.6.1.

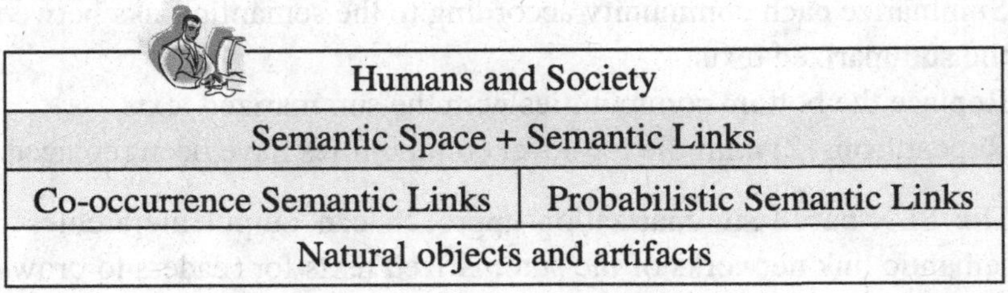

Humans and Society	
Semantic Space + Semantic Links	
Co-occurrence Semantic Links	Probabilistic Semantic Links
Natural objects and artifacts	

Fig. 2.19.6.1 Semantic links of different layers.

The probabilistic semantic link network reflects the conditional probabilistic relation. The co-occurrence semantic link network reflects the basic co-occurrence relation between events. The two types of semantic links are objective and mainly between objects or events. Some networks are semantics-rich while some are semantics-poor.

The social relation (denoted as *socialRel*) can be specialized for social networking as the following relations: *familyRel*, *workRel* and *communicationRel*. The *familyRel* can be specialized as the following links: *childOf*, *wifeOf*, *husbandOf*, *fatherOf*, *motherOf*, *brotherOf*, *sisterOf*, …, etc. The *child Of* link can be further specialized as the following links: *sonOf* and *daughterOf*. The *workRel* link is determined by the hierarchy of a work organization. In scientific research field, the *workRel* link can be specialized as the following links: *AuthorOf*, *CoAuthorOf*, *ColleagueOf*, *ReviewerOf*, *PIOf*, *memberOf*, …, etc.

Isolated node and link are meaningless. Semantic nodes and semantic links are regulated in a semantic link network, where the semantic space (classification hierarchy and rules) regulates their semantics. Reasoning on semantic link network is a kind of special operation for deriving semantic links. The derived semantic link network implies the original network in semantics. But, its semantics will change if new nodes or semantic links are added by humans or reasoning mechanisms.

Fig. 2.19.6.2 shows the scenario of waving semantic link network in society. Individuals establish their own SLNs by learning and understanding the relations between resources, and by establishing semantic links between individuals through interaction. Some semantic links are implicit, some are explicit, some are in mind, and some are record in text or other media.

The nodes and semantic links interact with each other to support intelligent behaviors. Interaction between individuals forms the global semantic link network, which may exhibit a certain pattern during evolution, e.g., semantic community (H.Zhuge, Communities and Emerging Semantics in Semantic Link Network: Discovery and Learning, *IEEE Transactions on Knowledge and Data Engineering*, 21(6)(2009)785-799). Relational reasoning usually carries out within a semantic community.

Both semantic link and semantic node play an important role in evolving the semantic link network. A semantic node can be an abstract concept, a physical object, a digital object, an event, or an individual in society.

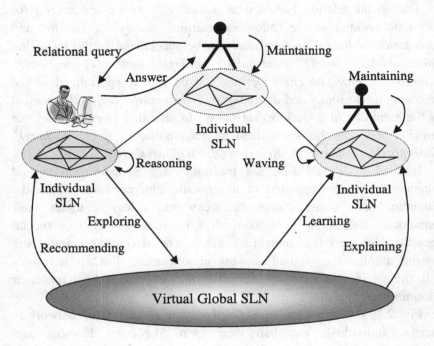

Fig.2.19.6.2 Waving semantic link networks in society.

Nodes in different cultures play different roles in forming the general pattern of a semantic link network.

In some cultures, the family relation plays the central role. In some cultures, the work relation plays the central role. In some cultures, the friend relation plays the central role. In some cultures, two of or all of the above relations play the equal roles.

All individual SLNs constitute the virtual global SLN, which provides exploring and learning context for individuals. Relational reasoning activities happen more often within individual SLNs than between individuals. Analogical reasoning carries out in and through the cyber space and the mental spaces by comparing different semantic link networks.

Some common SLNs can be abstracted as an abstract SLN for effective sharing and operation. Schema is a kind of such an abstraction.

The following is a basic approach for an individual to establish semantic links with other individuals.

(1) Add the name and address of other individuals to his/her communication list, determine the category of the semantic link between them, and then make specializations. The general *association* relation can be specialized as such relations as *friend*, *co-occur*, *friendOf* and *studentOf*.

(2) Add the metadata of other individual resources to his/her peer list, and determine the semantic link according to the relation between metadata, e.g., the citation relation between papers. Knowing the metadata of neighbors, a peer will communicate with their peers more efficiently.

(3) Record query/answer pairs as well as the individuals or the types of individuals who asked and answered as the experience to support intelligent activities.

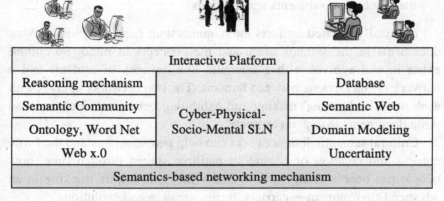

Interactive Platform		
Reasoning mechanism		Database
Semantic Community	Cyber-Physical-Socio-Mental SLN	Semantic Web
Ontology, Word Net		Domain Modeling
Web x.0		Uncertainty
Semantics-based networking mechanism		

Fig.2.19.6.3 The cyber-physical-socio-mental SLN and relevant techniques.

A cyber-physical-socio-mental semantic link network can be uncovered through analyzing various interactive behaviors in various spaces and the underlying networking mechanisms. Technical research and development can make use of current techniques such as social network, ontology, World Net, Web x.0, database, Semantic Web, domain modeling, uncertainty and semantics-based networking mechanisms like semantic peer-to-peer networks as depicted in Fig.2.19.6.3.

The interaction between human individuals and their artifacts forms the following cultural networks:

(1) *Reference network of artifacts* — a network formed by observing the natural objects and artifacts, writing documents about the artifacts, or citing the documents about the artifacts. The number of citations and readers determines the reputation of an artifact in the network.

(2) *Semantic link network of artifacts* — a network of relations between meta-information of artifacts. The attributes of an artifact can be inferred by relevant semantic links and the semantics of relevant artifacts.

(3) *Value network of artifacts* — The interactions between artifacts and the interactions between humans and artifacts constitute the value network of artifacts. The following factors influence the value of an artifact: the values of relevant artifacts as well as the authorities and the number of comments and citations.

Physically isolated artifacts interconnect with each other via relevant documents in the symbol space and the concepts in mind. So culture exists in and evolves with a semantic link network of artifacts and a network of interactions between humans. The two networks interact with each other by humans' making and exhibiting behaviors. Humans also write documents to explain artifacts.

Cultural semantic link networks can help people understand the form, content and creation of culture in multiple spaces through time, how people can benefit from them, and how they can inspire thinking in an advanced environment— carriers, forms, creation and evolution.

Market selection mechanism can be adopted to interpret the fitness in social and culture selection during their evolution. For example, the times of occurring culture features with the development of generations can be taken as selection criteria.

Although people wave and make use of semantic link networks consciously or subconsciously, we know little about their nature as a whole, how they operate and evolve, and how they help people to act intelligently.

The food web can be regarded as the degradation of the SLN as its links only reflect the trophic relationship. The rules on the food web reflect the influence between trophic levels.

The society can be abstracted as a SLN consisting of various social resources (including material resources and human resources), social relationships and social rules. Some social relations are explicit while some are implicit. Some social rules need to be explored. So, it is not easy to build a social SLN. It is a challenge issue to study the laws of the social SLN. Research on SLN can help understand the society.

SLN 3.0 concerns the fundamental issues about the world and human cognition: *How things in the social space (or other spaces) are related, maintained and evolving? How to make use of these relations to act intelligently?*

Previous research on brain network consists of three types of network: structural network, functional network, and effective network. *They are far from the semantics.*

Fuzzy Cognitive map represents causal relations between concepts (B. Kosko, Fuzzy Cognitive Maps, *International Journal of Man-Machine Studies*, 1986, pp. 65-75), but it is limited in ability to represent diverse relationships. SLN has potential to model the thought network by incorporating the semantic lens and solving some challenge issues discussed in (H.Zhuge, Discovery of Knowledge Flow in Science, *Communications of the ACM*, 49 (5) (2006) 101-107).

Since semantic relationships are not easy to be accurately indicated, statistical, inductive and analogical reasoning mechanisms are feasible candidate approaches. Complex network analysis could be useful implications (D. Liben-Nowell and J. Kleinberg, The Link-Prediction Problem for Social Networks, *J. Am. Soc. Inform. Sci. Technol.* 58 (2007)

1019; A. Clauset, C. Moore, and M. E. J. Newman, Hierarchical structure and the prediction of missing links in networks, *Nature*, 453(2008)98).

SLN 3.0 study also concerns modeling mental network or thought network. A dynamic SLN thought component has the following features:

(1)   A semantic node can contain concepts, axioms, lemmas, rules, methods, and even theory. Semantic nodes are dynamically ranked to reflect the up-to-date importance of nodes.

(2)   Semantic links mainly indicate the following relations: *subclassOf* (*subtypeOf*), *cause-effect*, *similar*, *reference*, *sequential*, and *partOf*.

(3)   A component can have built-in rules for reasoning and evolving.

(4)   The SLN evolves with adding and linking new concept nodes. Ranks of nodes change with the evolution. The evolution of SLN simulates the evolution of thought.

(5)   Two components can be merged into one by the following two links: reference from one component to the other, and reference from the third component to the two components. A reference link would generate more semantic links and semantic links between the two components would be enriched through reasoning.

Biology research shows that navigation of brain information is in triangle, which resembles the triangle semantic link network reasoning in the cyber space, social space, and mental space.

2.19.7   *Principles of emerging semantics*

Linking a semantic node or adding a semantic link to an SLN could generate new semantic links. A new semantic node could immediately know relevant semantic nodes through reasoning or flows through links. The following gives a new measure for nodes and links.

The richness of a semantic node is in positive proportion to the number and diversity of the semantic links it has and the richness of its neighbor nodes.

A richer semantic node could provide richer contents and more semantic relations for others.

The richness of a semantic link is in positive proportion to the following factors:

(1) *The number and richness of the semantic links it can reason with, the more the richer.*
(2) *The times of the relation appeared in SLN, the more the richer.*
(3) *The richness of its two ending nodes, the richer the richer.*

The following is the massive emerge principle:

The more diverse the richer.

A richer link contributes more richness to the connecting nodes. A richer node supports the richness of its connected links. So, this principle implicates the following strategy for a new semantic node to be rich.

Linking to enrich semantic links.

That is, new semantic link should be able to influence or reason with the potential neighbor semantic links.

Adding a new semantic link to SLN reflects the purpose of the new node. If the semantic link is unknown, the strategy for a new node to become rich can be simplified as follows:

Link to the richer node, as the richer node owns more diverse semantic links, which offer higher probability to influence or reason with the new semantic link.

The above principle can be explained by the following example:

A person with only one relation, e.g., family relation, usually has low and unstable social status. A person with multiple relations (e.g., not only family relation but also friend relation) usually has higher and relatively stable social status. So, if a person wants to raise social status, he/she should link to the person who has diverse relations rather than link to the person who is isolated or has only single relation, because this leads to higher probability to make new relations that can raise social status of involved persons. Generally, a node should have at least two kinds of relations to maintain social status in a social network.

In depth analysis of social relation needs to consider the negative and positive influence through a semantic link.

Fig. 2.19.7.1 shows three kinds of nodes. The massive emerging principle suggests that nodes C and D should take the priority to emerge as the candidates for node A to link. Selection decision also relies on the type of the relation between node A and the candidates.

Adding semantic links to an SLN tends to make shorter semantic paths.

Since implicit semantic links may be derived out from time to time with the evolution of the network, the richness of semantic nodes will be changed from time to time. This helps the new nodes to share the richness of network. Selecting appropriate nodes to connect, the network provides the chance for a new semantic node to become rich. Meanwhile, the new node helps the old nodes become richer, which in turn helps itself become richer.

The massive emerging principle maps a flat network into the metric space to help discover the emerging semantic nodes and links.

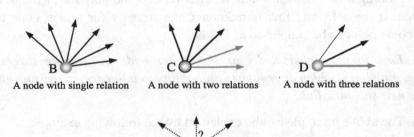

B — A node with single relation   C — A node with two relations   D — A node with three relations

Fig. 2.19.7.1 Linking to the node with diverse relations.

Multiple semantic paths may exist between semantic nodes in SLN. It is harder to explain the semantics of the semantic link path containing more different types of semantic links. The simplest principle is indicated by the following commonsense:

The less information a semantic link path contains, the easier people understand and remember.

The following is the simplest principle.

Among multiple semantic paths, the shortest path with the least types of semantic links takes the priority of emerging.

The above principle can be explained by information entropy. The richness changes with the evolution of the network, while the entropy of a semantic path is relatively stable unless the path itself changes.

The simplest emerging principle focuses on a particular semantic path while the richness emphasizes on the status of a semantic node or a semantic link in the whole network.

The simplest semantic path is the semantic link path with the least types of semantic links between two semantic nodes in the corresponding semantic closure SLN^+.

This massive principle reflects the law of movement of SLN, and the simplest principle reflects the law of recognizing and understanding an existence.

The following are principles from different facets.

The Distinguish Principle. *A semantic node or community has the priority of emerging if it is distinguished from others.*

A semantic community needs to maintain its distinguished characteristics. A humanized cyber society should enable any individual to autonomously select appropriate friends, and enable any community to maintain appropriate structure. So, individual and community should be able to predict situation and actively select new semantic links.

The Relevance Principle. *A semantic node or community has the priority of emerge if it is linked to an emerging semantic node through an existing or a potential semantic link.*

The above principles of emerging semantics can apply to the emerging of thought in modeling thought network. If the emerging path of semantic nodes is regarded as a thought, the relevance principle can be extended to the following:

An emerging semantic link path has the priority of emerging if it is linked to an emerging path through an existing or a potential semantic link.

2.19.8 *Discovering semantic communities* —*semantic localization*

Previous research on community discovery focuses on various approaches to partition a static graph through operating edges or nodes. The formation process of a community is seldom considered.

A significant semantic community is formed according to some rules. *The key to semantic community discovery is actually to find the rules of forming community.*

A semantic community concerns two aspects: *structure* and *semantics* restricted by rules and reasoning.

A *reasoning-restrict semantic community* satisfies the following conditions:

(1) *It is a connected graph.*
(2) *It excludes such semantic links that do not participate in any reasoning.*
(3) *The intra-community semantic links participate in reasoning with each other much more times than with the inter-community semantic links.*

The second condition implies that a semantic link belongs to the other community if it cannot reason with its neighbor semantic links. This condition can be used to discover semantic communities, where every semantic link participates in reasoning at least once. The third condition ensures that semantic links should be tight within community and should be loose between communities. This notion allows semantic communities to share a semantic node. This also means that given different sets of semantic links over the same set of nodes may represent different semantic communities.

The total number of semantic links participated in reasoning with a semantic link reflects its importance in the network or the extent of other semantic links relying on it. The following definition reflects the importance or reliance between semantic links, which is useful in discovering semantic communities in SLN.

The semantic betweenness of a semantic link in a given SLN is the number of times it can participate in reasoning.

Some reasoning rules are closely related while others are loosely related. A set of closely related rules influences the formation of a semantic community.

A rule-restrict semantic community carries out reasoning mainly within community.

The basic assumption is that the concepts in the same classification tree should be closely related to each other. Therefore, they should be in the same semantic community. An SLN is classification-restrict if all of its nodes and links appear in the same classification tree.

A classification-restrict semantic community satisfies the following:

(1) *Semantic nodes and relations belong to a common class in the classification trees.*
(2) *The semantic distance between any pair of intra-community nodes ≤ the semantic distance between any pair of intercommunity nodes.*

A semantic node and a relation can belong to multiple classes. The following is the algorithm to discover semantic communities by removing the semantic links with the lowest semantic betweeness with reference to its closure.

(1) Construct the SLN⁺ of the input SLN, record the semantic betweeness of all semantic links and list them in descending order. Record all of the semantic links that have reasoned with other semantic links.
(2) Remove the semantic links with zero semantic betweeness.
(3) Remove the semantic link(s) with the smallest semantic betweeness if this operation does not generate isolated nodes.
(4) Check the reasoning rule set and find all of the semantic links that have reasoned with the semantic link removed by step 3. Decrease the semantic betweenness of the semantic links that have reasoned with the removed semantic link(s) by 1.

(5) Repeat from step 2 until no semantic links is qualified to be removed or isolated node is found.

The above algorithm calculates SLN⁺ once. It can also avoid recalculating the semantic betweenness for all semantic links after the removal of one semantic link by checking the influenced semantic links at step 4 according to the rules. A tree of communities could be formed during the discovery process.

Many networks have such features: some nodes play more important role than others in forming communities. Another idea of community discovery is to find some initial communities, adjusting and combining communities to discover more reasonable semantic communities according to the semantic links in the SLN⁺.

The following algorithm inputs a community intensity η to help decide whether two communities should be combined to one. If more than η percent of nodes in one community are linked to the nodes in another community or vice versa, the two communities are likely to be combined to one in the evolution process.

(1) Calculate the degrees of all nodes (the total number of in-links and out-links) and rank them in descending order to form a degree queue (arbitrarily arrange the order of the nodes with the same degree).
(2) Construct semantic closure SLN⁺.
(3) The node with the highest degree and its neighbors constitute an initial community C_0. Remove these nodes from the degree queue. Let $t=0$.
(4) $t=t+1$. Let the first node k in the queue be the central node of a new community C_t. Remove k from the queue.
(5) For every neighbor of node k, put the neighbor into one community in $\{C_0, ..., C_t\}$, which has the largest number of nodes semantically linked to the neighbor in SLN⁺.
(6) Check every community C_j ($j=0, ..., t$). If more than η percent of the neighbors of node k belong to C_j or more than η percents of the nodes in C_j semantically link to node k in SLN⁺, then merge C_t to C_j and $t=t-1$.

(7) Repeat from step 4 until the number of communities satisfies user requirement or all nodes have been assigned to the communities.

Semantic communities in SLN can also be discovered by making use of the clustering features of the reasoning rules and the classification trees.

An SLN is rule-restrict if all of its semantic relations appear in its *Rules*.

A rule cluster of the reasoning rules is a set of rules, which can only reason with the rules within the rule cluster. The minimum rule cluster on rules is such a rule cluster that cannot be further partitioned into smaller rule clusters.

The above definition implies the following characteristics.

Characteristics

(1) *The minimum rule cluster is a connected graph of rules that can reason with each other.*

(2) *If there exists a rule that can reason with the rules in two rule clusters, the two rule clusters are the same or can be merged into one.*

(3) *There is no overlap between the precondition set and post-condition set of rules.*

An SLN can be very large, but its rule set is usually much smaller. The rule cluster can help efficiently determine relevant semantic communities.

The maximum partition of *Rules* is such a reasoning rule set $\{Rules_1, ..., Rules_n\}$ that each of which is a minimum rule cluster.

For a given rule-restrict SLN and a rule set Rules, if Rules can be clustered into a set of rule clusters $\{Rules_1, ..., Rules_n\}$, then SLN can also be partitioned into a set of semantic communities $\{SLN_1, ..., SLN_n\}$ and semantic reasoning of SLN_k depends only on $Rule_k$ ($k=1, 2, ..., n$).

Discovering semantic communities enables operations on SLN to be localized within a local SLN specific to a rule cluster. It also enables operations on the SLN to keep focusing on a specific semantic community while semantic communities keep changing.

The rule-restrictd SLN is partitioned into n semantic communities $\{SLN_1, ..., SLN_n\}$ according to the maximum partition on the rule clusters $\{Rules_1, ..., Rules_n\}$. Finding SLN closure SLN^+ is equivalent to finding each SLN_k^+ (k=1, ..., n), i.e., $SLN^+ = SLN_1^+ \cup ... \cup SLN_n^+$.

The following is a strategy for calculating semantic closure.

Discover semantic communities in SLN first, and then calculate the SLN^+ of each semantic community.

The following are some characteristics.

Characteristics

(1) *The operation result of deleting a semantic link in SLN is the same as deleting it in its semantic community.*
(2) *Adding a semantic link to SLN is the same as adding it to its semantic community. If a relation does not exist in Rules, itself is a community.*
(3) *If all relations in the new rule belong to a rule cluster, adding this new rule does not influence the other rule clusters.*

Strategies for adding a rule to Rules

(1) *If all relations in the new rule do not appear in the existing rule cluster, the new rule forms a new rule cluster.*
(2) *If all relations in the precondition of the new rule belong to a rule cluster, the new rule belongs to the rule cluster.*
(3) *If all relations in the precondition of the new rule belong to a rule cluster, and all relations in the post-condition of the new rule belong to another rule cluster, the new rule and the two rule clusters can be merged into one.*
(4) *If relations in the precondition or postcondition of the new rule belong to different rule clusters, merge these clusters and the new rule into one cluster.*

Although a large SLN may be defined by different people and at different times, operations on SLN can be localized within appropriate semantic communities regulated by the rule clusters.

Using classification semantics to discover communities in the SLN is the most direct and efficient way if its semantic space is available.

Semantic distance between communities is the semantic distance between corresponding concepts in the classification tree, each of which is the nearest common concept of the nodes of a semantic community.

Given a semantic distance function, the following approach can construct a semantic community hierarchy bottom-up for SLN.

(1) Take every semantic node of the given SLN as a semantic community.
(2) Merge the semantically closest semantic communities into one community according to the semantic distance measure.
(3) Repeat from step 2 until there are only two communities left.
(4) Recover the semantic links between semantic nodes within each community according to the given SLN.

The top-down approach to constructing the semantic community hierarchy consists of the following steps:

(1) Take SLN as an initial community.
(2) For every semantic link, calculate the semantic distance between the connecting nodes.
(3) Delete the semantic link with the longest semantic distance until the SLN is separated into two communities.
(4) For each current community, do from step 3 until every community only includes an isolated node.

The basic premise of the above two approaches is that two semantic nodes far away from each other in the semantic space should belong to different semantic communities, and the removal of any semantic link does not influence the semantic distances defined in the semantic space. More algorithms can be designed for discovering the semantic communities in SLN by using different levels of semantics.

For a general SLN, we can find the SLN-restrict first by using the semantic space, set the non-restrict SLN apart as a non-restrict community, and then restrict the non-restrict semantic nodes that link to the restrict nodes by semantic links. The percentage of the restrict SLN to the SLN reflects the restrict degree of the semantic space.

The above discussion shows a *semantic facet of the localization principle*.

2.19.9 SLN-based relation and knowledge evolution

Putting relation, knowledge, requirement, and services into the integrated cognitive processes in the cyber-physical society can understand them in-depth and therefore can make full use of them.

Social semantic link networks can be established among humans, annotations (tags), metadata, symbolized contents, knowledge and behaviors as shown in Fig.2.19.9.1 (H. Zhuge, The Knowledge Grid Environment, *IEEE Intelligent Systems*, 23(6)(2008)63-71).

Relations and knowledge generate and evolve through the networks with the following behaviors.

(1) Query and answer.
(2) Recommendation.
(3) Cooperation.
(4) Social behaviors such as employment and marriage.
(5) Reasoning over the semantic link networks.
(6) Information retrieval, extraction and summarization.
(7) Clustering humans and indicators (words) according to the usage relations between humans and indicators, the resource-mediated relations between humans, and the human-mediated relations between indicators. These clusters represent massive selection preference of semantics.
(8) Accumulating relations by discovering relations between symbolized contents, between humans, and between humans and meta-data, by clustering texts and then constructing content classification hierarchies, and, by discovering communities in the semantic link network.
(9) Accumulating problem-solving knowledge by asking questions and obtaining answers, making generalizations, and linking questions and answers to the semantic images in minds.

(10) Using relations to explain contents, using problem-solving knowledge to explain symbolized contents and relations, and using relations to complete the problem-solving knowledge.

(11) Managing a scalable structure of resource organization, which can adapt to the evolution of community semantics due to continuous change of humans and their recommended contents. Humans do not have to know the underlying structure of resource organization.

The SLN–based evolution substantially changes the way of knowledge acquisition in traditional knowledge engineering, from individual experts or knowledge engineers to massive contribution of knowledge. This change realizes a harmony:

One for everyone and from everyone.

Web 2.0 provides a Web-based platform for massive codification of knowledge.

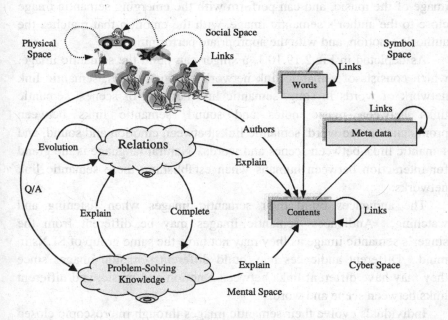

Fig. 2.19.9.1 Knowledge and relations evolve with operating a cyber-physical-social semantic link network.

2.19.10 *Building and performing semantic images*

Human individuals build and evolve semantic images in minds while interacting with each other in the social space and with the objects in the physical space and in the cyber space. Individuals may build different semantic images while involving in the same interaction process.

Let's observe how singers and audiences build and perform their semantic images.

Rhythm is the most basic language of human beings. It is widely used in performance arts. It is a kind of timed movement of such resources as event, sound and language in and through space.

Artists use rhythm and tune to organize music notes and words, and use speed to control the performing processes. Music instrument players and singers have established rich performing skill and semantic links between music notes and sounds in the mental spaces through learning process. A good music player or singer can quickly establish the semantic image of the music, and can perform with the emerging semantic image close to the author's semantic image, with the emotion that matches the author's emotion, and with the appropriate performing skill.

As depicted in Fig.2.19.10.1, a singer can build the semantic image, which consists of semantic link network of music notes, semantic link network of words in song, semantic link network of scenes, semantic links between music notes and sound, semantic links between pronunciation and word, semantic links between emotion and sound, and semantic links between scenes and words. Natural language is the grand for interaction between humans when establishing these semantic link networks.

The audiences build their semantic images when listening and watching. Audiences' semantic images may be different from the singer's semantic image as they may not have the same group of SLNs in mind. Different audiences may build different semantic images since they may have different links between emotion and music, and different links between scene and word.

Individuals evolve their semantic images through microscopic closed loops and macroscopic closed loops of interactions and flows (H.Zhuge,

Semantic linking through spaces for cyber-physical-socio intelligence: A methodology, *Artificial Intelligence*, 175(2011)988-1019).

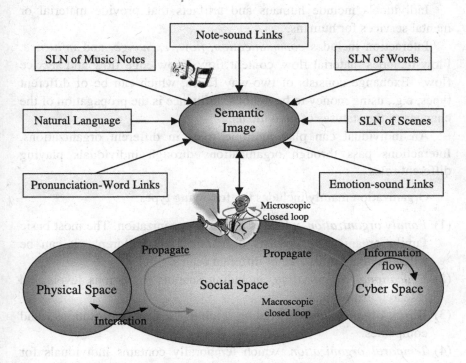

Fig. 2.19.10.1 Building and propagating semantic images.

Similar semantic images will be propagated through interaction between different individuals in the social space.

Although some audiences are not able to sing songs, they have built the similar semantic images because their emotion will respond to the songs to a certain extent when hearing them again. Some propagation will pass through the cyber space and social space. A music or song becomes popular when its semantic image has been built in large number of individuals in the society.

2.19.11 *Structure and networking rules of social space*

A society consists of *individuals, interactions, roles*, and *organizations.*

Individuals include humans and artifacts that provide material or mental services for humans.

Interaction includes *communication, flow, exchange*, and *influence*. Flow includes material flow, content flow, knowledge flow and service flow. Exchange consists of two-way flows, which can be of different types, e.g., using money to buy goods. Influence is the propagation of the changes of the statuses of individuals.

An individual can play multiple roles in different organizations. Interactions pass through organizations through individuals playing different roles.

Organization mainly includes the following types:

(1) *Family organization*, which is a natural organization. The most basic family organization consists of parents and children. It can be extended to a family tree of different scales.
(2) *Educational organization*, including schools of various levels and research institutions.
(3) *Work organization*, including public service institutions and companies.
(4) *Temporal organization*, which temporally contains individuals for special purpose, e.g., train, airplane, queue, and restaurant. In addition to the main purposes, temporal organizations also provide opportunities for individuals to communicate with each other.

Different organizations contain different social relations, e.g., family relation in family organization, colleague relation in work organization, and classmate relation in educational organization. The characteristics of different organizations are also suitable for propagating different types of knowledge.

Fig. 2.19.11.1 depicts the basic structure of social space, where the dotted arrows in red color representing flows. Flows will propagate through social relations (e.g., family relation, colleague relation, and classmate relation), the communication links, and the role links.

The following is the principle of flows through the structure.

Principle. *The effectiveness of propagating flows depends on the selection of appropriate individuals for interaction.*

The following are the rules for selecting appropriate individuals for communication:

Networking Rule 1. *The individuals who do not share concepts with the selector in the mental spaces should not be selected for communication.*

For example, a computer scientist should not select the individual without basic computer concepts for communication. The knowledge in an individual mental space is reflected by the roles of the individuals and the documents that he/she read or wrote.

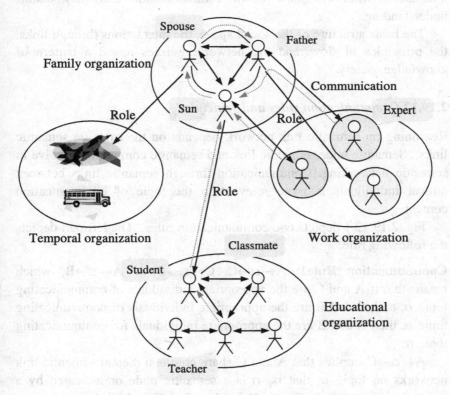

Fig. 2.19.11.1 Social space organization and knowledge propagation.

Networking Rule 2. *The individuals who communicated before or communicated with an individual (or device) familiar with the selector should take higher priority to be selected for communication.*

This is because the individuals who communicated before or those communicated with a familiar individual should share some concepts. For example, the colleagues, classmates, or the individuals in the same community should take higher priority for communication than strangers.

Networking Rule 3. *The individuals who speak the same language as the selector should take higher priority to be selected for communication than those who speak different languages.*

This is because individuals who speak different languages need translators, who will slow down communication and may distort understanding.

The basic structure of the social space, the interactions through links, the principles of flow, and the networking rules reveal a pattern of knowledge society.

2.19.12 *Communication rules and principles*

Reasoning on semantic link network depends on the rules on semantic links. Semantic node, semantic link and semantic community involve in semantic networking. Communication through semantic links between human individuals is more relevant to the topic of communication content.

Fig. 2.19.12.1 depicts two communication rules. The left part depicts the following rule.

Communication Rule1: $A \leftarrow \alpha \rightarrow C$, $C \leftarrow \alpha \rightarrow B$ $\Rightarrow$ $A \leftarrow \alpha \rightarrow B$, which means that if A and C are the appropriate individuals of communicating topic α, and, C and B are the appropriate individuals of communicating topic α, then A and B are the appropriate individuals for communicating topic α.

$A \leftarrow \alpha \rightarrow C$ implies that A and C share common mental semantic link networks on topic α, that is, α is a semantic node or indicated by a semantic community. $C \leftarrow \alpha \rightarrow B$ implies that C and B share common mental semantic link networks on α. Therefore, A and B share common mental semantic link networks on α, indicated by A←α→B. But, for semantic link reasoning, A—α→C, C—α→B ⇒ A—α→B may not be true because semantic link reasoning depends on reasoning rules. Using Rule1, no more topics can be generated during communication.

The left part of the figure depicts the following rule.

Communication Rule2: A←α→C, C←β→B ⇒ A←$\{\alpha,\beta\}$→B, which means that if A and C are the appropriate individuals for communicating topic α, and, C and B are the appropriate individuals for communicating topic β, then A and B are the appropriate individuals for communicating topics α and β.

Using Rule2, individuals A and C can communicate with each other on topic β in addition to α, and individuals C and B can communicate on topic α in addition to β.

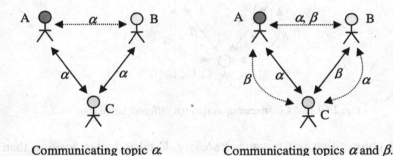

Communicating topic α.   Communicating topics α and β.

Fig. 2.19.12.1 Communication rules.

The Role of Language

Communication Rule 1 and Rule 2 assume that individuals use the same language. So far, language is the only way for humans to know each other. Language also plays the key role in constructing the structure of the social space, mental space and cyber space.

Fig.2.19.12.2 depicts communication through different languages, where "A: L_1", "B: L_2", and "C: L_1, L_2" denote that individual A speaks language L_1, B speaks language L_2, and C speaks language L_1 and L_2.

Individual A can communicate with C on topic α in language L_1, and individual C can communicate with B on topic β in language L_2. As the effect of knowledge fusion in C's mind, individual A can also communicate with C on topic β in language L_1, and the knowledge of B can flow to A through C. Individual C can also communicate with B on topic α in language L_2, and knowledge of A can flow to B through C. However, the knowledge flow through C depends on C.

Individual A and individual B cannot communicate with each other directly since they do not speak the same language. Individuals A and B can communicate with each other on topics α and β if C can play the translator role. In a knowledge creation organization, C can add own opinion when communicating with A or B rather than translate only.

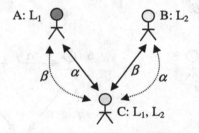

Fig. 2.19.12.2 Communication through different languages.

In a competitive self-organized society, C takes better position than A and B in obtaining knowledge because C can reserve some key symbolized contents and knowledge for keeping better position in competition. C can also attract more links because C can provide more content, knowledge, and services. In addition, C can get more profit by selling symbolized content (systemized semantic symbols), knowledge and services.

The above analysis indicates the following principles.

Communication Principle 1 (Language barrier of flows). The individual who knows more languages take better position in attracting flows of resources (contents, knowledge, services, etc).

Communication Principle 2 (Language barrier of centrality). The individual who knows more languages takes better position in gaining the centrality in the evolution of social networks.

Individuals will learn languages if the advantages of language become eminent. Therefore, we have the following principle.

Communication Principle 3 (Social effect of learning language). The advantages of the individuals who know more languages decrease with the increase of the number of individuals who know more languages. The advantage follows the law of marginal utility.

However, the above principles may not be eminent in a non-autonomous society because the activities of the individuals who know more languages may be restricted.

In addition to communication, languages profoundly affect the brain function and structure (J. Krizmana, et al. PNAS, 2012, DOI: 10.1073/pnas.1201575109; Crinion J, et al. Science 312(2006)1537–1540; Kim KHS, et al. Nature 388(1997)171–174).

However, language itself does not lead to intelligent behavior. Knowledge plays the key role in using language and performing intelligent behaviors.

Communication Principle 4 (Effectiveness). The effectiveness of communication depends on the consequence effects in the mental space, physiological space, psychological space and physical space.

Languages will evolve with various interactions in the Cyber-Physical Society.

2.19.13 *Influence between mental space and social space*

Humans communicate with each other through various languages, which are means of conveying concepts and thoughts in mind. Concepts play the key role in communication, and they are fundamental in philosophy although there are different explanations (http://plato.stanford.edu/entries/concepts/). What is the relation between concept and language? Some philosophers argue that natural language is necessary for having concepts, while others argue that concepts are prior to and independent of natural language.

The idea of interactive semantics argues that interaction takes place before the generation of language (H.Zhuge, Interactive Semantics, *Artificial Intelligence*, 174(2010)190-204), therefore *exploring interaction should take higher priority than studying language in semantics research.*

Interaction can be based on various indicators (language component, artifact, image, sound, etc). The following is the process of influence between the mental space and the social space through delivering indicators.

One person motivates concepts in mind according to internal motivation or in response to external stimulation, uses indicators (e.g., words) to indicate the concepts, and delivers the indicators to the other person(s) through the social network they are involved in. The person who receives the indicators activates the concepts in mind. The active concepts activate the other concepts through the mental semantic link network. The receiver may also use indicators to indicate the active concepts and deliver the indicator through social networks.

Continuously receiving indicators, the mind emerges semantic images. One semantic image can be linked to the other semantic images through the links between concepts to form a larger semantic image or a sequence of semantic images. The semantic images emerging one after another along the time dimension constitutes a *semantic movie.*

One or a set of indicators is meaningful if it can inspire semantic image or semantic movie in one's mind.

The following are some characteristics of the semantic link network of concepts in mind:

Characteristics

(1) *Diversity*. One indicator can activate multiple concepts in mind. Different orders in a set of indicators can render different semantic images. Sensing a sequence of indicators, different individuals may emerge different semantic movies in minds.

(2) *Priority*. The priority of emerging concepts is determined by the ranks of the concepts, the link structure, the times of being activated, and the current emerging concept. The often activated or high-rank concepts have higher priority. This priority is the basis of attention.

(3) *Temporality*. An active concept or semantic image can only last for a short period of time. Beyond the active period, the concepts will be inactive. The mind provides a stage for performing concepts or semantic images.

(4) *Relevancy*. A semantic image prepares to re-emerge when one of its concepts is activated. When one semantic image is emerging, the linked semantic images prepare to re-emerge. The priority of emerging a semantic image depends on the number of active concepts and their ranks.

(5) *Asynchrony*. There is a lag from sensing the indicator to emerging semantic image. If the speed of sensing is too fast, there will be no time to emerge semantic image. People can still sense the indicator even though no semantic image emerges. For example, if one scan text too fast, he/she has no time to emerge semantic images, therefore cannot understand it. This indicates that *the mind uses different components to process indicators and to emerge semantic images*.

Linking mental space to social space

Fig. 2.19.13.1 depicts the scenario that one mental semantic link network influences the other through social semantic link network. The larger nodes denote the currently more active concepts. A semantic image can be one concept or a set of related concepts. The nodes in yellow color denote semantic images.

Some concepts can be expressed in language while others are only in mind. *The concepts (i.e., internal-only concepts) that cannot be expressed in language may be linked to and influenced by those concepts that can be expressed by language*. The internal-only concepts can influence other concepts and render semantic images.

Activating a concept in different minds may have different effects because different minds have different semantic link networks and a concept has different emotional statuses in different minds. Therefore, a semantic link network of human individuals can pass through the influence of emotion.

Mental networks

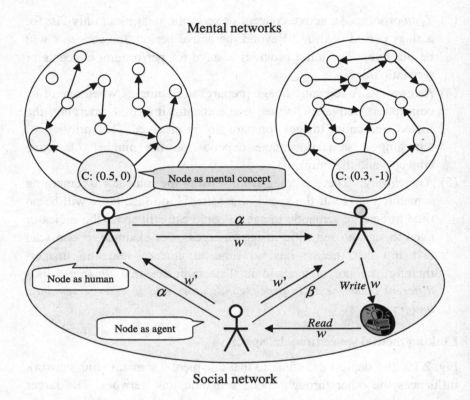

Fig. 2.19.13.1 Influence between mental semantic link networks through social semantic link network, where α denotes a semantic relation, C denotes a concept or semantic image in mind, and w denotes an indicator (e.g., word) that indicates C.

The interesting issue is how to use the influence through links to control emotions.

The following is a semantic link in the mental space, where $Rank_A$ and $Rank_B$ are the ranks of concepts A and B, α is the relation between the two concepts (e.g., sequential, co-occurrence, cause-effect), and ES is the emotional status, which can be divided into multiple levels from negative to positive, e.g., negative (-1), neutral (0), or positive ($+1$):

A(*Attributes*, $Rank_A$, ES_A) —α— B(*Attributes*, $Rank_B$, ES_B).

A concept has a rank determined by the number of connected concepts and their ranks. The inactive concepts do not influence the other concepts. The emotional status of a concept is influenced by the emotional statuses of the connected active concepts. The following is an approach to computing the emotional status of concept P at time $t+1$, where k denotes the active concepts linked to P, and f is a function that determines the influence from these concepts:

$$ES_P(t+1)= ES_P(t) + f(Rank_P(t), \sum_{k=1}^{n} Rank_k(t) \cdot ES_k(t)).$$

The rank of the emerging concept will get a certain rise. The rising rank will influence the rank of the connected concepts, and the influence will be propagated in the network.

In the semantic link network of concepts, the neutral concepts separate the positive concepts from the negative concepts. The high-rank negative concepts should reduce their ranks and then become neutral concepts before becoming positive concepts.

The emotional status of concepts could be changed by adapting links or ranks of the concepts.

Working in the social space, the social semantic link network consists of nodes as human individuals and links as social relations. It enables one person to communicate with the other person sharing common concepts by delivering indicators through certain semantic links. The following is the semantic link of the social semantic link network, where w is the indicator forwarding from person X to person Y at time t through relation α.

$$X(Rank_X, t) \longrightarrow \alpha{:}w(t) \rightarrow Y(Rank_Y, t).$$

The rank of the node in the social semantic link network is determined by the number of links it has and the ranks of the connected nodes. The potential energy of node and the motion energy of operating a semantic link network were proposed as a new measure of a dynamic network (H.Zhuge, Semantic linking through spaces for cyber-physical-socio intelligence: A methodology, *Artificial Intelligence*, 175(2011)988-1019).

A series of indicators $W=<w_1, ..., w_n>$ will be delivered from X to Y during a time period $\Delta t=[t_1, t_2]$, so the semantic link should consider a time period as follows:

$$X(Rank_X, \Delta t) —\alpha(\Delta t):W(\Delta t)\rightarrow Y(Rank_Y, \Delta t).$$

Y receiving W during Δt will emerge a concept (e.g, C in Fig. 2.19.13) or a semantic image consisting of the concepts indicated by these indictors.

2.19.14 *Application in cognitive-behavioral therapy*

Cognitive-Behavioral Therapy (CBT) is a kind of treatment for mental health problem (A.T. Beck, Cognitive Therapy and the Emotional Disorders. International Universities Press Inc., 1975). It combines cognitive therapy and behavioral therapy (M.B. Keller, et al., A comparison of nefazodone, the cognitive behavioral-analysis system of psychotherapy, and their combination for the treatment of chronic depression, *New England Journal of Medicine*, 342(20)(2000)1462–1470). Some empirical evidences show that CBT is effective for treating the problems concerning mood, anxiety, personality, and psychotic disorders.

Depression is a state of low mood and aversion to activity that can affect a person's thought, behavior, feeling and well-being. CBT is one method of treatments, at least an assistant means.

The semantic link network can be an analysis means for CBT. *The basic viewpoint is that depression is not only a mental problem but also a social problem.* Wrong links, ranks and interactions in the social space and the mental space could lead to depression. Adapting the links, ranks and interactions is a way to solve the problem.

The emotional statuses of the often emerging semantic images influence human mental status. Depression happens if negative mental concepts and semantic images often emerge. As the consequence, the ranks of the negative concepts and semantic images and the connected links become higher. The high-rank concepts and semantic images take the priority in the competition of emerging. The "rich get richer" phenomenon forms an *internal negative loop*, which makes depression more serious. An inter-person negative loop is formed through continuous interaction between persons on negative concepts.

A solution is to change the statuses of the semantic images from negative to neutral or positive by operating the social network that the patient involved in.

The following operations can influence the emotional status of a person:

(1) *Adapt interaction*. Reduce the times of interaction between the patient and the person who has many common high-rank negative concepts (often delivers negative emotion), and increase the times of interaction between the patient and the person who has many common high-rank positive concepts (often delivers positive emotion).

(2) *Adapt rank*. Reduce the rank of the person who delivers negative emotion through the social network the patient involved in. Raise the rank of the person who often delivers positive emotion through the social network. For example, change the person's position and responsibility in an organization.

(3) *Remove links*. Remove the link that often delivers negative semantic indicator in the social network. For example, change the patient's workplace to remove old work relations.

(4) *Increase links*. Increase the link that often delivers positive emotion in the social network. For example, encourage the patient to participate in more social activities to interact with the persons who can often deliver positive emotion. The linked persons should share common positive concepts.

(5) *Interact with appropriate resources*. Interact with the resources (e.g., text, video, audio) that indicate many positive semantic images.

(6) *Increase positive nodes*. Encourage the patient to learn new positive concepts and link to the persons that often deliver positive concepts.

(7) *Change the attributes of the negative concepts*. Abnormal attribute values of some concepts influence emotional statuses. Due to the bias of cognition, the attributes of some negative concepts do not

appropriately reflect the external world. The values of attributes may be changed by knowing more instances of the concept.

(8) *Invite the third party*, which is important in forming the loop of delivering positive indicators, and getting rid of the loop of delivering negative indicators.

The key is to know the high-rank negative concepts and semantic images in the patient's mind and the involved social network so that the other persons (e.g., family members) can avoid talking to the patients about the negative concepts and help change the social network through the above operations.

A web-based interactive e-health system can help detect the negative, neutral and positive concepts and semantic images in the patient's mind through a set of querying and answering, and then give necessary suggestions or play games with the patient. It is particularly useful in the places where appropriate therapists are not available.

Analyzing the mental semantic link network and the social semantic link network of the patient as well as the influence between the mental space and social space provides a new means of therapy.

2.20   Principles of Mental Concepts

Mental concepts are the basic components of semantic images in mind. Some concepts are the reflection and generalization of physical objects or events, while some others are too abstract to correspond to the physical objects or visible events. A mental concept is formed and enriched through learning, interaction and experience in multiple spaces. The process concerns the internal microscopic close-loop and the external macroscopic close-loop (H.Zhuge, Semantic linking through spaces for cyber-physical-socio intelligence: A methodology, Artificial Intelligence, 175(2011)988-1019).

A concept is rendered by the following facets of elements:

(1) *Attributes*, which render the concept through the attributes reflected in the physical space (e.g., car's color, shape, and internal space) and in the social space (e.g., price, reputation, and sales).

(2) *Links*, which connect to the other concepts through semantic links such as generalization and specialization. For example, the concepts of car should be linked to the concepts of road and human.

(3) *Functions*, which transform input into output, or change the statuses of attributes.

(4) *Operations*, which reflect the behaviors of changing statuses, and instruct the physiological organisms to act (e.g., instruct hands and legs to drive a car with certain speed).

(5) *Experiences*, which link feeling to the attributes and operations, e.g., the feeling of driving or moving.

Concepts are linked to form semantic images or semantic movies through interactions between the elements of multiple facets. The interactions form closed loops of experience. Fig. 2.20.1 shows the links between the concept of human individual and the concept of the external object. For example, human individual uses eyes to see the operation mechanisms and read the specifications, and use hands and legs to operate them. The eyes and the senses of time and space feel the effect of operation (e.g., motion). The relations between the process of motion and the process of the operations are established through continuous feeling and operations.

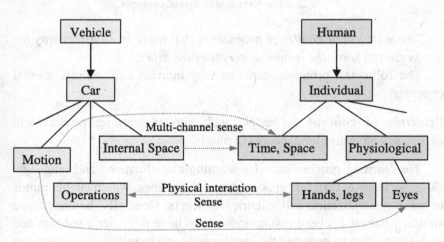

Fig.2.20.1 Linking concepts through interactions.

As shown in Fig.2.20.2, semantic link networks of concepts are built and keep evolving in lifetime with continuous learning and experiencing in the physical space and socio space and reading and writing through the symbol space.

Learning language helps the brain build the function of processing symbols according to the grammar and experience of reading and writing, and linking symbols to mental concepts.

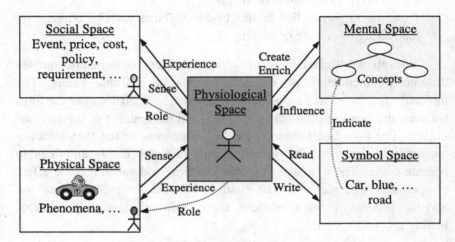

Fig. 2.20.2 The formation of mental concepts.

The most grand challenge problem is that there is no direct way for any person to know the mental concepts of the other.

The following principle explains why humans can indicate mental concepts.

Principle of concept 1. People with similar learning process and experience have similar concepts in minds.

The learning process includes learning classifications and language. Co-experience in different spaces generates feelings, which enable minds to make generalization and to enrich concepts. Generally, humans share similar genes and inherit similar culture, so have the inner condition and social condition to generate the similar concepts in minds. Therefore, we can generalize the principle by incorporating the physiological, social and physical aspects as follows:

Individuals have similar concepts in mind if they have similar physiological space, learning process and experience in physical space and social space.

Although there may have some innate concepts in mind, most concepts are generated through learning and experience. To interact with each other, humans use symbols (or sound) to indicate mental concepts. Learning establishes the mapping between words and mental concepts. However the mapping is not one-one mapping, one word can be used to indicate multiple mental concepts, and multiple words can be used to indicate one mental concept.

Emerging concepts with different emotions may have different influences in the psychological space and physiological space through behaviors. Studying the relation between mental concepts and behaviors can help people to understand each other.

People use a sequence of words to indicate a mental semantic image consisting of multiple concepts. Reading an article can emerge a network of semantic images in mind. People sharing more concepts have more common learning process and experience, so they know more common symbols.

Principle of concept 2. If two individuals have used more common symbols in multiple times of communication, their minds have more common mappings between concepts and symbols.

This principle indicates that people sharing more concepts can better understand each other when using symbols for communication, e.g., via emails. More times of communication provide stronger support for the mappings.

People in the same community should have used more common symbols for communication than those in different communities, so they share more concepts than those in different communities. According to the above principle, they can understand each other better than those in different communities.

People who have similar statuses in the social space should have similar activities, for example, students involve in learning activities, professors involve in teaching activities, and group leaders involve in similar activities although they are in different areas.

Principle of concept 3. Individuals have similar statuses in the social space often involve in similar events.

The statuses concern the ranks in the network, the link structure, and the statuses of the connected persons. This principle explains that great minds think alike.

Current technologies enable people to display the physiological behaviors of brain by using fMRI (functional magnetic resonance imaging) and EEG (electroencephalogram is a measure of brain waves), but there is a big gap between physiological behaviors and mental concepts. Fig. 2.20.3 shows the big gaps between mental concepts, physiological behaviors (e.g., brain images), and symbols.

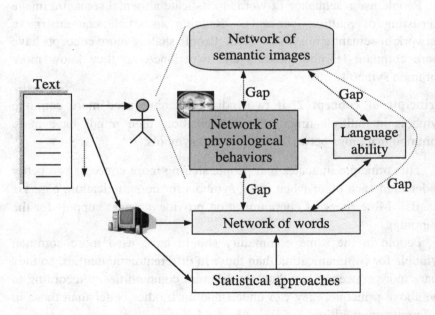

Fig. 2.20.3 Gaps between semantic image, brain image and symbols.

Scanning text, computers can easily remember all of the symbols and can form a network of symbols, but computers are not able to generate the semantic images as humans because the generation of the semantic images in mind concerns the spaces (e.g., social space, physiological space, and psychological space) that machines do not have and cannot experience, even if humans assign rules to them.

Only in some specific domains, machines can reduce the gaps by establishing one-one mapping between symbols and concepts. In the open domain, establishing one-one mapping is not feasible due to the diversity and richness of humans and society.

Knowing the semantic link networks of mental concepts is a way to effective interaction.

2.21 Discussion: Philosophy, Psychology, Language, and Semantics

Social relations are firstly studied by Laozi (576–BC), Confucius (551–479 BC), and Socrates (469 BC–399 BC). The formal generalization of relation can trace to the invention of set theory in 1874.

Hume (1711-1776) regarded *causation* as *a kind of mental association by associating constantly co-occurred events.*

"A caused B" is equivalent to "Whenever events of type A happen, events of type B follow", where the word whenever means by all possible perceptions.

He thought that humans have no perceptual access to the connection, but humans naturally believe in its objective existence. The causal relation can be also regarded as an expression of a functional change in mind, by which some events in experience could be referred.

He also believes that *two things are relational because they have constant conjunction (emerge into one, or one after the other at time, in space, or on logic), and one thing will remind people of another.*

SLN concerns all relations, the models of networking, and the laws and effects of networking. In the SLN method, relations can be in the social space, the cyber space, the physical space and the mental space. Relations in one space reflect the relations in the other space. Different minds may reflect different relations from the same set of individuals (objects, humans, events, etc.) in the same space. The mental space can reflect relations not only in one space but also through spaces. For example, the relations between behaviors in the social space can be detected by mining the data in the cyber space.

Wittgenstein (1889–1951) argued that the meaning of words is constituted by the function they perform within any given language-game (i.e., use cases). SLN uses a semantic space to determine the meaning of indicators (e.g., words) that indicate relations at the first stage. In the cyber-physical society, *the meaning of an indicator is rendered from not only the symbol space but also the physical space, social space and mental space.*

SLN is also relevant to the notion of *self*.

Hume regarded the self as nothing but *a bundle of interconnected perceptions linked by the property of constancy and coherence.*

John Locke (1632–1704) defines the self as conscious thinking thing that is sensible, concerned for itself, and conscious of emotion. He argued that the mind grows from empty through experience (J. Locke, An Essay Concerning Human Understanding, 1690).

Self is a basic cognition mechanism that reflects relations and determines the target of linking and the content of interactions. SLN can model and analyze self by creating the internal semantic link network and external semantic link network. *The internal network and the external network are linked through sense, reflection, and language interaction.*

How is self generated?

Physiological space and social space constitute the ground of generating self. Physiological system is the inner factor of generating self. For example, animals generate the motivation of eating food in the external physical space because of the sense of hungry generated from the physiological system. Social space is the external factor of generating self. For example, social competition and natural evolution generate the motivation of survival.

A self needs a reflection, from the cyber space, physical space, or social space. Self also needs confirmation in a community.

The cyber space has no physiological and social grounds to grow self.

Psychology is the study of mind and behavior. Research is often limited by the following factors: single dimension, isolated objects, small sample, and pre-defined tasks. The SLN provides tool and method for modeling and analyzing mind and behavior in a large relational network. In the cyber-physical society, behaviors and sense will be reflected in more spaces, and can pass through spaces. Therefore, psychologists can observe the real phenomena in addition to do experiments on behaviors with pre-defined tasks.

William Molyneux raised the following issue to Locke in 1688: "If a blind person were suddenly able to see, would he be able to recognize by sight the shape of an object he previously knew only by touch? Presented with a cube and a globe, could he tell which was which just by looking?" Locke answered: "He would not be able with certainty to say which was the globe, which the cube, whilst he only saw them," he said: "though he could unerringly name them by his touch."

This question may lead to fundamental thinking: *Whether there is an innate conception space common to both sight and touch or not*? Or, *whether we learn that relationship only through experience or not*? This concerns the core of philosophy of mind. Locke's opinion was confirmed by latter experiments (N.Bakalar, Study of Vision Tackles a Philosophy Riddle, *The New York Times*, April 25, 2011): The mind cannot immediately make sense of what the eyes see, and the recovered blind people cannot distinguish the two objects.

SLN and cyber-physical society can help study this philosophical issue. The following are two causes:

The first cause is that the channel of sight and the channel of touch are separated. This can be confirmed by the following test:

The child who never sees the real elephant cannot tell the feeling of touch by just watching a picture or video of an elephant.

The second cause is that the two things are isolated. If the blind person knows one relation (e.g., *aboveOf, leftOf, rightOf*) between the two objects as shown in Fig. 2.21.1, he/she should appropriately link the feeling of touch to the corresponding object although he may not recognize the two objects only by sight immediately. Afterwards, the person should be able to link the sight features to the touch features quickly. This indicates that humans can establish new concepts based on existing concepts.

People have built rich relations between semantic images of various granularities in mind through life-long learning and experience. These relations help people to emerge new semantic images. This is why people can understand each other in conversation even though some words are missed.

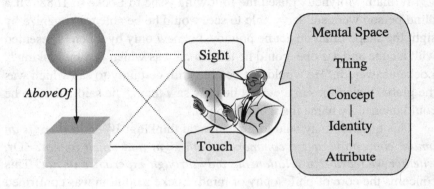

Fig. 2.21.1 Establishing new concepts with the help of relations.

The following mental process involves in establishing the initial concepts of the two physical objects:

(1) Link the touch features to the appropriate object in the physical space according to the relation between the object and the process of touching it (the motion and position of hand in the physical space).
(2) Link the touch features to the sight features through the relation between the objects.
(3) Attaching the sight features and the touch features to the objects as attributes.

The following is an important issue: *What are the most basic concepts or behaviors that enable humans to grow a network of versatile concepts?*

The following are *basic networking behaviors* in the mental space:

(1) Sense the objects in the physical space.

(2) Establish link between self and the objects, link one object to the other through self, and then establish the concept of space.

(3) Sense the individuals in the social space, link self to the individuals, and then link one individual to the other. Family relations will be established firstly.

(4) Link the features of sense to the features of emotions.

We should not forget an important fact that the blind person lives in a social space. People can obtain indirect experience through the social links. A blind person has a mental space and has established semantic images on many objects. The difference is that the concepts in their semantic images have no sight attributes. So, the recognition of objects needs the reflections from multiple channels and multiple spaces.

Natural language is a semantic indicating system created by humans for interaction. Humans acquire the ability of natural language through social interaction. Studies show that languages are processed in certain areas in human brain. Languages are generated and developed through interaction and evolution in a process of Darwin's natural selection.

With language, humans often interact with each other through the symbol space without participation of the physical space. This brings efficiency of interaction and expansion of human imagination, but leads to misunderstandings. People without experience in the physical space on the interaction topic rely on the symbol space to build semantic images. But, the symbol space is limited in ability to help humans to build the semantic images of versatile objects if people do not have relevant experience (direct mapping from the physical space). As shown in Fig.2.21.2, it is hard for individuals A and B to build appropriate semantic images according to the indicator "tiger" if they do not have the experience about tiger.

SLN can be regarded as a general language and method for exploring the semantics through spaces. The semantic space of the SLN can be regarded as the grammar of semantic indicators.

Human minds establish semantic images when sensing external stimulation, which evolves through the microscopic closed loop and macroscopic closed loop of super links through multiple spaces.

There are two types of semantic images: semantic images of physical objects and semantic images of indicators. Different people can generate the same semantic image of one physical object. This can be tested by behaviors and Q/A about the object. But, different people may generate different semantic images of one indicator. This is because different people may involve in different close-loops of hearing, speaking, reading and writing the indicator.

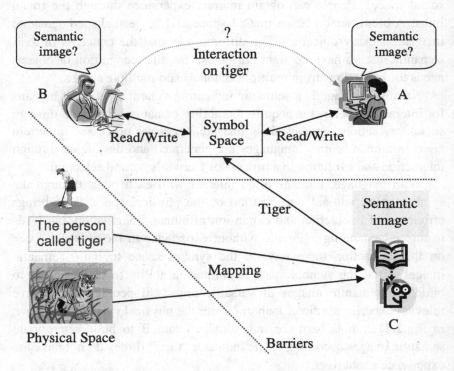

Fig. 2.21.2 The semantic images of physical objects and indicators. The dotted blue lines indicate the possible barriers.

A well-designed semantic indicator system like maps helps humans to build abstract semantic images although people have no direct experience. Some semantic indicator systems are created by team work, where collaborators may have different types of semantic images. As shown in Fig.2.21.2, participation of individual C in the interaction will help A and B to build the appropriate semantic image on "tiger". The possible barrier refers to the distances in the physical space and the social space, as well as to the change of the characteristics of individuals (e.g., the characteristics of human-raised animals are different from those of the wild animals).

The cyber-physical society will extend human ability by enabling experiencing the cyber space, the physical space and the social space, and reflecting themselves from these spaces while interacting with each other and with individuals in these spaces.

The SLN in the Cyber-Physical Society passes through the cyber space, physical space, socio space, and mental space for extending human ability. The objective existence of the network is linked to the subjective existence. So, research on SLN in the Cyber-Physical Society upgrades previous research in the cyber space. Only in the Cyber-Physical Society, some fundamental effects in the cyber space, social space, and mental space can be revealed.

When I was checking this chapter, Steve Jobs passed away on October 5, 2011. I watched the videos of his past activities several times. The most impressive one is his talk about *connecting the dots* in life toward success. His idea is in line with the following philosophical ideal of the Semantic Link Network:

Appropriately linking appropriate nodes through multiple spaces to wave the meaning of life.

When I was about to finish this chapter, John McCarthy passed away on October 23, 2011. He coined the artificial intelligence and invented the Lisp language. He foresaw service computing, grid computing, and cloud computing in 1961. In 1969, he studied philosophical problems of artificial intelligence. During 1963-1986, he studied commonsense, context, and causal laws, which are the basis of semantics and intelligent systems. John received the Turing Award in 1971. After 2001, he explored the emotions, Internet culture and social networking issues.

I tried to rebuild John's semantic image in my mind by reading his papers when I wrote the "Interactive Semantics" (*Artificial Intelligence*, 174(2010)190-204) and the "Semantic linking through spaces for cyber-physical-socio intelligence: A methodology" (*Artificial Intelligence*, 175(2011)988-1019). His insight on "Human-level AI" (*Artificial*

Intelligence, 171(18)(2007)1174-1182) and "Well-designed child" (*Artificial Intelligence*, 172(18)(2008)2003-2014) enlightens an important way of AI development.

It is an interesting issue to build his semantic image on AI by extracting semantic link networks from his papers so that AI researchers can interact with his semantic images.

John left us, but his important semantic images will be rebuilt and propagated through various explicit and implicit links in the mental space, cyber space and social space.

Humans have been relying on languages to indicate semantic images in minds. Only the important semantic images in minds are widely propagated and inherited through generations. In the cyber-physical society, individual mental spaces will be indicated by behaviors and languages. More individual mental spaces will be preserved, and retrieved more easily.

As a general method, SLN can be applied to many special networks such as biological network, brain network, physiological network, economic network, ecological network, and social networks. For example, by creating the gene networks of cancer features, the SLN method can help find the implicit relations, know the evolution rules of the network and the stage of the network in the evolution process, and indicate the way to control the evolution of the network.

Classification plays the key role in specifying the semantic space of the semantic link network. Multi-dimensional classifications can be formalized into a resource organization model.

The following chapter will introduce a multi-dimensional classification space: the Resource Space Model (RSM), in which coordinates of dimensions (axes) play roles like those of latitudes and longitudes in geographical maps as outlined at the beginning of this chapter.

Chapter 3

A Resource Space Model

Classification is one of the most basic methods for humans to recognize and organize various resources. The Resource Space Model is a resource organization model based on multi-dimensional classifications.

3.1. Examples of Using Multi-Dimensional Classifications

One-dimensional classification is often used. For example, supermarkets classify goods and arrange classes in a certain order according to customers' purchasing habit so that customers can easily get necessary goods. File system is a one-dimensional classification (hierarchical directory) system that enables both human and computer to easily manage various digital files in computer's disk.

The following are examples of using multi-dimensional classifications:

(1) Maps use two-dimensional space (*latitude*, *longitude*) or three-dimensional space (*latitude*, *longitude*, *elevation*) to actually specify locations on the earth.

(2) Experimental results are displayed and compared in two- or three-dimensional charts, and the display devices are two- or three-dimensional.

(3) Faceted web browsing view a set of web pages from different facets of contents.

(4) Sensor grids are used to collect overall signals of the brain.

(5) Stock market uses three-dimensional classification space (*time, company, price*) to reflect the real-time situation of the market.

Keyword search is popular in general-purpose web search. Fig.3.1.1 shows an example of searching the map by keywords.

A map classifies surface objects according to geographical coordinate space. With continuous expansion of the scope of human activities, more and more surface objects have not only physical features but also socio features. For example, a city has population, culture, economy, and education. Classification on socio features provides a socio dimension for users to accurately locate objects.

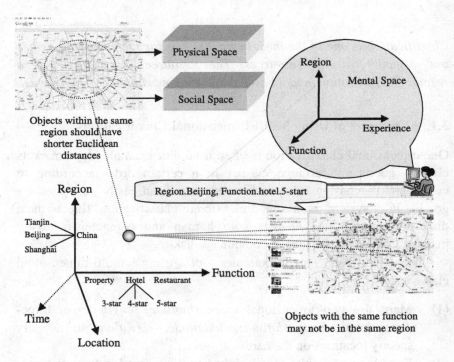

Fig. 3.1.1 Multi-dimensional classifications in map search.

Different spaces may use different distance measures such as Euclidean distance and semantic distance.

Two objects that are close in one space may not be close in the other space. The physical space is a metric space, where objects within the same region should have shorter Euclidean distances. Individuals within the same family or community are closer in the social space. Two individuals that are close in the social space (e.g., with the same social function) may not be close in the physical space (e.g., in the same region). A classification space with dimensions (*location, region, function*) can effectively organize various objects.

Map search concerns the mental space. Users have established classification spaces in minds through lifelong learning. They usually have consensus on classifications on social functions and physical regions. Querying a map is to find the points in the map that match the points in the physical space, the socio space and the mental space.

Users can search various objects by giving the keywords that indicate the coordinates in the dimensions or a part of the dimensions in mind. The social functions can be classified by physical regions, and physical regions can be classified by social functions.

More dimensions can be added to the classification space. For example, adding a time dimension enables users to accurately search historical maps.

The new version of Google map search enables users to select the classes of the search target, which can help narrow the search scope. To develop an underlying model to support efficient map search is a critical issue.

3.2. The Virtual Grid

The *Virtual Grid* is a platform independent interconnection environment, based on a resource organization model, which can effectively specify, share, use and manage a variety of resources (H. Zhuge, "Semantics, Resource and Grid", *Future Generation Computer Systems*, 20 (1)(2004)1-5). It has the following key parts:

(1) The *Resource Space Model* (RSM) — a resource space for effectively organizing and accurately locating resources. It can be a classification-based Resource Space Model. It can also be the integration of the semantic link network and the Resource Space Model. A resource space can be centralized or decentralized (H.

Zhuge and X. Li, RSM-Based Gossip on P2P Network. ICA^{3}PP 2007: 1-12).

(2) The *Resource Using Mechanism* (RUM) — a *faceted resource browser*, a *resource management engine*, a *Resource Operation Language* (ROL), a *ROL interpreter*, and an *application development environment.*

The resource browser provides an easy-to-use interface that helps end-users select resources and operations, specify parameters, and then have operations carried out. The resource management engine accepts instructions and then has them carried out according to the types of the resources to be operated on.

The ROL enables end-users to carry out simple operations, and application developers to compose a program to apply complex operations to resources.

The ROL interpreter supports not only complex applications in their use of resources, but also the resource browser in its use of resources. End-users can either run an application system to carry out operations of a specific kind or use the resource browser to operate directly on resources.

Developers build programs with the support of the development environment, which is in turn supported partly by the Virtual Grid and partly by application development tools.

A resource space has three views as discussed in "Resource Space Grid: model, method and platform" (H. Zhuge, *Concurrency and Computation: Practice and Experience*, 16(3)(2004)):

(1) The *user view*, a two- or multi-dimensional resource space, is used by the resource browser to make it easy for end-users to locate and use resources. The space will interact with the user's mental space during operation. It is hard for end-users to deal with multi-dimensional spaces without such help.

(2) The *universal view*, the entire *n*-dimensional resource space. A user view is a slice (or a subspace) of the universal view. Operating the same resource space, different users could have different user view.

(3) The *semantic view*, a semantic representation of a variety of resources to support effective interactions between human and machine as well as between machine and machine based on the semantic worldview, semantic image, and semantic lens mechanisms (H. Zhuge, "Interactive Semantics," *Artificial Intelligence*, 174(2010)190-204).

3.3 The Resource Space Model (RSM)

The Resource Space Model is the resource management mechanism using multi-dimensional classification space on resources.

3.3.1 *Resource spaces*

Definition 3.3.1 A resource space is an *n*-dimensional space in which every point has unique projection on every dimension.

The uniqueness implies that giving one coordinate at every dimension can uniquely determine one point, which contains a set of resources (possibly null). A resource space has a name, a type, a location (logical or physical), and an access privilege.

A dimension is classified by a set of coordinates. By establishing a good coordinate system for a resource space, we can precisely store and retrieve its resources by their coordinates. To distinguish coordinates or resources of the same name in different resource spaces, the coordinate or resource name can be used with the space name, for example: *coordinate-name. space-name*.

Further, we assume that an ontology service mechanism *Output = Ontology_Service (Input, k)* is available. The *Input* parameter is a word or phrase. The second parameter is a numeric variable used for controlling the output. If $k = 0$, the service puts out sets of words related to *Input* of the following kinds: synonym, abstract concept, specific concept, and instance. If $k = 1$, the ontology service puts out one more element — a quasi-synonym of the input word or phrase, if one exists.

In the discussion below, we use the following notations:

(1) A resource space is represented by $RS(X_1, X_2, ..., X_n)$, or RS for short, where RS is the name of the space and X_i is the name of an axis. $|RS|$ denotes the number of dimensions of RS.

(2) $X_i = \{C_{i1}, C_{i2}, ..., C_{im}\}$ represents an axis with its coordinates. Each element denotes a coordinate name in the form of a noun or a noun phrase. Any coordinate name must be defined in its domain ontology, as in the Word Net (www.cogsci.princeton.edu/~wn/).

Definition 3.3.2 Two axes are deemed the same if their names are the same and the names of the corresponding coordinates are the same based on a certain mapping. If two axes $X_1 = \{C_{11}, C_{12}, ..., C_{1i}\}$ and $X_2 = \{C_{21}, C_{22}, ..., C_{2j}\}$ have the same axis name and specify the same set of resources but have different coordinates, they can be joined into one: $X = X_1 \cup X_2$, denoted by $X_1 \cup X_2 \Rightarrow X$.

It is useful to form a relatively complete dimension when two persons classify a set of resources with different views. In the open domain applications, one name may be used to indicate different objects, and different names may be used to indicate the same thing, so the join operation should not just check the name of dimension.

Characteristic 3.3.1 An axis X can be split into two axes X' and X'' by dividing the coordinate set of X into two: the coordinate set of X' and that of X'', such that $X = X' \cup X''$.

A coordinate can be a hierarchy, with lower-level coordinates as subclasses of their common ancestor. We use $Sup(C)$ to denote the direct ancestor or immediate superior of C in a coordinate hierarchy. The name of each coordinate of a hierarchy can be differentiated from others of the same name by giving its name together with the names of all of its ancestors. The following definition shows the nature of coordinates in a hierarchy:

Definition 3.3.3 A coordinate C selects a class of resources (denoted by $R(C)$) such that if $C = Sup(C')$ then $R(C') \subseteq R(C)$.

From this definition, if $C = Sup(C')$ and $C' = Sup(C'')$ then $R(C'') \subseteq R(C)$.

For simplicity, an axis with hierarchical coordinates can be mapped onto an axis with flat coordinates by projecting its leaves onto the axis. But, this will lead to the lost of abstraction ability of the space.

Good resource space design should ensure correct resource sharing and management. Synonyms like "teacher", "instructor" and "tutor" should not be used together as flat coordinates, because that could lead to resource operations making mistakes.

Definition 3.3.4 A coordinate C is dependent on coordinate C' if $C \in Output = Ontology\_Service(C', 1)$.

Definition 3.3.5 If $X = (C_1, C_2, ..., C_n)$ is an axis and C_i' is a coordinate of another axis X', we say that X is a fine classification on C_i' (denoted by C_i'/X) if and only if:

(1) $(R(C_k) \cap R(C_i')) \cap (R(C_p) \cap R(C_i')) = \phi$ ($k \neq p$, and $k, p \in [1, n]$); and,

(2) $(R(C_1) \cap R(C_i')) \cup (R(C_2) \cap R(C_i')) \cup ... \cup (R(C_n) \cap R(C_i')) = R(C_i')$.

As the result of the fine classification, $R(C')$ is classified into n categories: $R(C_i'/X) = \{R(C_1) \cap R(C_i'), R(C_2) \cap R(C_i'), ..., R(C_n) \cap R(C_i')\}$.

Definition 3.3.6 For two axes $X = \{C_1, C_2, ..., C_n\}$ and $X' = \{C_1', C_2', ..., C_m'\}$, we say that X is a fine classification on X' (denoted by X'/X) if and only if X is a fine classification on $C_1', C_2', ...,$ and C_m'.

Characteristic 3.3.2 Fine classification is transitive, that is, if X''/X' and X'/X, then X''/X.

Fine classification is a basic mechanism of recognition and understanding.

Definition 3.3.7 Two axes X and X' are said to be orthogonal to each other (denoted by $X \perp X'$) if X is a fine classification on X' and vice versa, that is, both X'/X and X/X'.

For example, $KnowledgeLevel = <Concept, Axiom, Rule, Method> \perp Discipline = <ComputerScience, Mathematics, Physics>$ because $<Concept, Axiom, Rule, Method>$ is a fine classification of every

coordinate   of   the   *Discipline*   axis   and   the
<ComputerScience,   Mathematics,   Physics> is a fine classification of
every coordinate of the *KnowledgeLevel* axis. Another example is
Gender=<Male,   Female>   ⊥   *Student=<UndergraduateStudent,*
GraduateStudent>.

Because fine classification is transitive, we can assert the following:

Characteristic 3.3.3 Orthogonality between axes is transitive, that is, if
$X \perp X'$ and $X' \perp X''$, then $X \perp X''$.

3.3.2 *Normal forms*

To ensure a good design of a resource space, we need to define the
following normal forms for the space.

Definition 3.3.8

(1) A resource space is in first normal form (1NF) if no coordinate
    names are duplicated within any axes.
(2) A space in 1NF is also in second normal form (2NF) if no two
    coordinates are dependent on each other.
(3) A space in 2NF is also in third normal form (3NF) if any two axes
    are orthogonal.

These normal forms provide designers with guidelines for designing
a good resource space. The 1NF avoids explicit coordinate duplication.
The 2NF avoids implicit coordinate duplication, and prevents one
coordinate from semantically depending on another. The 3NF ensures
that resources are properly used.

Characteristic 3.3.4 If two spaces RS_1 and RS_2 hold the same type of
resources and they have n (≥ 1) axes in common, then they can be joined
as one RS such that RS_1 and RS_2 share these n common axes and
$|RS| = |RS_1| + |RS_2| - n$. RS is called the join of RS_1 and RS_2 and is denoted
by $RS_1 \cdot RS_2 \Rightarrow RS$.

Characteristic 3.3.5 A space RS can be separated into two spaces RS_1
and RS_2 (denoted by $RS \Rightarrow RS_1 \cdot RS_2$) such that they have n

$(1 \leq n \leq minimum\ (|RS_1|, |RS_2|))$ axes in common, $|RS| - n$ different axes, and $|RS_1| + |RS_2| = |RS| + n$.

The separation operation is also called disjoin in The Web Resource Space Model (H.Zhuge, Springer, 2008).

Characteristic 3.3.6 If two spaces RS_1 and RS_2 hold the same type of resources and satisfy: (1) $|RS_1| = |RS_2| = n$, (2) they have $n-1$ common axes, and (3) the distinct axes X_1 and X_2 satisfy the merge condition, then they can be merged into one RS by retaining the $n-1$ common axes and adding a new axis $X = X_1 \cup X_2$. RS is called the merge of RS_1 and RS_2, denoted by $RS_1 \cup RS_2 \Rightarrow RS$, and $|RS| = n$.

Characteristic 3.3.7 A resource space RS can be split into two spaces RS_1 and RS_2 that hold the same type of resources as that of RS and have $|RS| - 1$ common axes, by splitting an axis X into two axes X' and X'' such that $X = X' \cup X''$. This split operation is denoted by $RS \Rightarrow RS_1 \cup RS_2$.

Using these definitions and characteristics, we can prove the following three lemmas.

Lemma 3.3.1 Let $RS_1 \cdot RS_2 \Rightarrow RS$.

(1) RS is in 1NF if and only if both RS_1 and RS_2 are in 1NF.
(2) RS is in 2NF if and only if both RS_1 and RS_2 are in 2NF.
(3) RS is in 3NF if and only if both RS_1 and RS_2 are in 3NF.

Lemma 3.3.2 (1) $RS \Rightarrow RS_1 \cdot RS_2$ if and only if $RS_1 \cdot RS_2 \Rightarrow RS$; and, (2) $RS \Rightarrow RS_1 \cup RS_2$ if and only if $RS_1 \cup RS_2 \Rightarrow RS$.

The following lemma ensures that a resource space of many dimensions can be separated into several spaces of fewer dimensions that keep the same normal form as the original space. For instance, a five-dimensional space can be separated into two three-dimensional spaces that have an axis in common.

Lemma 3.3.3 If $RS \Rightarrow RS_1 \cdot RS_2$, we have:

RS is in 1/2/3NF if and only if both RS_1 and RS_2 are in that form.

From the definition of the normal forms, we have the following two lemmas about the merge and split operations.

Lemma 3.3.4 If $RS \Rightarrow RS_1 \cup RS_2$, and if RS is in 1/2/3NF, then RS_1 and RS_2 are in that form.

Lemma 3.3.5 If $RS_1 \cup RS_2 \Rightarrow RS$ and if RS_1 and RS_2 are in 3NF and RS is in 2NF, then RS is in 3NF.

Semantic overlaps may exist between resource definitions in some applications. In this case, the space designer must use quasi-synonyms as coordinates on an axis.

Lemma 3.3.6 Resources in a 3NF resource space can be accessed from any axis.

Proof. Let $X_i = \{C_{i1}, C_{i2}, \ldots, C_{ip}\}$, $1 \le i \le n$. If the RS is in 3NF, then for any two axes $X_k = \{C_{k1}, C_{k2}, \ldots, C_{kl}\}$ and $X_j = \{C_{j1}, C_{j2}, \ldots, C_{jm}\}$ $(1 \le k \ne j \le n)$, $X_k \perp X_j$. We have C_{kq} / X_j for every C_{kq} $(1 \le q \le l)$.
From the definition of fine classification, we have:
$R(C_{kq}) = (R(C_{kq}) \cap R(C_{j1})) \cup (R(C_{kq}) \cap R(C_{j2})) \cup \cdots$
$\cup (R(C_{kq}) \cap R(C_{jm}))$
$\quad = R(C_{kq}) \cap (R(C_{j1}) \cup R(C_{j2}) \cup \cdots \cup R(C_{jm}))$.
Then $R(C_{kq}) \subseteq (R(C_{j1}) \cup R(C_{j2}) \cup \cdots \cup R(C_{jm}))$ for $1 \le q \le l$.
Hence, we have $(R(C_{k1}) \cup R(C_{k2}) \cup \cdots \cup R(C_{kl})) \subseteq (R(C_{j1}) \cup R(C_{j2})$ $\cup \cdots \cup R(C_{jm}))$ for $1 \le k \ne j \le n$.
Similarly, we have: $(R(C_{j1}) \cup R(C_{j2}) \cup \cdots \cup R(C_{jm}))$
$\subseteq (R(C_{k1}) \cup R(C_{k2}) \cup \cdots \cup R(C_{kl}))$ for $1 \le k \ne j \le n$.
And then we have:
$(R(C_{j1}) \cup R(C_{j2}) \cup \cdots \cup R(C_{jm})) = (R(C_{k1}) \cup R(C_{k2}) \cup \cdots \cup R(C_{kl}))$
for $1 \le k \ne j \le n$.
So, if $R = (R(C_{j1}) \cup R(C_{j2}) \cup \cdots \cup R(C_{jm}))$, then for every axis $X_i = \{C_{i1}, C_{i2}, \ldots, C_{ip}\}$, $1 \le i \le n$, $R = R(C_{i1}) \cup R(C_{i2}) \cup \cdots \cup R(C_{ip})$. $\square$

This means that the resources that are accessible from any axis are the same. Hence a resource retrieval algorithm does not need to depend on the order of the axes.

Definition 3.3.9. A coordinate C is called weakly independent on another coordinate C' if $C \notin Output = Ontology\_Service\ (C', 0)$.

The second normal form has a weak analog.

Definition 3.3.10 The weak 2NF of a space is a 1NF, but in addition, for every one of its axes, any pair of coordinates are weakly independent on each other.

The inter-dependent coordinates can be merged into one coordinate to ensure the 2NF or semantic links can be established between coordinates (H.Zhuge and Y.Xing, Probabilistic Resource Space Model fro Managing Resources in Cyber-Physical Society, *IEEE Trans. on Service   Computing*, http://doi.ieeecomputersociety.org/10.1109/TSC.2011.12).   The third normal form also has a weak analog that can be useful in some applications.

Definition 3.3.11 The weak 3NF of a resource space is a weak 2NF, but in addition, all pairs of axes are orthogonal.

A 3NF resource space may contain points without resources, which lower the efficiency of resource management. We can further normalize a resource space by ruling out such empty points.

Definition 3.3.12 Let $X = (C_1, C_2, ..., C_n)$ be an axis and C_i' be a coordinate on another axis X'. We say that X is a regular and fine classification on C_i' (denoted by C_i'/X) if and only if

(1) $R(C_1) \cap R(C_i') = \phi, R(C_2) \cap R(C_i') \neq \phi, ...,$ and $R(C_n)) \cap R(C_i') \neq \phi$,

(2) $(R(C_k) \cap R(C_i')) \cap (R(C_p) \cap R(C_i')) = \phi$ $(k \neq p$ and $k, p \in [1, n])$, and
$(R(C_1) \cap R(C_i')) \cup (R(C_2) \cap R(C_i')) \cup ... \cup (R(C_n) \cap R(C_i')) = R(C_i')$.

Definition 3.3.13 For two axes $X = \{C_1, C_2, ..., C_n\}$ and $X' = \{C_1', C_2', ..., C_m'\}$, we say that X is a regular and fine classification on X' if and only if X is a regular and fine classification on $C_1', C_2', ...,$ and C_m'.

Definition 3.3.14 If two axes are regular and fine classification on each other, then the two axes are called *regularly orthogonal*.

Definition 3.3.15 The fourth normal form (4NF) of a resource space is a 3NF, but in addition, all pairs of axes are regularly orthogonal.

A generic *reference resource space* is the following four-dimensional resource space:

$RS = (category, level, location, time)$.

The category dimension is a classification of resources. Each coordinate on this axis represents a distinct category. A category coordinate can hold subcategories, and each subcategory can hold subcategories, and so on. A category together with all its lower subcategories forms a category hierarchy. Coordinates on the category axis are scalable because people usually consider resources across different levels. Except for certain basic subcategories, each coordinate of the category axis can be spread down onto a set of lower level coordinates, which can then be spread down again or collected back up to its higher level coordinates. Name duplication can be avoided by denoting a subcategory as a path, e.g., *category · subcategory*.

A resource can be located by its category dimension and level dimension. The location dimension determines the locations of resources in the cyber space, physical space, socio space or mental space. The level dimension can not only classify the category dimension but also the location dimension and the time dimension.

The generic reference resource space can have different specializations on category, level, location and time dimensions depending on the types of resource that it contains.

3.4 Criteria for Designing Resource Spaces

The normal forms defined above can now be used to consider in what ways a resource space may be good or bad. The following are criteria for a resource in a good resource space.

(1) The *understandable* criterion. First, *any resource in a resource space should be understandable*. At least the classifications of the resources should be known. That is, a resource space should not be given a resource that cannot be described or explained. The simple

reason is that only the understandable resources can help users. This criterion also excludes the resources that are irrelevant to users' knowledge structures. Second, *any axis should be understandable*. At least, the classification of any axis should be clear. Third, any coordinate should be understandable. That is, the intention and extension of any coordinate should be clear.

(2) The *resource positioning* criterion. Any resource in a resource space should belong to a point in the resource space. A point has projection at all axes. Such a resource is said to be "well positioned" in the resource space.

(3) The *resource use* criterion. The use of any resource in a resource space should obey all restrictions on its usage that were defined when it was created. For example, some resources can only be operated by particular software.

(4) *Minimum number of axes*, a point can be accurately located by minimum number of axes.

A resource space has a logical representation layer and a physical storage layer. If the two layers are not consistent, for example, if a resource exists in one layer but not in the other, then the RUM will be unable to operate on it properly. To ensure consistency, we set the following criteria.

(1) The *existence consistency* criterion. Any resource in a resource space should ensure the consistency of its existence in the schemas of different levels. In other words, if a resource is in one schema it must be in another schema. Resource operations should maintain this consistency.

(2) The *pervasive residence* criterion. The resources of a resource space should be allowed to reside on various hardware and software platforms.

(3) The *operability* criterion. An RUM should support at least three basic resource operations: get a resource from a resource space, put a resource into a space, and remove a resource from a space. These operations must also be available for managing through any view of a resource space.

3.5   Designing Resource Spaces

The following is a reference design process for logical-level applications:

(1) *Resource analysis.* Resource analysis is to determine the application scope, to survey possible resources, and then to specify all the relevant resources by using a *Resource Dictionary* (RD), which records them as a local resource space for the application. These resources can be described in XML, and the RD can be managed using the ROL or any other XML query language.

(2) *Top-down resource partitioning.* Due to the differences in structure, different designers may partition resources differently, so a uniform approach to partitioning is needed. The first step is to unify the highest-level partition. Humans, information, and natural or artificial objects are key factors in human society, and the resources of human society may be clearly partitioned in this way. The top-level partitioning of a domain can be regarded as a special case of this partitioning of human society. For example, an institute's resources can be classified at the highest level within three exclusive categories: human resources, information resources, and service resources. This step and the preceding one are carried out on each category and its subcategories and so on until the resources in the lowest level category are few enough for the application being designed.

(3) *Design bidimensional resource spaces.* People can manage bidimensional spaces better than higher dimensional spaces. So, we can first design a set of bidimensional resource spaces, and then consider joining them to form higher dimensional spaces. This design process has the following steps.

- *Name the axes.* Each axis name should reflect one category of the top-level partition of resources.
- *Name the top-level coordinates.* Each coordinate should reflect one subcategory of the category of its axis.
- *Name the coordinate within each hierarchy.* For each top-level coordinate, name its lower level coordinates until all the coordinates at all levels have been named.

- *Remove any dependence between coordinates*. Look for dependence between coordinates at all levels. Where it occurs, redesign the partitioning at that level and then name any new coordinates.
- *Make all axes orthogonal*. If any pair of axes is not orthogonal, reselect axes.

(4) *Join spaces*. If two spaces can be joined into one space, carrying out join operation to form a single resource space.

Making use of abstraction, and analogy between the existing (or reference) resource spaces and the new resource space, are important techniques for designing a good resource space (H. Zhuge, "Resource Space Model, Its Design Method and Applications", *Journal of Systems and Software*, 72(1)(2004)71-81).

3.6 Representation of Resources

The semantics of a resource could be seen as a black box if the semantics come from those of related resources, or as a glass box if they come from the features and functions of the resource itself. Combining the two ways could be more effective than either alone.

A resource template represents the common features of a class of resources of the same type. Resources defined in a space need a set of templates, organized as a hierarchy, where the lower level templates are expansions of higher level ones. Some applications can use the following root template:

> *ResourceTemplate*{
> *Resource-name*: *<string>* (*domain name*);
> *Description*: **;
> *Related-materials*: [
>   *Relationships*: [*LinkTo*:*<SemanticLinkType₁, Resource₁>*,
>   ......,
>   *LinkTo*:*<SemanticLinkTypeₘ,*
>   *Resourceₘ>*];
> *References*: [*material-name₁*: *<address₁>*,

......,

material-name$_n$:<address$_n$>]
          Others] }.

where an "address" can be a URL or a resource citation. For example, a
book citation takes the form: <Name: *String*; Author: *String*; Publisher:
String; PublisherAddress: *String* or URL>. A paper citation takes the
form: (JournalName: *String*; Volume: *Number*; Issue: *Number*;
PaperTitle: *String*; AuthorName: *String*; Publisher: *String*;
PublisherAddress: *String* or URL).

"Related-materials" specifies relationships between resources and
the references of the related resources. The relationship is a kind of
semantic link that describes the relationship between resources.

"Others" can be the relationships such as "Peer-resources: <name-
list>" and "Meta-resources: <name-list>".

To satisfy the pervasive residence criterion, the XML
(www.w3.org/XML) or XML-based markup languages like RDF
(Resource Description Framework) can be adopted to encode the
worldwide resource space and local resource spaces. An example of
representing a worldwide and a local knowledge space in XML is given
in (H. Zhuge, Resource Space Grid: Model, Method and Platform,
Concurrency and Computation: Practice and Experience, 16(13)(2004)).

In addition, the semantic link can be extended to the super link or the
complex link to connect resources in the physical space, the socio space,
and even the mental space in the future (H.Zhuge, Semantic linking
through spaces for cyber-physical-socio intelligence: A methodology,
Artificial Intelligence, 175(2011)988-1019).

3.7   The Resource Using Mechanism (RUM)

An RSM has two types of users: the end-users who use resources directly
through an enabling interface or indirectly through an application system,
and the application developers who build complex application systems
for end-users with the support of the RUM.

The ROL defines a set of basic operations for creating resource
spaces and for sharing and managing resources. Some of these operations

allow the user to create a local space and to get resources for that space from the universal view of all the local resource spaces. Others allow the user to put a set of resources into a local space, to remove those resources if privileged to do so, to browse resources, to join a local space to the universal view or to separate it from that view, to open a local space to a specific set of users, and to join several spaces into one.

Thus the ROL includes operations called Create, Get, Place, Remove, Browse, Log, Open, Join, Separate, Merge and Split. These can be supplied with a list of resources and their locations, but at least one resource must be listed. Resources can be retrieved by specifying constraints in the condition portion of an ROL statement (discussed in detail in Chapter 4).

A resource browser has the ROL interpreter carrying out ROL statements, but also helps users to locate resources they need and display the content of those resources in a template form. A resource browser has the following main functions.

(1) Provide an easy-to-use interface for users to specify what they want to do.
(2) Provide either a local view or the universal view of all resources.
(3) Check the format and grammar of the ROL statements.
(4) Deliver operations to the ROL interpreter, and take results back.
(5) Show the results of those operations.

The browser allows a user to:

(1) choose an operation by clicking a button,
(2) choose the resources to be operated on by specifying their coordinates in a resource space, and
(3) put in or select parameters to refine the operation.

The RUM is responsible for carrying out the operations fed to it by the browser and feeding back the content of resources according to their type. Different types of resource may need specific RUM operations. An implementation of the RUM must

(1) ensure an appropriate granularity of operating object (for instance, rules should be used together because a single rule may not be

meaningful and the deletion of a single rule may cause incompleteness of the component it belongs to),

(2) feed the resources back in a meaningful way, because the end-user may not be able to understand their original representation like formalism, and

(3) obtain any needed support from types of resource other than that of the resource being operated on.

The RUM can provide the following functions for experienced users:

(1) Apply reasoning, and supply explanation, based on the hierarchical structure of the space, the given rules and the experience extracted from the answers to users' queries.

(2) Make generalization and specialization on resources, classes and expressions.

(3) Convert raw resources into finely classified resources.

(4) Eliminate inconsistency and redundancy.

3.8   Comparisons

Viewing things from attributes and viewing things from classification represent different worldview of recognizing things. There are close relationship between the two views. The attribute view more focuses on individual and surface, while the classification view more concerns set and nature.

Identity is the foundation of the attribute view. Humans must assign every entity or attribute an identity. This is only feasible in close system as it is hard to establish consensus on identity in open system.

Abstraction on classifications takes the first priority of the classification view. The basic element of classification view is set, even though it can contain just one entity. A class can be assigned an identity, but a class can also be specified by its subclasses and super-class.

RSM is based on classifications, so the things managed by the RSM can be any form. The classification nature enables RSM to be suitable for managing contents by classification-based operations. This feature enables the RSM to manage semantics-rich Web resources. The classification nature enables the RSM to use various existing classification approaches. The classification nature also supports RSM to realize some automation, e.g., automatically generate the structure of resource space according to a set of given resources, and automatically upload resources into resource space. The automatic generation of resource space and adaptive resource space are research topics of RSM 2.0. The classification nature also enables RSM to manage resources in different spaces in the future cyber-physical society.

RDBM is based on identities and attributes of entities, so it is more suitable for managing atomic data and attribute-based operations. It basically does support abstraction on attributes.

Detailed comparisons are given in The Web Resource Space Model (H.Zhuge, Springer, 2008).

There are two commonalities between the RSM described here and the RDBM (R. Bocy, et al., "Specifying Queries as Relational Expressions", *Communications of the ACM*, 18(11)(1975)621-628; E.F. Codd, "A Relational Model of Data for Large Shared Data Banks", *Communications of the ACM*, 13(6)(1970)377-387). The first is that the operations are separated from the objects to be managed. The second is the form of the operational languages: both SQL-like (ANSI, The Database Language SQL, Document ANSI X3.315, 1986; A.Eisenberg, and J.Melton, Sql:1999, Formerly Known as Sql3, *SIGMOD Record*, 28(1)(1999)131-138). This enables RDB users to easily understand the syntax and semantics of the ROL. The mapping between RSM and RDBM is introduced in (H. Zhuge, Y.Xing and P.Shi, Resource Space Model, OWL and Database: Mapping and Integration, *ACM Transactions on Internet Technology*, 8(4)(2008)article no.20).

The classification nature of RSM can also help users and the RSM systems (RSMS) to determine the classes of keywords in keyword-based search, e.g., in the example given in the beginning of this chapter.

Differences between OLTP and OLAP were compared in J. Han, and M. Kambr, *Data Mining: Concepts and Techniques* (Morgan Kaufmann Publishers, 2000). The multidimensional data model used for data warehousing and OLAP differs from the RSM in its foundation, its managed objects, its normalization, its operational features, and the basis for its exchange of data.

The object-oriented methodology (G. Booch, J. Rumbaugh, and I. Jacobson, *The Unified Modeling Language: User Guide*. Reading, Mass.: Addison-Wesley, 1999) provides a method and mechanism for uniform domain modeling and system implementation. It reduces the complexity of systems of objects by using notions such as class and object to abstract a variety of entities, by encapsulating operations into each class, and by an inheritance mechanism. It supports reuse during software development. It does not have normal forms like RDBMS and RSM.

Object-relational databases (ORDBs) combine object-oriented and relational data base technologies (M. Stonebraker, P. Brown, and D. Moore, *Object-Relational DBMs: Tracking the Next Great Wave*, second ed., San Francisco: Morgan Kaufmann Publishers, 1999). In an ORDB, a table need not be in the first normal form of the relational data base model, and tables can be nested. Various nested normal forms have been studied as extensions of traditional flat normal forms in RDBMs (W.Y. Mok, "A Comparative Study of Various Nested Normal Forms", *IEEE Trans. on Knowledge and Data Engineering*, 14(2)(2002); Z.M. Ozsoyoglu, and L.Y. Yuan, "A New Normal Form for Nested Relations", *ACM Trans. Database Systems*, 12(1)(1987)111-136; Z. Tari, J. Stokes, and S. Spaccapietra, "Object Normal Forms and Dependency Constraints for Object-Oriented Schemata", *ACM Trans. Database Systems*, 22(4)(1997)513-569), but these extensions are based on relational algebra and a relational data model. The RSM differs from the ORDB in its methodology, foundation, its managed objects, its data model, its normalization, and its operational features.

The resource browser helps users work on resources. Major differences between the resource browser and the typical current Web browser are as follows:

(1) the objects used by the resource browser are various resources, while the Web browser uses Web pages;
(2) the resource browser locates various resources by classification, while the Web browser locates Web pages by URL;

(3) the resource browser can locate resources and then operate on them by setting appropriate parameters, but the Web browser can only display Web pages according to URLs;

(4) the resource browser supports a uniform classification view on resources, while the Web browser only supports the viewing of a single Web page at a time; and

(5) the resource browser is supported by the RSM, while the current Web browser lacks the support of a coherent data model.

The design method for the RSM does not include a conceptual model, so a designer's experience and the reference model play key roles in designing a good resource space. The hierarchical resource organization approach is in line with top-down resource partitioning as described above, and with the "from general to specific" style of thought.

For application development, the ROL is not only an SQL-like language but also it uses XML syntax to support programming based on a semi-structured data model. The XML query language XQL is a concise language and is developed as an extension of the XSL pattern language. It builds upon the capability of identifying classes of nodes by applying Boolean logic, filters, and indexing to collections of nodes.

The ROL borrows its syntax and semantics from standard SQL. The statements of the ROL are SQL-like and have the SQL SELECT-FROM-WHERE pattern. The ROL can perform operations like those of the classical relational database, such as nested queries, aggregates, set operations, join and result ordering.

The ROL also borrows the following features from XML query languages:

(1) management of structured and semi-structured data;
(2) abstract data types;
(3) the XML-based data format and the result semantics;
(4) the skelom functions to associate a unique ID with a given resource space;
(5) document selection; and,
(6) partial path specification.

A detailed comparison is given in "Resource Space Grid: Model, Method and Platform" (H.Zhuge, *Concurrency and Computation*: *Practice and Experience*, 16(14)(2004) 1385-1413).

3.9   Dealing with Exponential Growth of Resources

Exponential growth of resources is an obstacle to effective management of resources. How to manage exponential expansion of resources becomes an important challenge. Some scientists like Jim Gray regarded the study of intensive data as a new science — the fourth paradigm for scientific exploration.

The RSM can solve the problem in theory by classifying resources and increasing the number of dimensions with the expansion of resources.

If expansion rate of resources is e^n, we could use a resource space with at least n-dimensions and each dimension having at least n coordinates to manage resource explosion since the following holds when $n \geq e$: $n^n \geq e^n$. Generally, if the expansion rate of resources is x^n, the following holds when $n \geq x$:

$$n^n \geq x^n.$$

If continuous expansion of resources accompanies appropriate classifications, this kind of expansion is controllable. For example, a 10-dimensional resource space with 10 coordinates at each dimension has 10^{10} points. If each point manages 100 resources in average, the resource space can contain 10^{12} resources. Increase one more dimension and one more coordinate at each dimension will enable the space to contain 11^{11} points. A 20-dimensional resource space with 20 coordinates at each dimension has 20^{20} points.

Furthermore, the increment of dimensions does not overload resource management. Any point can be accurately located by given its coordinates at each dimension.

Generally, resources are classified in different spaces. In each space, resources are classified by time, external feature, internal structure, and community. Further, resources are classified with the generation and evolution of dimensions.

Although people are facing unlimited expansion of resources, there are some limitations that can be used to deal with this expansion.

(1) Resources should have finite life spans, which could reduce expansion of resources to a certain extent.
(2) The expansion of dimensions is relatively slow compared with the rapid expansion of resources. That is, a new dimension may emerge when many resources are added.
(3) Users' interests, requirements and time of using resources are limited. That means users need the most interested resources and to get them rapidly.

Therefore, the following are ways to deal with the issue of rapid expansion of resources:

(1) Discovering self-organized communities of resources, and assigning constraints on the communities to regulate their evolution. This implies a dynamic data model. The problem is to find an appropriate schema for a community. Relational databases use data types to regulate data. Finding the schema for semantics-rich network is the basis for effectively managing the linked resources.
(2) Discovering the critical points to control the complex networks connecting resources.
(3) Linking appropriate resources to individuals according to their interests and requirements. This can be implemented by building a personal resource space that only includes resources matching the owner's interest and requirement. The personalized crawler searches those resources and uploads them into the personal resource space in time.
(4) Classifying resources according to resources' life span, reputation, and goodness to the society. The resources that are active, and have high reputation take the priority to be selected.
(5) Removing redundant resources.
(6) Recycling useless resources to meet the need of individuals if possible (e.g., editing text or video resources). Removing the useless and harmful resources is necessary in managing expanding

resources. An example of the necessity is that people often remove junk emails to keep email box clean.

According to the report in *Nature* (May 12, 2011), MIT and Northeastern University have developed a computational model that can analyze any type of complex network and find the critical points that can be used to control the entire system. An algorithm has been designed to determine how many nodes in a network need to be controlled for total network control. The number of points needed depends on the network's degree distribution, which describes the number of connections per node. The researchers found that sparse networks require more controlled points than denser networks.

Data clean is a way to ensure the usefulness of data (V.Raman and J.M.Hellerstein, Potter's wheel: An interactive data cleaning system, *VLDB2001*, Roma, Italy).

Different from the other notions of dimension like that in SVM (C. Cortes and V.Vapnik, Support-Vector Networks. *Machine Learning*, 20(3)(1995) 273-297), dimension in RSM is a classification tree that can be mapped into an ontology hierarchy. The structure of the dimension in RSM reflects generalization and specialization on resources.

Harmony between the expansion of resources and the development of the environment is important for the future interconnection environment (H. Zhuge and X. Shi. Toward the eco-grid: a harmoniously evolved interconnection environment. *Communications of the ACM*, 47(9)(2004)78-83). A unified resource model called soft-device has been proposed for modeling resources in the future interconnection environment (H.Zhuge, Clustering Soft-Devices in Semantic Grid, *Computing in Science and Engineering*, 4(6)(2002)60-62).

A schema mechanism of the Semantic Link Network was suggested (H. Zhuge and Y. Sun, The schema theory for semantic link network. *Future Generation Computer Systems*, 26(3)(2010)408-420). If the physical characteristics of complex network such as the diameter and centrality can be considered, the schema can better reflect the nature of network. Further, it will be much better if the schema can adapt itself according to the change of network. We can image that a large-scale complex network of resources can be operated like database if an appropriate schema can be found. The classification-based Resource Space Model is likely to help implement this idea and support faced navigation on the network.

3.10 Extension of the Resource Space Model

3.10.1 *Formalizing resource space*

Let O be a domain terminology set, with a mapping from O onto the domain ontology that explains the domain's semantics. The resource space can be formalized as follows.

Definition 3.10.1 Let $S = 2^O$ be the power set of O. The resource space defined on O is represented as $RS(X_1, X_2, ..., X_n)$, where RS is the name of the space and $X_i = \{C_{i1}, C_{i2}, ..., C_{ip}\}$ is an axis, $1 \leq i \leq n$, C_{ij} is the root of the hierarchical structure of coordinates on X_i, $C_{ij} = \{<V_{ij}, E_{ij}> \mid V_{ij}$ is the set of coordinates, E_{ij} is the set of relations from coordinate $v_t \in V_{ij}$ to $v_s \in V_{ij}$ such that $R(v_t) \supseteq R(v_s)\}$, $1 \leq j \leq p$, where $R(v)$ is a class of resources represented by v. Every point in RS is an element of the Cartesian product $X_1 \times X_2 \times ... \times X_n$, represented as $p(x_1, x_2, ..., x_n)$.

Tuples of relational data models reflect the attributes of entities. In the RSM, x_i in a point $p(x_1, x_2, ..., x_n)$ reflects partitioning resources from one axis. Resources represented by a point $p(x_1, x_2, ..., x_n) \in RS$ can be represented as $R(p(x_1, x_2, ..., x_n)) = R(x_1) \cap R(x_2) \cap ... \cap R(x_n)$, where $R(x_i)$ is a class of resources represented by x_i, $1 \leq i \leq n$.

3.10.2 *Resource space schemas and normal forms*

A resource space schema formally describes a resource space. The major task in the logical design of a space is to specify its schema, and to define the axes and coordinates.

Application domains require that resources in a space schema satisfy certain integrity constraints. The schema sho+uld satisfy all these constraints, so it is defined as follows:

Definition 3.10.2 A resource space schema is a 5-tuple: $RS <A, C, S, dom>$, where

(1) RS is the space name;
(2) $A = \{X_i \mid 1 \leq i \leq n\}$ is the set of axes;
(3) $C = \{C_{ij} \mid C_{ij} \in X_i, 1 \leq i \leq n\}$ is the set of coordinates;
(4) S is the power set of the domain ontology O; and,
(5) dom is the mapping from the axes A and coordinates C into S, dom: $A \times C \rightarrow S$, for any axis $X_i = \{C_{i1}, C_{i2}, ..., C_{ip}\}$, $dom(X_i, C_{ij}) \in S$, where $1 \leq i \leq n$ and $1 \leq j \leq p$.

In applications, (4) and (5) should be determined before the schema is designed, so that the schema can be simplified as a triple: $RS <A, C>$.

The schema is relatively stable, while resource spaces can be dynamic due to the resource operations on the space. The design of a resource space is to determine its schema.

An axis with hierarchical coordinates can be transformed into an axis with flat coordinates if only the leaf nodes of each hierarchy are considered. Here we discuss only the flat case, and assume that an RS is always in 2NF. The equivalent definitions of the normal forms can be given.

For the space $RS(X_1, X_2, ..., X_n)$, we use $R(X_i)$ to denote resources represented by axis X_i, where $X_i = \{C_{i1}, C_{i2}, ..., C_{ip}\}$, $1 \leq i \leq n$. $R(X_i) = R(C_{i1}) \cup R(C_{i2}) \cup ... \cup R(C_{ip})$. First, we define fine classification.

Lemma 3.10.1 For two axes $X_i = \{C_{i1}, C_{i2}, ..., C_{ip}\}$ and $X_j = \{C_{j1}, C_{j2}, ..., C_{jq}\}$ of the space RS, if $R(X_i) = R(C_{i1}) \cup R(C_{i2}) \cup ... \cup R(C_{ip})$ and $R(X_j) = R(C_{j1}) \cup R(C_{j2}) \cup ... \cup R(C_{jp})$, $X_j/X_i \Leftrightarrow R(X_j) \subseteq R(X_i)$ hold.

From this we can redefine the notion of orthogonality.

Lemma 3.10.2 For two axes $X_i = \{C_{i1}, C_{i2}, ..., C_{ip}\}$ and $X_j = \{C_{j1}, C_{j2}, ..., C_{jq}\}$ in the space RS, $X_j \perp X_i \Leftrightarrow R(X_j) = R(X_i)$.

Proof: The lemma is approved as follows:
(1) If $X_j \perp X_i$, then we have X_j/X_i and X_i/X_j from the definition of orthogonality. From lemma 3.10.1 we have $R(X_j) \subseteq R(X_i)$ and $R(X_i) \subseteq R(X_j)$. So, $R(X_j) = R(X_i)$.
(2) If $R(X_j) = R(X_i)$, then $R(X_j) \subseteq R(X_i)$ and $R(X_i) \subseteq R(X_j)$. From lemma 3.10.1, we have X_j/X_i and X_i/X_j. That means $X_j \perp X_i$. From (1) and (2), we have $X_j \perp X_i \Leftrightarrow R(X_j) = R(X_i)$. $\square$

The above lemma indicates that "two axes are orthogonal" is equivalent to that the expression ability of two axes is the same.

Clearly $X_i \perp X_j \Leftrightarrow X_j \perp X_i$, which means the orthogonal operation $\perp$ is symmetrical. From all this follows a new proof of the transitivity of *fine classification* and the *orthogonal* operation.

Theorem 3.10.1 The fine classification and orthogonal operations are transitive.

Proof: From Lemma 3.10.1 and Lemma 3.10.2, we can get $X_j/X_i \Leftrightarrow R(X_j) \subseteq R(X_i)$ and $X_j \perp X_i \Leftrightarrow R(X_j) = R(X_i)$. Because the set operations "$\subseteq$" and "$=$" are transitive, fine classification and the orthogonal operation is transitive. $\square$

From this follows the definition of the third normal form.

Theorem 3.10.2 For space $RS\,(X_1, X_2, ..., X_n)$, RS is in 3NF $\Leftrightarrow R(X_1) = R(X_2) = ... = R(X_n)$, that is, every axis X_i can retrieve all the resources in RS.

Proof: Proof includes the following two aspects:

(1) If RS is in 3NF, then $X_1 \perp X_2 \perp ... \perp X_n$. From Lemma 3.10.2, $R(X_1) = R(X_2) = ... = R(X_n)$.
(2) Similarly, if $R(X_1) = R(X_2) = ... = R(X_n)$, we get $X_1 \perp X_2 \perp ... \perp X_n$, and because $\perp$ is both transitive and symmetrical, then, for any two axes X_i and X_j in RS, $X_i \perp X_j$. That means RS is in 3NF.

From (1) and (2), it follows that RS is in 3NF $\Leftrightarrow R(X_1) = R(X_2) = ... = R(X_n)$. $\square$

Theorem 3.10.2 can be restated as a definition of the 3NF.

Beyond the three normal forms, other normal forms of the resource space schema can be defined for the convenience of partitioning and other operations.

Definition 3.10.3 (2$^+$NF) A space $RS\,(X_1, X_2, ..., X_n)$ is in 2$^+$NF, if it is in 2NF and $X_2/X_1, X_3/X_2, ..., X_n/X_{n-1}$.

The above definition means $R(X_1) \supseteq R(X_2) \supseteq \ldots \supseteq R(X_n)$ from Lemma 3.10.1. If RS is in 2^+NF, then, because fine classification / is transitive, we have: for every two axes X_i and X_j, $1 \le i \ne j \le n$, either X_i/X_j or X_j/X_i. So / is a full ordering on the set $\{X_1, X_2, \ldots, X_n\}$. On the other hand, it is obvious that if / constitutes a full ordering on the axes of RS, then RS is in 2^+NF. In the following, we discuss the properties of the 2^+NF under the operations on resource spaces.

Corollary 3.10.1 For two spaces RS_1 and RS_2, let $RS_1 \cdot RS_2 \Rightarrow RS$. Then, although both RS_1 and RS_2 are 2^+NF, RS needs not be in 2^+NF.

Proof: Suppose $RS_1 = \{X_1, X_2\}$ and $RS_2 = \{Y_1, Y_2\}$, where X_i and Y_i are axes and satisfy X_2/X_1, Y_2/Y_1 and $X_2 = Y_2$. Then, we can join RS_1 and RS_2. Let $RS_1 \cdot RS_2 \Rightarrow RS$, so that $RS = \{X_1, X_2, Y_1\}$.

(1)   If either $R(X_1) \subseteq R(Y_1)$ or $R(Y_1) \subseteq R(X_1)$, either $R(X_2) \subseteq R(X_1) \subseteq R(Y_1)$ or $R(X_2) \subseteq R(Y_1) \subseteq R(X_1)$. From Definition 3.10.3, RS is in 2^+NF.

(2)   Otherwise, if both $R(X_1) \subseteq R(Y_1)$ and $R(Y_1) \subseteq R(X_1)$ are false, then neither Y_1/X_1 nor X_1/Y_1. Since / is a full order on the axes of RS, if RS is in 2^+NF then RS is not in 2^+NF, a contradiction.

Therefore, from (1) and (2), RS is in 2^+NF. $\square$

Corollary 3.10.1 tells us that 2^+NF does not persist under the Join operation. But if we add some conditions, 2^+NF will persist.

Corollary 3.10.2 (Join) Let $RS_1 = \{X_1, X_2, \ldots, X_n\}$ and $RS_2 = \{Y_1, Y_2, \ldots, Y_m\}$ be two 2^+NF resource spaces, and $RS_1 \cdot RS_2 \Rightarrow RS$. If $Y_1 = X_n$ or $X_1 = Y_m$, then RS is in 2^+NF.

Proof: (1)   If $X_1 = Y_m$, then from $RS_1 \cdot RS_2 \Rightarrow RS$, we have $RS_2 = \{Y_1, Y_2, \ldots, Y_{m-1}, X_1, X_2, \ldots, X_n\}$. Since RS_1 and RS_2 are in 2^+NF, we have $X_n/X_{n-1}/\ldots/X_2/X_1$ and $Y_m/Y_{m-1}/\ldots/Y_2/Y_1$, then, from the transitivity of / we have: $X_n/X_{n-1}/\ldots/X_2/X_1 = Y_m/Y_{m-1}/\ldots/Y_2/Y_1$. From definition 3.10.3, RS is in 2^+NF. (2) Also, if $Y_1 = X_n$, RS is in 2^+NF for the same reason as (1). $\square$

Corollary 3.10.3 If $RS \Rightarrow RS_1 \cdot RS_2$, and RS is in 2^+NF, then RS_1 and RS_2 are also in 2^+NF.

Proof: Suppose $RS = \{X_1, X_2, ..., X_n\}$. Because RS is in 2^+NF, and $/$ is a full ordering on RS, and $RS \Rightarrow RS_1 \cdot RS_2$, then the axes of RS_1 are a subset of the axes RS, so $/$ is also a full ordering on the axes of RS_1, and RS_1 is in 2^+NF. For the same reason, RS_2 is also in 2^+NF. $\square$

Corollary 3.10.3 tells that 2^+NF persists under the operation Separate. From the definitions of Join and Separate, we can get $RS_1 \cdot RS_2 \Rightarrow RS$ if and only if $RS \Rightarrow RS_1 \cdot RS_2$. Then, from corollary 3.10.3, we have the following corollary.

Corollary 3.10.4 For resource spaces RS_1 and RS_2, let $RS_1 \cdot RS_2 \Rightarrow RS$. If either RS_1 or RS_2 is not in 2^+NF, then RS is not in 2^+NF.

From the above corollaries, we can get the following:

Corollary 3.10.5 If $RS \Rightarrow RS_1 \cdot RS_2$, and RS is not in 2^+NF, then either RS_1 or RS_2 or both could be in 2^+NF.

Corollary 3.10.6 For resource spaces RS_1 and RS_2, let $RS_1 \cup RS_2 \Rightarrow RS$. Then, if RS_1 and RS_2 are in 2^+NF, RS is in 2^+NF.

Proof: Suppose $RS_1 = \{X_1, X_2, ..., X_n\}$ satisfies $X_n/X_{n-1}/.../X_2/X_1$, and $RS_2 = \{Y_1, Y_2, ..., Y_n\}$ satisfies $Y_n/Y_{n-1}/.../Y_2/Y_1$. Since $RS_1 \cup RS_2 \Rightarrow RS$, RS_1 and RS_2 have $n-1$ common axes and one different axis. Suppose that $X_i = Y_i, 1 \le i \ne k \le n$, and $X_k \ne Y_k$. Then, $RS = \{X_1, ..., (X_k \cup Y_k), ..., X_n\}$. Because $X_{k+1}/X_k/X_{k-1}$ and $X_{k+1} = Y_{k+1}/Y_k/Y_{k-1} = X_{k-1}$, from Lemma 3.10.1, we have: $R(X_{k-1}) \supseteq R(X_k) \supseteq R(X_{k+1})$ and $R(X_{k-1}) \supseteq R(Y_k) \supseteq R(X_{k+1})$.
So, $R(X_{k-1}) \supseteq (R(X_k) \cup R(Y_k)) \supseteq R(X_{k+1})$, which means $R(X_{k-1}) \supseteq R(X_k \cup Y_k) \supseteq R(X_{k+1})$. From Lemma 3.10.1 $X_{k+1}/(X_k \cup Y_k)/X_{k-1}$, so, $X_n/ ... /X_{k+1}/(X_k \cup Y_k)/X_{k-1}/ ... /X_1$, hence RS is in 2^+NF. $\square$

This corollary tells us that 2^+NF persists under the Merge operation.

Corollary 3.10.7 Let $RS \Rightarrow RS_1 \cup RS_2$. Although RS is in 2^+NF, neither RS_1 nor RS_2 need be in 2^+NF.

Proof: Suppose $RS = \{X_1, X_2, X_3\}$, $X_3/X_2/X_1$ and $X_2 = X_2' \cup X_2''$. Then, $RS_1 = \{X_1, X_2', X_3\}$ and $RS_2 = \{X_1, X_2'', X_3\}$.

(1) If either $R(X_3) \subseteq R(X_2')$ or $R(X_2') \subseteq R(X_3)$, then, we have: either $R(X_3) \subseteq R(X_2') \subseteq R(X_1)$ or $R(X_2') \subseteq R(X_3) \subseteq R(X_1)$ respectively. From Definition 3.10.4, we have: RS_1 is in 2^+NF.

(2) Otherwise if neither $R(X_3) \subseteq R(X_2')$ nor $R(X_2') \subseteq R(X_3)$, then neither X_2'/X_3 nor X_3/X_2'. Since $/$ is a full ordering on the axes of RS_1, if RS_1 is 2^+NF then RS_1 is not in 2^+NF.

According to (1) and (2), RS_1 need not be in 2^+NF. For the same reason, RS_2 needs not be in 2^+NF. $\square$

Corollary 3.10.7 tells us that the 2^+NF does not persist under the Split operation. From Corollary 3.10.7 we have the next corollary.

Corollary 3.10.8 Let $RS \Rightarrow RS_1 \cup RS_2$, let RS be in 2^+NF, and let $RS = \{X_1, ..., X_{k-1}, X_k, X_{k+1}, ..., X_n\}$, $X_n/X_{n-1}/.../X_2/X_1$, $X_k = X_k' \cup X_k''$, $RS_1 = \{X_1, ..., X_{k-1}, X_k', X_{k+1}, ..., X_n\}$, and $RS_2 = \{X_1, ..., X_{k-1}, X_k'', X_{k+1}, ..., X_n\}$, if $X_{k+1}/X_k'/X_{k-1}$, then RS_1 is in 2^+NF, and if $X_{k+1}/X_k''/X_{k-1}$, then RS_2 is in 2^+NF.

From these three corollaries, we have the following:

Corollary 3.10.9 For two spaces RS_1 and RS_2, let $RS_1 \cup RS_2 \Rightarrow RS$. Although neither RS_1 nor RS_2 is in 2^+NF, RS could be.

Corollary 3.10.10 Let $RS \Rightarrow RS_1 \cup RS_2$. Although RS is not in 2^+NF, either RS_1 or RS_2 or both could be.

The 2^+NF is the weakened form of the 3NF. We can also define a strengthened form of the 3NF as follows:

Definition 3.10.4 A space RS $(X_1, X_2, ..., X_n)$ is 4NF if it is a 3NF, and for any point $p(x_1, x_2, ..., x_n) \in RS$, $R(p(x_1, x_2, ..., x_n)) = R(x_1) \cap R(x_2) \cap ... \cap R(x_n) \neq \Phi$.

Because a 4NF space is also in a space 3NF, it has the same properties as 3NF in a space under resource space operations.

3.10.3 *Topological properties of resource spaces*

If we define a distance between two points in an n dimensional space $RS(X_1, X_2, ..., X_n)$, then the distance can be used to define a topological space. We focus on the 2NF space, and first define a distance d on axis X_i, $1 \leq i \leq n$, then construct from d a distance D on the whole space RS.

For a given set G, if there exists a function $d: G \times G \rightarrow \Re^+$, where $\Re^+$ represents the set of non-negative real numbers, then d is called a distance on G if it satisfies the following three axioms:

Axiom 1. $d(g_1, g_2) = 0 \Leftrightarrow g_1 = g_2$.
Axiom 2. $d(g_1, g_2) = d(g_2, g_1)$.
Axiom 3. $d(g_1, g_2) \leq d(g_1, g_3) + d(g_3, g_2)$, for any g_1, g_2 and $g_3 \in G$.

For an axis $X = \{C_1, C_2, ..., C_n\}$, C_i is a coordinate hierarchy denoted as $<V_i, E_i>$, where V_i is a set of sub-coordinates, and E_i is the subclass relation between sub-coordinates. We define the function d on X as follows.

Definition 3.10.5 For points x_1 and x_2 on axis X,

$d(x_1, x_2) =$

$$
\begin{cases}
0, & \text{if } x_1 = x_2. \\
\infty, & \text{if } x_1 \in V_i, x_2 \in V_j \text{ and } i \neq j. \\
\min\{length(\Gamma) \mid \Gamma = (x_1, x_1', \cdots, x_m', x_2)\} & \text{if } x_1 \text{ and } x_2 \in V_i, \text{ and } x_1 \neq x_2.
\end{cases}
$$

where $<x_1, x_1'>, <x_j', x_{j+1}'>, <x_m', x_2> \in E_i, 1 \leq j \leq m-1$, $length(\Gamma)$ is the length of the path Γ with a weight on each link. And, we make a reasonable assumption: if x_1 and $x_2 \in V_i$ and $x_1 \neq x_2$, there is a path $\Gamma = (x_1, x_1', ..., x_k', x_2)$ from x_1 to x_2. So $d(x_1, x_2) < length(\Gamma) < \infty$.

Theorem 3.10.3 d is a distance on axis X.

In the following, we first give the definition of function D on RS, and then prove that it is a distance on RS.

Definition 3.10.6 For any two points $p_1(x_1, x_2, ..., x_n)$ and $p_2(y_1, y_2, ..., y_n)$ in the space $RS(X_1, X_2, ..., X_n)$, we define

$$D(p_1, p_2) = (\sum_{i=1}^{n} d^2(x_i, y_i))^{\frac{1}{2}},$$

where d is the distance on axis X_i, $1 \leq i \leq n$.

Theorem 3.10.4 D is a distance on RS.

So the space $RS(X_1, X_2, ..., X_n)$ is a metric space (RS, D) with distance D. The distance D in RS defines a discrete topological space (RS, ρ). The following discusses the properties of the topological space (RS, ρ).

According to the definition of distance d, we have $d(x_1, x_2) < \infty \Leftrightarrow x_1$ and x_2 belong to the same coordinate hierarchy.

Definition 3.10.7 For two points $p_1(x_1, x_2, ..., x_n)$ and $p_2(y_1, y_2, ..., y_n)$ in the resource space RS, p_1 is said to be linked to p_2 if $D(p_1, p_2) < \infty$. For a set of points P in RS, P is called a linked branch if for any two points p_i and p_j in P $(i \neq j)$, p_i is linked to p_j.

From Definition 3.10.7 comes the following corollary.

Corollary 3.10.11 In a space $RS(X_1, X_2, ..., X_n)$, if a set of points P constitutes a linked branch, then for any two points $p_1(x_1, x_2, ..., x_n)$ and $p_2(y_1, y_2, ..., y_n)$ in P, x_i and y_i $(1 \leq i \leq n)$ belong to the same coordinate hierarchy.

Proof: If P is a linked branch, then for any two points $p_1(x_1, x_2, ..., x_n)$ and $p_2(y_1, y_2, ..., y_n)$ in P, $D(p_1, p_2) < \infty$. Since

$$D(p_1, p_2) = (\sum_{i=1}^{n} d^2(x_i, y_i))^{\frac{1}{2}},$$

we can get $d(x_i, y_i) < \infty$, $1 \leq i \leq n$. Hence, x_i and y_i belong to the same coordinate hierarchy. $\square$

Corollary 3.10.11 tells us the following rules:

If two points in a space are linked to each other, then their corresponding coordinates belong to the same coordinate hierarchy.

It is obvious that the connective relation (denoted by ~) is an equivalent relation on the topological space RS. So, $RS/\sim$ is a quotient space of *RS*. The next corollary describes the structure of the quotient space *RS/~*.

Corollary 3.10.12. The quotient space $RS/\sim$ =
$\{\ p^{'}(C_{i1}^1, C_{i2}^2, \cdots, C_{in}^n)\ |\ C_{ik}^k$ is a root coordinate on axis X_k in $RS(X_1, X_2, ..., X_n)$, $1 \leq k \leq n\}$, where $p'(x_1, x_2, ..., x_n)$ in $RS/\sim$ is the linked branch including point $p(x_1, x_2, ..., x_n)$ in *RS*.

Proof: Proof consists of the following two aspects:

(1) It is clear that any point $p^{'}(C_{i1}^1, C_{i2}^2, \cdots, C_{in}^n)$ is in $RS/\sim$. So $RS/\sim \supseteq \{\ p^{'}(C_{i1}^1, C_{i2}^2, \cdots, C_{in}^n)\ |\ C_{ik}^k$ is a root coordinate on axis X_k in $RS\}$.

(2) For any point $p(x_1, x_2, ..., x_n)$ in $RS(X_1, X_2, ..., X_n)$, from Corollary 3.8.11, we get that there exists a root coordinate C_{i1}^1 on axis X_1, ..., and C_{in}^n on axis X_n, such that x_1 is in C_{i1}^1, ..., and x_n is in C_{in}^n. So $p(x_1, x_2, ..., x_n)$ is in the linked branch of $p^{'}(C_{i1}^1, C_{i2}^2, \cdots, C_{in}^n)$, which means $p^{'}(x_1, x_2, \cdots, x_n) = p^{'}(C_{i1}^1, C_{i2}^2, \cdots, C_{in}^n)$. Then, we have $RS/\sim \subseteq$ $\{\ p^{'}(C_{i1}^1, C_{i2}^2, \cdots, C_{in}^n)\ |\ C_{ik}^k$ is a root coordinate on axis X_k in $RS\}$.

From (1) and (2), $RS/\sim = \{\ p^{'}(C_{i1}^1, C_{i2}^2, \cdots, C_{in}^n)\ |\ C_{ik}^k$ is a root coordinate on axis X_k in $RS(X_1, X_2, ..., X_n)$, $1 \leq k \leq n\}$. $\square$

In the quotient space $RS/\sim$, we can define a distance D_- on $RS/\sim$ as induced from the distance D on *RS*. $D_-(p_1', p_2') = min\ \{D(p_1, p_2) | p_1 \in p_1'$ and $p_2 \in p_2'\}$, where p_1' and p_2' represent the linked branches including p_1 and p_2 respectively. Then, for any $p_1', p_2' \in RS/\sim$, $p_1' \neq p_2'$, $D_-(p_1', p_2') = \infty$, $D_-(p_1', p_1') = 0$, which means that $RS/\sim$ is a discrete topological space with the distance D_- on it.

The resource space *RS* enables us to locate resources by coordinates. The quotient space *RS/~* enables us to search in a more abstract space.

Theorem 3.10.5 A point exists in *RS* if and only if it belongs to a point of *RS/~*.

Proof: Proof consists of the following two aspects:

(1) For a $p(x_1, x_2, ..., x_n)$ in RS, from Corollary 3.10.12, there exists $p'(C_{i1}^1, C_{i2}^2, \cdots, C_{in}^n)$ in $RS/\sim$ such that $p(x_1, x_2, ..., x_n)$ is in the linked branch of $p'(C_{i1}^1, C_{i2}^2, \cdots, C_{in}^n)$. So $p(x_1, x_2, ..., x_n)$ belongs to a point of $RS/\sim$.

(2) Suppose $p(x_1, x_2, ..., x_n)$ belongs to a point $p'(x_1, x_2, ..., x_n)$ in $RS/\sim$. From Corollary 3.10.12, all the points in the linked branch $p'(x_1, x_2, ..., x_n)$ are in RS, so $p(x_1, x_2, ..., x_n)$ exists in RS.

From (1) and (2), we can infer that a point is in RS if and only if it also belongs to a point in $RS/\sim$. □

This theorem provides a top-down refinement search strategy for a large-scale space:

From the quotient space down to the resource space.

The strategy also ensures that all resources in space RS can be found through $RS/\sim$.

3.11   Integrity Constraints for the Resource Space Model

The integrity constraints for the RSM are of four kinds: *entity*, *membership*, *referential* and *user-defined*. These work together so that the RSM can correctly and efficiently specify and manage resources.

3.11.1 *Entity integrity constraints*

In relational databases, keys play a fundamental role in the data model and in conceptual design. They enable tuples to refer to one another and ensure that operations can accurately locate tuples.

As a coordinate system, naturally the RSM supports precise resource location. However, it is not always necessary to have the user painstakingly specify all the coordinates of a point, especially when an axis is added. The RSM needs better resource location.

Definition 3.11.1. Let $p \cdot X_i$ be the coordinate of p at axis X_i in $RS(X_1, X_2, ..., X_n)$, that is, the projection of p on X_i. If $p_1 \cdot X_i = p_2 \cdot X_i$ for $1 \le i \le n$, then we say that p_1 is equal to p_2, denoted by $p_1 =_p p_2$.

Using this definition, a *candidate key* of the RSM can be defined as follows.

Definition 3.11.2. Let CK be a subset of $(X_1, X_2, ..., X_n)$, and let p_1 and p_2 be non-null points in $RS(X_1, X_2, ..., X_n)$. CK is called a candidate key of RS if we can derive $p_1 =_p p_2$ from $p_1 \cdot X_i = p_2 \cdot X_i$, where $X_i \in CK$.

A candidate key is specific enough to identify non-null points of a given space.

The *primary key* is a candidate key specified by the designer of the space. The axes of the primary key are called *primary axes*.

Point constraint. If axis X is a primary axis of the space RS, then no X coordinate of any point in RS should be null.

This constraint is used to ensure that primary keys can distinguish non-null points in a given space. One type of null value is "at present unknown".

In the RSM one can infer some keys from the presence of others. This is of great importance in query optimization, especially when creating new spaces. Inference rules for candidate keys come from the following four theorems.

Theorem 3.11.1. If a set of axes CK is a candidate key of the space RS, then any axis set that includes CK is also a candidate key of RS.

From the definition of Join we have the following theorem.

Theorem 3.11.2. Let RS_1 and RS_2 be two spaces which can be joined to produce a new space RS. If CK_1 and CK_2 are candidate keys of RS_1 and RS_2 respectively, then $CK = CK_1 \cup CK_2$ is a candidate key of RS.

From the definition of Merge we have the following theorem.

Theorem 3.11.3. Let RS_1 and RS_2 be two spaces that can be merged into one space RS. Let X_1 and X_2 be two different axes of RS_1 and RS_2 respectively, and let $X_c = X_1 \cup X_2$. If CK_1 and CK_2 are candidate keys of RS_1 and RS_2 respectively, then $CK = (CK_1 - \{X_1\}) \cup (CK_2 - \{X_2\}) \cup \{X_c\}$ is a candidate key of RS.

From the definition of Split we have the following theorem.

Theorem 3.11.4. Let RS_1 and RS_2 be two spaces created by splitting the space RS. Suppose that the axis X_c of RS is split into X_1 and X_2 belonging to RS_1 and RS_2 respectively. Let CK be a candidate key of RS. If $X_c \notin CK$, let $CK_1 = CK_2 = CK$, otherwise let $CK_1 = CK - \{X_c\} \cup \{X_1\}$ and $CK_2 = CK - \{X_c\} \cup \{X_2\}$. Then CK_1 and CK_2 are candidate keys of RS_1 and RS_2 respectively.

Proof. Let A be the set of all axes of RS and A_1 be the set of all axes of RS_1. Assuming that CK_1 is not a candidate key of RS_1, there must be two non-null points p_1 and p_2 in RS_1 which satisfy both $(\forall X \in CK_1)$ $(p_1 \cdot X = p_2 \cdot X)$ and $(\exists X^* \in A_1)$ $(p_1 \cdot X^* \neq p_2 \cdot X^*)$. Let p_1' and p_2' in RS have the same coordinate values as p_1 and p_2 respectively. Clearly, $(\forall X \in CK)$ $(p_1' \cdot X = p_2' \cdot X)$ if $CK_1 = CK$ or $CK_1 = CK - \{X_c\} \cup \{X_1\}$.

(1) When $CK_1 = CK$, if $X^* \neq X_1$, then $p_1' \cdot X^* \neq p_2' \cdot X^*$, otherwise $p_1' \cdot X_c \neq p_2' \cdot X_c$;
(2) When $CK_1 = CK - \{X_c\} \cup \{X_1\}$, then $X^* \neq X_1$. So $p_1' \cdot X^* \neq p_2' \cdot X^*$.

From (1) and (2), $p_1' \neq_p p_2'$. Clearly, this conclusion contradicts the assumption that CK is a candidate key of RS. So, CK_1 is a candidate key of RS_1. Similarly, we can prove that CK_2 is a candidate key of RS_2.

In resource space systems, there are often spaces created by join, merge and split operations. Theorems 3.10.2, 3.10.3 and 3.10.4 provide an efficient means of deriving candidate keys of these spaces.

In the RSM, a resource entry denoted by a 3-tuple *Resource_Entry* <*ID, Index, Description*> is used to index into a resource representation layer. The *ID* field is used to specify the entries at a given point. Two entries at different points could have the same *ID*. The *Index* field is the index data linked to the representation layer. Description of resources concerns internal semantics and external semantics. To facilitate operations on resources, the *Description* can simply use a set of attributes to reflect a resource, while leave the detailed descriptions to the representation layer. In the following discussion, $re \cdot ID$, $re \cdot index$ and $re \cdot SD$ denote the *ID, index* and *Description* of entry re respectively.

Resource entry constraint 1. No ID should be null, and for any two entries re_1 and re_2 at the same non-null point, $re_1 \cdot ID \neq re_2 \cdot ID$.

This constraint requires that all entries in a given non-null point should have distinct *ID*s. This ensures that any operation can precisely locate its target entry.

Resource entry constraint 2. No index of an entry should be null, and for any two entries re_1 and re_2 at the same non-null point, $re_1 \cdot index \neq re_2 \cdot index$.

This constraint requires that:

(1) every entry should include index data linking to the representation layer, and
(2) no two entries at the same non-null point should have the same index data.

Otherwise, it will lead to information redundancy and unnecessary maintenance of consistency between resource entries at the same point.

The syntactic structure of the index data of entries depends on the implementation of the representation layer. For instance, an XML-based implementation of a representation layer commonly uses XPath expressions, whereas filenames are often used for file-based implementations.

To analyze the index of a resource entry, not only the syntactic structure but also the semantics should be considered. For example, an absolute path differs from a relative path syntactically. However, these two types of paths may indicate the same data.

Resource entry constraint 3. The semantic description *SD* of any entry should not be null, and no two entries re_1 and re_2 at the same non-null point should be the same or imply each other, that is, neither $re_1 \cdot SD \Rightarrow re_2 \cdot SD$ nor $re_2 \cdot SD \Rightarrow re_1 \cdot SD$.

This is the entity integrity constraint for the *Description* of an entry. It is optional but stricter than constraint 2. Since a $re \cdot SD$ embodies the semantic existence of an entry in a resource space, clearly $re \cdot SD$ should not be null. Furthermore, entries at a given non-null point should neither be the same nor imply each other. For example, a resource and its copies are allowed to coexist at a non-null point by constraint 2, but not by constraint 3.

3.11.2 *The membership integrity constraint*

In relational databases, a tuple can be inserted into a table only if all fields of the tuple satisfy the domain constraints of the table. So the relationship between the tuple and the table should be checked before insertion.

In the RSM, a resource space holds the classification of its resources. The existence of entry *re* at point *p* means that the resource indexed by *re* belongs to the type represented by *p*. An entry can be placed at a point by the following operation:

PLACE *re* <*ID, Index, Description*> **AT** $p\,(C_{1,i1}, C_{2,i2}, ..., C_{n,in})$.

If there were no restrictions, an entry could be placed at any point of the space. So, checking the memberships of resource entries plays an important role in the RSM.

$R_\Delta\,(RS)$, $R_\Delta\,(C)$ and $R_\Delta\,(p)$ denote the sets of resources currently stored by space *RS*, coordinate *C* and point *p* respectively. For any entry *re*, if *re* has been placed at the point *p*, then $re \in R_\Delta\,(p)$.

Membership constraint. Let *re* <*ID, Index, Description*> be a resource entry. For any point $p\,(C_{1,i1}, C_{2,i2}, ..., C_{n,in})$ in a given space, putting *re* into the space should be constrained by the definition of the point $R\,(p)$, that is, $re \in R_\Delta\,(p) \rightarrow re \in R\,(p)$.

An entry *re* can be placed at point *p* only if *re* belongs to the type that *p* represents. Constraining membership in this way can ensure correct resource classification. When a place or update operation is applied to an entry, this constraint should be checked.

3.11.3 *Referential integrity constraints*

In relational databases, it is often required that a value that appears in one relation for one set of attributes should also appear for another set of attributes in another relation. This condition is called a referential integrity constraint.

In the following discussion, three types of referential integrity constraints for the RSM are considered.

In the RSM, the basic function of an entry is to index a resource in the representation layer. For any entry *re* <*ID, index, Description*>, *re · index* is the index of the resource. Resource entry constraint 2 ensures that *re · index* is non-null. But it cannot ensure that *re · index* makes sense. This is mainly because modifications to entries or representation layers may cause the indices of entries to become dead links. The first referential integrity constraint is intended to eliminate dead links

Referential constraint 1. For every entry *re* in a resource space system, there exists a resource in the representation layer which is referred to by its index (*re · index*).

The resource space layer refers to the representation layer. The above constraint ensures that *re · index* makes sense for any entry *re*. This constraint should be checked when a *re* is placed or a *re · index* updated.

When changes take place in a representation layer, this integrity should also be satisfied. The layer can be viewed as a Semantic Link Network (SLN). An SLN consists of semantic nodes and semantic links. A semantic node can be an atomic node (a piece of text or image) or complex node (another SLN). For most applications, the domain is a subset of the whole resource representation layer. This subset SLN is denoted by SLN*.

In the resource representation layer, any resource denoted by a 3-tuple *Resource* (*ID, Description, Resource-Entry-List*) can be regarded as a semantic node. The *ID* is the identifier of a resource in a given SLN*. It is helpful for locating the target resource. The *Description* is the detailed description of a resource, used to facilitate operations. The *Description* of a resource can be represented by an SLN. There may exist many indices (resource entries) in the resource space layer to a resource in the representation layer. The *Resource-Entry-List* of a resource is used to record all entries indexing this resource.

For any entry, an item of the *Resource-Entry-List* should include the name of its space, the coordinate of its point, and its *ID*. So, from the *Resource-Entry-List*, all corresponding entries can be obtained. In the following $res \cdot ID$, $res \cdot SD$ and $res \cdot REL$ denote the *ID*, *Description* and *Resource-Entry-List* of resource *res* respectively.

There exists a variety of relations between resources. The following discussion is about the relations of similarity and inclusion. Two functions, *Similarity* and *Inclusion*, are introduced to evaluate the similarity and inclusion between resources. *Similarity* (res_1, res_2) returns a real number between 0 and 1 giving the similarity between resources res_1 and res_2. *Inclusion* (res_1, res_2) returns a real number between 0 and 1 giving the degree of inclusion of resource res_2 in resource res_1.

For a given threshold value δ, if *Similarity* $(res_1, res_2) \geq \delta$, then resources res_1 and res_2 are regarded as equal. And, if *Inclusion* $(res_1, res_2) \geq \delta$, then res_2 is viewed as a subset of res_1. Both equality and inclusion between resources lead to semantic redundancy and unnecessary maintenance of consistency between resources in a given SLN*. To eliminate this redundancy, the following constraint is introduced.

Resource redundancy constraint. Let res_1 and res_2 be two resources in the SLN*. For a given threshold value δ, both *Similarity* $(res_1, res_2) < \delta$ and *Inclusion* $(res_1, res_2) < \delta$.

Before placing a resource in the SLN* or after updating a resource, this constraint should be checked. In the case of placement, if the above constraint has been violated, the operation will be canceled. But suppose resource res_1 is to be updated to res_1'. If there already exists a resource res_2 such that either *Similarity* $(res_1', res_2) \geq \delta$ or *Inclusion* $(res_1', res_2) \geq \delta$, the alternative actions are:

(1) the update operation is canceled, or
(2) after the update of res_1, resource res_2 is deleted.

If the second action is taken, the alternative actions are:

(1) all resource entries indicated by $res_2 \cdot REL$ are deleted, or
(2) all resource entries indicated by $res_2 \cdot REL$ are redirected to res_1'.

Thus, dead links in the space layer will be avoided after the changes take place in the representation layer.

The first referential integrity constraint specifically between resource spaces relates to the join operation.

Referential constraint 2. If RS_1, RS_2 and RS are three spaces that satisfy $RS_1 \cdot RS_2 \Rightarrow RS$, then $R_\Delta (RS) \subseteq R_\Delta (RS_1) \cup R_\Delta (RS_2)$.

RS is derived from RS_1 and RS_2, and this referential constraint maintains the dependency of RS on RS_1 and RS_2. Thus, when an entry is placed in RS or removed from RS_1 or RS_2, this constraint should be checked.

The second type of referential integrity constraint applies to 3NF spaces. We first define the *foreign* key of the RSM.

Definition 3.11.3. Let S be a subset of axes of the space RS_1, but not the primary key of RS_1. If there exists another space RS_2 such that $R(RS_1) = R(RS_2)$ and S is the primary key of RS_2, then S is called the foreign key of RS_1, RS_1 is called the referencing space of RS_2 and RS_2 is called the referenced space of RS_1.

From this definition, we have the following theorem.

Theorem 3.11.5. Let $S = \{X_1, X_2, ..., X_m\}$ be the foreign key of the referencing space $RS_1 (X_1, X_2, ..., X_m, X_{m+1}, ..., X_n)$, and $RS_2 (X_1, X_2, ..., X_m, Y_{m+1}, ..., Y_t)$ be the corresponding referenced space. For two non-null points $p(C_1, C_2, ..., C_m, C_{m+1}, ..., C_n)$ and $p'(C_1, C_2, ..., C_m, C'_{m+1}, ..., C'_t)$ in RS_1 and RS_2 respectively, $R(p) \subseteq R(p')$.

This theorem indicates the inclusion relationship between points in the referencing space and their counterparts in the referenced space. The next constraint aims to maintain the legal referential relationship between the referencing space and its referenced space.

Referential constraint 3. Let $S = \{X_1, X_2, ..., X_m\}$ be the foreign key of the referencing space $RS_1 (X_1, X_2, ..., X_m, X_{m+1}, ..., X_n)$, and $RS_2 (X_1, X_2, ..., X_m, Y_{m+1}, ..., Y_t)$ be the corresponding referenced space. For two non-null points $p (C_1, C_2, ..., C_m, C_{m+1}, ..., C_n)$ and $p' (C_1, C_2, ..., C_m, C'_{m+1}, ..., C'_t)$ in RS_1 and RS_2 respectively, $R_\Delta(p) \subseteq R_\Delta(p')$.

This constraint ensures that if an entry *re* appears at a certain point *p* in the referencing space, then *re* must exist as the counterpart of *p* in the referenced space.

3.11.4 *User-defined integrity constraints*

Any resource space system should conform to the entity, membership and referential integrity constraints. In specific applications, different space systems should obey certain context-relevant constraints. These constraints are called user-defined integrity constraints. The following introduces three frequently used types of user-defined constraints. Two spaces shown in Fig. 3.11.4 are used to illustrate these constraints.

In Fig. 3.11.4 (a), the resource space *Salary-Post* is used to hold data about employees. Every point classifies these employees by their salary and post. In Fig. 3.11.4 (b), *Keeper-Warehouse* is used to hold data about goods. Each point of *Keeper-Warehouse* classifies these goods by their keeper and warehouse.

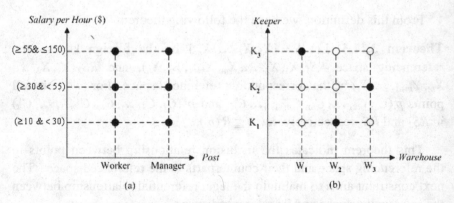

Fig. 3.11.4 Examples of bidimensional resource spaces.

User-defined constraints require the attribute values in the resource description to satisfy some rules. The function *GetAttribute* (*re*, *attr*) returns the value of attribute *attr* specified in the *Description* of the entry *re*. The Boolean function *JudgeRelation* (*operand*$_1$, *operand*$_2$, *relational-operator*) judges whether *operand*$_1$ and *operand*$_2$ satisfy the relation specified by *relational-operator*. This constraint can be described as follows:

> <Constraint expression> ::=
>   *JudgeRelation*(*GetAttribute*(*re, attr*), user-defined-constant-value,
>   <Relational-Op>) |
>   <Constraint expression> ∨ <Constraint expression> |
>   <Constraint expression> ∧ <Constraint expression> |
>   ¬<Constraint expression>;
> <Relational-Op> ::= < | > | = | ≤ | ≥ |≠.

Take Fig.3.11.4(a) for example. If the resource space designer requires of *Salary-Post* that the salary per hour of any worker should not be lower than \$12 and that the salary per hour of any manager should not be lower than \$50, then this user-defined constraint for entry *re* is:

(*JudgeRelation* (*GetAttribute* (*re, post*), "worker", =)
  ∧ *JudgeRelation* (*GetAttribute* (*re, salary per hour*), 12, ≥)) ∨ (
  JudgeRelation (*GetAttribute* (*re, post*), "manager", =)
  ∧*JudgeRelation* (*GetAttribute* (*re, salary per hour*), 50, ≥)).

Before the entry *re* can be placed in *Salary-Post* or updated, the system should check whether the above constraint has been violated.

In some applications, rich semantic relations among entries should be taken into consideration. Operations on an entry may require other operations on semantically relevant entries. This type of user-defined constraint is called a resource-entry-based constraint. For example, suppose *RS* is a space holding all the registration data about students of a school and *RS'* is another holding all the health data of the same students. Let *re* be the entry holding a particular student's registration data and *re'* be the entry holding his/her health data. The health data depend on the validity of the registration data, that is, $re' \in R_\Delta (RS') \rightarrow re \in R_\Delta (RS)$. So this constraint should be checked before *re'* is placed or after *re* is deleted.

As resource sets, points are often required to satisfy some application relevant rules from the viewpoint of set theory. Take Fig. 3.11.4 (b) for example. Suppose that a warehouse could have only one keeper in *Keeper-Warehouse* and that each keeper is in charge of only one warehouse.

For any K_i, there exists at most one W_j such that $R_\Delta(p(K_i, W_j)) \neq \varnothing$, and for any W_m there exists at most one K_n such that $R_\Delta(p(K_n, W_m)) \neq \varnothing$. We define the following function:

$$NotNull(p) = \begin{cases} 1, & R_\Delta(p) \neq \varnothing \\ 0, & R_\Delta(p) = \varnothing \end{cases}$$

And, use p_{ij} to denote the point $p(K_i, W_j)$. Then, the formal description of this constraint is as follows:

$$\forall i (\sum_{j=1}^{3} NotNull(p_{ij}) \leq 1) \land \forall j (\sum_{i=1}^{3} NotNull(p_{ij}) \leq 1).$$

Thus, before any goods can be placed in *Keeper-Warehouse*, the system must check whether the above constraint is violated or not.

The effectiveness of resource use also depends on the users' classifications in their mental spaces and the semantic relationships between resources. A way is to establish the "Fuzzy Resource Space Model and Platform". Further discussion can be found in (H. Zhuge, *Journal of Systems and Software*, 73(3) (2004)389-396).

3.12 Storage for Resource Space and Adaptability

An efficient storage mechanism is critical for resource space systems. To store resource space is to find an appropriate way to index multidimensional and hierarchical structure so as to support various queries. There are multiple ways to implement the storage of a resource space. The following are several feasible ways.

Making use of the storage mechanism of relational database to store resource space. This just needs to transform resource space into relational tables. The underlying resource management mechanism is implemented by the database system. In this case, a resource space is just like a multi-dimensional classification view. However, a good resource space may not correspond to a good relational database due to their different normal form definitions. The mapping between the Resource Space Model and the relational database has been introduced in "Resource Space Model, OWL and Database: Mapping and Integration" (H.Zhuge, et al., *ACM Transactions on Internet Technology*, 8(4)(2008) article no.20).

Making use of XML and its operation mechanisms. The hierarchical structure supports the representation of resource space, while the efficiency of resource space operation will depend on the efficiency of XML operation mechanisms.

Making use of peer-to-peer mechanism *to store resource space.* This is suitable for decentralized applications. Several proposals have been proposed, e.g., in RSM-Based Gossip on P2P Network (H.Zhuge, *The 7th International Conference on Algorithms and Architectures for Parallel Computing*, IC^{3}PP07, Hangzhou, China, 2007). The structured and unstructured P2P resource space systems have been introduced in The Web Resource Space Model (H.Zhuge, Springer, 2008).

Developing new indexing mechanisms to support the characteristics of the resource space. Solutions such as CTree and C*Tree have been proposed (H.Zhuge, The Web Resource Space Model, Springer, 2008; Q.Zeng and H.Zhuge, C*-tree: A Multi-Dimensional Index Structure for Resource Space Model, SKG2010). The spatial indexes like R-tree (A.Guttman, R-trees: a dynamic index structure for spatial searching, SIGMOD'84, pp.47-57) are more suitable for indexing flat and continuous dimensions. Generally, a resource space with hierarchical coordinate structure can be transformed into a hierarchical structure of spaces where the spaces at each level only have flat axes, and each low-level space corresponds to a point in a high-level resource space. This structure keeps the semantics of the original resource space but may lead to high space complexity.

An ideal RSM storage mechanism should be adaptive to the following operations on the resource space: Add, delete, or modify an axis or coordinate. That is, the change of index should be minimal when changing the structure of the space.

Multi-dimensional indexes such as RTree and R*Tree are not suitable for storing resource space directly (N. Beckmann, et. al. The R* tree: an efficient and robust index method for points and rectangles. *SIGMOD*, 1990, pp322-331), because there may not be meaningful order on the coordinates at the same axis, therefore the Most Minimum Rectangle is meaningless.

The following issues should be considered to effectively store a resource space.

(1) How to store an axis, its coordinates, and the hierarchical relations? Given a coordinate (concept), all direct sub-coordinates, its direct super-coordinates, and all ancestor coordinates should be rapidly retrieved.
(2) How to quickly return all resources indicated by a given coordinate? How to support fast intersection of queries on multiple axes?
(3) How to efficiently support dynamic updating of coordinates in a resource space?
(4) How to index continuous and discrete axes and to support effective resource retrieval?
(5) How to enable the indexing mechanism to support efficient range query?

A way to implement the indexing mechanism is to integrate the following three approaches.

(1) Using RTree to index continuous axes.
(2) Encoding the axis with discrete coordinates by the hierarchical encoding mechanisms. ORDPATH is a hierarchical encoding mechanism based on prefix for labelling XML nodes (P.O'Neil, et. al., ORDPATHs: Insert-Friendly XML Node Labels, *SIGMOD*, 2004, pp.903-908). It is derived from the Dewey Order Encoding, a global

hierarchical encoding method (C.D. Batty, An introduction to the Dewey decimal classification. Melbourne, Cheshire, 1966).

(3) Using inverted table to index resources indicated by each coordinate.

Much work has been done on indexing and querying on XML data. The approach to integrating structure indexes and inverted lists was introduced (R.Kaushik, et al., SIGMOD'04, France).

An important issue is the normal form checking of a changing resource space. A resource space may need changing with the change of resources and human cognition. Changing a resource space has the following influence.

(1) Removing an axis can be regarded as the result of the disjoin operation. The normal forms of the new space can be verified by Lemma 3.3.3. This operation actually generalizes the classification of the space. As the consequence, resources will no longer be classified by the removed axis, and the granularity of classification is enlarged.

(2) Adding an axis may break 3NF since the new axis may not be orthogonal to existing axes. Adding an axis X to a space S can be regarded as the join of S and a bi-dimensional space consisting of X and one axis in S. The normal forms can be verified by Lemma 3.3.1.

(3) Removing a coordinate from a dimension will not break the 1NF, 2NF, 3NF and 4NF if the resources on the coordinates can be appropriately moved to the rest coordinates or put into an undefined coordinate.

(4) Adding a coordinate to a dimension implies that classification on the dimension needs revision. Adding a coordinate may lead to the increment of null points corresponding to the coordinate. So, this operation may break the 4NF. So, all the normal forms need verifying.

3.13 Application: Faceted Navigation

Traditional web browsing displays one web page for once operation: inputting the URL in browser or clicking the interested hyperlink in the current web page. Search engines display a list of hyperlinks according to the ranks of the pages by ranking the web pages sharing the same keywords.

Faceted navigation (also called faceted browsing or faceted search) is an important approach to improving traditional web searching and browsing by refining the search results through a process of multi-step facet selection. It allows users to view the contents of a set of resources at each step from a specific facet.

Although lacking fundamental theory and model on the underlying resource organization, some application systems have implemented faceted navigation through defining faceted metadata and traditional indexing approaches (K.-P. Kee, et. al., Faceted metadata for image search and browsing, CHI03' *Proceedings of the SIGCHI Conference on Human Factors in Computing Systems*, 2003; E. Oren, et al., Extending Faceted Navigation for RDF Data, ISWC2006; D.F.Huynh and D.R.Karger, Parallax and companion: Set-based browsing for the data web, WWW09; Dakka, W., et al. Faceted Browsing over Large Databases of Text-Annotated Objects, *ICDE 2007*; Dachselt, R. et al. FacetZoom: a continuous multi-scale widget for navigating hierarchical metadata, CHI08, 2008).

The Resource Space Model naturally supports faceted navigation as the model and theory for resource organization due to its multi-dimensional classification characteristic. Scholar search shows that the work published in 2002 (H. Zhuge, A knowledge grid model and platform for global knowledge sharing. *Expert Systems Applications*, 22(4)(2002)313-320) is the first faceted navigation system. The work published in the first edition of this book (2004, chapter 3) is the first theoretical work on faceted browsing, navigation and search.

Fig.3.13.1 is the interface of the early faceted browsing system developed in 2001. It is based on three dimensions: the left hand column is one dimension, and the middle grid contains two dimensions. Users can accurately locate a set of resources by selecting the interested point. Users can also operate the axes and space by the operation buttons.

Fig. 3.13.2 shows an example of using a three dimensional resource space (*Topic*, *Language*, *Time*) to organize web pages. Users don't need to remember the URLs of the web pages. Once the interested point is located, all the required web pages are in the point.

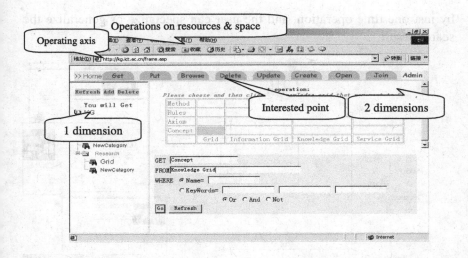

Fig. 3.13.1 The initial faceted browsing system developed in 2001.

The faceted navigation system based on the Resource Space Model consists of the following three main components:

(1) A Resource Space Management System RSMS including the storage mechanism, management mechanism, constraint mechanism, and query language.
(2) A crawler is responsible for searching relevant web pages according to one point or several points in the space and uploading the obtained web pages into the point or points.
(3) A friendly user interface that helps users to conveniently locate the point by selecting the coordinates at each axis and to view the search result.

Users can get all of the required web pages by giving coordinates on the dimensions determining the point in the space. For example, using (*Language.Chinese*, *Topic.Stock*, *Time.2006-12-13*) can get all the web pages on stock market in Chinese on December 13 in 2006. There are two major advantages of the RSM-based faceted navigation systems: the crawler has clear searching target, the user can get all required web pages by just one time operation, and the user can specialize or generalize the search result.

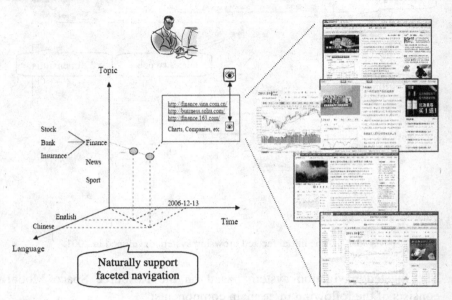

Fig.3.13.2. Underlying resource organization model for faceted navigation of web pages.

Furthermore, decentralized systems can be developed to support decentralized faceted navigation.

Fig. 3.13.3 shows two interface examples. The right hand side is three dimensional. Users can locate a small cube by rotating the cube and making separation from any dimension. The six sides of one basic cube represent six different facets of the same set of resources. The left hand side is suitable for more than three dimensions. Users can select the coordinates in the dimensions in the lower left area by clicking the dimensions and moving the pointers along the selected dimensions.

Faceted browsing, navigation, and search are not only significant in the cyber space but also useful in the other spaces in the future cyber-physical society (H.Zhuge and Y.Xing, Probabilistic Resource Space Model for Managing Resources in Cyber-Physical Society, *IEEE Transactions on Service Computing*, http://doi.ieeecomputersociety.org/10.1109/TSC.2011.12). The study of the Resource Space Model is fundamental for faceted browsing, navigation and search.

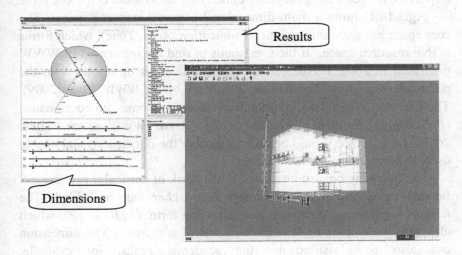

Fig.3.13.3. Interfaces for faceted navigation.

In depth research concerns the issue of how humans establish the dimension.

3.14   Application: Personal Resource Space

3.14.1 *The idea*

An important way to solve the issue of expanding ocean data is to establish personal resource space, which can provide the necessary resources for particular user. The reason is that the number of resources needed by an individual is limited due to limited personal time and energy.

Current operating systems are based on file system, which provides resource management mechanism like the My Computer in MS Windows for users to mange personal files. However, the file system is a one-dimensional directory system, which classifies files top-down into pre-named folders. Once user goes into one folder, he/she can only see the inside files and folders. The classifications (directory) cannot be refined from the other dimensions. Although the interface can be improved, to create an appropriate underlying data model is the key issue.

Fig.3.14.1 shows a multi-dimensional personal resource space. The core space has three dimensions: (*Publication, Area, Time*), which forms a 3NF resource space. If the user wants to find the references in WWW published in 2009, he/she can quickly locate a set of resources in the point determined by (*Publication: Reference, Area: WWW, Time: 2009*). The user can also refine his search by selecting some sub-coordinates: (*Publication: Reference.technical_report, Area: WWW.search, Time: 2009*). A interface should be able to display the dimensions and enable users to easily select the coordinates.

The user may be also interested in the work of particular researchers. In this case, one more dimension *Researcher* can be added. The *Researcher* dimension can take the following form: (*A, B, … , Z*), which classifies researchers by the first alphabet of surname. The dimension can also be classified by the academic ranks, for example, (*Turing_Award_Winner, ACM_Awards_Winner, IEEE_Awards_Winner, ACM_Fellow, IEEE_Fellow, Professor, Others*).

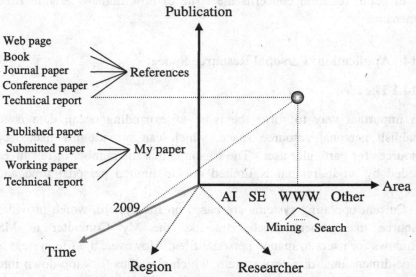

Fig.3.14.1 A researcher's personal resource space.

If the user is also interested in the work of particular region, one more dimension *Region* can be added. The first level coordinates of the *Region* dimension are the names of the countries he/she is interested in. However, adding the *Researcher* dimension will break the 3NF because some researchers have no publications in some areas.

The following issue is important:

Can the names of researchers be the coordinates?

The answer is yes, because the name of a researcher here represents a set of his/her publications rather than an individual. Similarly, the name of a country represents the set of its publications rather than its entity. It is important for designers to distinguish entity and set in RSM. Even the 2009 at the time dimension, it represents a set of resources. The following are rules:

(1) The names of dimensions and coordinates represent sets.
(2) The name of any resource represents the entity of the resource.

With this personal resource space, the user can put the resources in the right point, and retrieve the interested resources accurately according to the interested dimensions and coordinates.

To create an intelligent personal resource space, the following issue needs to be solved:

Can machines know the meaning of dimensions?

The dimensions and coordinates are named by users. There will be no problem for users to know the relations between a coordinate and the resources it represents. How to enable machines to automatically put resources into and retrieve them from the right points is an important issue. The key of the solution is the representation of resources and the representation of coordinates. If machines know the representations, they can calculate the semantic distance between representations, then put resources into or retrieve resources from the right points.

The candidate representation approaches include the SVM (Support Vector Machine), LSA (Latent Semantic Analysis), ontology or metadata based approaches, and the classification based on Wikipedia and ODP (Open Directory Project).

In specific domain, e.g., in bioinformatics, it is easy for users to establish consensus on some form of simple representations. But, it is hard in open domain applications.

The following are informal approaches to represent dimension and its coordinates:

(1) Define the pattern or pattern tree of the dimension. A dimension can be represented as $X(pattern)[C_1(pattern), ..., C_n(pattern)]$, where a *pattern* can be a *pattern tree* as discussed in the Probabilistic Resource Space Model for Managing Resources in Cyber-Physical Society (H.Zhuge et. al., *IEEE Trans. on Service Computing*, doi.ieeecomputersociety.org/10.1109/TSC.2011.12). For example, a set of sequentially appeared words $(w_1, ..., w_n)$ can be the pattern of coordinate indicating the textual resources. It can be extended to the following forms: $(w_1|w_1', ..., w_n|w_n')$ and $(w_1 \rightarrow w_1', ..., w_n \rightarrow w_n')$, where w_1 and w_1' are words, symbol "|" represents "or", and symbol "$\rightarrow$" represents implication, that is, one word semantically implies the other. A semantic link network of small set of words can also be a pattern.

(2) Give a set of rules to describe the features of the resources. So, a dimension should be represented as $X(Constraint)[C_1(Constraint), ..., C_n(Constraint)]$, where *Constraint* consists of a set of constraints for regulating resources. This is useful when the patterns are difficult to express.

(3) Give a process to select the appropriate resources. A dimension can be represented as $X(Process)[C_1(Process), ..., C_n(Process)]$, where a *Process* maps input resources into [yes, no]. If the output is yes, the input resource can be put into the coordinate. This approach can be used to classify complex resources.

The meaning of coordinate depends not only on the dimension but also on the other dimension. For example, the name of a researcher indicates a set of resources that are also regulated by the publication dimension. So, a point can provide more semantics for the crawler than a coordinate.

In many cases, classification is inexact, even for humans. A probabilistic value can be assigned to each resources belonging to a coordinate, e.g., $(R \in C, conf)$, where $conf \in [0, 1]$ is a confidence degree. It is important to give a higher priority to the resource with higher confidence degree.

3.14.2 *Uploading linked resources*

Resources are not isolated. There are explicit and implicit relations between resources. These relations represent the external semantics of resources. For example, if paper R cites paper R' and R has been put into coordinate C, then R' can be put into C. That is, $(R \longrightarrow R') \wedge R \in C \Rightarrow R' \in C$. The following reference increases the confidence of putting R' into C:

$$(R \longrightarrow R') \wedge (R'' \longrightarrow R') \wedge R \in C \wedge R'' \in C \Rightarrow R' \in C.$$

The following are two rules to include resources in a network into a coordinate:

Rule1: If all the neighbors of resource r have been put into coordinate C, r should be put into C with a certain confidence. The more neighbors, the higher the confidence degree.

A resource has a certain centrality in the semantic link network of resources (H.Zhuge and J.Zhang, Topological Centrality and Its e-Science Applications, *Journal of the American Society for Information Science and Technology*, 61(9)(2010)1824-1841). The resource with higher centrality is more important in the network. The following rule can be derived from Rule1.

Rule2: If all the neighbors of resource r and the neighbors of r' have been put into coordinate C, and the centrality of r is higher than r', then putting r into C should have higher confidence than putting r' into C.

Fig.3.14.2.1 explains the rules of putting the linked resources into coordinate. The resource networks consist of nodes and solid lines. The dotted lines denote that the linked nodes have been put into coordinate C. The dark nodes in different networks have different confidences: the confidence of the node in the right hand side network is higher than that of the middle network, which is higher than the confidence of the node in the left hand side network.

The rules are useful in determining the classes of the resources when the semantics of the linked resources have been determined.

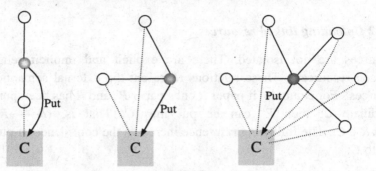

Fig.3.14.2.1 Putting the linked resources into coordinate *C*.

As shown in Fig. 3.14.2.2, if all the neighbors of a resource have been put into coordinate *C*, it should be put into *C* rather than the other coordinates. Evaluation should be made when some of its neighbors or the neighbors of some of its neighbors have been put into another coordinate. One way is to put the resource into the coordinate that contains the most of its neighbors. The other way is to put the resources into all the relevant coordinates with different confidences, which can be calculated by *the number of neighbors belonging to C / total number of neighbors*. This is reasonable since recognition of classification is usually incomplete. With the change of the network, the confidence degrees should be changed.

The confidence can also be evaluated by fuzzy and probabilistic approaches. Fuzzy Resource Space Model and Probabilistic Resource Space Model have been proposed to deal with uncertain resources (H. Zhuge, Fuzzy resource space model and platform, *Journal of Systems and Software*, 73(3)(2004)389-396; H.Zhuge and Y.Xing, Probabilistic Resource Space Model for Managing Resources in Cyber-Physical Society, *IEEE Transactions on Service Computing*, doi.ieeecomputersociety.org/10.1109/TSC.2011.12).

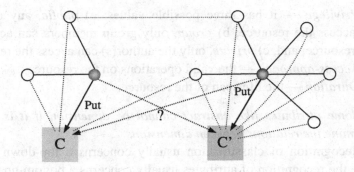

Fig.3.14.2.2 Putting the linked resources into different coordinates.

From social development point of view, human understanding and representation abilities are established in a process of experience and learning. It is natural to transfer the problem of representation into an evolution process. So, we can create a process to enable machines and users to interact with each other. For example, the process can start from the current classification in the user's file directory, and make adjustment according to the increasing resources during using. The difficulty is that adaptation depends on the tracing of user's interest during long-term use of the space.

3.15 The Dimension

Recognition of classification and attributes are two basic ways for humans to recognize the world. For example, resources in the cyber space concern the following attributes:

(1) *Name* — the identifier differentiating one resource from another.
(2) *Author* — the name(s) of the creator(s).
(3) *Abstract* — a general description of the content or function of a resource. It could be a set of keywords, natural language description, formal description, semantic link network, or template.
(4) *Version* — the number that identifies the evolution of the resource.
(5) *Location* — the addresses in the cyber space.

(6) *Privilege* — it has three possible values: a) *public*, any user can access the resource; b) *group*, only group members can access the resource; and, c) *private*, only the author(s) can access the resource.

(7) *Access-approach* — the valid operations on the resource.

(8) *Duration* — the life span of the resource.

Some attributes like abstract cannot be dimension if it is hard to determine the relations between dimensions.

Recognition of classification usually concerns a top-down process while the recognition of attributes usually concerns a bottom-up process. *A dimension is meaningful only when it is related to a space and its resources.* An attribute is meaningful only when it is related to the resource entity and the attribute value. The two ways reflect two levels of a unified cognition process.

A common attribute of a set of resources is a candidate of being a dimension or a coordinate of a dimension when a space is concerned. For example, *gender* can be a dimension of the human resource space although it is used as an attribute of a human individual. When *gender* is a dimension, it represents all the resources in the space. When *gender* is an attribute, an attribute value will be linked to the individual, e.g., *gender=male* for Zhuge. When people use attribute to describe a set of resources, they concern a resource space, and the attribute is actually a dimension if it can cooperate with the other dimensions. An individual has many attributes, while a resource space only needs a small number of dimensions, because *a space should use a minimum number of dimensions to locate resources.*

Usually, the dimensions of a resource space are determined by the creator (designer) who is familiar with the resources and the requirements of users. Humans have established many consensuses on classifications through continuous learning and experience. These consensuses are the basis for the generation of dimensions in the cyber space and in the socio space.

A critical issue is: *Can machines automatically discover the dimensions on a given set of resources?* If they can, resource spaces can be automatically generated. That will be a breakthrough in information management. Unfortunately, it is hard if machines do not know the resources and the users.

However, the following approaches can help machines to automatically discover the dimensions in resources.

(1) Using a small set of resources with known dimensions that reflect the user's viewpoint to train machines.
(2) Making use of online massive classifications such as Wikipedia and ODP (Open Directory Project). One advantage is that the online classifications keep evolving with the development of the society.
(3) Making use of domain classification like ACM Computing Classification System.
(4) Making use of domain ontology mechanisms.
(5) Making use of the current classification and clustering techniques.
(6) Analyzing the external links of resources.
(7) Making use of community discovery techniques.
(8) Tracing user browsing and searching behaviors, including used keywords, selection of hyperlinks, downloaded resources, and the folders selected for the resources.

An important issue in generating the dimensions of a resource space is to *leverage the weight of different dimensions*.

A good resource space should ensure that its resources are evenly distributed so that the search efficiency and efficacy can be guaranteed. Otherwise, the following case may occur: some points are overloaded, while others are empty. Therefore, the depth and width of the coordinate hierarchies should be largely balanced. One over length or over width coordinate tree should be maintained by the separation or merge operations. A resource space is appropriate if the length and width of a coordinate hierarchy are less than nine.

Another important issue is the orthogonal relations between dimensions. Humans are able to determine the orthogonal relation between dimensions because they continuously classify things and sharing their opinions in lifetime. Classification may change in an open system. For example, a new dimension color emerges to classify swan when black swans appear. Lemma 3.10.2 provides an approach to check the orthogonal relation between dimensions according to their ability of specifying resources.

Chapter 1 has discussed the relation between dimension and space. The generation of dimension is also relevant to the motion of resources and their self-organization. Human behaviors are the original force of the motion and self-organization in the cyber space and socio space. Human behaviors drive the formation of dimensions in the cyber space and in the socio space.

Generally, the Resource Space Model concerns the issue of how to establish an appropriate classification space for the resources of an application domain, to normalize the space, and to enable users to easily operate the space to manage the contents of various resources, no matter what forms they have.

So far, the Resource Space Model has a complete theory, model and method.

Chapter 4

The Single Semantic Image

Intelligent individuals have the ability of classifying feelings through multiple channels, generating a single semantic image by linking relevant semantic images and abstracting semantic images to classes, retrieving the required semantic image on demand, and acting based on the emerging semantic images.

A major goal of the underlying resource management mechanism of the Knowledge Grid environment is to efficiently obtain, store and manage various resources (may be in different spaces) on demand through semantic images. The single semantic image is the fusion of semantic images of different facets on one resource or a set of resources.

4.1   Obtaining Single Semantic Image from Multi-Facet Views

Humans can only see one facet of a physical object at one location because of the physical characteristics of object, light and eyes. Obtaining multi-facet images of object can help humans to build panoramic views. Humans can obtain the semantic images of multiple facets by changing the location of view, and can link these views to form semantic images in mind.

The mental semantic link networks are formed and evolved through life-time experience, and they operate over the neuron networks of brain. With the mental semantic link networks, humans can emerge a single semantic image in mind based on the panoramic views of the current feeling or the semantic image of one facet.

271

Semantic integration has been studied in neuroscience (T.Sitnikova, et. al., Two Neurocognitive Mechanisms of Semantic Integration during the Comprehension of Visual Real-world Events, *Journal of Cognitive Neuroscience*, 20(11)(2008)2037-2057). However, it is hard to derive the semantic images from neuron networks through reasoning and abstraction.

Pursuing the representation of multiple facets is the advanced stage of art development. Artists like Pablo Picasso tried to represent semantic images of multiple facets on flat painting. As shown in Fig.4.1, the artist inputs the feelings from experiencing in the real world, generates multiple semantic images, and outputs the single semantic image through painting processes. People may emerge multiple semantic images while watching the painting reflecting multi-facet views.

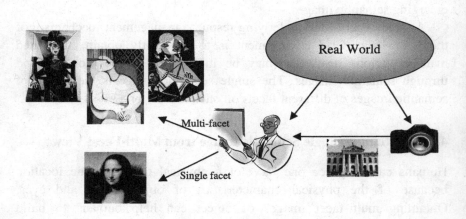

Fig. 4.1 Efforts towards single semantic image.

The cyber space can help humans to view multiple facets of an object at one location by deploying sensors (cameras) at the appropriate locations in the space of the object(s). However, the deployment of sensors and the generation of semantic image still rely on human mind.

4.2 Combining SLN and RSM

The Resource Space Model and the Semantic Link Networking model reflect different semantic images of the same set of resources from the classification and the link point of views. A way to implement the *single semantic image* (SSeI) is to integrate different semantic models into one complex semantic space model.

The Resource Space Model (RSM) organizes versatile resources through multi-dimensional classifications and normal forms. It enables users to use a set of coordinates at the dimensions of the space to determine one or a set of resources. The SLN model organizes resources by using semantic links, normal forms and the rules of networking. Potential semantic links can be derived from the existing semantic links. The formation of the classification space and the formation of the semantic link space are two facets or phases of constructing a unified complex semantic space.

The combination of RSM and SLN forms a rich semantic layer with the advantage of *classification*, *linking* and *reasoning*, which are fundamental mechanisms of intelligence. There are many ways to realize the combination. One solution is to map the resources or points in the classification space into the nodes or instances of nodes in the SLN, or map the nodes in SLN into the points in the classification space. Users can first limit the scope of interest by locating a category in the multi-dimensional classification space, and then browsing the SLN within the scope of the category. Users can also explore the SLN with knowing the categories of nodes and communities in the SLN from the RSM.

The integration of RSM and SLN establishes a kind of semantic map or knowledge map as shown in Fig. 4.2. The integrated model provides a fundamental semantic model for many applications such as faceted search, information fusion, and knowledge services. The up-level multi-dimensional classifications can provide multi-facet information for users and support abstraction through multiple dimensions. The low-level semantic link network can provide rich semantic links and reasoning mechanisms for intelligent applications.

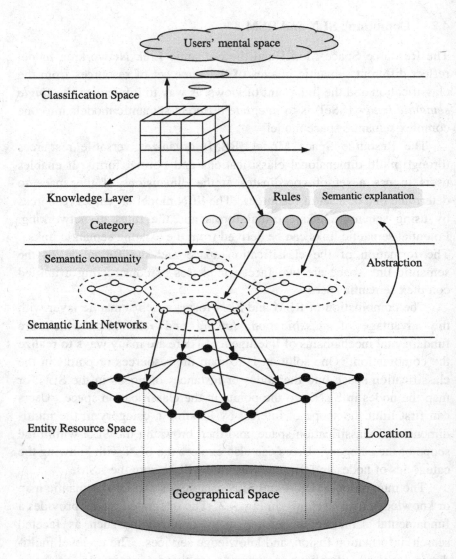

Fig. 4.2 The semantic spaces of multiple layers.

Users make and use the multi-dimensional classification space and the semantic link network according to the semantic images in their mental spaces. The orthogonal classification space can help users focus their intention, while the SLN reflects various semantic relationships (explicit or tacit) between various resources and classes.

The normalization theories of RSM and SLN support the implementation of single semantic image for accessing relevant semantic contents. Knowledge can emerge from the images through semantic networking, reasoning, specialization and generalization.

Similar to the idea of SSeI, the Complex Semantic Space Model (CSSM) integrates the Resource Space Model and the Semantic Link Network model (Keynote at the 20th *IEEE International Conference on Collaboration Technologies and Infrastructures*, June 27th-29th, 2011, Paris, France). The difference is that the CSSM extends the resources in the cyber space to the physical space, social space, and mental space. The idea is to use one model to manage versatile resources in diverse spaces. Herein, we hope to extend the SSeI and CSSM to include multiple semantic models that can support each other.

More types of spaces like the Euclidean space can be incorporated into the complex semantic space to model the real physical space and socio space.

Incorporating the geographical space into the complex semantic space as shown in Fig.4.2 can link geographical information (e.g., geographical location) to the semantic link network (non-Euclidean space) and the classification space (non-Euclidean space), so that people can search with geographical information. Some geographical information is relevant to society and culture.

4.3   The SSeI Mechanism

The single semantic image has three basic semantic mechanisms: *classification*, *linking* and *reasoning*, which are the most basic semantic mechanisms for humans to organize and understand resources.

The notion of the *single semantic image* can be understood in the light of related concepts in database systems. At the heart of a database system is a collection of tables. Views of those tables are "virtual relations" defined by query expressions (J.D. Ullman, "Principles of

Database and Knowledge-Base Systems", *Computer Science Press, Inc.*, 1988). The viewing mechanism has the following advantages.

(1)   Only relevant data are collected from different tables.
(2)   Interaction between users and database systems is simplified.
(3)   Different users of a database can get different views of it.
(4)   Data independence is supported.
(5)   Security can be more easily enforced.

However, this viewing mechanism can only be applied to formal relational tables, and it is not suitable for unstructured or semi-structured resources. Also, only someone who knows the structure of a database can create a new view of it. This limits the scope of the viewing mechanism.

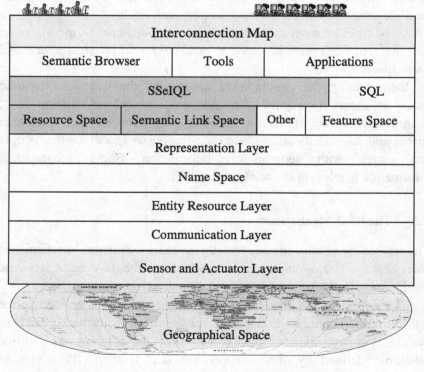

Fig. 4.3. General architecture of the SSeI mechanism.

The SSeI mechanism integrates multi-dimensional classification space, semantic link network, and other models (e.g., relational data model) by establishing mappings between their semantic primitives (H.Zhuge, Y.Xing and P.Shi, Resource Space Model, OWL and Database: Mapping and Integration, *ACM Transactions on Internet Technology*, 8/4, 2008).

An SSeI should be dynamically formed according to requirements.

Fig.4.3 shows the mechanism's general architecture. The entity resources are various kinds of data files with names in the name space. The representation layer is the description of the structure of the entity resources. The "Other" block means the other spaces. In a particular application domain, names in the name space should be unique.

Resources of different spaces can be operated on uniformly at the SSeI level. The following form can be used to express the semantic relation between points in different spaces:

$$P\,(S\!:C) \longrightarrow \alpha \rightarrow Q\,(S'\!:C').$$

Where C and C' are expressions that accurately locate points P and Q in spaces S and S' respectively, and α denotes the semantic link between P and Q. If S is a three-dimensional classification space, C can be represented as (c_1, c_2, c_3), where c_1, c_2, and c_3 are coordinates at the three axes of S.

The distance space is the geometric abstraction of the physical space. Although distance can be regarded as a kind of semantic link and distance space can be regarded as a special case of the classification space (by assigning order to dimension). An orthogonal distance space (in short *DS*) is intuitive and convenient for humans to use in applications.

A complex semantic space integrating the distance space, the Resource Space Model, and the Semantic Link Networking model can better model the cyber-physical-socio space than any single model.

Generally, the SSeI mechanism based on the multi-dimensional classification space (denoted as RSM), the semantic link space (denoted as SLN), and DS can be defined as the following structure:

<{*RSM, SLN, DS*}→ *SSeI, OP*>, which satisfies:

(1) For any two resources r_1 and r_2, if there are two points (classes) p_1 and p_2 in *RSM* that includes r_1 and r_2, then p_1 and p_2 are in *SSeI*.

(2) If r_1—α→r_2 is in *SLN*, then r_1—α→r_2 is in *SSeI*. If there is a rule in SLN: r_1—α→r_2, r_2—α→r_3 ⇒ r_1—α→r_3, then the rule is in *SSeI*.

(3) If r_1, r_2 and r_3 are in *DS*, then r_1, r_2 and r_3 are in *SSeI*, and the distance relations are kept, e.g., $d(r_1, r_2) + d(r_2, r_3) \geq d(r_1, r_3)$.

(4) *OP* is the set of operations of *RSM*, *SLN*, *DS* and *SSeI*. Operations on different spaces are defined and used separately.

An SSeI mechanism supports multiple SSeIs, which can be reorganized by operations like the *Join*, *Merge* and *Split* operations of the RSM.

4.4 The Single Semantic Image Query Language

To operate semantic images in the cyber space needs a language that can be processed by computer and can be understood by humans. However, it is a challenge to create an ideal language for operating semantic images.

The SSeI query language (SSeIQL, pronounced *say-quill*) is a language in which a user describes which contents are to be retrieved from where. SSeIQL can select one or more spaces, and can define and modify the structure of the spaces.

SSeIQL includes the following components and capabilities:

(1) *Space Definition Language* SDL. It provides commands for defining and modifying the structures of spaces, and for deleting spaces.

(2) *Space Manipulation Language* SML. It provides commands for combining and separating spaces.

(3) *Resource Manipulation Language* RML. It provides commands for adding resources to, and removing them from, spaces, and for modifying mappings within spaces.

(4) *View Definition*. SSeIQL includes commands for defining views to map resources from one space into the other.

(5) *Authorization*. SSeIQL includes controls for specifying privileges for accessing resources and views.

(6) *Integrity Constraints.* SSeIQL includes controls for specifying constraints to preserve the integrity of resources in spaces. Updates that violate such integrity constraints will be blocked.

The syntax and semantics of SSeIQL are like those of SQL, which is popular in IT professionals. SSeIQL is defined in an extended BNF notation, where "[ ]" means optional. The words in bold capitals are fixed SSeIQL keywords.

A SSeIQL *query* has three clauses:

(1) The **SELECT** clause lists the query target required in the answer.
(2) The **FROM** *CSS* clause specifies the complex semantic space *CSS* to be used in the selection. *CSS* is determined by its axes X_1, X_2 , ..., and X_m, denoted as $CSS(X_1, X_2 , ..., X_m)$. Multiple spaces can be used in one query.
(3) The **WHERE** *<conditional expression>* clause conditions the answer in terms of coordinates of resources and the semantic relationships required between the coordinates at the axes.

A typical SSeIQL query has the following form:

> **SELECT** $x_1, x_2, ..., x_n$
> **FROM** $CSS_1, CSS_2, ... , CSS_m$
> **WHERE** *<conditional expression>*.

Each x_i names a resource, an attribute, a point (in the space), a link, a community (of semantic link network), or coordinate. Each CSS_i names a complex semantic space. A **SELECT** * clause specifies that all targets appearing in the **FROM** clause are to be selected.

The *ACM Computing Classification System* can be construed as a normalized three-dimensional information space: *ACM–CCS* (*Category*, *Publication*, *Country*). The query "Find all journal papers in the resource space ACM–CCS on *Semantic Web and from China*" can be written in SSeIQL as follows:

> **SELECT** Point *p* **FROM** *ACM–CCS*
> **WHERE** *p*=(*Category* = "*Semantic Web*" & *Publication* = "*Journal*" & *Country*="*China*").

If we need to find all of the points that link to p with relation l, the following command can be used.

SELECT POINT * FROM *ACM–CCS*
WHERE * ~*l*~ (*Category* = *"Semantic Web"* & *Publication* = *"Journal"* & *Country="China"*).

If we need to find all the resources (e.g., papers) that cite *resource r*, the following command can be used, where "*~*cite*~*r*" represents the semantic link between * and *r*.

SELECT RESOURCE * FROM *ACM–CCS*
WHERE *~*cite*~ *r* in (*Category* = *"Semantic Web"* & *Publication* = *"Journal"* & *Country="China"*).

If we want to find the community c that a set of coordinates involves in, the following command can be used. The result is a resource set consisting of all journal papers satisfying the condition.

SELECT Community *c* **FROM** *ACM–CCS*
WHERE (*Category* = *"Semantic Web"* & *Publication* = *"Journal"* & *Country="China"*) in *c*.

SSeIQL provides for the nesting of subqueries. A subquery is a **SELECT/FROM/WHERE** expression that is nested within another query.

A SSeIQL program is a composition of SSeIQL statements. Execution sequence within a SSeIQL program is specified as follows:

Sequential process:
    <SSeIQL statement>; {*<SSeIQL statement>*;}
Branch-statement:
    IF *<conditional expression>*
    THEN *<SSeIQL statement>*
    ELSE *<SSeIQL statement>*
    END IF;

Loop-statement:
> **DO** <*SSeIQL statement*>
> **WHILE** <*conditional expression*>;

Begin-End-statement:
> {*Sequential-process*}

4.5 SSeIQL Syntax Specification

The syntax of SSeIQL introduced herein can be a reference for readers to design better languages.

4.5.1 *Space definition*

SSeIQL's RML provides commands to specify and modify complex semantic spaces, in particular, the schema and axes for each space, the coordinates associated with each axis, and the integrity constraints.

An advanced space may include some services, so a space can be defined by using the following command:

> **CREATE SPACE** *CS* [**AT** *USL*]
> **WITH DIMENSION** $X_1 = \{C_{11}, ..., C_{1u}\}, ..., X_n = \{C_{n1}, ..., C_{nv}\}$
> [**WITH SERVICE** $S_1, S_2, ..., S_n$]
> > <*integrity constraint$_1$*>
> > ......
> > <*integrity constraint$_m$*>.

Where *CS* is the name of the complex semantic space; X_i is the name of its axis; C_{ij} is the coordinate or coordinate hierarchy of axis X_i; *USL* is the location of the space; $S_1, S_2, ...$ and S_n are services; and, the integrity constraints are applied to the new space.

The **DROP** command deletes all data about its spaces. Not only is all resource mappings in *CS* deleted, but also the schemas for *CS*.

> **DROP SPACE** *CS*

The **MODIFY** command is used on an existing space to add or drop axes or coordinates. In the case of adding, all resource mappings in the space assign *null* as the value for the new axes or coordinates.

An axis can be added to a space by using the following command:

MODIFY SPACE *CS*
ADD AXIS $X_i < C_{i1}, ..., C_{ij} >$
[**ADD SERVICE** $S_1, S_2, ..., S_n$]

Where *CS* is the name of an existing space; X_i is the name of the axis to be added; $< C_{i1}, ..., C_{ij} >$ is the coordinate list of the additional axis; and, $S_1, S_2, ...,$ and S_n are services to be added.

Coordinates can be added to an axis of a space by using the following command.

MODIFY SPACE *CS*
ADD COORD $< C_u, ..., C_v >$ **TO** X_i [$< sup\_C_u, ..., sup\_C_v >$].
[**ADD SERVICE** $S_1, S_2, ..., S_n$]

Where *CS* is the name of an existing space, $< C_u, ..., C_v >$ is the coordinate hierarchy to be added, X_i is the name of the axis it is to be added to, and $< sup\_C_u, ..., sup\_C_v >$ specifies the direct ancestor of each of $< C_u, ..., C_v >$. If $< sup\_C_u, ..., sup\_C_v >$ is omitted, $< C_u, ..., C_v >$ will be appended to X_i.

An axis can be dropped from a space by using the following command:

MODIFY SPACE *CS*
DROP AXIS X_i.
[**DROP SERVICE** $S_1, S_2, ..., S_n$]

Where *CS* is the name of an existing space; X_i is the name of an axis of the space; and, $S_1, S_2, ...,$ and S_n are services to be dropped.

Coordinates can be dropped from an axis of a space by using the following command.

MODIFY SPACE *CS*
DROP COORD $< C_u, ..., C_v >$
FROM X_i [$< sup\_C_u, ..., sup\_C_v >$].

Where *CS* is the name of an existing space, $< C_u, ..., C_v >$ is the coordinate hierarchy to be dropped, X_i is the name of an axis of the space, and $< sup\_C_u, ..., sup\_C_v >$ is the direct ancestor of $< C_u, ..., C_v >$.

The axes or services of a space can be listed by using the following command:

USING *CS* **LIST AXES** | **SERVICES**

Where *CS* is the name of an existing space.

The coordinates of a given axis in a space can be listed using the following command:

USING *CS* **LIST COORD OF** X_i.

Where *CS* is the name of an existing space, and X_i is an axis in *CS*.

4.5.2 *Multiple space manipulation*

Multiple spaces can be manipulated by using the following operations:

(1) The Merge operation

If two axes $X_1 = <C_{11}, C_{12}, ..., C_{1n}>$ and $X_2 = <C_{21}, C_{22}, ..., C_{2m}>$ have the same axis name but different coordinates, then they can be merged into one: $X = X_1 \cup X_2 = <C_{11}, C_{12}, ..., C_{1n}, C_{21}, C_{22}, ..., C_{2m}>$.

The **MERGE** operation makes spaces $CS_1, ..., CS_n$ at $USL_1, ..., USL_n$ respectively into a single space *CS* and places the new space at *USL* subject to any specified conditions. It can be written in SSeIQL as follows:

MERGE $CS_1, ..., CS_n$ [**AT** $USL_1, ..., USL_n$]
INTO *CS* [**AT** *USL*]
[**WITH SERVICE** $S=S_1 \cup ... \cup S_n$]
WITH *new_axis* (*CS*) $= X_{1\mu} (CS_1)$ &...& $X_{nv} (CS_n)$
CONSTRAINT *axis_number*
    CHECK $|CS_1| = ... = |CS_n| = |CS|$
CONSTRAINT *common_axis_number*
    CHECK *number* (*common_axes*) $= |CS| -1$.

Where $|CS_i|$ is the number of axes of space CS_i, $X_i(CS_j)$ indicates an axis of CS_j to be merged, the **CONSTRAINT** clause specifies *common_axis_number* as the constraint name, and the predicate of the **CHECK** clause must be satisfied for the spaces to be merged.

(2) The Split operation

A space CS can be split into two spaces CS_1 and CS_2 that store the same type of resources as CS and have $|CS| - 1$ common axes by splitting one axis X into two: X' and X'', such that $X = X' \cup X''$.

The **SPLIT** operation splits one space CS at USL into each CS_i at each $URSL_i$. The axis X of CS will be split into $X_{1\alpha}(CS_1), \ldots, X_{n\beta}(CS_n)$. We can write the SSeIQL **SPLIT** expression as follows:

> **SPLIT** CS [**AT** USL]
> **INTO** $CS_1, \ldots, CS_n$ [**AT** $USL_1, \ldots, USL_n$]
> **WITH** X (CS) **JOIN-INTO** $X_{1\alpha}(CS_1) = $ <coordinate_set$_1$> **&** ...
>   **&** $X_{n\beta}(CS_n) = $ <coordinate_set$_n$>
> [**WITH SERVICE** S **JOIN-INTO** S_1 **OF** $CS_1, \ldots, S_n$ **OF** CS_1]
> [**WITH SERVICE** $S = S_1 \cup \ldots \cup S_n$]
> **CONSTRAINT** *axis_split*
> **CHECK** X (CS) $= X_{1\alpha}(CS_1) \cup \ldots \cup X_{n\beta}(CS_n)$

The **CHECK** clause requires that no coordinate or axis be removed in the split operation.

(3) The Join operation

If two spaces CS_1 and CS_2 store the same type of resources and they have k ($k \in [1, minimum(|CS_1|, |CS_2|)$) common axes, then they can be joined together as one CS such that CS_1 and CS_2 share these k common axes and $|CS| = |CS_1| + |CS_2| - k$. CS is called the join of CS_1 and CS_2.

The **JOIN** operation can be written in SSeIQL as follows:

> **JOIN** $CS_1, \ldots, CS_n$ [**AT** $USL_1, \ldots, USL_n$]
> **INTO** CS [**AT** USL]
> **WITH COMMON AXES** $(X_1, \ldots, X_\mu)$
> [**WITH SERVICE** $S = S_1 \cup \ldots \cup S_n$]
> **CONSTRAINT** *common_axis_number*
> **CHECK** *number* (*common_axes*) $\leq |CS| - 1$.

(4) The Separate operation

A space CS can be separated into two spaces CS_1 and CS_2 that store the same type of resource as that of CS such that they have n ($1 \leq n \leq min$

($|CS_1|$, $|CS_2|$)) common axes and $|CS| - n$ different axes, and $|CS| = |CS_1| + |CS_2| - n$.

The **SEPARATE** operation separates the space *RS* at *USL* into CS_1, ..., CS_m at USL_1, ..., USL_m respectively, subject to specified conditions. It can be written in SSeIQL as follows:

> **SEPARATE** *CS* [**AT** *USL*]
> **INTO** CS_1 (X_{11}, ..., $X_{1\mu}$), ..., CS_m (X_{m1}, ..., X_{mv})
> [**AT** USL_1, ..., USL_m]
> **WITH COMMON AXES** (X_1, ..., X_k)
> [**WITH SERVICE** *S* **JOIN-INTO** S_1 **OF** CS_1, ..., S_n **OF** CS_1]
> [**WITH SERVICE** $S=S_1 \cup ... \cup S_n$]
> **CONSTRAINT** *axis_disjoin*
>   **CHECK** $X(CS) = X_{1\alpha}(CS_1) \cup ... \cup X_{m\beta}(CS_m)$

The constraint *axis_disjoin* requires that the operation should not remove any axis of the original space.

(5) The Union operation

If two spaces CS_1 and CS_2 store the same type of resources and have n ($n = |CS_1| = |CS_2|$) common axes, they can be united into one space *RS* by eliminating duplicates. *CS* is called the union of CS_1 and CS_2, and $|CS| = n$. The Union operation can be written in SSeIQL as follows:

> **UNION** CS_1, ..., CS_n [**AT** USL_1, ..., USL_n] **INTO** *CS*
> [**WITH SERVICE** $S=S_1 \cup ... \cup S_n$]
> **CONSTRAINT** *axis_number*
>   **CHECK** $|CS_1| = ... = |CS_n| = |CS|$
> **CONSTRAINT** *common_axis_number*
>   **CHECK** *number* (*common_axes*) = $|CS|$

The Union operation requires that the spaces to be united have the same number of axes and the same axis names.

4.5.3 *Resource modification*

The SSeIQL RML is used to modify resource mapping in a space. Resource mapping can be inserted, removed, or changed. The services managed by the space are different from the services of the space.

(1) Insertion

A newly created space is empty. We can use the **INSERT** command to insert resources in the entity space into the space.

> **INSERT** $R_1..., R_m$ **INTO** $CS_1, ..., CS_m$ [**AT** $USL_1, ... , USL_m$]
> [**WHERE** <*conditional expression*>].

To insert resources into a space, we either directly specify a resource set to be inserted or write a query that gives the set of resources to be inserted. The simplest **INSERT** statement is for a single resource set. Suppose that we wish to insert a resource set {*ResourceID*} into space $CS(X_1, X_2, X_3)$ at (c_1, c_2, c_3). We write the statement as follows:

> **INSERT** {*ResourceID*} **INTO** $CS(X_1, X_2, X_3)$
> **COORD** $< X_1:c_1, X_2:c_2, X_3:c_3>$.

Instead of specifying a resource set directly, we can use a **SELECT** statement to extract a set of resources.

> **INSERT INTO** $CS(X_1, X_2, X_3)$
> **COORD** $< X_1:c_1, X_2:c_2, X_3:c_3>$
> **BY SELECT** $R_1, R_2, ..., R_n$
> **FROM** $CS_1, CS_2, ... , CS_m$
> [**WHERE** <*conditional expression*>].

(2) Deletion

In SSeIQL, a deletion is expressed by the following statement:

> **DELETE** R **FROM** $CS_1,..., CS_m$ [**AT** $USL_1,..., USL_m$]
> [**WHERE** <*conditional expression*>].

The deletion statement means that if the specified resource exists at the specified point of the given space and the user has the authority to delete it, then it will be deleted.

(3) Update

In SSeIQL, the following **UPDATE** statement is used to change a resource index in a given space.

UPDATE *CS*
REPLACE R_1 **WITH** R_2
[**WHERE** *<conditional expression>*].

The **WHERE** clause of the **UPDATE** statement means the same as the **WHERE** clause of the **SELECT** statement.

4.5.4 *Operating semantic link space*

In SSeIQL, the semantic relationship between resources can be specified by the following command:

CREATE | DELETE SLINK α
WHERE PRIOR $P <P_u, ..., P_v>$
    AND NEXT $S < R_u, ..., R_v>$.

Where α denotes the semantic relationship between two resources; and, $P<P_u, ..., P_v>$ and $S<R_u, ..., R_v>$ denote the coordinates of the predecessor and the successor in the space being operated.

The following two statements are for logging a space on a community and opening a space to other spaces.

LOG *RS* [**AT** *URSL*] **ON/OFF** [*community*]

OPEN *S* [**AT** *USL*]
TO $S_1, ..., S_m$ [**AT** $USL_1, USL_2, ..., USL_m$].

4.5.5 *View definition*

A view in SSeIQL can be defined by using the **CREATE VIEW** command. To define a view, the name of the view as well as the query that computes the view is required. The form of the **CREATE VIEW** command is as follows:

CREATE VIEW *v* **AS** *<query expression>*.

Where *<query expression>* is any valid query expression, and v is a view name.

As a simple example, consider the view consisting of m axes of a resource space. The view named *RS–view* is defined as follows:

CREATE VIEW *RS–view* $(X_1, …, X_m)$ **AS**
SELECT $X_1 = < c_{11}, …, c_{1,k_1} >, …, X_m = < c_{m,1}, …, c_{m,k_m} >$
[SELECT SERVICE $S_1, … , S_n$**]**
FROM *RS*

The list of axis names can be omitted. We define a view over two spaces by using the **MERGE** operation as follows:

CREATE VIEW *RS–view* $(X_1, …, X_m)$ **AS**
SELECT $X_1, X_2, …, X_m < C_{X_m,1}, C_{X_m,2}, …, C_{X_m,i} >$ **FROM** CS_1
MERGE
SELECT $Y_1, Y_2, …, Y_m < C_{Y_m,1}, C_{Y_m,2}, …, C_{Y_m,j} >$ **FROM** CS_2
[SELECT SERVICE $S_1, … , S_n$**]**
WHERE $X_1 = Y_1, …, X_{m-1} = Y_{m-1}$
AND $X_m.axis\_name = Y_m.axis\_name$

The new axis $axis_m$ is formed by
$$X_m \bigcup Y_m = < C_{X_m,1}, …, C_{X_m,i}, C_{Y_m,1}, …, C_{Y_m,j} >.$$

We define a view combining two spaces by using **JOIN** operation as follows:

CREATE VIEW *RS–view* $(X_1, …, X_m)$ **AS**
SELECT $X_1, X_2, …, X_m < C_{X_m,1}, C_{X_m,2}, …, C_{X_m,i} >$ **FROM** CS_1
JOIN
SELECT $Y_1, Y_2, …, Y_n < C_{Y_n,1}, C_{Y_n,2}, …, C_{Y_n,j} >$ **FROM** CS_2
[WITH SERVICE $S_1, … , S_n$ **FROM** CS_1**]**
[WITH SERVICE $S_1', …, S_n'$ **FROM** CS_2**]**
WHERE $X_1 = Y_1, …, X_i = Y_i$ *(i<=minimum (m, n))*

Once a view has been defined, we can use the view name to refer to the virtual space that the view represents. View names may appear at any place where a space name may appear. A **CREATE VIEW** clause creates a view definition in the resource dictionary, and the view definition stays in the resource dictionary until a **DROP VIEW** command removes it.

If there is any modification to resources in a space, the set of resources in the view changes as well. Views are typically implemented as follows: When a view is defined, the resource dictionary stores the definition of the view. Whenever a viewed space is used in a query, it is replaced by the stored view expression.

One important topic needs further research: the normal forms of the complex semantic space, and the relationship between the normal forms and the introduced operations.

4.6 The Programming Environment

SSeIQL needs a programming environment to implement complicated functions. The environment should have its own semantic images to intelligently support user-friendly programming (e.g., graphical programming), control and explain the execution of programs, and the management of semantic images of distributed resources (H.Zhuge, Interactive Semantics, *Artificial Intelligence*, 174(2010)190-204). It should be able to establish links between natural language, graphs, resources, and processes in the cyber space, and the semantic images in mind that reflect the real world.

Ideally, it should enable the programmer to obtain appropriate resources in different spaces on demand and describe in a single executable program, and to feel the effects of execution in multiple spaces. Fig. 4.6 depicts the scenario of programming with single semantic image in the environment. The semantic images including shapes and words emerge in mind when people see real objects or think the relationships between objects in the physical space.

Scientists have made great effort in building a creative programming environment. The Pygmalion early used the notion of icon, introduced the drag-and-drop as a way of passing arguments to functions, conceived of programming as a process of animation, and introduced the idea of programming by example. The programming by example is to enable users to describe what they want to do, and demonstrate the phases of the process on the example. The programming environment records the phases and generalizes them into a program. Lessons from Pygmalion were pointed out in (H.Lieberman, A Creative Programming Environment, in HCI Remixed, T.Erickson and D.W.McDonald (Ed), 2008).

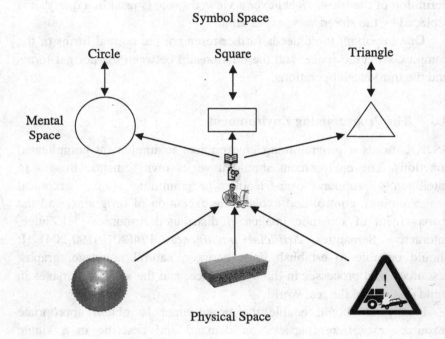

Fig. 4.6 Programming with single semantic image through Cyber-Physical-Socio Space.

The SSeIQL programming environment is a cyber-physical-socio environment, which is the extension of the man-machine environment and the man-computer symbiosis (J.C.R.Licklider, Man-Computer Symbiosis, *Transactions on Human Factors in Electronics*, vol. HFE-1, pp.4–11, March, 1960).

Object-oriented method is an attempt to unify real-world modeling and programming in computer. Soft-device is also an attempt to unify hardware and software (H.Zhuge, Clustering Soft-Devices in the Semantic Grid, *Computing in Science and Engineering*, Nov/Dec, (2002)2-4). The notion of object and soft-device can be extended to include the features, processes and rules in the cyber space, physical space, socio space, and mental space.

The following are references for designing and implementing a programming environment:

1. Smalltalk is an object-oriented, dynamically typed, reflective programming language, and development environment (A.Goldberg, SMALLTALK-80: the interactive programming environment, Addison-Wesley Longman Publishing Co., Inc. Boston, MA, USA, 1984). It includes a big class repository to support efficient development. Many software development ideas are benefit from it.

2. JXTA is a network programming platform specifically designed for P2P systems. Heterogeneous devices can interoperate through JXTA protocols. Implementation can be carried out over TCP/IP, HTTP, Bluetooth, HomePNA, and many other protocols (L.Gong, JXTA: a network programming environment, *IEEE Internet Computing*, 5(3)(2001)88-95).

3. OSLN is an Object-Oriented Semantic Link Network language for defining complex objects on the Web (X. Sun, OSLN: An Object-Oriented Semantic Link Network language for complex object description and operation. *Future Generation Computer Systems*, 26(3)(2010)389-399). Objects are regarded as the basic semantic components with internal members and functions that are declared to express attributes and semantic processes. Semantic links are defined to describe relationships among objects. Features of object-oriented programming languages are incorporated into OSLN, allowing users to write semantic programs for describing the structures of objects, object operations and manipulations. Users can write scripts as using traditional programming languages.

4. Orchestration and choreography are useful guidelines for creating business processes from Web services. The orchestration refers to

an executable business process that can interact with both internal and external Web services. Orchestration represents control from one party's perspective. Choreography is collaborative and allows each involved party to describe its part during interaction (C.Peltz, Web Services Orchestration and Choreography, *Computer*, 36(10)(2003)46-52).

4.7   The Single Semantic Image Browser

The common function of current Web browsers is to obtain a Web page coded with HTML from a Web location and then to display it for reading. The browsers work only for humans, always in read-only mode, and without regard to the semantics of Web pages. On the other hand, Web pages do not encode machine-understandable semantics. Future browsers will need to help people and virtual roles to describe, obtain and predict the resources of interest.

The future Web browser will be a semantic browser that enables users to exploit a variety of distributed resources through their semantic images rather than their location and medium, and can intelligently assist users to effectively accomplish operations such as the description, publication, capture, visualization and maintenance of semantic images.

An ideal semantic browser can actively capture, normally organize, effectively share, dynamically cluster, and uniformly manage globally distributed versatile resources, can adapt the organization structure and service process to change, can intelligently provide necessary contents and explanations for users, and can help users to interact with each other.

In the current Web, semantics is lost and distorted as pages are added or modified because resource providers cannot encode machine-understandable semantics into Web pages, and the Web browsers and search engines are not able to understand the HTML-based Web pages.

People can understand each other to some extent even if they speak different languages. This phenomenon implies that a primitive common semantic space exists behind versatile communication media such as spoken and sign languages and body language. If resource providers can describe resources in a common semantic space, then a variety of resources can implement semantic interconnection. A common semantic space has several semantic layers. If we establish these semantic layers above the entity resources, then the semantic browser can browse resources based on the semantic layer.

Existing mark-up languages like XML and RDF can help establish: a name space where resources are uniquely identified; a structural space where structural information of resources is specified; and a relational space where associations between resources are described. We still need to create new techniques to support semantic description in a logical semantic space where logical relationships are described and reasoning carried out, and in a process semantic space where the processes that integrate multiple resources or services are described and carried out.

Users either provide resources or consume resources. Resource providers indicate the semantics of the newly added resources and the consumers browse in complex semantic spaces. The providers and consumers can be humans, virtual roles and devices. A complex semantic space helps the semantic browser to provide the following distinctive capabilities:

(1) Users can exploit resources according to their privilege and the resources' semantic description.
(2) A variety of resources can be given a single semantic image in which the semantic layers unify and interconnect resources, and eliminate semantic isolation.
(3) Resources can be clustered on demand according to the user's needs and the semantic description of relevant resources.

Current technologies supporting the definition of process semantics include: Workflow which can further execute and monitor the process; PetriNets which can verify the correctness of concurrent process semantics; and description logic which allows resource providers to specify a terminological hierarchy using a restricted set of first order formulas.

A semantic browser consists of a semantic description tool, an intelligent browsing engine, and a browser interface.

The *semantic description tool* allows resource providers to establish a semantic link network or to add new nodes to an existing network. To simplify the use of large-scale semantic networks, the component-based description approach can be adopted. Just like software components, semantic components have the characteristics of "encapsulation", which requires the interconnection between components to be realized by its "interface" consisting of an input and an output (a fail exit or a succeed output). The internal nodes and links of a semantic component satisfy process and logical correctness.

The intelligent semantic browser engine includes an intelligent user profile mechanism that helps the browser understand the user's requirements and automatically traces and analyzes the user's resource handling, and evolves according to the analysis.

An advanced *browser engine* should include the following functions:

(1) Generate a complex semantic space according to user's interest and the patterns in resources.
(2) Support visualization of appropriate views of the complex semantic space.
(3) Carry out semantic reasoning and display hints to help users decide on the next browsing step.
(4) Express users' operational requirements in a structural way.
(5) Help users to describe and obtain the semantic images of resources of interest.
(6) Support four-layer browsing: high-level orthogonal classification space browsing, middle-level relational, logical and process semantic space browsing, low-level structure browsing, and deep resource (like text or image) browsing. It is able to provide implicit relations for users.
(7) Support diversity of users (people, virtual roles, and intelligent devices). Some people can use the depiction interface while the others can use the structural internal description.
(8) Adapt the content organization to the change of user interest.

The semantic browser supports advanced applications. The following are two of its applications:

(1) *E-learning.* The teacher can use the semantic browser to conveniently put teaching materials together, and the students can use it to browse the teaching materials at multiple semantic levels with necessary hint. Moreover, the teaching process and the organization of teaching materials will be adapted according to the progress and effectiveness of learning.

(2) *Web service manmagement.* Users employ the semantic browser to define the service process needed for a business process. The browser retrieves the required services in the UDDI repositories (Universal Description, Discovery and Integration), clusters retrieved fragments, and integrates them according to the process definition. It can also adapt the service process according to the change of the user's demand.

4.8 SSeI in a Peer-to-Peer Semantic Link Network

The scalability and autonomy of a Peer-to-Peer (P2P) network make it a promising infrastructure for a scalable Knowledge Grid environment.

The original motivation for most early P2P systems such as Gnutella (www.gnutella.com) and Napster (www.napster.com) was only for file sharing. Peer Data Management Systems (PDMSs) aim at an adaptable architecture for decentralized data sharing, and usually consist of a set of peers, with each peer having an associated XML schema.

Integrating heterogeneous data in large-scale P2P networks is a challenging problem because the data held in the peers are autonomous, scalable, dynamic and heterogeneous. Heterogeneous data management in a PDMS presents the following three key problems:

(1) Identifying semantically relevant peers autonomously.
(2) Routing a query accurately and efficiently from the originating peer to relevant other peers to reduce network flooding.
(3) Integrating heterogeneous data returned from different peers to provide users and other peers with an SSeI data usage mode (P2P systems do not have a global schema like that of traditional data integration systems).

Previous research on P2P computing systems and PDMSs mainly considered the following issues: data models for P2P databases, peer clustering, peer searching, query routing algorithms, and peer schema mediation mechanisms (W.S. Ng et al., PeerDB: A P2P-Based System for Distributed Data Sharing, *Proc. of International Conference on Data Engineering, ICDE*, 2003, Bangalore, India, March 2003; I. Stoica et al., Chord: A Scalable Peer-to-Peer Lookup Protocol for Internet Applications, *IEEE/ACM Transactions on Networking*, 11(2003)17–32). The above issues remain resolved.

A P2P Semantic Link Network (P2PSLN) is a directed network, where nodes are peers or P2PSLNs, and edges are typed semantic links specifying semantic links between peers (H. Zhuge, Active E-Document Framework ADF: Model and Tool, *Information and Management*, 41(1) (2003)87-97). In a P2PSLN, each peer is an active and intelligent soft-device, which can dynamically and intelligently establish semantic connections with others. A *semantic link* between two peers is a pointer with a type (α) directed from one peer (predecessor) to another (successor).

A peer can be a server when providing data, information and services, a mediator when forwarding queries, and a client when receiving information, knowledge and services from other peers.

Each peer in a P2PSLN has two main modules: a *communication* module and a *data management* module. Peers communicate with each other through SOAP (Simple Object Access Protocol) messages. Users can query a peer through a GUI (Graphical User Interface) or by using SSeIQL.

The data management module of each peer is responsible for managing the queries and the answers. Upon receiving a query, the data management module performs the following tasks:

(1) *Query Processing* — Analyze the query and extract its parameters.
(2) *Query Translation* — Match the query to the XML schema of the current peer to check whether it might be able to answer the query. If not, the query will be forwarded to the successors that are likely to be able to answer the query or to forward the query suitably.
(3) *Query Evaluation* — Put the query to the current peer for answering.

(4) *Peer Selection* — Select promising successors according to the semantic relationship and similarity between the current peer and possible successors.

(5) *Query Reformulation* — Reformulate a query posed on the current peer over schemas of its immediate successors.

(6) *Query Forwarding* — Autonomously forward the query to the selected successors according to the routing policy and a predefined TTL (Time To Live) value.

Upon receiving an answer from a successor, the data management module of the peer initiating the query will analyze the answer to detect inconsistent data. If a successor was sent the query but returned few answers, the current peer will send SOAP messages to it to find out whether it still exists in the current P2PSLN and whether there are any schema changes, and then update the schema mapping, semantic link type and the similarity degree between them. Finally, the data management module will combine the data in the answers and so it provides users or peers with data from multiple sources in a single semantic image.

An approach including automatic semantic link discovery, a method for constructing and maintaining P2P semantic link networks, a semantic peer similarity measurement approach for efficient query routing, and peer schema mapping algorithms for query reformulation and heterogeneous data integration has been proposed (H. Zhuge, et al., Query Routing in a Peer-to-Peer Semantic Link Network, *Computational Intelligence*, 21(2)(2005)197-216.).

The proposed approach has the following characteristics:

(1) Enriches the relationships between peers' data schemas by using semantic links.

(2) Uses not only nodes, but also XML structure, in measuring the similarity between schemas to efficiently and accurately forward queries to relevant peers.

(3) Deals with semantic and structural heterogeneity and data inconsistency so that peers can exchange and translate heterogeneous information using a single semantic image.

The integration of the P2P semantic link network and the classification space provides a scalable semantic layer for the Knowledge Grid environment. An integrated normalization theory is useful and important to the SSeI.

4.9   Abstraction Level, Time, Epistemology, Location and Space

The semantic image of a resource will be different if it is viewed from different abstraction levels and times. Considering the *level* and *time* as additional dimensions, a point takes the following form:

$$P(C_1, C_2, ..., C_n, level, time).$$

The semantic link between nodes may vary with the abstraction levels and times, denoted as follows, where relation α is the function of *level* and *time*.

$$P_1(C_1, C_2, ..., C_n, level, time)\text{—}\alpha(level, time)\text{—}P_2(C_1', C_2', ..., C_n',$$
level, time).

The semantic images of sequential times constitute a dynamic semantic image, which is the basis of recognizing the real world.

Epistemology is the basis of explanation. Semantic images also vary with epistemologies, that is, the semantic images generated with different epistemologies would be different. Adding the epistemology dimension, a point takes the following form:

$$P(C_1, C_2, ..., C_n, level, time, epistemology).$$

The level, time and epistemology dimensions require operations on the SSeI to impose the following criteria.

Criterion 4.1 *Join*, *Merge* and *Split* operations should be carried out at the same level.

Criterion 4.2 If SSeIs are bound by durations, then, the result of *Join*, *Merge* and *Split* operations are bounded by the overlap of these durations.

Criterion 4.3 Abstraction of one or more SSeIs generates a view at the next higher level of the SSeI.

It is hard to establish consensus between individuals with different epistemologies, so we have the following criterion.

Criterion 4.4 Only SSeIs of the same epistemology can be joined or merged.

The locations contain rich semantics, which record the behaviors of individuals (points). Different points at the close locations may involve in the same event. For example, people in theater, classroom, and airplane. A point at the certain level, time and location is denoted as follows:

$$P(C_1, C_2, \ldots, C_n, level, time, location).$$

Artifact spaces like houses, workshops, theaters, trains and airplanes provide diverse functions for humans to extend abilities. The semantic image of an artifact space is rendered in a single form in the mental space although the sources may come from different types of spaces.

Human intelligence and ability are extended in diverse spaces by creating spaces and operating them. Human daily life and work more and more rely on connecting various spaces.

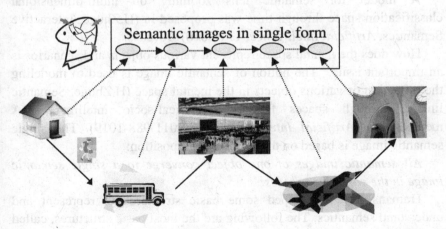

Fig.4.9 Human abilities are extended in various spaces.

The event of attending a conference involves in a series of spaces as depicted in Fig. 4.9. The creation of new spaces like the Web conference will enhance human ability and efficiency of connecting different spaces.

The semantic image in single form also implies that only one mechanism is needed to operate all semantic images although they may reflect different spaces.

Time and location can largely determine the space in which an individual is being contained. Sensors will be able to detect the location and to distinguish the type of spaces. This enables the Knowledge Grid environment to recommend the appropriate information to appropriate person in the appropriate space and at appropriate time. The environment can also know what the person is doing through the spaces.

4.10   A Semantic Lens

The mechanism of semantic lens was proposed for simulating human ability of changing the focus while observing and thinking.

A semantic lens should have the ability of abstraction, the ability of focusing, the ability of coordinating semantic images, the ability of zooming, the ability of reasoning, and the ability of emerging semantic images.

A model for semantic lens zooming on multi-dimensional classification space through time was proposed in (H.Zhuge, Interactive Semantics, *Artificial Intelligence*, 174(2010)190-204).

How does the mental space represent various objects and scenarios is an important issue. The notion of semantic image is used to modeling the reflection of various objects in the mental space (H.Zhuge, Semantic linking through spaces for cyber-physical-socio intelligence: A methodology, *Artificial Intelligence*, 175(2011)988-1019). The single semantic image is based on the following proposition:

All semantic images of one object converge to a single semantic image in the cognitive process.

Humans have developed some basic structures to represent and understand semantics. The following are the most basic structures, called interactive semantic base:

(1) *Number* and *set*. Basic concepts on set such as member, subset, union, intersection, and difference are commonsense.

(2) *Class*, *object*, *instance* and *attribute*. An object belongs to a class. Both class and object have attributes. An attribute has a name and a value. Basic attributes like color are reflection of existence. Commonsense on attributes is reached through interaction.

(3) *Relation* based on class and set. Various relations connect classes and objects to form structure. The basic relations consist of space relation, subclass or superclass relation, member relation, and mapping.

(4) *Structure* constructed based on class, object, attribute, and relation.

(5) *Classification*, which is fundamental to recognize, differentiate, and understand natural semantics and social semantics.

(6) *Rules* for operating commonsense, primitives and constructs as well as for reflecting instinct stimulus-response.

(7) *Reasoning*. New relations can be derived from various relations by various reasoning, including logical, deductive, inductive, and analogical reasoning.

Based on above structures, various semantic link networks are coordinated and the relation between the observer's interest and the following factors are established through interaction.

(1) The formation order of semantic links. For the same semantic link network, different formation orders may indicate different semantics.

(2) Semantic communities. Communities are formed and changed with the evolution of the semantic link network.

(3) Complex reasoning on semantic links. It integrates multiple types of reasoning to pursue the satisfied results rather than correct results.

(4) Co-occurrence relation among nodes, semantic links and experiences.

(5) Analogy between SLNs, reflecting the distinguished features of intelligence.

(6) Time of nodes' presence. For the same set of nodes, different times of participation lead to different evolution processes of a semantic link network.

(7) Workflows among nodes, representing the work process of active nodes.

(8) Direct and indirect relation between individuals and between objects. Showing one type of SLN, relevant SLNs will emerge according to coordination rules and relations (explicit or implicit) regardless of their types. Nodes and semantic links of SLN can have corresponding points in the classification space.

The semantic lens can show semantic image from different dimensions and abstraction levels. The time dimension records the time of interaction, event occurrence, and adding a semantic link to the semantic link network so that the semantic lens can show semantic image through time.

A semantic lens model based on the self-organized semantic link network and the adaptive multi-dimensional classification space is depicted in (H.Zhuge, Interactive Semantics, *Artificial Intelligence*, 174(2010)190-204). It extends the ability of individuals in building, retrieving and organizing semantic images.

The semantic lens can observe the single semantic image based on the integration of multiple models. Users can select either the link paradigm or the classification paradigm as the current operation interface based on the single semantic image at any step of operation as shown in Fig. 4.10. The dotted arrows represent the inter-coordinate semantic links and the inter-point semantic links.

A semantic lens may emerge different semantic images if different ontologies and rules are given. Considering the rules and ontology, the single semantic image can be extended to the following form:

<{RSM, SLN, DS}→ SSeI, Rules, Ontology, OP>, where

1. *Rules* consists of three parts: (1) *reasoning rule set* for deriving semantic links; (2) *influence rule set* for reflecting the influence of semantic link operations on the resource spaces, and the influence of resource space operations on the semantic link network; and, (3) *operation rule set* for regulating operations.

2. *OP* includes the operations on the spaces, on the *Rules* and on the *Ontology*.

3. *Ontology* is a class hierarchy that is consistent with the coordinate hierarchies in the resource spaces.

The semantic links can be between resource spaces, between points, between axes, between coordinates, or between resources.

In every space, each coordinate has a *weight* — *a function of the number of resources it specifies and the times of being accessed.* Therefore, *a point has a weight determined by the weights of its projections on every axis.*

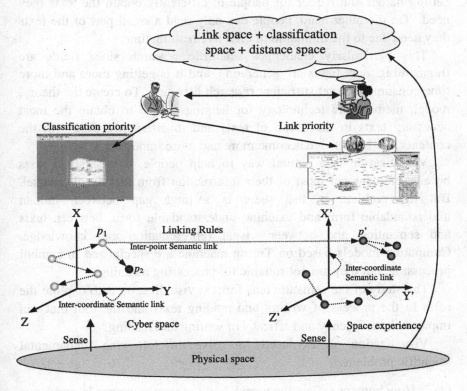

Fig. 4.10 A semantic lens based on multiple models.

The e-presence techniques can capture the videos, photos, audios, texts about human presence and replay them after synchronization. The problem is how to automatically link diverse types of resources and coordinate semantic link networks according to diverse interests that may change from time to time. The semantic lens can enhance the intelligence of individuals when they interact with each other and operate resources.

4.11   A Semantic Lens for Text Visualization

A grand challenge of social development is the contradiction between the unlimited expansion of texts and the limitation of human life. It is getting harder and harder for people to efficiently obtain the texts they need. On the other hand, people can only read a small part of the texts they need due to the limitation of effective reading time.

This particularly challenges scientific research since fields are fragmenting, new fields are generating, and it is getting more and more time-consuming to get sufficient research literature. To create the theory, model, method and technology for helping people to obtain the most necessary texts in the ocean of texts and to efficiently transform the contents into knowledge become more and more important.

Visualization is a natural way to help people to understand texts because humans get most of their information from the visual channel. But the problem is that there is a huge gap between human understandable form and machine understandable form, between texts and semantics, and between visual representation and knowledge. Computing models based on Turing machine are specialized in symbol processing, but they are not suitable for processing meaning.

The study of the semantic lens for text visualization is to explore the rules in the process of writing and reading texts and the tool that can improve the efficiency and efficacy of writing and reading.

Visualization of text needs to solve the following fundamental scientific problems:

(1)   How humans reflect the world, build semantic images in mind, use languages to indicate semantic images, and rebuild the semantic images indicated in text?

(2)   How do humans generate knowledge from text?

(3)   How to raise the efficiency of understanding text?

(4)   How to create an adaptive semantic space, and map texts into the space to support text visualization?

(5)   How to fuse versatile forms of information, and transform the fusion result into the required knowledge?

(6)   How to map the relations, reasoning and principles in different spaces and to coordinate them in a coherent intelligent process?

(7)   How to rebuild the knowledge flows of authors through a reading flow? Knowledge flow will be discussed in chapter 5.

(8)   How to discover various explicit and implicit relations, knowledge flow, and knowledge communities in an open set of texts?

Research should explore the basic principles, theories, models, methods, and software tools to solve above scientific problems. Research will also solve technical problems such as visualizing not only static texts but also dynamic links and knowledge flows through links.

Achievements will lead to a revolution of information and knowledge sharing, breakthrough in computing model, and influence IT industry, for example, the invention of a new generation search engine.

Fig. 4.11 depicts an example of using a four-dimensional complex semantic space to support visualization of texts. More dimensions can be added to the space. The visualization process includes the following steps:

(1) Mapping words, sentences and corpuses in text into the space.
(2) Integrating them with the experiences (scenarios) in the space.
(3) Building the semantic image.
(4) Displaying the semantic image.

The underlying semantic links between language units of different granularities and relevant reasoning rules reflect some basic semantics.

Much research regards words as the basic research object. However, one word can indicate diverse semantics. The semantics of words are bounded in one sentence. So, it is appropriate to use sentence as the basic language unit for accurately indicating semantic image.

By defining concepts and the dependent set of sentences, and constructing the semantic link network of dependent sentences and semantic link network of concepts, we can design a semantic lens with multiple functions for helping people comprehend articles. Integrating with the semantic link networks of articles, the semantic lens can help people efficiently read large-scale articles (B.Xu and H.Zhuge, The Textual Semantic Lens, the *7th International Conference on Semantics, Knowledge and Grids*, Beijing, China, Oct.24-26, 2011).

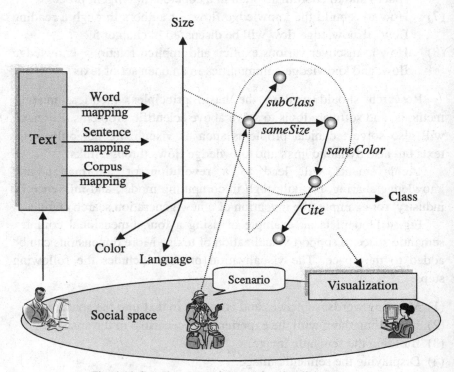

Fig. 4.11 Complex semantic space for visualizing texts.

Relevant research concerns automatic abstracting, which focuses on extracting important units from text, but it does not concern multi-facet contents and neither reflects users' personal needs as users' requirements may change. For instance, different users may want to read different facets of one article, especially a novel and encyclopedia. Faceted navigation mostly deals with text-annotated data or RDF data, but seldom considers facets in text and the communities in the content of text.

A textual semantic lens can be designed to help users to effectively read text. Humans can gradually comprehend text through seeking the answers to the following questions:

What is it about? The first step of understanding is to identify the concepts in text.

What are the links established between concepts?

What can we know from the linked concepts?

How does a semantic image emerge in mind?

These questions concern the following four basic functions.

(1) *Conceptualization*. Reader maps the words and sentences in texts into the appropriate points in the complex semantic space in the mental space and links them to the experiences in the points to form concepts. The complex semantic space has the ability to make abstraction and specialization of concepts. A writer can use multiple words or sentences to indicate one concept.

(2) *Grounding*. The micro-ground of a sentence is formed by previously read sentences that indicate the concepts. People can generate the *micro-ground* of every sentence in text while reading. Micro-grounds can be merged into larger grounds for better understanding by linking points in different micro-grounds.

(3) *Linking sentences*. A sentence can be comprehended if all of its concepts have been comprehended. To comprehend a concept in a sentence, the reader should comprehend the concept in previous sentences, as a concept is enriched through writing or reading. *Dependence links* between sentences are being established while reading. So, a sentence level semantic link network evolves with reading. This is a basic intelligent behavior involved in reading. Of course, different sentences have different importance in rendering the main idea.

(4) *Establishing structure*. The structure of a text includes the tree structure of the topic and its components, and the sequential links between paragraphs, and between sections.

(5) *Semantic distance between concepts*. The distance between concepts can be defined according to the number sentences that include them.

For example, if one sentence includes two concepts, the distance between them can be regarded as 1. If two sentences include two concepts, the distance between them can be regarded as 2. The weight of a link can be measured by the distance definition and the times of the link appeared in the text (several sentences may include two concepts). So, a weighted semantic link network of concepts can be established by the distances between concepts.

(6) *Zooming*. Reader's attention can be zoomed through the structure of text, e.g., from a sentence to a paragraph (larger scale) or a micro-ground, or from a paragraph or a micro-ground to a sentence. Zooming can also be on the semantic communities of different scales in the semantic link networks. Zooming can also be on the centrality of different granularities in a semantic link network.

The semantic lens can also reach articles. Integrating SLN of articles, the SLN of sentences, and the SLN of concepts has the following advantages:

(1) An article can be understood from the origin of the topic and previous works on the topic by tracing the explicit or implicit citation link between articles.

(2) Communities in the SLN of articles provide richer ground for people to understand and raise the efficiency of understanding.

(3) The SLN of articles can extend the scope of knowledge of reader, and can inspire thinking by giving rich semantic links within the area or cross-areas.

4.12 Single Semantic Image through Multiple Channels

Humans can establish a single semantic image through multiple channels. Senses from different channels are independent of each other. If vision, tasting and hearing about an object are separated, people cannot recognize it.

A fundamental intelligence is the ability of linking senses through different channels and forming closed loops through behaving, sensing, and emerging semantic images in mind.

Behaving through one channel like writing accompanies sensing through another channel like views. Practice like dictation helps establish the links between behaviors and senses through different channels. This is why blind people cannot write in normal natural language.

The semantics of sense will be enhanced when linking the new semantic image to the existing semantic images. Different people may generate different semantic images when sensing the same thing.

The future cyber-physical-socio intelligence will be able to reflect the semantic images in the mental space as a cyber image while people interact with each other and with other individuals in the society. Managing semantic images in the cyber space can support various individuals to behave intelligently.

In addition to computing and communication, human ability of controlling behaviors and sensing situations can be extended in the cyber-physical society. Semantic images can be enriched by forming various closed flows through multiple channels.

One sense may inspire multiple semantic images. Multiple senses may correspond to one semantic image, which can be reflected by a semantic link network of points in the complex space.

Fig. 4.12 depicts the emerging semantic images while co-experiencing in multiple spaces. Semantic images evolve with the closed flows through sensing, emerging semantic images, linking new semantic images to existing semantic images, and behaving in multiple spaces. For example, when people look at an apple falling from the tree, the semantic images emerge in the mental space including the feeling of movement, the scene of tree and apple, the sound of hitting land, the symbol of apple, the structure of the scene, geometric line of falling, and the accompanying process.

The closed loops are also in various flows through social networking in the cyber-physical society. *How to control the formation and evolution of the loops is a challenging issue.*

Macroscopic closed loops concern the material flows in the physical space, information flow in the cyber space, goods flows and money flows in the socio space, and knowledge flows in the mental space. Humans co-experience in the cyber space, physical space and socio

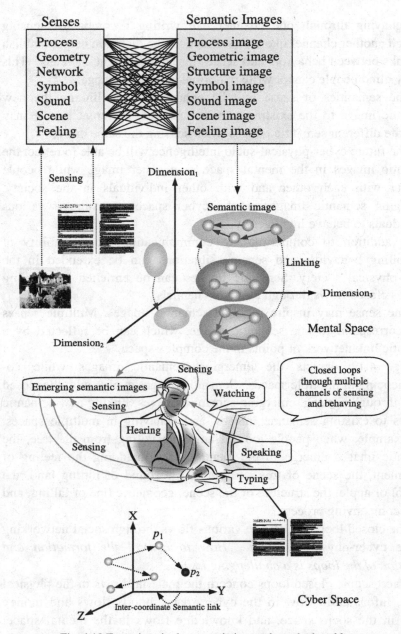

Fig. 4.12 Emerging single semantic image through closed loops.

space, transform information into knowledge, and create techniques for transforming materials into goods. Goods provide services for humans and incur money flow in the socio space. Closed loops are formed by decomposing goods into materials after end of use.

Macroscopic closed loops concern the inter-space influence. Significant change of the patterns in one space will influence the patterns in the other space. Changes in the physical space will influence the cyber space and the socio space. Changes in the socio space like population increase will influence the physical space and the cyber space. Changes in the socio space and the cyber space will influence interaction between humans, which will influence the mental space. The change of the mental space will influence the cyber space and the socio space.

4.13 Philosophical Discussion

We have discussed Molyneux's issue and Locke's opinion in chapter 2. Here we use the notion of single semantic image to extend the explanation of the formation process of concepts in mind.

Establishing the mental concepts concerns the following mental process:

(1) Separating external objects from self. This ability can be seen as innate. Touching self is different from touching external object because touching self is in a closed loop of sensing and building semantic image.
(2) Establishing some initial classes by generalizing the features of objects in daily life. The blind people can distinguish the class of active objects from the class of passive objects.
(3) Determining the features (e.g., touch) of the objects. Compare the features of the objects with the features of the existing classes. If the features of one object match the features of one class, the person can attach the touch features to the class.
(4) If there is no matching class, the person will create a temporal class and put the object into the class as an instance.

(5) Link the touch features to the corresponding object according to the relation between the object and the process of touching it in the physical space (i.e., the position of hand).

(6) Link the touch features to the sight features through the relation between the objects.

(7) Attaching the sight features and the touch features to the objects.

If a temporal class is built, the blind people will refine the temporal class when he/she touches other cubes and globes.

Chapter 5

Knowledge Flow

Knowledge is power, but knowledge is not just statically stored. It evolves through being shared and developed by various roles, people, and resources within the cyber-physical-socio environment.

A *knowledge flow* is a passing of knowledge between people or through machines. It has three crucial attributes: *direction* (sender and receiver), *carrier* (medium) and *content* (shareable). Good knowledge flow enables intelligent participants (people, roles and devices) to cooperate effectively.

5.1 Concept

Although knowledge flow is intangible, any teamwork relies on it, even if team members are unaware of its happening. *Team members share knowledge through various forms of networking, where knowledge flows through links.* Knowledge flow works like the conveyor belts in a production line. Any team member can put knowledge onto the appropriate belt to have it automatically conveyed to the team member who needs it. Team members can be helped by knowledge from the "conveyor belts" connected to them when working on a task. The linkages of such "knowledge conveyor belts" together with the team members as active nodes make up a knowledge flow network. Designing the network properly, and controlling its operation effectively, will raise the efficiency of knowledge sharing within teams (H. Zhuge, A Knowledge Flow Model for Peer-to-Peer Team Knowledge Sharing and Management, *Expert Systems with Applications*, 23(1)(2002)23-30).

Effective knowledge flow will avoid redundant knowledge passing between team members, recognizing that different members may be given different kinds of tasks and need different kinds of knowledge. Members then do not need to spend time and energy in searching for knowledge in a traditional centralized repository.

The carrier can be the Internet, local networks, various wireless networks, and even sensor networks. The content being shareable means that the knowledge can be understood by all team members. A connective network ensures that the content can be passed from any team member to any other member. Fig. 5.1 depicts a scenario of a question-answering knowledge sharing. Question and answering can be delivered through email. Knowledge in personal mental space evolves with continuous question-answering process.

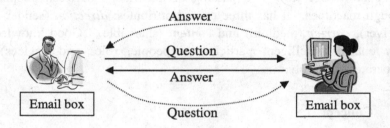

Fig. 5.1 Knowledge sharing through question and answering processes.

Knowledge content can be specified as being within a knowledge space where each point places knowledge of a specific type and level at a specific location (H. Zhuge, A Knowledge Grid Model and Platform for Global Knowledge Sharing, *Expert Systems with Applications*, 22(4)(2002)313-320). Such a specification meets the following needs:

People working in different roles need knowledge at different levels.

People working at different kinds of tasks need different kinds of knowledge.

Thus the knowledge of a flow *KF* has a field (a two-dimensional region in a knowledge space) defined by a type field *TFd* and a level field *LFd*:   *Field* (*KF*) = <*TFd*, *LFd*>, where *TFd* = <*t* | *t* is a knowledge type> and *LFd* = <*level* | *level* is a knowledge level>.

The operation $TFd_1 \cup TFd_2$ is a set union such that the order of the knowledge types of each along the knowledge type axis is maintained. Similarly, the set operations $\cup$, $\cap$, $-$ can be carried out between any two *TFd*s and between any two *LFd*s.

Let <TFd_1, LFd_1> and <TFd_2, LFd_2> be the fields of two knowledge flows KF_1 and KF_2. The following operations hold:

(1) <TFd_1, LFd_1> $\cup$ <TFd_2, LFd_2> = <$TFd_1 \cup TFd_2$, $LFd_1 \cup LFd_2$>;
(2) <TFd_1, LFd_1> $\cap$ <TFd_2, LFd_2> = <$TFd_1 \cap TFd_2$, $LFd_1 \cap LFd_2$>;
(3) <TFd_1, LFd_1> $-$ <TFd_2, LFd_2> = <$TFd_1 - TFd_2$, $LFd_1 - LFd_2$>;
(4) <TFd_1, LFd_1> $\subseteq$ <TFd_2, LFd_2>
$$\text{if and only if } <TFd_1 \subseteq TFd_2, LFd_1 \subseteq LFd_2>.$$

A knowledge node, the sender or receiver of a flow, can also generate and request knowledge. What a node can put out depends on what knowledge it has stored and what it can get in. A node can be an automaton that holds its own store of knowledge and uses an agent to help team members use that knowledge.

When a knowledge node is working it is said to be *active*. Otherwise, it is *inactive*. A node switches between these states. Active nodes can self-organize a knowledge organization that can effectively share knowledge.

The following are properties of a good knowledge flow network.

(1) A knowledge flow network is *connective* if there is a flow pass through every pair of nodes. A connective knowledge flow network requires a connective actual network, but a connective actual network does not ensure a connective knowledge flow network.

(2) A knowledge flow network is *complete* for a task if it is connective and its nodes correspond to the team members or their roles in the task. A complete network means that no team member is isolated from the knowledge of any other.

(3) A complete knowledge flow network is the *smallest* if it has the fewest possible flows between nodes. A smallest network can not only eliminate isolation but also achieve effective team knowledge sharing.

(4) A smallest complete knowledge flow network has no redundant paths between any two nodes.

5.2   A Knowledge Flow Process Model

Knowledge can flow through any of the following four types of connections:

Sequential connection. Two flows, KF_1 and KF_2 merge into one, KF_1/KF_2, such that 1) $Field(KF_1/KF_2) = Field(KF_1) = Field(KF_2)$, or 2) $Field(KF_1/KF_2) = Field(KF_2)$ if $Field(KF_1) \subseteq Field(KF_2)$.

Join-connection. Two or more flows converge to form one, denoted as $KF_1 \wedge KF_2 \wedge ... \wedge KF_n \Rightarrow KF$, such that $Field(KF_1 \wedge KF_2 \wedge ... \wedge KF_n \Rightarrow KF) = Field(KF_1) \cup Field(KF_2) \cup ... \cup Field(KF_n) = <LFd_1 \cup LFd_2 \cup ... \cup LFd_n, TFd_1 \cup TFd_2 \cup ... \cup TFd_n>$.

Split-connection. A flow KF can be split into two or more flows, denoted as $KF \Rightarrow KF_1 \vee KF_2 \vee ... \vee KF_n$, such that $Field(KF \Rightarrow KF_1 \vee KF_2 \vee ... \vee KF_n) = Field(KF_1) \cup Field(KF_2) \cup ... \cup Field(KF_n) = <LFd_1 \cup LFd_2 \cup ... \cup LFd_n, TFd_1 \cup TFd_2 \cup ... \cup TFd_n>$.

Broadcast. A flow KF can be broadcast to many flows $KF_1, KF_2, ..., KF_n$ such that $Field(KF = (KF_1, KF_2, ..., KF_n)) = Field(KF_1) = Field(KF_2) = ... = Field(KF_n)$.

The differences between workflow (www.wfmc.org) and knowledge flow are as follows:

(1) A knowledge flow can take in the knowledge generated at a node as it flows through it. A knowledge flow may change its content when it passes through a node. Workflows regulate the work order among members.
(2) Much knowledge flow content comes from team members' experience carrying out a task and cannot be anticipated. Workflow networks reflect existing business domains and can be designed.
(3) Knowledge flow content comes from team members, while workflow content reflects either data or execution dependence between activities (tasks).

For teamwork, the knowledge flow can be made consistent with the workflow by having the same roles in both networks.

5.3 Peer-to-Peer Knowledge Sharing

Team members are called peers if they do the same work for the same type of tasks at the same level of the organizational hierarchy. Knowledge sharing makes use of the knowledge within a team to solve problems more quickly or effectively. Sharing between peers is more effective than that between non-peers for the following reasons.

(1) Peers' work on the same types of tasks so their experiences are more relevant for sharing with each other to solve their problems.
(2) Peers have some similar knowledge structures so can understand each other more easily when sharing knowledge.
(3) Peers have more interests in common so they can more effectively share knowledge. For example, two programmers can better share programming knowledge than either can with a manager.

Organizational innovation is one of the key issues of knowledge management. A successful large-scale knowledge organization tends to have fewer middle layers than an unsuccessful one. Organizations in some domains, like orchestras, may even have no middle layers at all (P.F. Drucker (ed.), Harvard Business Review on Knowledge Management", *Boston, MA: Harvard Business School Press*, 1998). So peer-to-peer knowledge sharing is also a useful aim in structuring a large-scale organization.

Example. Software development by distributed teams focuses on work cooperation and resource sharing between physically dispersed team members during the development. Research on such work focuses only on aspects of technique. Human cognitive characteristics are seldom addressed. The following are reasons for incorporating knowledge flow into software development by distributed teams:

(1) *Software development is a knowledge-intensive process.* Team members can improve their work not only by using software tools but also through cognitive cooperation.

(2) *Cognitive cooperation cannot be planned.* Team members' development knowledge is gained and gathered as their work proceeds, so cognitive cooperation among them cannot be planned, though it must be encouraged. Cooperation in the form of knowledge flows is essential.

(3) *A distributed team requires effective and low cost communication.* Planned and disciplined knowledge flow can cut the cost of communication and can better reflect the actual work process of project development.

(4) *A development team should be supported by a formal experience accumulation procedure.* All team members can use the experience of their predecessors accumulated while working on previous projects, so that the team can avoid fruitless work and adapt to any change of participants or of roles.

There are five cognitive levels of knowledge in software development, given here from low to high.

(1) *Coding knowledge* helps members to share programming skills. The skills of this level are in the form of problem-solution pairs.

(2) *Reuse knowledge* helps members to reuse code components.

(3) *Knowledge of methods* enables team members to apply known problem solving techniques. Such knowledge is in the form of problem-method pairs, where a method can be a process, a pattern, or an algorithm.

(4) *Rules for development and cooperation* encourage team members to share knowledge and experience, which flow on to others to improve their software development generally. Rules for cooperation can make sharing more efficient, and are very useful for bringing new members successfully into a team.

(5) *Decision and evaluation knowledge* is meta-knowledge gained from developing the knowledge of the other four levels. It reflects the manner of making decisions during the development process, and provides guidance in making new decisions, even in quite new circumstances.

5.4 Knowledge Intensity

Knowledge flows can be used to transfer capability and expertise in an orderly and effective way. The major obstacle is the absence of criteria for assessing the effectiveness of a knowledge flow network and for ensuring its optimal operation. Effectiveness lies in essence in having a good path for needed knowledge to flow from where it resides to where it is needed—across time and space and within and between organizations as necessary.

Knowledge intensity is a critical parameter in this process, whereby a team member with profound knowledge is qualified to occupy a position of very high intensity in the flow network. Good management will keep knowledge flowing from those who are more knowledgeable to those who are less, and so avoid wasted flows.

The notion of intensity reflecting degree of knowledge leads to principles that provide objective laws for the existence and development of effective knowledge flow.

To set up a reasonable scope for research, the following assumptions specify the nature of equality, autonomy, and generosity in knowledge flow networking.

Assumption. *Nodes in a knowledge flow network are able to acquire, use and create knowledge.* It is reasonable to assume that people in an organization all have some ability to generate, use and spread knowledge.

Assumption. *Knowledge nodes share knowledge autonomously.* This limits research to the passing and sharing of knowledge among nodes independently, without outside influence. Then we can just focus on team members' effectiveness and the needs of the task at hand when designing knowledge flow networks.

Assumption. Nodes share useful knowledge without reserve.

Knowledge within a team usually covers several areas, classified according to discipline. Knowledge can be also classified into five levels as outlined above (H. Zhuge, A Knowledge Grid Model and Platform for Global Knowledge Sharing, *Expert Systems with Applications*, 22(4)(2002)313-320).

Knowledge area and level are two dimensions of knowledge space. An area i and a level j determine a *unit knowledge field* (or unit field for short) denoted by $UFd\,(i,j)$.

Knowledge intensity is a parameter that expresses a node's degree of knowledge and reflects the corresponding person's cognitive and creative abilities in a unit field. The intensity of a knowledge node and its change determine the node's "rank" in a network. It is in direct proportion to the aggregate knowledge held by the node.

A node with superior knowledge and ability to learn, use and create knowledge will be of high intensity. Thus, we estimate the intensity of a node in a unit field by assessing how much knowledge in the unit field is held by the node.

The knowledge intensity of a node will be different in different unit fields. We use the following four-dimensional orthogonal space *KIS* to represent the knowledge intensity of a knowledge node:

KIS (knowledge-area, knowledge-level, knowledge-intensity, time).

Any point in this space represents the knowledge intensity of a node in a certain unit field at certain time. At the given time t, the intensity of node u in unit field $UFd\,(i,j)$ for a given *task* is *KI* (*task, u, i, j, t*).

In every unit field some nodes need to pass knowledge to others. We can define a knowledge flow network for every unit field with flows that avoid unnecessary knowledge passing. Cooperation within a task can involve many networks, one for each unit field.

5.5   Knowledge Flow Principles

It is ineffective if knowledge flow through persons with the same knowledge structure. Therefore, we have the following principle.

Principle. *Knowledge only flows between two nodes when their intensity differs in at least one unit field.*

This can be formally expressed as follows. Let u and v be two knowledge nodes, and KI (*task, u, i, j, t*) and KI (*task, v, i, j, t*) be their intensity in UFd (i, j) at time t. If the following formula holds, knowledge will flow between u and v.

$$\exists i \exists j (KI(task, u, i, j, t) - KI(task, v, i, j, t)) \neq 0$$

Principle. A knowledge flow network is effective if and only if every flow is to a node of lower intensity than its source.

This can be formally expressed as follows. If u_k is any node in a knowledge flow network, with u_{k-1} its predecessor, then the network is effective if the following formula holds.

$$\forall k (KI(task, u_{k-1}, i, j, t) - KI(task, u_k, i, j, t)) > 0 .$$

Just as for water or electricity, knowledge naturally flows from high intensity nodes to low intensity nodes.

Principle. *The intensity difference between any two nodes in a knowledge flow network always tends to zero. That is, the following formula holds:*

$$\forall i \forall j \lim_{t \to \infty} (KI(task, v, i, j, t) - KI(task, u, i, j, t)) = 0 .$$

Let nodes u and v be the two ends of a knowledge flow in unit field UFd (i, j). If they share their useful knowledge *without reserve*, the one with lower intensity will learn from the other, and the difference in their knowledge intensity in UFd (i, j) will become smaller and smaller with the passing of time. This effect will be apparent in a closed environment, one in which there is no flow into the network from outside. In such an environment, all nodes are likely to have similar knowledge in the long term simply from learning together and sharing. All flow could stop. This principle implies that a team will improve its performance more by learning from outside the team than by only exchanging knowledge within the team.

Principle. *If knowledge depreciation is ignored, the intensity in any unit field at any node will never decrease.*

If KI (*task, u, i, j, Δt*) is the change in knowledge intensity of node u in UFd (*i, j*) in a period of time $\Delta t > 0$, then KI (*task, u, i, j, Δt*) should not be negative. So we have:

$$KI(task, u, i, j, \Delta t) = KI(task, u, i, j, t + \Delta t) - KI(task, u, i, j, t) \geq 0$$

Knowledge depreciation can be ignored if the flow duration is rather short or the depreciation rate in the unit field is quite low.

When the intensity at a node changes to a certain extent, the knowledge flow network should be reformed if it will improve the flow.

In a competitive team, each node will attempt to increase its intensity so as to raise its position and rewards. This incentive inspires team members to learn, create and contribute as much as possible.

5.6   Computational Model of Knowledge Intensity

5.6.1 *Computing knowledge intensity in a closed environment*

We first discuss the simple case where node v is the only predecessor of node u, u is the only successor of v, and the knowledge intensity of node v is a constant. The knowledge intensity of node u in unit field UFd (*i, j*) at time t, KI_{closed} (*task, u, i, j, t*), has the following features:

(1) KI_{closed} (*task, u, i, j, t*) monotonically increases.
(2) KI_{closed} (*task, u, i, j, t*) tends to that of its predecessor in the long term. So the eventual stable value of KI_{closed} (*task, u, i, j, t*) is that of its predecessor, that is, $KI_{fs} = KI_{closed}$ (*task, v, i, j, 0*).
(3) The rate of increase of KI_{closed} (*task, u, i, j, t*) is in direct proportion to two factors; one is its current intensity and the other is the ratio of its difference from its possible stable value of KI_{fs} to the value of KI_{fs}.

From the above analysis, we obtain the following non-linear differential equation, where λ is the proportionality coefficient and KI_{u0} is the initial intensity of u:

$$\begin{cases} \dfrac{dKI_{closed}(task,u,i,j,t)}{dt} = \lambda(\dfrac{KI_{fs} - KI_{closed}(task,u,i,j,t)}{KI_{fs}})KI_{closed}(task,u,i,j,t) \\ KI_{u0} = KI_{closed}(task,u,i,j,0) \end{cases}$$

The following is the solution of above equation:

$$KI_{closed}(task,u,i,j,t) = \dfrac{KI_{fs}}{1 + (\dfrac{KI_{fs}}{KI_{u0}} - 1)e^{-\lambda t}} \cdot$$

While the knowledge intensity at the source node v changes with time, consequent intensity change at u comes after that at its predecessor. Let the intensity of node v in unit field $UFd(i,j)$ at time t be $KI_{closed}(task, v, i, j, t)$. Then, we have the following equation:

$$\begin{cases} \dfrac{dKI_{closed}(task,u,i,j,t)}{dt} = \lambda(\dfrac{KI_{closed}(task,v,i,j,t) - KI_{closed}(task,u,i,j,t)}{KI_{closed}(task,v,i,j,t)})KI_{closed}(task,u,i,j,t) \\ KI_{u0} = KI_{closed}(task,u,i,j,0) \end{cases}$$

The following is the general solution of the above equation, where C_1 is a constant:

$$\begin{cases} KI_{closed}(task,u,i,j,t) = \dfrac{1}{C_1 e^{-\lambda t} + \lambda e^{-\lambda t}\displaystyle\int_0^t \dfrac{e^{\lambda t}}{KI_{closed}(task,v,i,j,t)}dt} \\ KI_{u0} = KI_{closed}(task,u,i,j,0) \end{cases}$$

We can get the solution of $KI_{closed}(task, u, i, j, t)$ by replacing $KI_{closed}(task, v, i, j, t)$ in the above formula with the appropriate expression.

For example, in a closed team composed of three nodes, let a be the predecessor of b, and b be the predecessor of c. Let $KI_{closed}(task, a, i, j, t)$ be a constant KI_{a0}. Then, we get b's intensity function from the above formula as follows:

$$KI_{closed}(task,b,i,j,t) = \dfrac{KI_{a0}}{1 + (\dfrac{KI_{a0}}{KI_{b0}} - 1)e^{-\lambda t}} \cdot$$

And c's intensity function is

$$KI_{closed}(task,c,i,j,t) = \frac{KI_{a0}KI_{b0}}{KI_{b0} + (KI_{a0} - KI_{b0})\lambda te^{-\lambda t} + \dfrac{(KI_{a0} - KI_{c0})KI_{b0}}{KI_{c0}}e^{-\lambda t}} .$$

5.6.2 Computing knowledge intensity in an open environment

In an open environment, a knowledge node can learn from the external environment as well as from within its team.

Let $KI_{open}(task, u, i, j, t)$ (in short, $KI(u, t)$) be the knowledge intensity value of node u in $UFd(i, j)$ at time t in an open environment. It is composed of the intensity coming from within the team (denoted by $KI_{in}(u, t)$) and that from the external environment (denoted by $KI_{out}(u, t)$). The overall intensity at node u is thus

$$KI(u,t) = KI_{in}(u,t) + KI_{out}(u,t) .$$

In an open environment, the nodes that have higher intensity will absorb knowledge more rapidly than those with lower. The rate of increase of $KI_{out}(u, t)$ is in direct proportion to u's intensity. And when the intensity of predecessor node v is higher than that of u, $KI_{in}(u, t)$ can be computed as described above.

Therefore, we can obtain the following non-linear differential equations, where λ and δ are proportionality coefficients and KI_{u0} is the initial knowledge intensity of u:

$$
\begin{cases}
\begin{cases}
KI(u,t) = KI_{in}(u,t) + KI_{out}(u,t) \\
\dfrac{dKI_{out}(u,t)}{dt} = \delta KI(u,t) \\
\dfrac{dKI_{in}(u,t)}{dt} = \lambda(\dfrac{KI(v,t) - KI(u,t)}{KI(v,t)})KP(u,t) \\
KI_{u0} = KI(task,u,i,j,0)
\end{cases}, & if\ KI(v,t) - KI(u,t) > 0 \\[2em]
\begin{cases}
KI(u,t) = KI_{in}(u,t) + KI_{out}(u,t) \\
\dfrac{dKI_{out}(u,t)}{dt} = \delta KI(u,t) \\
KI_{in}(u,t) = 0 \\
KI_{u0} = KI(task,u,i,j,0)
\end{cases}, & if\ KI(v,t) - KI(u,t) \leq 0
\end{cases}
$$

Its general solution is as follows, where C_2 is a constant:

$$\begin{cases} KI(u,t) = \dfrac{1}{C_2 e^{-(\delta+\lambda)t} + \lambda e^{-(\delta+\lambda)t} \displaystyle\int_0^t \dfrac{e^{(\delta+\lambda)t}}{KI(v,t)}\,dt}, & \text{if } KI(v,t) - KI(u,t) > 0 \cdot \\[4mm] KI_{u0} = KI(u,0) \\[2mm] KI(u,t) = KI_{u0}e^{\delta t}, & \text{if } KI(v,t) - KI(u,t) \le 0 \end{cases}$$

By appropriately replacing $KI(v, t)$ in the above formula, we can get the solution for $KI(u, t)$.

Using this approach, we can compute changes in knowledge intensity at nodes of a network in a closed or open environment based on their initial intensities, their learning ability and their predecessor nodes' intensities.

The following will discuss how to estimate the initial knowledge intensity.

5.6.3 *Knowledge Intensity Evaluation*

Knowledge can be explicit or tacit. Explicit knowledge is expressible, linguistic, and simple to encode. Tacit knowledge comes more from experience and intuition, and is therefore much more difficult to pass on (K.C. Desouza, Facilitating Tacit Knowledge Exchange, *Communications of the ACM*, 46(6)(2003)85-88; I. Nonaka, A Dynamic Theory of Organizational Knowledge Creation, *Organization Science*, 5(1)(1994)14-37).

Explicit knowledge is easy to assess by using objective methods such as statistics. Tacit knowledge is difficult to assess because it is often at least partly subconscious (M. Mitri, Applying Tacit Knowledge Management Techniques for Performance Assessment, *Computers & Education*, 4(2003)173-189).

Combining an objective evaluation approach with a subjective one could be a good way to assess knowledge intensity (H. Zhuge, A Dynamic Evaluation Approach for Virtual Conflict Decision Training, *IEEE Transactions on Systems, Man and Cybernetics*, 30(3)(2000)374-380; H. Zhuge and J. Liu, A Fuzzy On-line Collaborative Assessment Approach for Knowledge Grid, *Future Generation Computer Systems*, 20(1)(2004)101-112).

The objective approach uses the quantity and quality of a node's explicit knowledge. The subjective approach uses questionnaires for completion by the node itself and by others, and assessment of achievement. Although the tacit knowledge and the cognitive and creative abilities of a node are hard to assess, they can be inferred subjectively to some extent. The node with more knowledge always emits better information and one with more ability always gets better evaluations.

5.7   Knowledge Spiral Model

Knowledge spirals are formed when knowledge flows through networks. A node can deliver knowledge to its successors either by forwarding knowledge from a predecessor, or by passing on its own.

Fig. 5.7 depicts a knowledge spiral, which consists of nodes with two types of flow:

(1) *External*—knowledge passed between nodes.
(2) *Internal*—knowledge created at a node, for example through abstraction, analogy, synthesis or reasoning.

The knowledge spiral model is very similar to the hypercycle model (K. Oida, The Birth and Death Process of Hypercycle Spirals, in: R.K. Standish, M.A. Bedau, H.A. Abbass, edd., *Artificial Life VIII*, MIT *Press*, 2002). The self–replication arc and the catalytic–support arc of the hypercycle correspond to the knowledge passing and the knowledge processing respectively. The differences are twofold: self–replication in a hypercycle is carried out within nodes but knowledge passing is between nodes; and catalytic–support in a hypercycle happens between nodes but knowledge processing happens within nodes.

An effective knowledge spiral should maintain the intensity differences between nodes and ensure that only needed knowledge is passed between nodes. The processing at a knowledge node can be modeled as an automaton. Knowledge can also be modeled in a conflict environment (H. Zhuge, Conflict decision training through multi-space cooperation, *Decision Support Systems*, 29(2000)111-123).

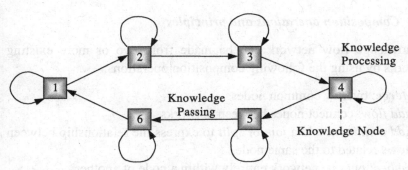

Fig.5.7 Knowledge spiral process model.

In general, work and knowledge both flow within a team (H. Zhuge, Workflow-based cognitive flow management for distributed team cooperation, *Information and Management*, 40(5)(2003)419-429). A team member can take on one or more roles, and a role can also be part of other roles. Some roles take part in knowledge flow spirals and others carry out the tasks specified in work lists.

A knowledge flow spiral can be in one of the following four states.

(1) *Static*: creating and storing knowledge.
(2) *Active*: fulfilling roles.
(3) *Suspension*: waiting for something.
(4) *Termination*: reaching either the successful or the unsuccessful exit node.

5.8   Knowledge Flow Network Planning

Planning the knowledge flow network for a team means describing and designing a network free of unnecessary flows so that the network is efficient and effective. The success of the planning depends on the experience of the planner. Planning a large network is time consuming and may need a team of planners. Without an agreed abstraction method, planners will find it hard to work together and to bring about a coherent plan. These difficulties are the main obstacles to planning successful large knowledge flow networks.

5.8.1 *Composition operations and principles*

A knowledge flow network can be made from two or more existing networks by using the following composition operations.

(1) *Merge*: overlay common nodes.
(2) *Add flow*: connect nodes between networks.
(3) *Add condition*: add a *join* or *split* to express the relationship between flows related to the same node.
(4) *Embed*: put one network entirely within a node of another.
(5) *Graph operations*: combine networks with union, intersection, or subtraction.

Flows should be added whenever nodes have unit fields in common. Conditions should be added when a node is itself a network.

Composing knowledge flow networks also involves composing their roles. Let Rel_i be the relationship between the roles in $RoleSet_i$, $Roles_1 = <RoleSet_1, Rel_1>$ and $Roles_2 = <RoleSet_2, Rel_2>$ the role models of two networks KFN_1 and KFN_2 of the same team (maybe created by different planners), and KFN the union of KFN_1 and KFN_2 (that is, $KFN_1 \cup KFN_2$). The role model of KFN can be obtained by using the following union operation:

$$Roles = Roles_1 \cup Roles_2 = <RoleSet_1 \cup RoleSet_2, Rel_1 \cup Rel_2>.$$

People, teams and tasks are the three main considerations in building a knowledge flow network. Composition of networks should respect the following principles:

The flow effectiveness principle. Composition of knowledge flow networks should ensure the effectiveness of the composed network. Effectiveness will be achieved if flows in the same chain share the same knowledge space or subspace so that the right knowledge can be delivered to the node in need of it, and so that the content of a flow can be stored at the right node. Where there are intensity differences between nodes, knowledge flow is only effective from the node with higher intensity to that with lower.

The organizational effectiveness principle. Composition of knowledge flow networks will not be effective unless it meets the regulations and targets of the team. If the composition requires that the team expands, then the expansion should help meet regulations and targets, for example in respect of profit, security and copyright.

The task relevancy principle. Knowledge gained by the composite team should help the team complete its tasks. If knowledge resulting from the composition does not help task completion, then the composition is ineffective.

The mutual benefit principle. All members of the team should benefit from the composition, for example by gaining helpful knowledge or by increase in some reward. Otherwise, the team may suffer from lessened cooperation in the long run.

The minimum coverage principle. The composite knowledge flow network should be the smallest that includes all the nodes and flows of the original networks. In other words, there must be no redundant flows or nodes. Otherwise effective knowledge sharing cannot be assured in the composite network.

The trust principle. Effective cooperation requires that team members trust each other as much as possible.

5.8.2 *Knowledge flow network components*

A large–scale building block used in the design of knowledge flow networks is the knowledge flow component. It is a knowledge flow network that is *independent*, *encapsulated*, and *complete*.

Independence. Processing within a component should be relatively independent of that in other components. Consequently, the density of knowledge flow paths within a component is usually higher than that between components.

Encapsulation. It can itself be used as a knowledge node. A knowledge flow component can be normalized to have just one initial node and one successful final node. Any external knowledge flow can only use the component through those two nodes.

Completeness. The knowledge flow process is complete in both build–time (definition phase) and run–time (execution phase).

A knowledge flow network component is called *definition complete* if:

    (1)   every internal node has at least one input and one output flow;
    (2)   every internal flow except from the final node goes to an internal node;
    (3)   the final node can be reached from the initial node; and,
    (4)   there is no isolated node or subnetwork.

Execution completeness requires that all restrictions and conditions be met during execution, and that the execution of the knowledge flow component can be treated as that of a single knowledge node.

Components can be used to compose a knowledge flow network. Using known and well-understood patterns of flow can help planners to compose effective new networks in the same way as using design patterns leads to effective software engineering (E. Gamma, et al., Design patterns: elements of reusable object-oriented software, *Pearson Education*, 1995). It can also promote understanding between planners. A knowledge flow network pattern is an abstraction of a mode of teamwork. In the pattern, every node should be reachable from every other node via a path of nodes and flows under certain constraints. The flow characteristic of the pattern is peer–to–peer.

Further work needs to be done on the following aspects:

(1) Mathematical models for adapting a knowledge flow network to new conditions;
(2) Algorithms for matching patterns and components and for selecting usable ones; and,
(3) Approaches that consider intention, trust and belief (B. J. Grosz and S. Kraus, Collaborative plans for complex group action, *Artificial Intelligence*, 86(1996)269-357).

5.8.3 *The team organization principle*

Trust between team members is an important factor that affects team cooperation. People more trusted by current team members should be preferred when recruiting.

The distribution of page ranks of the Web obeys the "power-law" and "the rich get richer" rules, and so do aspects of many other networks (L.A. Adamic and B.A. Huberman, Power-Law Distribution of the World Wide Web, *Science*, 287(24) (2000)2115).

The distribution of trust levels is somewhat similar to that of Web page ranks because nodes with high trust levels have more opportunities to cooperate than nodes with low trust levels.

However, knowledge differences tend to level off, a *"the poor get richer"* rule, because a node with less knowledge can gain from nodes with more (that is, knowledge intensity always tends to equilibrium).

The following principle can now be affirmed.

Principle. *A team prefers the recruit who has more knowledge and is highly trusted by more team members.*

5.9 Resource-Mediated Knowledge Flows

Knowledge flows can be generated and carried out by asking and answering; knowledge flowing from the person/role who answers a question to the person / role who asks the question.

Some relationships between resources reflect knowledge flows between resources' authors. For example, citation relationships between scientific papers reflect knowledge flows from an author of a paper being cited to an author of the paper that cites it. A citing paper is a confluence of incoming knowledge flows and a source of output knowledge flows conveying the innovation of its author(s). So, a resource–mediated knowledge flow management tool would be very useful in managing knowledge and in exploring the nature of innovation in scientific research.

Hyperlinks between resources reflect a kind of weak citation relationship. Semantic relationships between resources can be set up to refine the citation relationship by using text–mining approaches (J. Han and M. Kambr, Data Mining: Concepts and Techniques, *Morgan Kaufmann Publishers*, 2000).

In resource-mediated mode, knowledge flows through four types of links: *question answering links, citation links, hyperlinks,* and *semantic links,* as shown by the broken lines in Fig. 5.9.1.

Algorithms for computing the ranks in a knowledge flow network can be designed with reference to the PageRank algorithm (J. Kleinberg and S. Lawrence, The structure of the Web, *Science,* 294(30)(2001)1849-1850).

A Knowledge Grid environment has three flows: *knowledge, information* and *service.* The Cyber-Physical Society further includes material flow, energy flow, and monetary flow.

Exploring their common features can lead to the design and implementation of a uniform flow model. In-depth investigation of knowledge flow involves interdisciplinary research into management, cognition, psychology and epistemology.

Recognizing and understanding knowledge flow between scientists is valuable for science. Citations between scientific articles imply a knowledge flow from the authors of the article being cited to the authors of the articles that cite it. Discovering knowledge flow in scientific papers was studied in (H.Zhuge, Discovery of Knowledge Flow in Science, *Communications of the ACM,* 49(5)(2006)101-107).

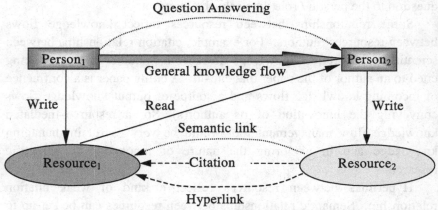

Fig. 5.9.1 Resource-mediated knowledge flows.

The knowledge implicitly flows through the citation network with the following activities of nodes: learning, reasoning, fusing, generalizing, inventing, and problem-solving. With the evolution of a scientific research area, the knowledge flow network evolves with the citation network and acts differently in different phases.

Knowledge flow networks are extended with continuous expansion of the citation network. Scientists can interest and publish in several areas, and thus be involved in different knowledge flow networks. This enables knowledge to flow through knowledge networks of different areas to promote interdisciplinary research.

One characteristic is the *reachability* — knowledge of author A's article can reach C when C cites B's article and B cites A's article. If B also cites D, knowledge of D can also reach C. B actually fuses knowledge from A and D.

The reputation of a node in knowledge flow network is relevant to the centrality (e.g., citation number), but a highly cited node (e.g., a survey paper) may not be the source of knowledge. So, the roles of nodes should be differentiated.

Implicit semantic links exist between scientists, scientific activities, and scientific entities such as journals and research institutions. These semantic links constitute a scientific semantic map. Knowledge flows along semantic links such as "co-author" and "supervise" prior to other links to constitute a knowledge map. Such a knowledge map is dynamic, and it could be discovered by analyzing these links.

The contact network and the virus spread characteristics determine the spread of epidemics, so the evolution of the contact network influences an epidemic. Appropriately adapting the contact network can control an epidemic.

Knowledge flows through a semantic link network can be reflected by such models as knowledge dissemination and query routing. Changing a semantic link network may influence the efficiency of query routing. The knowledge dissemination model resembles the spread of infectious diseases. Changing the semantic link network will influence the knowledge flowing through it.

Knowledge flows work on knowledge-level cooperation, which pass through the interaction among team members and come with activity-level cooperation. So, integration of knowledge flow network and workflow network is necessary in real applications (H. Zhuge, et al., A timed workflow process model. *Journal of Systems and Software*, 55(3) (2001)231-243; H.Zhuge, Workflow-and agent-based cognitive flow management for distributed team cooperation, *Information and Management*, 40(5)(2003)419-429).

Knowledge flows fuse frequently when used, and their contents are not predictable. Effectively managing knowledge flows within a team can lead to effective team knowledge management and eventually raise the effectiveness and efficiency of teamwork.

Coordinating and fusing knowledge flows, data flows, and control flows, and integrating knowledge flows and workflows, are powerful means for making an effective teamwork.

With the development of the Web, the growth of human knowledge is relying on Web search (B. Sparrow, et al., Google Efects on Memory: Cognitive Consequences of Having Information at Our Fingertips, *Science*, August 5, 2011; J.Bohannon, Searching for the Google Effect on People's Memory, *Science*, July 15, 2011).

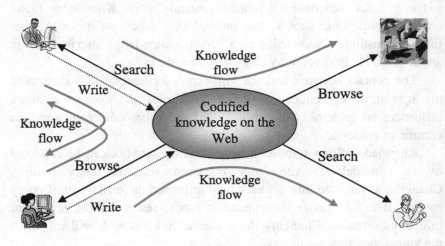

Fig.5.9.2 Web-centered knowledge flow. The codified knowledge on the Web evolves with continuous users' contribution and activities.

The codified knowledge on the Web is like an external brain. Posting knowledge on the Web and searching knowledge from the Web, knowledge flows through users and the Web. Fig. 5.9.2 shows this type of knowledge flow. The arc arrows in red-color represent knowledge flows. The knowledge flow network of this type is simple in structure but knowledge flow is dense due to large number of users.

Different from the centralized structure, Chapter 8 will introduce a peer-to-peer knowledge sharing network.

Knowledge flow spirals are formed when knowledge flows through a network. A knowledge node (scientist) can deliver knowledge to its peers by forwarding knowledge it has received, or by posting knowledge it generates on the Web. The received knowledge inspires a node to generate new knowledge. Knowledge flow can be in form of broadcasting (e.g., keynote), writing or reading the Web contents, or query routing (e.g., email). A knowledge spiral includes two types of flow:

(1) *external knowledge flow* — knowledge flowing between nodes; and,
(2) *internal knowledge flow* — knowledge arising within a node as the result of processing.

Scientific activities involve in the following spirals:

(1) A *rising* spiral has an increasing rate of citations over time. It involves in a rising research group. In contrast, a *descending spiral* has a decreasing rate of citations. It involves in a declining research group.
(2) A *rising and expanding* spiral is a rising spiral that includes an increasing number of authors over time. It involves in a rising and expanding research group.
(3) A *falling and shrinking spiral* is a descending spiral that is losing contributors. It involves in a declining and shrinking group.
(4) An *authoritative* spiral requires that all of its nodes remain authoritative. It involves in an authoritative research group.
(5) An *original* spiral has at least one source node. It involves in the presence of an initiator.

(6) *A downstream* spiral contains contributors who often cite others but are seldom cited by others.

Knowing above knowledge flow spirals can help scientists to explore knowledge evolution in research community development, and to make appropriate research plan.

5.10   Exploring Knowledge Flows

5.10.1 *Market mechanism*

Optimizing knowledge flow process to avoid unnecessary knowledge flow and stimulating individuals to actively contribute knowledge are two approaches to maintain an effective knowledge flow network.

Previously, we assume that knowledge nodes are all willing to contribute knowledge. Actually, people would probably hesitate to do this way, especially when they consider the cost of generating knowledge and worry about losing position in organization. Incentive mechanism will influence the performance of a knowledge flow network.

Except altruistic behaviors, individual motivation of sharing knowledge includes the following aspects: expectation of gaining material or monetary rewards; expectation of gaining appreciation, recognition, reputation, etc; and, expectation of gaining knowledge reciprocity with others when needed.

Studies have shown that organizations actually behave as potential knowledge markets, with buyers, sellers, and brokers. Online knowledge exchange markets, classification of users, reputation mechanisms, and dynamic pricing algorithms are topics of research (V.L.Smith, An Experimental Study of Competitive Market Behavior, *Journal of Political Economy*, 70(1962)11-137).

A knowledge service is the integration of systematic knowledge and the mechanism of using the knowledge to perform a task. Knowledge service is static in definition but it is dynamic during supplying. Different from ordinary services, the service receiver could obtain some knowledge from the provider by the underlying knowledge flow network during knowledge service process.

Different from exchanging knowledge that faces the trouble of speculation and unfair price because of high cost of knowledge creation and low cost of knowledge duplication, knowledge services are more suitable for marketing.

Knowledge service in society purses profit, and service and market are inseparable. This inspires us to establish a knowledge service market over knowledge flow network to stimulate knowledge flow and knowledge services. (H. Zhuge and W. Guo, Virtual Knowledge Service Market—For Effective Knowledge Flow within Knowledge Grid, *Journal of Systems and Software*, 80 (2007) 1833–1842).

Establishing knowledge service market mechanism over knowledge flow network is a way to maintain an effective knowledge flow network. A knowledge service market has the following effects:

1. *Stimulating cooperation.* Virtual money earned from selling knowledge services can qualify nodes to buy when they needed, which is a kind of indirect reciprocity (M.A. Nowak and K.Sigmund, Evolution of indirect reciprocity, *Nature*, 427(27)(2005)1291-1298). With the expectation of future gain, people tend to sell knowledge services.
2. *Win-win.* Buyers can obtain needed knowledge service to accomplish their tasks and sellers can promote reputation and friendship that can affect the possibility of obtaining knowledge services at a lower price.
3. *More pay for more work.* The quantity of virtual money and the degree of reputation reflect the contribution of people. More contribution can earn more rewards, and can thus purchase more knowledge services. Those never provide services for others will not be served, so free-riding can be avoided.

5.10.2 *Knowledge growth*

Exploring knowledge flow concerns fundamental understanding of knowledge. There are many problems remain resolved. For example, when can humans contribute to maintain an effective knowledge flow network? Obviously, infants could not.

Humans need to grow knowledge to a certain extent before they can participate in and contribute to effective knowledge flow networking. The process of growing knowledge includes the following steps:

(1) Establish or enrich concepts.
(2) Establish or enrich classifications, on concepts and on classifications.
(3) Establish or enrich links, between entities, between entities and concepts, between concepts, and between classifications.
(4) Learn to reasoning, from simple relational reasoning and inductive reasoning to logical reasoning and complex reasoning, and carry out reasoning to derive new classifications and links.
(5) Establish the initial notions of dimension and space, and establish spaces.
(6) Establish or enrich methods for solving problems.
(7) Ask questions according to the established concepts and reasoning.
(8) Receive answer, and link the question-answer to relevant concepts and methods for enrichment.

Chapter 6

Exploring Scale-Free Networks

Scale-free networks are often dominated overall by relatively few nodes that are linked to relatively many other nodes. This chapter describes the properties of diverse scale-free networks and reviews the development of methods for modeling such networks, covering random graph theory, small-world effects, the idea of preferential attachment, and the dynamic evolution of these networks. By extending the current scale-free network model, we explore an abstract live network—a possible high-level model for Knowledge Grid development.

6.1 Concepts

Complex networks are common in nature and society. The World Wide Web is a complex network, where nodes are Web pages connected by hyperlinks pointing from one page to another. The Internet is also a complex network, where a large number of routers and computers are linked by various physical and wireless links. Another wonderful example is the brain, which is an enormous network of microscopic nerve cells connected by axons and in many other ways, and the nerve cells are themselves networks of molecules connected by biochemical reactions.

The importance and pervasiveness of complex networks in both natural and artificial fields have drawn the attention of many scientists. But so far, we are still far from uncovering all the rules and principles. The past few years have witnessed dramatic advances: increased computing power allows us to gather, share and analyze data on a scale far larger than before. A variety of complex networks—from information networks (for example, the World Wide Web, citation networks) to biological networks (for example, a cell's metabolic system) to social networks (for example, actors in Hollywood)—have been discovered to share an important property:

Systems are dominated overall by relatively few nodes that are linked to relatively many other nodes.

Networks containing such dominant nodes are called *scale-free* in the sense that some nodes have a very large number of links, whereas most nodes have relatively very few. It has been shown that such scale-free networks are remarkably robust against accidental failure but vulnerable to coordinated attack.

How then do the distinctive characteristics of such a network come about? (L.A. Adamic, B.A. Huberman, Power-law Distribution of the World Wide Web, *Science*, 287(2000)2115; R. Albert, H. Jeong, A.L. Barabási, Diameter of the world-wide web, *Nature*, 401(1999)130-131). Several statistical methods for characterizing and modeling network structure will be discussed in this chapter.

Traditionally, complex networks with no specific governing rules have been described as random graphs, proposed as the simplest and most direct realization of a complex network. This idea has its roots in the work of two Hungarian mathematicians, Paul Erdös and Alfréd Rényi. In their model, pairs of nodes to be linked are randomly chosen. The most intriguing question here is whether or not such a simple operation is enough to produce a scale-free structure. If not, we will return to the question posed in the previous paragraph.

One basic measure of the structure of a complex network that has assumed particular importance is its degree distribution, $P(k)$ (D.S. Callaway, et al., Are randomly grown graphs really random?, *Phys. Rev.*, E64, 041902, 2001; P.L. Krapivsky and S. Redner, Organization of growing random networks, *Phys. Rev.*, E63, 066123-1-066123014, 2001; W.E. Leland, et al., On the self-similar nature of Ethernet traffic, *IEEE/ACM Transactions on Networking*, 2(1994)1-15; A.L. Barabási and R. Albert, Emergence of Scaling in Random Networks, *Science*, 286 (1999)509-512), defined as the number of nodes that are linked to k other nodes. In a network where links are placed randomly, the majority of nodes have approximately the same number of links and the whole system takes on a deeply democratic structure. Therefore its degree follows a Poisson distribution with a peak at some k (A.L. Barabási and E. Bonabeau, Scale-free networks, *Scientific American*, May, (2003)50-59; A.L. Barabási, R. Albert and H. Jeong, Mean-field theory for scale-free random networks, *Physica A*, 272(1999)173-187).

Perhaps the most significant advance that promotes the adoption of various modeling measures is the discovery that for most large networks the degree distribution deviates somewhat from a Poisson distribution. For example, a recent project to map the Internet found that its degree distribution follows a power law. Power laws are quite different from the bell-shaped distributions that characterize random networks. In particular, a power law does not have a peak, as the Poisson distribution does, but is instead described by a continuously decreasing function. This discovery allows various scale-free models to be constructed, and could well lead to a universal theory of network evolution.

This chapter reviews theoretical developments in statistical theory used to characterize complex networks, and then describes a scenario and modeling approach for the future Knowledge Grid environment.

6.2 The Topologies of Some Real Networks

The rapid development in speed and capability of computers and networks allows us to collect and generate data on a global scale, so the exploration of the underlying architecture of various complex systems has become active and fruitful. Herein reviews the study of some representative networks with structures that are scale-free.

6.2.1 *The Internet*

The Internet is a net of interconnected nodes: hosts (users' computers), servers (computers or programs providing a network service) that may also be hosts, and routers that direct traffic across the Internet as shown in Fig. 6.1 (M. Faloutsos, P. Faloutsos and C. Faloutsos, On power law relationships of the Internet topology, *Comput. Commun. Rev.*, 29 (1999)251-262; Q. Chen, et al., The origin of power laws in Internet topologies revisited, in *Proceedings of the 21st Annual Joint Conference of the IEEE Computer and Communications Societies*, 2002).

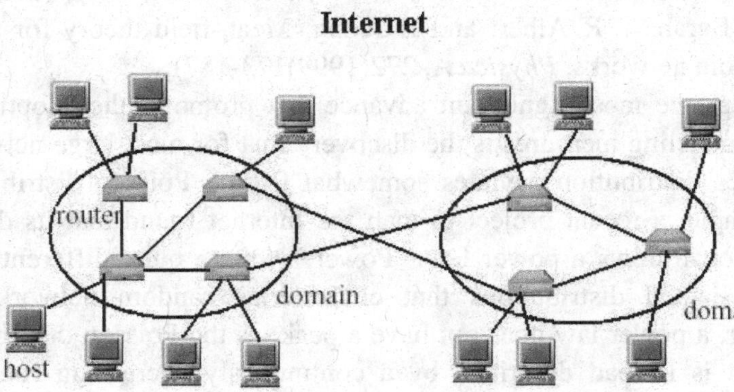

Internet

Fig. 6.1 Naive scheme of the structure of the Internet.

The topology of the Internet may be studied at two different levels. At the router level, the nodes are the routers and computers, and the links are the wires and cables that physically connect them. At the domain level, each domain (or autonomous system), composed of very many routers and computers, is considered to be a single node. A link is drawn between two domains if there is at least one route that connects them (R. Govindan and H. Tangmunarunkit, Heuristics for Internet Map Discovery, *Proceedings of the IEEE INFOCOM Conference*, 2000, pp.1371-1380; S.H. Yook, et al., Modeling the Internet's large-scale topology, cond-mat/0107417).

At the domain level, the Internet is a relatively small sparse network with the following basic characteristics. In November 1997, it consisted of 3015 nodes and 5156 links, the average degree distribution was 3.42, and the highest degree of a node was 590. In April 1998, there were 3530 nodes and 6432 links, the average degree was 3.65, and the highest degree was 746. In December 1998 there were 4389 nodes and 8256 links, the average degree was 3.76 and the highest degree was 979. The degree distribution of this network was reported to be of power law form, $P(k) \sim k^{-\gamma}$, where $\gamma = 2.2$ (M. Faloutsos, P. Faloutsos and C. Faloutsos,

On power-law relationships of the Internet topology, *Computer Communications Review*, 29(1999)251-262).

At the router level, going by relatively poor data from 1995 (J.J. Pansiot and D. Grad, On routes and multicast trees in the Internet, *Computer Communications Review*, 28(1998)41-50), the Internet consisted of 3888 nodes and 5012 links, with the average degree 2.57 and the highest degree 39. The degree distribution of this network was fitted by a power law with $\gamma = 2.5$. Note that the estimate based on the highest degree value gives a quite different value, $\gamma = 1 + \ln 3888 / \ln 39 = 3.3$, so that the empirical value of the γ exponent is not very accurate. In 2000, Govindan and Tangmunarunkit found that the Internet had by then about 150,000 routers connected by 200,000 links (R. Govindan and H. Tangmunarunkit, Heuristics for Internet Map Discovery, *Proceedings of the IEEE INFOCOM Conference*, 2000, pp.1371-1380). The degree distribution was found to "lend some support to the conjecture that a power law governs the degree distribution of real networks". If this is true, one can estimate from this degree distribution that its γ exponent is about 2.3.

6.2.2 *The World Wide Web*

The World Wide Web is the largest network for which topological information is available. The nodes of network are the Web pages and its links are the hyperlinks pointing from one page to another, as shown in Fig. 6.2.2.1.

The size of this network was close to one billion nodes at the end of 1999 (S. Lawrence and C.L. Giles, Searching the World Wide Web, *Science*, 280(5360)(1998)98-100; S. Lawrence and C.L. Giles, Accessibility of Information on the Web, *Nature*, 400(8)(1999)107-109). Interest in the World Wide Web as a network boomed after it was discovered that the degree distribution of Web pages followed a power law over several orders of magnitude. Since the links of the World Wide Web are directed, the network is characterized by two degree distributions. That of outgoing links, $P_{out}(k)$, signifies the probability that a Web page has k outgoing hyperlinks. That of incoming links, $P_{in}(k)$, is the probability that k hyperlinks point to a page. Several studies have established that both $P_{out}(k)$ and $P_{in}(k)$ have power law tails: $P_{out}(k) = k^{-r_{out}}$ and $P_{in}(k) = k^{-r_{in}}$.

World Wide Web

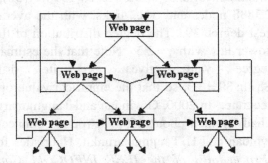

Fig. 6.2.2.1 Naive scheme of the structure of the WWW.

Albert et al. studied a subset of the World Wide Web containing 325,729 nodes and have found $\gamma_{out} = 2.45$ and $\gamma_{in} = 2.1$ (R. Albert, H. Jeong, and A.L. Barabási, Diameter of the world-wide web, *Nature*, 401(1999)130-131). Kumar et al. used a 40-million-page crawl by Alexa Inc., obtaining $\gamma_{out} = 2.38$ and $\gamma_{in} = 2.1$. A later survey of the World Wide Web topology by Broder et al. used two Altavista crawls over a total of 200 million pages, obtaining $\gamma_{out} = 2.72$ and $\gamma_{in} = 2.1$ (A. Broder, et al., Graph structure of the Web, *Proceedings of the 9th WWW conference*, 2000, pp.309-320; R. Kumar, et al., Extracting large-scale knowledge bases from the Web, *Proceedings of the 25th VLDB Conference*, 1999, pp.639-650).

Fig. 6.2.2.2 shows the degree distributions of incoming and outgoing links from two different sources: squares stand for the results of Albert et al., and circles for the results of Broder et al. (R. Albert and A.L. Barabási, Statistical Mechanics of complex networks, *Reviews of Modern Physics*, 74(2002)48-94).

Adamic and Huberman used a somewhat different representation of the World Wide Web, with each node representing a separate domain name and considering two nodes to be linked if any of the pages in one domain linked to any page in the other. While this method lumped together pages that were in the same domain, a nontrivial aggregation of the nodes, the distribution of incoming links still followed a power law with $\gamma = 1.94$ (L.A. Adamic and B.A. Huberman, Power-law Distribution of the World Wide Web, *Science*, 287(2000) 2115).

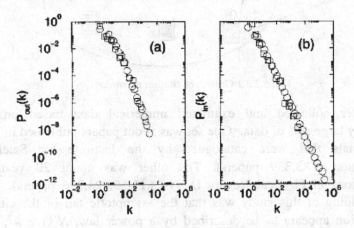

Fig. 6.2.2.2 Degree distribution of Web pages.

6.2.3 *Networks of citations of scientific papers*

In the network defined by citation relationships between scientific papers, nodes stand for scientific papers and directed links from the starting node to the ending node denote the link from the citing paper to the cited paper. There is a sequencing constraint for papers: in general, a paper can only cite papers published before it, though occasionally a citation will specify *in print* or *preprint*. Hence, the citation network takes on a distinctive feature—no closed loops.

The growth of citation networks is very simple. As illustrated in Fig. 6.2.3.1, a new node joins the net only if it contains at least one reference to an older node. This is the only way to create new nodes and links. Since citations between old papers will never be updated, new links between old papers will not appear. The number of citations of any paper is the in-degree of the corresponding node of the network.

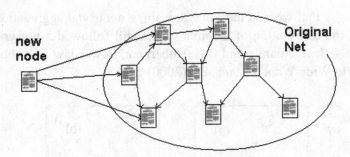

Fig. 6.2.3.1 Growth of citation networks.

Render collected and examined numerical data based on two relatively large sets of data. One set was about papers published in 1981 in journals that were catalogued by the Institute for Scientific Information (783,339 papers). The other was about 20 years of publications in Physical Review D, (vols.11-50, 24,296 papers). The main finding of this study was that the asymptotic tail of the citation distribution appears to be described by a power law, $N(k) \sim k^{-\gamma}$, with $\gamma = 3$ (S. Redner, How Popular is Your Paper? An Empirical Study of the Citation Distribution, *European Physics Journal B*, 4(1998)131-134). This conclusion is reached indirectly by means of a Zipf plot measure (see Fig. 6.2.3.2).

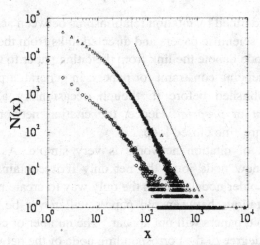

Fig. 6.2.3.2 Citation distribution from the 738,339 papers in the ISI data set ($\triangle$) and the 24,296 papers in the PRD data set (o). After Render's paper.

A more recent study by Vazquez extended these studies to the outgoing degree distribution as well, finding that it has an exponential tail (A. Vazquez, Statistics of citation networks, 2001, cond-mat/0105031).

6.2.4 *Networks of collaboration*

As an object of scientific study, collaboration networks have a great advantage in their copious and relatively reliable data. The links between collaborators can be vividly depicted by a bipartite graph (see Fig. 6.2.4) containing two distinct types of nodes — collaborators (denoted by empty circles) and collaborations (denoted by filled circles) (M.E.J. Newman, et al., Random graphs with arbitrary degree distribution and their applications, *Phys. Rev. E*, 64(2001), no.026118, cond-mat/0007235).

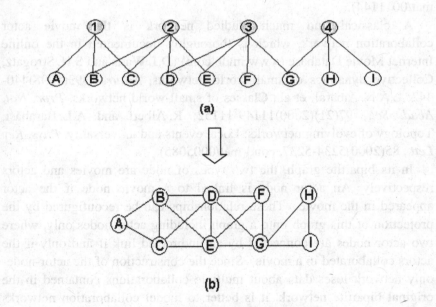

Fig. 6.2.4 A bipartite graph (a) and its projection (b).

Collaborations are of different sets of collaborators, so the collaboration nodes link to the individual collaborator nodes. Note that the bipartite graph stresses the relation between two roles, not the interactions between collaborators, so direct links between nodes of the same kind are absent and the links are undirected. The bipartite graph can also be transformed into its corresponding network by removing collaborations and linking collaborators that are linked to the same collaboration (see Fig. 6.2.4 (b)) (M.E.J. Newman, The structure of scientific collaboration networks, *Proc. Nat. Acad. Sci. U.S.A.*, 98(2001)404-409; M.E.J. Newman, Scientific collaboration networks: I. Network construction and fundamental results, *Phys. Rev. E*, 64(2001), 016131. M.E.J. Newman, Scientific collaboration networks: II. Shortest paths, weighted networks, and centrality, *Phys. Rev. E*, 64(2001), 016132; M.E.J. Newman, Who is the best connected scientist? A study of scientific coauthorship networks, *Phys. Rev. E*, 64(2001), 016131, cond-mat/0011144).

A classical and much studied network is the movie actor collaboration network, which is thoroughly documented in the online Internet Movie Database (www.imdb.com) (D.J. Watts and S.H. Strogatz, Collective dynamics of small-world networks, *Nature*, 393(1998)440-442; L.A.N. Amaral, et al., Classes of small-world networks, *Proc. Nat. Acad. Sci.*, 97(21)(2000)11149-11152; R. Albert and A.L. Barabási, Topology of evolving networks: Local events and universality, *Phys. Rev. Lett.*, 85(2000)5234-5237, cond-mat/0005085).

In its bipartite graph, the two types of node are movies and actors respectively. An actor node is linked to a movie node if the actor appeared in the movie. These relationships can be reconfigured by the projection of this graph onto a graph including actor nodes only, where two actor nodes are connected by an undirected link if and only if the actors collaborated in a movie. Since the construction of the actor-node-only network loses data about multiple collaborations contained in the original bipartite network, it is better to model collaboration networks using the full bipartite structure.

Similar examples are the Boards of Directors of companies in which two directors are linked if they belong to the same board (G.F. Davis and H.R. Greve, Corporate élite networks and governance changes in the

1980s, *Am. J. Sociol.*, 103(1997)1-37), and co-ownership networks of companies in which individuals as co-owners are linked, and collaborations of scientists in which scientists as the co-authors in the same paper are linked (A.L. Barabási, et al., Evolution of the social network of scientific collaborations, *Physica A*, 311(2002)590-614; V. Batagelj and A. Mrvar, Some analyses of the Erdös collaboration graph, *Social Networks*, 22(2000)173-186).

The degree distribution in the movie/actor network, with the number of nodes $N = 212,250$ and the average degree $k = 28.78$, was observed to obey a power law form with exponent $\gamma = 2.4$ (A.L. Barabási and R. Albert, Emergence of Scaling in Random Networks, *Science*, 286(1999)509-512). The degree distribution of mathematical journals containing 70,975 different authors and 70,901 published papers was investigated and described by a power law with exponent $\gamma = 2.4$. *Neuroscience* journal issues from 1991 to 1998, containing 209,293 authors with 3,534,724 citations and 210,750 papers, were scanned in and the degree distribution was fitted by a power law with exponent $\gamma = 2.4$ (A.L Barabási, et al., Evolution of the social network of scientific collaborations, *Physica A*, 311(2002)590-614; H. Jeong, Z. Neda and A.L. Barabási, Measuring preferential attachment for evolving networks, *Europhysics letters*, 61(2003)567-572, cond-mat/0104131).

6.2.5 *Networks of human language*

The human language as a carrier of information can also be thought of as a network made up of word nodes or some other components linked by semantic links. There are various ways to link such nodes when constructing a network based on a language bank. For instance, one may link neighboring words within sentences. In this case there will be a link between two nodes if and only if the words are next to one another in at least one sentence in the language bank. Or, one may also link the second nearest neighbors for each word in a sentence, which gives rise to two types of links.

Ferrer and Sole constructed a Word Web for the English language based on the British National Corpus (R. Ferrer and R.V. Sole, The small-world of human language, *Working Papers of Santa Fe Institute*,

www.santafe.edu/sfi/publications/Abstracts/01-03-004abs.htm).   The
nodes are English words, and the undirected links are connections
between every pair of nodes that have their words as neighbors in
sentences of the corpus.   Two slightly different networks, called the
unrestricted word network (UWN) and the restricted word network
(RWN), yielded $N_{UWN} = 478,773$, $N_{RWN} = 460,902$ nodes, and $E_{UWN} = 1.77$
$\times 10^7$, $E_{UWN} = 1.61 \times 10^7$ links.   The two networks, however, gave very
similar results for the distribution of degrees after about three quarters of
the 10^7 words of the British National Corpus (a collection of text samples
of both spoken and written modern British English) had been processed.
The degree distribution of the UWN and RWN showed two sections with
different power law exponents: $\gamma_1 = -0.15$ for the first and $\gamma_2 = -0.27$
for the second (see Fig. 6.2.5).

Based on these results, Dorogovtsev and Mendes proposed a simple
stochastic theory of the evolution of human language based on the view
of language as an evolving network of interacting words
(S.N. Dorogovtsev and J.F.F. Mendes, Language as an evolving Word
Web, *Proc. Royal Soc. London B*, 268(2603)(2001), cond-mat/0105093).
To characterize the Word Web, they adopted the idea of preferential
attachment: the more links a node acquires, the more likely it is to be
linked to subsequently.

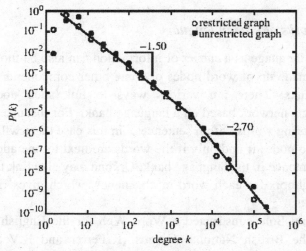

Fig. 6.2.5 Degree distribution for the word network. After R. Ferrer and R.V. Sole's
paper.

The idea can be described as follows. At each time step, a new node (word) is added to the network, and the total number of nodes t plays the role of time. The new node is linked to some old one i with the probability proportional to its degree k_i. In addition, $c\,t$ new links are created between old nodes, where c is a coefficient that characterizes the network. These new links between old nodes i and j are formed with probability proportional to the product of their degrees $k_i k_j$. Note that all the links are undirected.

Dorogovtsev and Mendes concluded that the basic characteristic of the word net structure, namely its degree distribution, does not depend on the rules of the language but is determined entirely by the general principles of the evolutionary dynamics of the word network.

6.2.6 *Other networks*

Besides the above representative networks, there exist, however, many other kinds of network, which also play important roles in their own fields.

Biological networks, for example, are a useful and valuable kind of network, which recently attracted much attention (H. Jeong, et al., The large-scale organization of metabolic networks, *Nature*, 407(2000)651-654).

Food webs are useful to quantify the interaction between various species. In a food web the nodes are species and the links represent predator-prey relationships between species (N.D. Martinez, Artifacts or attributes? Effects of resolution on the Little Rock Lake food web, *Ecological Monographs*, 61(1991)367-392).

A genomic regulatory system can be regarded as an extremely large directed network, where the nodes are the distinct components of the system, and the links point from the regulating to the regulated component (S.A. Kauffman, *The Origins of Order: Self-organization and Selection in Evolution*, Oxford University Press, Oxford, 1993).

Long distance telephone call patterns are another class of large directed graph, which have long been constructed in the telecommunications industry. In these graphs, the nodes are phone numbers and every completed phone call is a link directed from the caller to the receiver (W. Aiello, F. Chung and L. Lu, A random graph model for massive graphs, *Proceedings of the 32nd ACM Symposium on the Theory of Computing*, New York, 2000, pp.171-180).

The power grid is regarded as a complex network whose nodes are generators, transformers and substations, and whose links are high-voltage transmission lines (D.J. Watts, *Small Worlds*, Princeton University Press, Princeton, 1999).

One interesting study of the class diagram (a notation in software engineering) of the public Java Development Framework 1.2 revealed that its optimization design process turns out to be a scale-free network (S. Valverde, R.F. Cancho and R.V. Sole, Scale-free Networks from Optimal Design, *Europhysics Letters*, 60(2002)512-517, cond-mat/0204344).

In addition, electronic circuits are also viewed as undirected graphs. Their nodes are electronic components (resistors, diodes, capacitors, and the like, in analog circuits and logic gates in digital circuits) and their undirected links are wires (R. Ferrer, C. Janssen and R.V. Sole, The topology of technology graphs: Small-world patterns in electronic circuits, *Phys. Rev.*, E, vol.64, no.32767).

6.3   Random Graph Theory

Traditionally, networks of complex topology have been treated as completely random graphs. This paradigm has its roots in the work of two Hungarian mathematicians, Paul Erdös and Alfréd Rényi, who were the first to study the statistical aspects of random graphs by probabilistic methods (P. Erdös and A. Rényi, On random graphs, *Publications Mathematicæ* 6(1959)290-297; P. Erdös and A. Rényi, On the evolution of random graphs, *Publications of the Mathematical Institute of the Hungarian Academy of Sciences*, 5(1960)17-61).

In the Erdös-Rényi (ER) graph model:

(1) The total number of nodes N is fixed;
(2) The probability that any two nodes are linked is p.

Consequently the total number of links n is a random variable with the expectation value $E(n) = pN(N-1)/2$. The degree distribution is binomial:

$$P(k) = \binom{N-1}{k} p^k (1-p)^{N-1-k}$$

So the average degree is $k = p(N-1)$. For large N, the distribution takes the Poisson form with a bell shape, $P(k) = e^{-k} \bar{k}^k / k!$. The clear prediction of the ER model is that, because of the random placement of links, the resulting system will be deeply democratic: most nodes will have approximately the same number of links and it will be extremely rare to find nodes that have significantly more or fewer links than the average.

What's more, the ER model demonstrates that many properties of diverse random graphs appear quite suddenly at a threshold value of $p_c \sim c/N$. That is, for $p < p_c$ the graph is composed of many isolated clusters, while at p_c large clusters form, which towards the limit become a single cluster.

Fig. 6.3 shows the graph evolution process for the ER model. As illustrated in Fig. 6.3 (a), we start with $N = 10$ isolated nodes. Then pairs of nodes are linked with probability p. Figures (b), (c) and (d) show three results for $p = 0.1, 0.15$ and 0.2 respectively. We notice the emergence of clusters with increasing p. In this context, a linked cluster unites half of the nodes at $p = 0.15$. In the limit $p = 1$, the graph becomes fully linked.

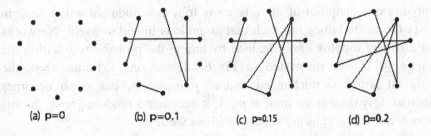

(a) p=0   (b) p=0.1   (c) p=0.15   (d) p=0.2

Fig. 6.3 An example of graph evolution for the ER model.

6.4   The Small-World Theory

The small-world phenomenon (D.J. Watts, Networks, dynamics, and the small-world phenomenon, *Am. J. Sociol.*, 105(1999)493-592; D.J. Watts, *Small Worlds*, Princeton University Press, Princeton, 1999) is common among networks in nature.

"Small" means that almost every node in such a network is to some degree "close" to every other, even to those that are perceived as likely to be far away. Thus "small" describes the global property of such networks: remarkably *short path lengths*. Also, in such networks there is fairly *high clustering locally*.

To facilitate description, we introduce here a clustering coefficient giving the extent to which nodes link together locally. The clustering coefficient is defined as the probability that the immediate neighbors of one node are also neighbors of one another. Interestingly enough, small-world networks simultaneously possess the features of random networks —short path length; and of ordered lattices—high clustering.

Watts and Strogatz studied the inherent relationships between these three systems and developed a one-dimensional link-rewiring process that can interpolate between regular and random networks (D.J. Watts and S.H. Strogatz, Collective dynamics of 'small-world' networks, *Nature*, 393(1998)440-442). The Watts-Strogatz (WS) model begins with a one-dimensional lattice of n nodes with each linked to its k nearest neighbors by undirected links (for example, in Fig. 6.4.1 (a) $n = 20$ and $k = 4$). And then with probability p each link is rewired until every link in the original lattice has been treated once. Rewiring here means moving one endpoint of the link away to a new node chosen at random over the entire lattice but such that no node is linked to itself. Networks of different topology are obtained by tuning the probability p within the range $[0, 1]$. As illustrated in Fig. 6.4.1, for one extreme $p = 0$, the original lattice is unchanged; but as p increases, the graph becomes increasingly disordered until at $p = 1$, it becomes a random graph. In this sense, random graphs are small worlds as well.

Fig. 6.4.2 shows the clustering coefficient $C(p)$ as circles, and the path length $L(p)$ as squares, both functions of the rewiring probability p. For clarity, both C and L are divided by their maximum value which is taken as $C(0)$ and $L(0)$ respectively. As p increases smoothly from 0 to 1, the path length drops rapidly, though clustering declines relatively slowly, but when p is near 0, clustering is almost stable. This result suggests that the rewiring of a few links can have a great influence on the local property, but little on the global property. According to Watts and Strogatz, small-world networks are those having large clustering and short path length. Besides rewiring, adding links uniformly at random on an ordered lattice can also lead to a small-world network (see Fig. 6.4.1 (b)).

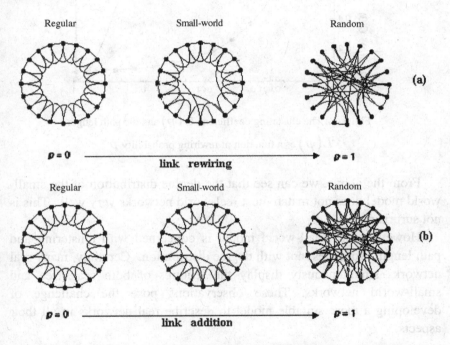

Fig. 6.4.1 Small-world networks realized through interpolating between a regular lattice and a random network.

The degree distribution of the WS model depends strongly on p (A. Barrat and M. Weigt, On the properties of small-world networks, *Eur. Phys. J. B*, 13(2000)547-560). When $p=0$, each node has the same degree k, and the degree distribution is a delta function centered at k,

$P(k) = \delta(k - z)$ where z is the coordination number of the lattice, while for $0 < p < 1$, $P(k)$ becomes broader but is still peaked around z. Ultimately, as p approaches 1, the degree distribution $P(k)$ approaches that of a random graph.

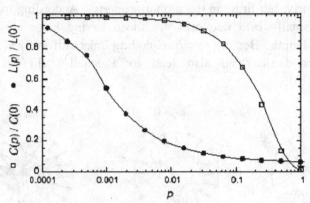

Fig. 6.4.2 The clustering coefficient $C(p)$ and the path length $L(p)$ as a function of rewiring probability p.

From the above, we can see that the degree distribution of the small-world model does not match most real-world networks very well. This is not surprising.

However, the small-world model is concerned with clustering and path length properties, not with degree distribution. Certainly, many real networks simultaneously display the features of both scale-free and small-world networks. These observations pose the challenge of developing a more suitable model to describe real networks in all their aspects.

6.5 Modeling Measures for Live Scale-Free Networks

Over the past few years, scientists have discovered that various complex networks, both natural and artificial, share an important property—some nodes have very many links to other nodes, while most nodes have just a handful—which exhibits a pronounced power law scaling. The dominant nodes can have hundreds, thousands, or even millions of links. In this sense, the networks appear to have no scale.

Scale-free networks have some important characteristics. They are, for instance, remarkably resistant to accidental failure but extremely vulnerable to coordinated attack. We review here some of the main modeling measures for scale-free systems and attempt to gain an insight into the actual rules that govern the growth of such systems.

6.5.1 *The Barabási-Albert model*

The power law degree distribution was first observed in networks by Barabási and Albert, who proposed an improved version of the Erdős-Rényi (ER) theory of random networks to account for the scaling properties of a number of systems, including the link structure of the Web (A.L. Barabási, R. Albert and H. Jeong, Mean-field theory for scale-free random networks, *Physica A*, 272(1999)173-187; A.L. Barabási and R. Albert, Emergence of Scaling in Random Networks, *Science*, 286(1999)509-512). They argued that the key factor in capturing the topological evolution of scale-free networks is the hypothesis that highly linked nodes increase their connectivity faster than less linked peers, a phenomenon called preferential attachment.

The scale-free BA model introduced by Barabási and Albert, incorporating growth with preferential attachment, leads naturally to the observed scale invariant distribution. The model is defined in the following two aspects:

(1) Growth: Starting with a small number (m_0) of nodes, at each time step we add a new node with m ($\leqslant m_0$) links that will be linked to the nodes already present in the system.

(2) Preferential attachment: When choosing the nodes to which the new node links, we assume that the probability Π that a new node will be linked to node i depends on the connectivity k_i of that node, and will be $\Pi(k_i) = k_i / \sum_j k_j$.

Then, at time step t the expected total number of nodes and links are $t + m_0$ and mt respectively. Barabási and Albert developed a mean-field method to calculate $p(k) = 2m^2 t / (k^3 \times (m_0 + t))$ with $\gamma = 3$. Simulations were carried out validating this result. Fig. 6.5.1 (a) shows degree distributions $p(k)$ with $N = m_0 + t = 300,000$ and $m_0 = m = 1$ (circles), $m_0 = m = 3$ (squares), $m_0 = m = 5$ (diamonds) and $m_0 = m = 7$ (triangles). The slope of the dashed line is $\gamma = 2.9$. Fig. 6.5.1 (b), for $m_0 = m = 5$, and system sizes $N = 100,000$ (circles), $N = 150,000$ (squares) and $N = 200,000$ (diamonds) shows that $p(k)$ is independent of time, and consequently independent of the system size.

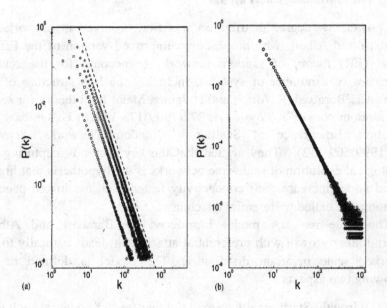

Fig. 6.5.1 Numerical simulations of the BA model(After Barabási and Albert).

The BA model is successful in explaining the emergence of power law statistics in the link structure of growing networks.

However, when applied to the Web, it fails to predict a scaling exponent that agrees with the observed value. But we should emphasize that the preferential attachment mechanism proposed by Barabási and Albert is the basic idea of the modern theory of evolving networks.

6.5.2 *Generalizations of the Barabási-Albert model*

6.5.2.1 *Link rewiring*

Because the measured and predicted exponents disagreed, Albert and Barabási later introduced an extended model of network evolution that gives a more realistic description of the Web, incorporating the addition of new nodes, new links, and the rewiring of links. They made some modifications to the rules of growth. The starting conditions of the extended model were the same, but it was revised to have three phases instead of the previous two phases (Topology of Evolving Networks: Local Events and Universality, *Phys. Rev. Lett.*, 85(2000)5234-5237):

(1) With probability p, the network adds m ($\leqslant m_0$) new links:

$$\left(\frac{\partial k_i}{\partial t}\right) = pm\frac{1}{N} + pm\frac{(k_i+1)}{\sum_j(k_j+1)}$$

where N is the size of the system. A node is randomly selected as the starting point of the new link that corresponds to the first term in the equation above (for example, a web developer decides to add a new hyperlink to a page). To reflect the second term, the other end of the link is selected with the following probability:

$$\Pi(k_i) = \frac{k_i+1}{\sum_j(k_j+1)}$$

because new links prefer to point to popular nodes, those with a high number of links. The process is repeated m times.

(2) With probability q, m links are rewired:

$$\left(\frac{\partial k_i}{\partial t}\right) = -qm\frac{1}{N} + qm\frac{k_i+1}{\sum_j(k_j+1)}.$$

Here we randomly select a node i and a link l_{ij}. Then, we remove this link with probability given by the first term and replace it with a new link l_{ij}' that connects i to node j' chosen with the probability given by the second term. Here m has the same significance as in rule (1).

(3) With probability $1 - p - q$, a new node is added:

$$\left(\frac{\partial k_i}{\partial t}\right) = (1-p-q)m\frac{k_i+1}{\sum_j(k_j+1)}$$

The new node, together with m new links connected to it is added into the system.

In the model, the probabilities p and q can be varied within the intervals $0 \leqslant p < 1$ and $0 \leqslant q < 1 - p$. Note that Albert and Barabási chose the probability $\Pi(k_i)$ to be proportional to $(k_i + 1)$ to ensure that all the nodes in the network can acquire links, even isolated nodes ($k_i = 0$). We also note that for $p = 0$ and $q = 0$, the model is reduced to the first one discussed above with the prediction of $\gamma = 3$.

By combining the contribution of the three processes, the network model evolves according to

$$\partial k_i/\partial t = (p-q)m/N + m(k_i+1)\Big/\sum_j(k_j+1) .$$

The total number of nodes $N(t) = m_0 + (1-p-q)t$ and the total number of links $\sum_j k_j = (1-q)2mt - m$, indicating that for large t, the initial condition for the constants m_0 and m is irrelevant. Its theoretical resolution has the following form:

$$P(k) = \left[k + \kappa(p,q,m)\right]^{-\gamma(p,q,m)},$$

which predicts for $q < q_{max} = \min\{1-p, (1-p+m)/(1+2m)\}$ the degree distribution follows a generalized power law, while for $q > q_{max}$, however, the equation is not valid, but numerical simulations indicate that $P(k)$ approaches an exponential. In addition, the exponent $\gamma(p,q,m)$ characterizing the tail of $P(k)$ for $k >> \kappa(p,q)$ changes continuously with p, q, and m, predicting a range of exponents between 2 and ∞. From this result, we can see that this model offers a more realistic description of various real networks.

6.5.2.2 *Node attractiveness*

Dorogovtsev et al. modified the BA model by specifying that the probability that a new link points to a given k-degree node is proportional to the following characteristic of the node: $A_k = A^{(0)} + k$, called attractiveness (S.N. Dorogovtsev, J.F.F. Mendes, A.N. Samukhin, Structure of growing networks with preferential linking, *Phys. Rev. Lett.*, 85(2000)4633-4636). All nodes are added with some initial attractiveness $A^{(0)}$ but its attractiveness increases later, proportionally to its degree k.

In the particular case of the BA model, $A^{(0)} = m$. The calculations indicate that the degree distribution follows $P(k) \sim k^\gamma$ with $\gamma = 2 + A^{(0)}/m$. Consequently the initial attractiveness does not destroy the scale-free nature of the degree distribution, but only changes the degree exponent. What is more, this exponent value is consistent with the empirical value of the exponent of the distribution of incoming links provided $A^{(0)}/m$ is sufficiently small.

In response to S. Bornholdt and H. Ebel (World Wide Web scaling exponent from Simon's 1955 model, *Phys. Rev. E*, 64(2001), 035104(R)), Dorogovtsev et al. further proposed a more generalized model and showed that this model is essentially the same as the Simon model (S.N. Dorogovtsev, et al., WWW and Internet models from 1955 till our days and the 'popularity is attractive' principle, *Condensed Matter Archive*, 2000, cond-mat/0009090). The only mismatch is in the definitions of the time scales, and the differences in these do not influence the result. The model they considered is a combination of a preferential component (denoted by n_r) and a non-preferential component (denoted by m). The expression for the degree exponent thus is $\gamma = 2 + (n_r + n + B)/m$.

The Bornholdt-Ebel model is the particular case of $n_r = 0$, $n = 1$ and $B = 0$ with probability $\alpha = 1/(1+m)$, while the BA model is in fact the case of $n_r = 0$ and $n + B = m$.

6.5.3 *The idea of random fraction for web growth*

While highly diverse information is added to the Web in an extremely complex and undisciplined manner, there may be certain rules hidden in the Web. Huberman and Adamic determined the distribution of site sizes based on two databases, Alexa and Infoseek, which covered 259,794 and 525,882 sites respectively (B.A. Huberman and L.A. Adamic, Growth dynamics of the World-Wide Web, *Nature*, 401(1999)131). Both data sets displayed a power law over several orders of magnitude. They used a simple stochastic growth model to explain this distribution.

Their assumption is that the day-to-day fluctuation in site size is proportional to the size of the site. One would not be surprised to find that a site with a million pages has lost or gained a few hundred pages on any given day. On the other hand, finding an additional hundred pages within a day on a site with just ten pages would be unusual, to say the least. Thus, they assume that the number n of pages on the site on a given day is equal to the number of pages on that site on the previous day, plus or minus a random fraction of n.

Two additional factors they considered are: first, sites appear at different times and grow at different rates; second, the number of Web sites has been growing exponentially since its inception, which means that there are many more young sites than old ones. When factoring the age of each site into the Web growth process, $P(n)$, the probability of finding a site of size n, obeys a power law. Thus, Huberman and Adamic draw the conclusion that considering sites with a wide range of distributions in growth rates yields the same result: a power law distribution in site size.

6.5.4 *The Krapivsky-Redner model*

Krapivsky et al. studied three models to investigate the evolution rules of the World Wide Web (P.L. Krapivsky and S. Redner, Organization of growing random networks, *Phys. Rev. E*, 63(2001), 066123; P.L. Krapivsky and S. Redner, Rate equation approach for growing networks, *Lecture Notes in Physics*, Springer, 2003; P.L. Krapivsky, et al., Connectivity of growing random networks, *Phys. Rev. Lett.*, 85(2000)4629-4632; P.L. Krapivsky, et al., Degree distributions of growing networks", *Phys. Rev. Lett.*, 86(2001)5401-5404). They quantified the structure of Web growth by the rate equation approach. These models are:

(1) The GN (growth network) model. At each time step, one node is added and immediately linked to an old node according to an attachment probability $A_k \sim k^\gamma$ that depends only on the degree of the "target" node.

(2) The WG (Web graph) model. This extends the GN model and allows link directionality that leads to independent in-degree and out-degree distributions. Network growth occurs by two distinct processes that are meant to mimic how hyperlinks are created in the Web:

① With probability p, a new node is introduced and it immediately links to an earlier target node. The linking probability depends only on the in-degree of the target.

② With probability $q = 1 - p$, a new link is created between already existing nodes. The choices of the originating and target nodes depend on the out-degree of the former and the in-degree of the latter.

(3) The MG (multi-component graph) model. Nodes and links are introduced independently.

① With probability p, a new unlinked node is introduced.

② With probability $q = 1 - p$, a new link is created between existing nodes. As in the WG model, the choices of the issuing and target nodes depend on the out-degree of the former and in-degree of the latter. Step ① allows for the formation of many clusters.

Note that very different behaviors arise for $\gamma < 1$, $\gamma = 1$, and $\gamma > 1$. Krapivsky et al. focus only on the strictly linear kernel $A_k \sim k$.

For a homogeneous GN model, $P(k) \sim k^{-3}$, while for a heterogeneous GN model, where each node is endowed with an intrinsic and permanently defined "attractiveness" η, the attachment rate is modified to be $A_k(\eta) = \eta k$ and the degree distribution is no longer a strict power law, but exhibits a logarithmic correction: $P(k) \sim k^{-(1+m(\eta))} (\ln k)^{-\omega}$.

As for the WG and MG models, the attachment rate $A(i, j)$, defined as the probability that a newly introduced node links to an existing node with i incoming and j outgoing links, depends only on the in-degree of the target node, $A(i, j) = A_i = i + \lambda_{in}$, while the creation rate $C(i_1, j_1 | i_2, j_2)$, defined as the probability of adding a new link from $a(i_1, j_1)$ node to $a(i_2, j_2)$ node, depends only on the out-degree of the issuing node and the in-degree of the target node, $C(i_1, j_1 | i_2, j_2) = C(j_1, i_2)$. The parameters λ_{in} and λ_{out} are stochastic factors. By tuning model parameters to reasonable values, Krapivsky et al. obtain distinct power law forms for the in-degree and out-degree distributions with exponents that are in good agreement with current data for the Web.

6.5.5 *The Simon model*

Simon proposed a class of stochastic models that resulted in a power law distribution function, which was originally described in terms of the underlying process leading to the distribution of words in a piece of text (H.A. Simon, On a class of skew distribution functions, *Biometrika*, 42(1955)425-440; H.A. Simon, T. Van Wormer, Some Monte Carlo estimates of the Yule distribution, *Behavioral Sci.*, 8(1963)203-210).

Simon's stochastic process was essentially a birth process, which had the following algorithm: consider a text that is being written and has reached a length of N words. $f(i)$ denotes the number of different words that have each occurred exactly i times in the text. Thus $f(1)$ denotes the number of different words that have occurred only once. The text is continued by adding another word. With probability p this is a new word, while with probability $1-p$ this word is already present. In this case, Simon assumes that the probability that the $(N+1)$th word has already appeared i times is proportional to $i \times f(i)$, that is, the total number of words that have occurred i times.

As described above, the Simon model was originally proposed without any relation to networks. However, it is possible to formulate the Simon model for networks in terms of nodes and directed links. Bornholdt and Ebel first addressed the problem of WWW growth by sketching a simple stochastic process of adding new nodes and links, based on the Simon model (S. Bornholdt and H. Ebel, World Wide Web scaling exponent from Simon's 1955 model, *Phys. Rev. E*, 64(2001), 035104(R)).

The following steps are iterated:

(1) With probability α, a new node is added with a link pointing to it from a node chosen in an arbitrary way.

(2) Otherwise (with probability $1 - \alpha$) a new link is added into the network between two existing nodes; The issuing node chosen randomly, the target node chosen with probability proportional to its degree, that is, for k-degree nodes, the probability is $p_k = \dfrac{kf(k)}{\sum_i if(i)}$.

Note that this model does not specify where the links originate, so, it does not include modeling out-degree statistics. The Simon model represents a form of the "rich-get-richer" phenomenon, but it does not imply the preferential attachment used in the BA model, whose node-chosen-probability is only proportional to node's degree k. In addition, from the viewpoint of Bornholdt and Ebel, the linking process is in two distinct parts: first, finding a node that has obeyed the rule (2), and second, deciding whether to link this page or not. This process depends, however, on many other variables such as contents and age. In the models discussed above, for example, the BA model, both steps occur at once, and link a page with a probability proportional to its popularity.

6.5.6 *An example from software engineering*

Software architecture graphs can be conceived as complex networks where blocks are software components and links are relationships between software components. Communication between these components drives program functionality. After analyzing the class diagram of the public Java Development Framework 1.2 and a computer game, Valverde et al. discovered that, apart from preferential attachment, local optimization design in a software development process could also lead to scale-free or small-world structures (S. Valverde, et al., Scale-free Networks from Optimal Design, *Europhysics Letters*, 60(2002)512-517, cond-mat/0204344). Scale-free topology originates from a simultaneous minimization of link density and path distance, while small-world structure takes shape only if link length is minimized.

6.5.7 *Other growth models with constraints*

For many real networks, either nodes or links have a finite life time (for example, biological networks) or links have a finite capacity (Internet routers or nodes in the electrical power grid). The concept of finite life span in such models means nodes and links are not only added to the network, but may also be removed from the network.

6.5.7.1 *Decaying networks*

In real networks, for example, the Internet, links are not only added but may break from time to time. That certainly changes the structure of such networks. Dorogovtsev and Mendes proposed a decaying network model with undirected links based on the BA model (S.N. Dorogovtsev and J.F.F. Mendes, Scaling behavior of developing and decaying networks, *Europhys. Lett.*, 52(2000)33-39). The model evolves for the following reasons.

Firstly, it grows as in the BA model, that is, at each time step a new node is added and is undirectedly linked to an old node with a probability proportional to its connectivity k. In addition, a new parallel component of the evolution is introduced—the removal of some old links. At each time step, $|c|$ links between old nodes are removed with equal probability. $c\,(\leq 0)$ may be also non-integer and it can be regarded as the probability for removing links. The resultant degree exponent is $\gamma = 2 + 1/(1+2c)$. The limiting value of c is -1, since the rate of removal of links cannot be higher than the rate of addition of new nodes and links, leading to $\gamma \rightarrow \infty$.

6.5.7.2 *Aging networks*

Dorogovtsev and Mendes studied the growth of a reference network with aging of sites defined in the following way (S.N. Dorogovtsev and J.F.F. Mendes, Evolution of reference networks with aging, *Phys. Rev. E.*, 62(2000)1842-1845). Each new site of the network is linked to some old site with probability proportional (i) to the connectivity of the old site, as in the BA model, and (ii) to power law $\tau^{-\alpha}$, where τ is the age of the old site and the parameter α is in the interval $[0, \infty]$. Rule (ii) expresses the concept of aging in real reference networks as papers or actors will gradually lose their ability to attract attachment.

Both numerical and analytical results show that the structure of the network depends on α. When α increases from $-\infty$ to 0, the exponent γ of the degree distribution ($P(k) \sim k^\gamma$ for large k) grows from 2 to the value for the network without aging, that is, to 3 for the BA model. The following increase of α to 1 makes γ grow to ∞. For $\alpha > 1$, the scaling disappears and $P(k)$ becomes exponential, and the network has a chain structure.

6.5.7.3 *Fitness networks*

In the first version of BA model, older nodes increase their connectivity at the expense of newer ones, as older nodes have more time to acquire links and they gather links at a faster rate than newer nodes. In reality, however, a node's degree and growth depend not only on age, but also on content, advertisement, and so on.

For example, on the WWW, some documents acquire a large number of links in a very short time through good content, successful marketing, and other factors. Bianconi and Barabási attributed this phenomenon to an inherent competition mechanism working with some intrinsic quality of the nodes in the network (G. Bianconi and A.L. Barabási, Bose-Einstein condensation in complex networks, *Phys. Rev. Lett.*, 86(2001)5632-5635; G. Bianconi and A.L. Barabási, Competition and multiscaling in evolving networks, *Europhys. Lett.*, 54(2001)436-442). To address this phenomenon, they offered a fitness model, in which nodes have differing ability (fitness) to compete for links. Each node i is endowed with a fitness and unchanged factor η_k since its inception. Initially, there are few nodes in the network. At each step, a new node k is added with fitness η_k, where η is chosen from the distribution $\rho(\eta)$. Each node k is linked to m already existing nodes in the network. The probability of linking to a node i is proportional to the degree and the fitness of node i,

$$\Pi_i = \frac{\eta_i k_i}{\sum_j \eta_j k_j}$$

This combines preferential attachment with the fitness factor, that is, even a relatively new node with few links can acquire links at a high rate if it has high fitness. The continuum theory predicts 'the degree distribution is

$$P(k) \sim \frac{k^{-C-1}}{\ln(k)},$$

(where C is a constant), that is, a power law with a logarithmic correction. While the fitness model allows for recently added nodes with high fitness to take a central role in the network topology, the price paid is a large number of free parameters in the model.

6.5.7.4 *Age or cost constrained networks*

Amaral et al. studied a variety of real world networks and divided them into three classes: scale-free networks, broad-scale networks and single-scale networks (L.A.N. Amaral, et al., Classes of Small-World Networks, *Proceedings of the National Academy of Sciences*, 97(2000)11149-11152).

They further attributed the source of this classification to certain constraints on preferential attachment that resulted in free scale behavior and added two factors to the model: aging of the nodes and imposing a cost on the adding of links to the nodes or on increasing the link capacity of a node.

In the movie actor network, for example, every actor's career lasts a limited time, which implies that in such a network, no matter how many links a node has received, sooner or later it will receive no new links at all. An example of the second factor is in the network of world airports. Constrained in space and time, airports must limit the number of landings or departures per hour and the number of passengers in transit. Therefore, the physical cost of adding a link (flight) and the limited capacity of a node (airport) will limit the number of possible links attaching to a given node.

Amaral et al. then consider a network in which nodes have two states: active and inactive, with inactive nodes refusing new links. All nodes are initially active but become inactive. Two factors were considered to lead to inactivity:

(1) The time a node may remain active decays exponentially, which is called aging.
(2) A node becomes inactive when it reaches a maximum number of links, which is called cost.

There may have certain critical values of degree k which distinguish the three classes of networks mentioned above. Near the critical point k, the degree distribution follows a power law. A little away from the critical point, the distribution becomes broad in scale. Far from the critical point, the distribution becomes singular in scale.

6.6 Modeling Actual Scale-Free Networks

The large and rapidly increasing number of Web pages, the use of HTML, the characteristics of Web structure and the mode of Web information services have made it hard to support effective, efficient and intelligent services. To get past the shortcomings of the Web, scientists are working towards a future interconnection environment (T. Berners-Lee, et al., Semantic Web, *Scientific American*, 284 (5)(2001)34-43; I. Foster, et al., Grid Services for Distributed System Integration, *Computer*, 35(2002)37-46).

Computer scientists are exploring the fundamental issues of the future interconnection environment. For example, what ideal computing model goes beyond the scope of the client/server, Grid and peer-to-peer computing models? And, what resource organization model gives the advantages of both autonomy and normalization?

One vision of the future interconnection environment is described as a platform-independent *Virtual Grid* environment of requirements, roles and resources. With machine-understandable semantics, resources can dynamically cluster and fuse to provide on-demand and appropriate services by understanding the requirements and functions of each other. Services based on a uniform resource model can access all resources through a single semantic entry point. Through virtual roles, a resource can intelligently help people accomplish complex tasks and solve problems by participating in versatile resource flow cycles to use appropriate knowledge, information, and computing resources (H. Zhuge, Semantics, Resource and Grid, *Future Generation Computer Systems*, 20(1)(2004)1-5).

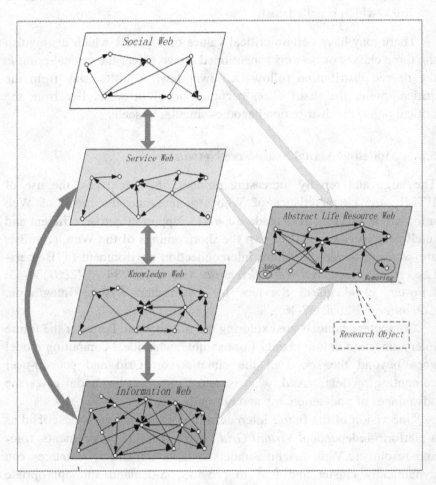

Fig. 6.6 A four-layer network architecture.

The future interconnection environment needs networks of diverse design to cooperate in supporting complex and intelligent applications. Fig. 6.6 depicts a four-layer network architecture, where the Social Web, Service Web, Knowledge Web and Information Web work in cooperation. The research objective here is to abstract the four networks: semantically rich and living networks of "live" resource nodes with semantic links between the nodes. Every node has a life span from birth (addition to the network) to death (removal from the network). Nodes can represent versatile resources including live sub-networks. Investigating the rules of evolution of such a network will reveal useful implications for developing the future interconnection environment.

A node's life is determined by the number of links to it. When all the links to a node have been deleted it "dies" because it is can no longer be reached from other nodes, and hence it can itself be removed from the network.

A network with add and delete operations can better support a *competitive environment*: the more robust a node (having many more links with its environment), the more likely it is to survive; conversely, the less robust, the more likely it is to be deleted. By investigating the abstract life network, we can better predict the distributions of other special Webs as shown in Fig. 6.6, and also provide evidence for evaluating and selecting the experimental data set to be used to simulate the future interconnection environment.

6.6.1 *An urn transfer model for a live scale-free network*

In our model, the inter-resource semantic relationships are reflected by a variety of semantic links such as *cause-effect links*, *implication links*, *subtype links*, *similar-to links*, *instance links*, *sequential links*, and *reference links* (H. Zhuge, Active e-document framework ADF: model and tool, *Information & Management*, 41(1)(2003)87-97). We can consider the distribution of these different types of semantic link separately but in a similar way. The differences between the seven types of link lie in the values of their parameters. We can use an asymptotic formula to describe their respective distributions.

In our urn transfer model, urns contain balls with pins attached to them. In representing the semantic link network, urns stand for sets of resource nodes with the same number of semantic links, their balls standing for resource nodes, and their pins standing for semantic links. We assume a countable number of urns: urn_k ($k = 0, 1, 2, 3, ...$), where each ball in urn_k has k pins attached to it.

Initially, at time step $t = 0$, all the urns are empty except urn_0 which has one ball in it. Let $F_k(t)$ be the number of balls in urn_k at time step t, thus $F_0(0) = 1$, $F_k(0) = 0$, $k \neq 0$, and let p, p' and α be parameters, with $0 < p < 1$, $0 < p' < 1/2$ and $\alpha > 0$. Note that p is the expectation of adding a new ball into urn_0 each time step, p' is the delete factor and α is the non-preferential factor. Then, at each time step one of following behaviors may occur in this model: add a new ball having no pins attached into urn_0 or add/remove one pin to/from a selected ball, then transfer the ball into the urn containing balls with its number of pins. To be more precise, a new ball is added to urn_0 with the probability:

$$p_{i+1} = 1 - \frac{(1-p)\sum_{k=0}^{t}(k+\alpha)F_k(t)}{t[(1-p)(1-2p')+\alpha p]+\alpha(1-p)}, \text{ where } 0 \leq p_{i+1} \leq 1 \tag{6.1}$$

and urn_k being chosen with the following probability:

$$\frac{(1-p)(k+\alpha)F_k(t)}{t[(1-p)(1-2p')+\alpha p]+\alpha(1-p)} \tag{6.2}$$

Note that the denominator is the expected value of $\sum_{k=1}^{t}(k+\alpha)F_k(t)$. Thus, one ball from urn_k is transferred to urn_{k-1} (that is to say, one pin is removed from the ball) with probability p, $k > 0$; or transferred to urn_{k+1} (one pin is added) with probability $1-p$, that is,

$$P_{transdown} = \frac{p'(1-p)(k+\alpha)F_k(t)}{t[(1-p)(1-2p')+\alpha p]+\alpha(1-p)} \text{ and}$$

$$p_{tran\,sup} = \frac{(1-p')(1-p)(k+\alpha)F_k(t)}{t[(1-p)(1-2p')+\alpha p]+\alpha(1-p)} \quad (6.3)$$

In the boundary case, $k=0$, one ball is either removed from the urn_0 with probability $p_{transdown}$ or transferred to urn_1 with probability $p_{tran\,sup}$ after attaching a pin to it.

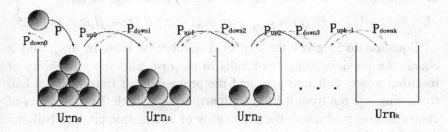

Fig. 6.6.1 The urn-transfer process.

To show this more clearly, we illustrate the urn transfer process in Fig. 6.6.1. An arrow denotes a ball being chosen and transferred, with the probability shown alongside. The placement of the arrow shows the urns involved. Solid arrows denote pins or balls being added, while dashed arrows denote pins or balls being removed. For example, the figure shows the number of balls in urn_1 changing with both a probability of increase (that is, $p_{tran\,sup0} + p_{transdown2}$), and a probability of decrease (that is, $p_{tran\,sup1} + p_{transdown1}$).

For $k>0$, we have the following expected value of $F_k(t+1)$ at time step t.

$$E_t(F_k(t+1)) = F_k(t) + \frac{(1-p')(1-p)(k-1+\alpha)}{t[(1-p)(1-2p')+\alpha p]+\alpha(1-p)}F_{k-1}(t)$$

$$- \frac{(1-p)(k+\alpha)}{t[(1-p)(1-2p')+\alpha p]+\alpha(1-p)}F_k(t)$$

$$= F_k(t) + \beta_t((1-p')(k-1+\alpha)F_{k-1}(t)$$

$$+ p'(k+1+\alpha)F_{k+1}(t) - (k+\alpha)F_k(t)) \tag{6.4}$$

where $\beta_t = (1-p)\big/\big[t((1-p)(1-2p') + \alpha p) + \alpha(1-p)\big]$. Equation (6.4) gives the expected number of balls in urn_k ($k>0$) as the previous number of balls in that urn plus the probability of increasing the number of balls in urn_k. This is equal to the probability of choosing urn_{k-1} to add a pin plus that of choosing urn_{k+1} to remove one pin with the probability of choosing urn_k subtracted. In the boundary case $k=0$, we have

$$E_t(F_0(t+1)) = F_0(t) + p_{t+1} + p'\beta_t(1+\alpha)F_1(t) - \beta_t\alpha F_0(t) \tag{6.5}$$

Equation (6.5) gives the expected number of balls in urn_0, and it equals the previous number of balls in the urn_0 plus the probability of inserting a new ball into urn_0 and the probability of transferring a ball (removing one pin from it first) from urn_1 to urn_0, with the probability of choosing urn_0 subtracted: the probability of adding one pin to a ball and that of deleting one ball in urn_0.

$$\text{Let} \quad \beta = \frac{1-p}{(1-p)(1-2p') + \alpha p},$$

We have $t\beta_t \approx \beta$ for large t. Indeed, for $t \geq 1$, $\beta - t\beta_t = \alpha\beta\beta_t$.

We prove that $E(F_k(t))/t$ tends to a limit f_k as t tends to infinity in section 6.6.5. As a direct result of this, $\beta_t E(F_k(t))$ tends to βf_k as t tends to infinity. Moreover, if the convergence is fast enough, $E(F_k(t+1) - E(F_k(t))$ will tend to f_k as t tends to infinity, and we can use these facts to obtain the value of f_k. Let

$$E(F_k(t)) = t(f_k + \varepsilon_{k,t}) \tag{6.6}$$

where $\varepsilon_{k,t}$ tends to zero as t tends to infinity. So, by letting t tend to infinity, we can get the following from equation (6.4):

$$f_k = \beta[(1-p')(k-1+\alpha)f_{k-1} + p'(k+1+\alpha)f_{k+1} - (k+\alpha)f_k] \tag{6.7}$$

and the following equation from equation (6.5):

$$f_0 = p + \beta p'(1+\alpha)f_1 - \beta\alpha f_0 \tag{6.8}$$

by virtue of $E(p_t) = p$. But it is difficult to solve equation (6.7) to obtain a perfect analytic expression directly without some simplification.

Because p' as a parameter should generally be small in comparison with $1-p'$, we could make an approximation as follows:

$$f_k \approx \beta[(1-p')(k-1+\alpha)f_{k-1} - (k+\alpha)f_k], \quad f_0 \approx p - \beta\alpha f_0$$

Consequently

$$f_k \approx \frac{\beta(1-p')(k-1+\alpha)f_{k-1}}{1+\beta(k+\alpha)}, \quad f_0 \approx \frac{p}{1+\alpha\beta}.$$

Recursively we obtain:

$$f_k \approx (1-p')^k \frac{p}{1+\alpha\beta} \times \frac{\Gamma(k+\alpha)\Gamma((1+\beta+\alpha\beta)/\beta)}{\Gamma(\alpha)\Gamma((1+\beta+\alpha\beta+k\beta)/\beta)}$$

$$= (1-p')^k \frac{p\Gamma(k+\alpha)\Gamma(\rho+\alpha+1)}{(1+\alpha\beta)\Gamma(\alpha)\Gamma(k+1+\rho+\alpha)} \tag{6.9}$$

where Γ is the Gamma function and $\rho = 1/\beta$. Through the asymptotic behavior of the Gamma function when x is large, we have:

$$\Gamma(x) = \sqrt{2\pi}x^{x-1/2}e^{-x+u(x)} \tag{6.10}$$

$$u(x) = \sum_{n=0}^{\infty}(x+n+1/2)\ln(1+\frac{1}{x+n}) - 1 = \frac{\theta}{12x}, \quad 0 < \theta < 1$$

By virtue of (6.10), equation (6.9) can be turned into:

$$f_k \approx \frac{p}{1+\alpha\beta}(1-p')^k \times$$

$$\frac{\Gamma(\rho+\alpha+1)(k+\alpha)^{k+\alpha-0.5}e^{-(k+\alpha)+u(k+\alpha)}}{\Gamma(\alpha)(k+1+p+\alpha)^{(k+1+\rho+\alpha)-0.5}e^{-(k+1+\rho+\alpha)+u(k+1+\rho+\alpha)}}$$

By only retaining the most influential part of the approximating equation above, we can get the following asymptotic formula:

$$f_k \sim Ck^{-(1+\rho)}(1-p')^k \tag{6.11}$$

where C is a constant and ~ stands for asymptosis. Thus we can use f_k, a function of k with p, α and p' as parameters, to describe the distribution of resource nodes with the same number of semantic links.

Obviously, we can also conclude that $f_k > f_{k+1}$, that is, asymptotically there are more balls in urn_k than that in urn_{k+1}. Without the deletion of semantic links, that is, when $p=0$, the extended model reduces to the stochastic model proposed in (M. Levene, et al. A stochastic model for the evolution of the Web, *Computer Networks*, 39(2002)277-287). Thus when $\alpha=0$ and $p'=0$ the extended model reduces to Simon's original model.

6.6.2 *A directed evolving graph for a live scale-free network*

Now we further pursue our research objective by using a different approach to the urn transfer model. We employ the rate equation method to describe Web growth in light of the evolution characteristic. At each time step, the state of the network is given by a directed evolving graph $G = (N, E)$, where N is the node set and E is the link set. For simplicity, we use the following notations:

$F_{i,j}(t)$: the expected number of nodes with i incoming semantic links (that is, in-degree) and j outgoing semantic links (that is, out-degree) at time step t;

$F(t)$: the expected total number of nodes in the graph at time step t;

$I(t)$ and $J(t)$: the expected in-degree and out-degree of the entire graph at time step t respectively;

α_{in} and α_{out}: the non-preferential factors for in-degree and out-degree respectively.

At each time step of the evolution, one of two kinds of operation for nodes and links may occur:

(1) with probability p, a new unlinked node is introduced,
(2) with probability $(1-p)(1-p'')$, a node is chosen to receive a new link, and with probability $(1-p)p'$, a node is chosen to have an existing link deleted.

In addition, the probability of link addition/deletion from an issuing node to a target node is proportional to $(k+\alpha)$, which is a combination of a preferential component k and a non-preferential component α. For the issuing node, k stands for its out-degree and α stands for α_{out}, while for the target node, k stands for its in-degree and α stands for α_{in}.

Since the long-term behavior is most significant, we look only at the asymptotic regime ($t \to \infty$) where the initial condition is irrelevant. Therefore, the expected total number of nodes $F(t) = \sum F_k(t) = pt$.

Further, the expectation of the total number of incoming/outgoing links $E(\sum kF_k(t)) = (1-p)(1-p')t - (1-p)p't = (1-p)(1-2p')t$.

Consequently,

$$E\left(\sum_k (k+\alpha)F_k(t) \right) = \left[(1-p)(1-2p') + \alpha p \right] t.$$

According to the rules of evolution outlined above, the rate equation for the joint degree distribution $F_{i,j}(t)$ is

$$\frac{dF_{i,j}}{dt} = (1-p')(1-p)\frac{(i-1+\alpha_{in})F_{i-1,j} - (i+\alpha_{in})F_{i,j}}{\left[(1-p)(1-2p') + \alpha_{in}p \right]t}$$

$$+ (1-p')(1-p)\frac{(j-1+\alpha_{out})F_{i,j-1} - (j+\alpha_{out})F_{i,j}}{\left[(1-p)(1-2p') + \alpha_{out}p \right]t}$$

$$+ p'(1-p)\frac{(i+1+\alpha_{in})F_{i+1,j} - (i+\alpha_{in})F_{i,j}}{\left[(1-p)(1-2p') + \alpha_{in}p \right]t}$$

$$+ p'(1-p)\frac{(j+1+\alpha_{out})F_{i,j+1} - (j+\alpha_{out})F_{i,j}}{\left[(1-p)(1-2p') + \alpha_{out}p \right]t} + p\delta_{i,0}\delta_{j,0} \qquad (6.12)$$

The first group of terms on the right side relates to the changes in the in-degree of target nodes by creation of a new link between already existing nodes (probability $1-p'$). For instance, the creation of a new link to a node with in-degree $i-1$ leads to a gain in the number of i in-degree nodes. This occurs with rate $(1-p')(1-p)(i-1+\alpha_{in})F_{i-1}$, divided by the appropriate normalization factor $\Sigma_{i,j}(i+\alpha_{in})F_i(t) = i + \alpha_{in}F$.

The second group of terms describes the same cases for out-degree changes, but the normalization factor is replaced by $\Sigma_{i,j}(j + \alpha_{out}) F_j(t) = i + \alpha_{out} F$.

The third and fourth groups relate to deletion processes for in- and out-degrees respectively. Hence, the prefixed factor is $p'(1-p)$. The last term relates to the contribution of new nodes. In the boundary case for the isolated nodes in the network described here, that is, $F_{0,0}$, the link deletion behavior might be regarded as isolated nodes being removed from the network.

For clarity, we resolve the joint distribution $F_{i,j}(t)$ straightforwardly into separate in-degree and out-degree distributions by means of summing i and j respectively:

$$\sum_j \frac{dF_{i,j}}{dt} = \frac{dI_i}{dt}, \ \sum_i \frac{dF_{i,j}}{dt} = \frac{dO_j}{dt}$$

Thus, the in-degree distribution $I_i(t)$ satisfies:

$$\frac{dI_i}{dt} = (1-p')(1-p)\frac{(i-1+\alpha_{in})I_{i-1} - (i+\alpha_{in})I_i}{\left[(1-p)(1-2p') + \alpha_{in}p\right]t}$$
$$+ p'(1-p)\frac{(i+1+\alpha_{in})I_{i+1} - (i+\alpha_{in})I_i}{\left[(1-p)(1-2p') + \alpha_{in}p\right]t} + p\delta_{i,0}$$

And the out-degree distribution $O_j(t)$ satisfies:

$$\frac{dO_j}{dt} = (1-p')(1-p)\frac{(j-1+\alpha_{out})O_j - (j+\alpha_{out})O_j}{\left[(1-p)(1-2p') + \alpha_{out}p\right]t}$$
$$+ p'(1-p)\frac{(j+1+\alpha_{out})O_{j+1} - (i+\alpha_{out})O_j}{\left[(1-p)(1-2p') + \alpha_{out}p\right]t} + p\delta_{j,0}$$

Therefore, the in- and out-degree distributions evolve in the same manner except for the difference between the factors α_{in} and α_{out}, which reflects the fact that the governing rules of this model are symmetric. Hence it is safe to say that both the incoming and outgoing links share the same evolutionary trend in their degree distribution and the only difference lies in the values of non-preferential factors. In what follows, we therefore employ α to represent α_{in} or α_{out} and F_k to represent I_i or O_j. Thus we only need to consider $F_k(t)$.

$$\frac{dF_k}{dt} = (1-p')(1-p)\frac{(k-1+\alpha)F_{k-1}}{\left[(1-p)(1-2p')+\alpha p\right]t}$$

$$+p'(1-p)\frac{(k+1+\alpha)F_{k+1}}{\left[(1-p)(1-2p')+\alpha p\right]t}$$

$$-(1-p)\frac{(k+\alpha)F_k}{\left[(1-p)(1-2p')+\alpha p\right]t} + p\delta_{k,0} \tag{6.13}$$

Although equation (6.13) is an exact differential equation for the generating function of degree distribution $F_k(t)$, it is quite difficult to solve it exactly. Using measures like those adopted in simplifying the urn transfer model, we simplify equation (6.13) as follows:

$$\frac{dF_0}{dt} = p - \frac{(1-p)\alpha F_0}{\left[(1-p)(1-2p')+\alpha p\right]t}$$

$$\frac{dF_k}{dt} = \frac{(1-p')(1-p)(k-1+\alpha)F_{k-1}-(1-p)(k+\alpha)F_k}{\left[(1-p)(1-2p')+\alpha p\right]t} \tag{6.14}$$

The exact solution to equation (6.14) can be obtained.

$$F_0(t) = \frac{p\left[(1-p)(1-2p')+\alpha p\right]}{\left[(1-p)(1-2p')+\alpha\right]}t + C_0$$

If $F_0(0) = 0$, then $C_0 = 0$. As a result, the solution to the above recursion may be expressed in terms of the following ratios of gamma functions:

$$F_k = (1-p')^k F_0 \frac{\Gamma(k+\alpha)\Gamma\left(\alpha/(1-p) + 2(1-p')\right)}{\Gamma\left(k + \alpha/(1-p) + 2(1-p')\right)\Gamma(\alpha)} \qquad (6.15)$$

with

$$F_0(t) = \frac{p\left[(1-p)(1-2p') + \alpha p\right]}{\left[(1-p)(1-2p') + \alpha\right]} t$$

It is clear from equation (6.15) that we can substitute $F_k(t)$ for $f_k * t$, that is $F_k = f_k * t$. We then get the same asymptotic formula as that of the urn transfer model:

$$f \sim Ck^{-(1+\rho)}(1-p')^k.$$

which resembles a power law.

We now compare the two modeling measures.

Firstly, they are based on different mechanisms. In the urn transfer model, we use operations on balls and pins in each urn to stand for the evolution, while the directed evolving graph model more clearly reflects the addition and removal of nodes and links. In this sense, the urn transfer model is more abstract.

Secondly, in the urn transfer model, pins denote either incoming links or outgoing links but don't distinguish between them. In fact, the main difference between the two kinds of link lies in the values of the parameters. In the directed evolving graph, however, the addition or deletion of a link can have an effect on both the incoming and outgoing link distributions.

6.6.3 *Experiments and analysis*

For the purpose of validating the feasibility of our models, we designed and ran a simulation program with 10^6 time steps to mimic the dynamic evolution. Due to the similarity of the results between the urn transfer model and the directed evolving graph model, we need consider only the latter. The values of the parameters are based on the empirical data from the current hyperlink Web because of course data from the future interconnection environment is not available. We chose an initial condition for the evolving graph in which there is only a single node, although the asymptotic long-term behavior does not depend on this initial condition.

Furthermore, an accurate solution for the original equation (6.13) can be iteratively produced using mathematical tools. Note that the only difference between in- and out-degree distributions lies in the different values for α, which will be illustrated in the figures below.

Fig. 6.6.3.1 (a) shows the in-degree distribution on a double logarithmic scale as derived from the *Web graph* model (P.L. Krapivsky and S. Redner, A statistical physics perspective on Web growth, *Computer Networks*, 39(2002)261-276) with $p = 0.125$, $\alpha = 0.75$ and $p' = 0.01$. Points are results from numerical simulations and the solid lines are precise results from equation (6.13). The two curves are basically consistent. Fig. 6.6.3.1 (b) is an amplified illustration, which is the same as (a) except for being on a linear scale.

We need further to check the validity of our revision of equation (6.13). Fig. 6.6.3.2 compares equations (6.13) and (6.15) for in-degree distribution. The x coordinates stand for the number of incoming links, that is, in-degree, and y coordinates for the number of nodes that have the same in-degree. The solid lines are the results from iteration, that is, equation (6.13), while the dotted ones are for the revised version, that is, equation (6.15). In Fig. 6.6.3.2 (a), $p = 0.125$, $\alpha = 0.75$ and $p' = 0.1$, and for clarity a portion of the graph is shown as a magnified inset. Note that the insets in subsequent figures are of a similar nature. Fig. 6.6.3.2 (b) is for $p = 0.125$, $\alpha = 0.75$ and $p' = 0.2$. It becomes clear that the smaller the value of link deleting factor p', the more similar the two curves.

As far as outgoing links are concerned, Fig. 6.6.3.3 shows the out-degree distribution for $p = 0.125$, $\alpha = 3.55$ and $p' = 0.01$ on both a double logarithmic scale (a) and a linear scale (b), which evolves in a fashion similar to the in-degree distribution.

Again, we compare equation (6.13) and equation (6.15) for out-degree distribution in Fig. 6.6.3.4, where the x coordinates stand for the number of outgoing links, that is, out-degree, and y coordinates for the number of nodes with the same out-degree. Fig. 6.6.3.4 (a) is for $p = 0.125$, $\alpha = 3.55$ and $p' = 0.1$, while Fig. 6.6.3.4 (b) is for $p = 0.125$,

$\alpha = 3.55$ and $p' = 0.2$. Comparing these, we arrive at the same conclusion as for the in-degree distribution.

From all these comparisons we can therefore draw a conclusion: the evolution of the in- and out-degree distributions of our model is in agreement with the revised analytical solution. The discrepancy between the numerical simulations and the precise iterations may partly be a result of inadequate numbers of iterations. Thus running the simulations for a much larger number of iterations might give more satisfying results.

In the following, we make a further comparison between the current hyperlink distribution in the Web graph model and the semantic link distribution in our model. Fig. 6.6.3.5 (a) shows the in-degree distribution, while Fig. 6.6.3.5 (b) illustrates the out-degree distribution. We can clearly see the offset between the current Web model and our model. The key reason may be both node and link removal behaviors in our model. Obviously, the bigger the deletion value is, the larger the offset. In addition, the value of the slope for our model is always smaller in magnitude than that of the current hyperlink Web.

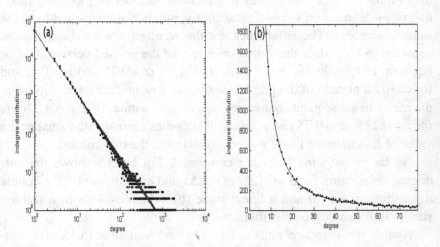

Fig. 6.6.3.1 In-degree distribution for simulation and precise iteration.

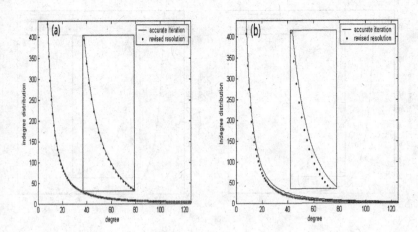

Fig. 6.6.3.2 In-degree distributions for precise iteration and revised analytical resolution.

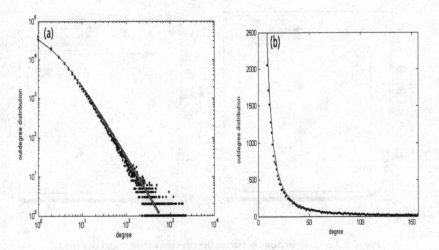

Fig. 6.6.3.3 Out-degree distribution for simulation and accurate iteration.

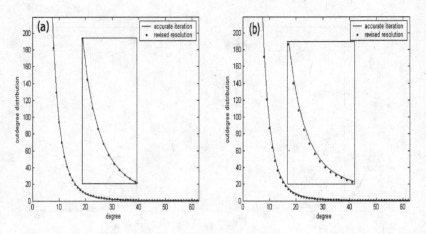

Fig. 6.6.3.4 Out-degree distribution for precise iteration and revised analytical resolution.

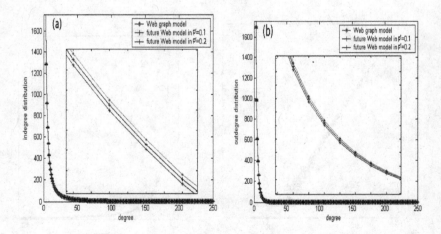

Fig. 6.6.3.5 Comparisons between the previous model and our model.

6.6.4 *Further consideration and comparisons*

In the live scale-free network, resource nodes may be deleted directly rather than by deleting links step by step. That means that not only isolated nodes may be deleted. In this case, we employ the following urn transfer model.

Using the same terms as in section 6.6.1, we can describe the model in this way: while at stage $k+1$ of the stochastic process for $k \geq 1$, for urn_i, $i > 0$, one of two kinds of operation may be carried out at each time step: add one pin to a selected ball with probability $p_{transup}$, then transfer the ball into urn_{i+1}, or delete the selected ball with probability $p_{transdown}$ rather than transferring it to urn_{i-1}; in the limiting case, one more operation is performed: add a new ball having no pin attached into urn_0 with probability p_{k+1}. Thence we get the expected value of $F_i(k+1)$ at stage k for $i > 0$ in the following equation:

$$E_k(F_i(k+1)) = F_i(k) + \beta_k((1-p')(i-1+\alpha)F_{i-1}(k) - (i+\alpha)F_i(k)) \quad (6.16)$$

In the boundary case, we have

$$E_k(F_0(k+1)) = F_0(k) + p_{k+1} - \beta_k \alpha F_0(k) \quad (6.17)$$

Using a method similar to that of section 6.6.1, we can derive the following equation from equation (6.16) as k tends to infinity

$$f_i = \beta[(1-p')(i-1+\alpha)f_{i-1} - (i+\alpha)f_i] \quad (6.18)$$

and from equation (6.13) as k tends to infinity we derive:

$$f_0 = p - \beta \alpha f_0 \quad (6.19)$$

Making use of the characteristic of the Gamma function as shown in equation (6.10), we can solve equation (6.18) to obtain an asymptotic formula with equation (6.19) as an initial condition.

$$f_i \sim C i^{-(1+\rho)}(1-p')^i$$

which could also be used to describe the distribution of future resource nodes with the same number of incoming or outgoing links.

Though the asymptotic formula is the same as the formula deduced in section 6.6.1, the delete probability in this urn transfer strategy could be large. In contrast, the asymptotic formula in section 2 could apply only when the delete probability p' is small compared to $1-p'$.

We can also compare the link distributions between the empirical data (denoted by *previous*) of the current hyperlink Web and the asymptotic formula (denoted by *revised*) derived from our growth model using the delete mechanism proposed in this section when the delete probability is relatively large. We show the comparison in Fig. 6.6.4.1.

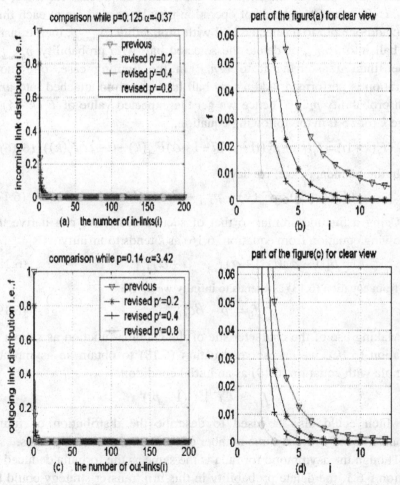

Fig. 6.6.4.1 Distributions of the previous model and our model with new delete mechanism.

Another possibility for the live scale-free network is to control the rich/poor gap (this term is employed to describe the gap between nodes with very different numbers of links), since the preferential attachment mechanism will certainly lead to the 'rich get richer' phenomenon. Here we attempt a simulation as follows: if the number of links coming in to a node reaches a certain value, no further incoming links will be attached to it. As expected, the distribution as in Fig. 6.6.4.2 no longer obeys a power law, and its tail in fact rises a little. This observation indicates that "wealth" has been shared among relatively rich nodes.

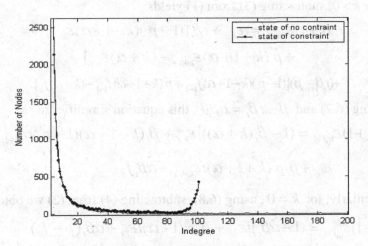

Fig. 6.6.4.2 Power law changes with added constraints.

6.6.5 *Proof of the proposition*

Proposition. *For all* $k \geq 0$, $\lim_{t \to \infty} E(F_k(t))/t = f_k$

Proof. Using (6.6) to rewrite (6.4) and (6.5), we obtain: for $k > 0$,

$$(t+1)(f_k + \varepsilon_{k,t+1}) = t(f_k + \varepsilon_{k,t}) + t\beta_t[(1-p')(k-1+\alpha)(f_{k-1} + \varepsilon_{k-1,t})$$
$$+ p'(k+1+\alpha)(f_{k+1} + \varepsilon_{k+1,t}) - (k+\alpha)(f_k + \varepsilon_{k,t})], \tag{1}$$

and for $k = 0$,

$$(t+1)(f_0 + \varepsilon_{0,t+1}) = t(f_0 + \varepsilon_{0,t}) + p - t\beta_t\alpha(f_0 + \varepsilon_{0,t})$$

$$+t\beta_t p^{'}(1+\alpha)(f_1 + \varepsilon_{1,t}), \tag{2}$$

Equations (6.7) and (6.8) may be written in a similar form as

$$(t+1)f_k = tf_k + \beta(1-p^{'})(k-1+\alpha)f_{k-1}$$

$$+\beta p^{'}(k+1+\alpha)f_{k+1} - \beta(k+\alpha)f_k, \tag{3}$$

and $(t+1)f_0 = tf_0 + p - \beta\alpha f_0 + \beta p^{'}(1+\alpha)f_1,$ $\qquad$ (4)

For $k > 0$, subtracting (3) from (1) yields:

$$(t+1)\varepsilon_{k,t+1} = t\varepsilon_{k,t} + t\beta_t[(1-p^{'})(k-1+\alpha)\varepsilon_{k-1,t}$$

$$+p^{'}(k+1+\alpha)\varepsilon_{k+1,t} - (k+\alpha)\varepsilon_{k,t}]$$

$$+(t\beta_t-\beta)[(1-p^{'})(k-1+\alpha)f_{k-1}+p^{'}(k+1+\alpha)f_{k+1}-(k+\alpha)f_k]$$

using (6.7) and $\beta - t\beta_t = \alpha\beta\beta_t$, this equation simplifies to

$$(t+1)\varepsilon_{k,t+1} = (1-\beta_t(k+\alpha))t\varepsilon_{k,t} + \beta_t(k-1+\alpha)(1-p^{'})t\varepsilon_{k-1,t}$$

$$+\beta_t p^{'}(k+1+\alpha)t\varepsilon_{k+1,t} - \alpha\beta_t f_k \tag{5}$$

Similarly, for $k = 0$, using (6.8), subtracting (4) from (2) we obtain:

$$(t+1)\varepsilon_{0,t+1} = (1-\alpha\beta_t)t\varepsilon_{0,t} + \beta_t p^{'}(1+\alpha)t\varepsilon_{1,t} + \alpha\beta_t(p-f_0) \tag{6}$$

From (5), by virtue of $0 < \beta_t < 1/(t/C_0 + \alpha)$ for $t \geq 1$ and
$0 < \beta < C_0$ where C_0 is a constant for definite parameters, and the fact
that $f_k < 1$, $0 \leq p^{'} < 1/2$, $0 < p < 1$ and $\alpha > 0$, we have: for $0 < k \leq t$,
(where t may tends to infinity and k should have the upper bound in
reality)

$$(t+1)|\varepsilon_{k,t+1}| \leq (1-\beta_t(k+\alpha))t|\varepsilon_{k,t}| + \beta_t(1-p')(k-1+\alpha)t|\varepsilon_{k-1,t}|$$

$$+\beta_t p'(k+1+\alpha)t|\varepsilon_{k+1,t}| + \alpha\beta_t \tag{7}$$

for $k = 0$, from (6) we have:

$$(t+1)|\varepsilon_{0,t+1}| \leq (1-\alpha\beta_t)t|\varepsilon_{0,t}| + \beta_t p'(1+\alpha)t|\varepsilon_{1,t}| + \alpha\beta_t(p-f_0) \tag{8}$$

We now define $\delta_t = \max_{k\geq 0}|\varepsilon_{k,t}| = \max_{0\leq k\leq t+1}|\varepsilon_{k,t}|$ (9)

Let $C = \max\left\{\dfrac{\alpha}{(\alpha-p'(1+\alpha))(1+\alpha\beta)}, \dfrac{\alpha}{1-2p'}, 1\right\}$ (In reality, the first

element will be positive), we will show by induction on t that

$$t\delta_t \leq C \tag{10}$$

From (9) and (6.6), we obtain that $\delta_1 = \max\{1-f_1, f_2\} < 1$, so (10) holds for $t = 1$.

Now we assume that (10) holds for some $t \geq 1$, so for $k = 0$, from (8) we get

$$(t+1)|\varepsilon_{0,t+1}| \leq (1-\alpha\beta_t)C_1 + \beta_t p'(1+\alpha)C_1 + \alpha\beta_t(p-f_0)$$

$$\leq (1-\alpha\beta_t)C_1 + \beta_t p'(1+\alpha)C_1 + \alpha\beta_t p(1-\dfrac{1}{1+\alpha\beta})$$

(since $f_0 > p/(1+\alpha\beta)$)

$$\leq C_1 \quad \text{where } C_1 = \dfrac{\alpha}{(\alpha-p'(1+\alpha))(1+\alpha\beta)}.$$

For $0 < k \leq t$, from (7) we obtain:

$$(t+1)|\varepsilon_{k,t+1}| \leq (1-\beta_t(k+\alpha))C_2 + \beta_t(1-p')(k-1+\alpha)C_2$$

$$+ \beta_t p'(k+1+\alpha)C_2 + \alpha\beta_t$$

$$\leq (1-(1-2p')\beta_t)C_2 + \alpha\beta_t$$

$$\leq C_2 \quad \text{where } C_2 = \dfrac{\alpha}{1-2p'}.$$

Therefore, $(t+1)\delta_{t+1} \leq C$.

In conclusion, as t tends to infinity, δ_t tends to 0 for all k. So far, we have proved that

$$\lim_{t \to \infty} E(F_k(t))/t = f_k, \text{ for } k \geq 0.$$

6.7 Summary and Implications

Studies of real-world complex networks relate to the Internet, the World Wide Web, social networks, collaboration networks, citation networks, and a variety of biological networks. Statistical data revealed that most networks are scale-free. Models have been proposed to explain how such networks organize themselves and what the expected effects of the resulting structure will be. R. Albert and A.L. Barabási have given an extensive pedagogical review from physics literature. They have proved the simplicity and the power of statistical physics for characterizing evolving networks. ("Statistical mechanism of complex networks", *Reviews of Modern Physics*, 74(2002)48-94). Another review of models of growing networks that uncovered some generic topological and dynamical principles was "Evolution of networks" (S.N. Dorogovtsev and J.F.F. Mendes, *Advances in Physics,* 51(2002)1079-1187).

Starting with a brief description of these representative networks, we have provided a broader view of network growth. The large discrepancy between scale-free networks and random networks is a big challenge to classical graph theory.The preferential attachment mechanism (preferential linking to nodes with a higher number of links) indeed produces a desired property: the scale-free structure of real networks. However, the models created by it can be applied to real networks only at a macroscopic and qualitative level. These simple models are far from reality. Therefore, the actual rules and complex relations behind real scale-free networks deserve further investigation.

We have studied an instance of the future interconnected environment: an abstract overlay where nodes stand for versatile resources having lifespans, and links imply certain semantic relationships between nodes. By defining and investigating two types of models, a stochastic growth model and a directed evolving graph model, we have obtained the same scale-free distribution rule. Simulations and comparisons validate the proposed models.

An important obstacle encountered in the investigation of the future interconnection environment is the lack of proper experimental data. Besides introducing the growth rule of the live scale-free network, the proposed models can also provide the evidence for evaluating and selecting experimental data that can simulate the future interconnection environment.

Many application models and overlays can be built to describe a complex network. For example, different infection models can be used for the same contact network to study disease propagation (H.Zhuge and X.Shi, Fighting Epidemics in Knowledge and Information Age, *Computer*, 36(10)(2003)114-116). To apply these models we must try to find the complete evolution rules of these complex networks. For example, it could help us to answer the question: Is there any degeneration phase in the evolution of these networks? We believe there is, because the development of anything real is essentially limited. But the keys to the answer are the degeneration rule and the modeling of the - degeneration phase.

On the other hand, different semantic views can be taken of the one network to meet the needs of different applications (H.Zhuge, Semantic Grid: Scientific Issues, Infrastructure, and Methodology. *Communications of the ACM*, 48(4)(2005)117-119). An important growth characteristic of a semantically rich network is that a new node is likely to link to the most semantically relevant nodes rather than to the highly linked ones, which is not at all what preferential attachment models. Does this characteristic influence the growth of the networks, and to what extent?

Many interesting issues challenge current theories and techniques (H.Zhuge, Future Interconnection Environment, *Computer*, 38(4)(2005)27-33; H.Zhuge, Interactive Semantics, *Artificial Intelligence*, 174(2010)190-204; H.Zhuge, Semantic linking through spaces for cyber-physical-socio intelligence: A methodology, *Artificial Intelligence*, 175(2011)988-1019.).

In social networks, networks evolve with interactions between individuals. One important issue is to know the effect of operations on networks. For example, merging two networks, whether the characteristics of two networks can be reserved in the new network or not. Research has shown that the scale-free property can hold for several merge operations but in other merge operations degree distribution is deviated from power-law distribution (X.Sun and H.Zhuge, Merging Complex Networks, in *Proceedings of International Conference on Semantics, Knowledge and Grids*, SKG2011, Beijing, China).

Chapter 7

Topological Centrality in Social Network

The rich get richer phenomenon widely exists in social networks. There are two ways for a node in social network to become richer: linking to more nodes; and, linking to more important nodes. A node may get rise if it links to some important nodes than links to many but less important nodes. Both nodes and links play an important role in forming network centrality. Topological centrality is a network centrality measure that reflects relative centrality of nodes and links according to the influence between nodes, between links, and between node and link.

7.1 Principles of Influence

In social network, influence needs to pass through node by node. So, propagation of influence takes time and energy, and the node closer to the source of influence will be influenced sooner.

Therefore, social network has the following two principles of influence.

(1) *Short-term locality* — Influence is localized in the short-term.
(2) *Long-term globality* — Influence may be globalized in the long-term.

The short-term and long-term refer to not only time but also the number of influenced nodes (individuals). A global influence should reach a certain percentage of the whole nodes. The influence of a social behavior is at first localized, and then, it may be globalized due to the long-term movement of social network.

Social preference also influences the scope of influence. For example, if most peers prefer to spread information to most of its peers, a global influence will be formed.   Global influence usually carries out within a community with common interest.

Nodes with different socio energy have different scopes of influence. An individual's socio energy concerns potential energy (measured by centrality and interaction) and motion energy (measured by influence of operations).

The above principles have been explained from the privacy, socio energy, and information access point of views in (H.Zhuge, Semantic linking through spaces for cyber-physical-socio intelligence: A methodology, *Artificial Intelligence*, 175(2011)988-1019).

The motion of social network forms some centralities.

7.2   Basic Concept

In a connected social network, the weights of nodes and links influence each other. Each time of influence between each pair of nodes can be regarded as one time of influence (i.e., *iteration* in simulation algorithm). If the order of nodes' weights keeps stable after many times of iteration, the network reaches the *stable state* and the nodes with the highest weights can be regarded as the *topological centers* of the network. An undirected graph may have one or more topological centers. The number of centers depends on the structure of the network.

An undirected social network has or can be transformed into one of the following structures.

1.   A network with *circular* structure has n topological centers as shown in Fig. 7.1 a.
2.   A network with *symmetric* structure has two topological centers as shown in Fig. 7.1 b.
3.   Otherwise, the network has a unique topological center as shown in Fig.7.1c. The black nodes are the topological centers. The darker is the node, the higher the topological centrality is.

The networks with the circular structure have n ($n \geq 3$) topological centers. A network with symmetric structure has two topological centers. The other two types of network have one topological center.

When a network is in the stable state, the topological centrality (TC) of node is the ratio of its weight to the largest weight of nodes. The topological centers have the largest weight 1.

The topological centrality of link is the ratio of its weight to the largest weight of link.

In an undirected graph, the length of the shortest path between two nodes is the geodesic distance between them. If two nodes are unreachable, their geodesic distance is regarded as $+\infty$.

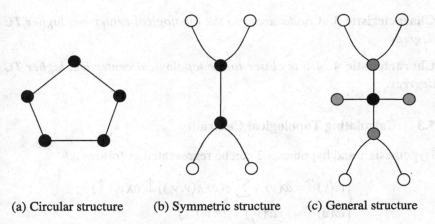

(a) Circular structure   (b) Symmetric structure   (c) General structure

Fig. 7.1 Three typical topological structures in social network.

The TC of node or link reflects the geodesic distance from a node to its nearest topological center. The higher is the TC, the closer it is to the nearest topological center.

According to the logicality principle of influence, we have the following hypothesis.

Hypothesis 1. *The topological centrality of a node is positively correlated to the topological centrality degrees of its neighbor nodes.*

The above hypothesis leads to the following two characteristics.

Characteristic 1. *A node linking to nodes with higher TC degrees gets higher TC degree.*

Characteristic 2. *A node linking to more nodes gets higher TC degree.*

According to the locality of influence between node and link, we have the following hypothesis.

Hypothesis 2. *If two nodes of a link have higher TC degrees, the link has higher TC; and, if a link has higher TC, its two ends (nodes) also have higher TC degrees.*

This hypothesis leads to the following two characteristics.

Characteristic 3. *A node closer to the topological center has higher TC degrees.*

Characteristic 4. *A link closer to the topological center has higher TC degrees.*

7.3   Calculating Topological Centrality

Hypothesis 1 and hypothesis 2 can be represented as follows:

$$\begin{cases} \omega(v) \uparrow = \omega(v) + \sum g(\omega(e(v,v_i)) \uparrow, \omega(v_i) \uparrow) \\ \omega(e) \uparrow = f(\omega(v_s) \uparrow, \omega(v_t) \uparrow) \end{cases},$$

where v is a node, v_i are neighbors of v, ω $(e(v, v_i))$ is the weight of the link between v and v_i; $\uparrow$ means the positive correlative relations; l is a link, v_s and v_t are two ends (nodes) of l respectively; and f and g are two functions.

During the calculation process of TC degree, the weights of nodes and links will increase after each time of iteration, but the descending order of weights of nodes will converge to stable state. The weights of nodes can be normalized by dividing the largest weight of nodes. If the normalized weights of nodes converge, the descending order of weights of nodes will keep stable, and the weights of links will also converge. The converged weights of nodes and links are the TC degrees of nodes and links respectively.

The normalization of weights of nodes satisfies the following characteristics:

(1) If the normalized weights of nodes converge, the order of nodes with descending weights of nodes will also converge. The normalization process does not change the order of weights of nodes, but the weights of nodes are mapped into the interval (0; 1].
(2) If the normalized weights of nodes converge, the weights of links also converge. The weights of links are the sum of the weights of its two ends (nodes). Since the normalized weights of nodes converge, the weights of incident links will also converge.
(3) If the normalized weights of nodes converge, the TC degrees of links converge, because the normalization of weights of links maps the weights of links into (0; 1], and this keeps the order of weights of links.

The following approach calculates the TC in a connected social network $G = (V, E)$, which has n nodes and m ($m \geq n - 1$) links. Let $V = \{v_1, v_2, \ldots, v_n\}$, $E = \{e_1, e_2, \ldots, e_m\}$, and A be the corresponding adjacency matrix. The element of A is a_{ij}, satisfying $a_{ij} = 1$ when $\{i, j\} \in E$ and $a_{ij} = 0$ when $\{i, j\} \notin E$.

The following formula implements the iterative calculation of TC of nodes and links, where $temp\_\omega_i$ and ω_i are the weights of v_i before and after normalization, and $temp\_\omega_{e(i,j)}$ and $\omega_{e(i,j)}$ are the weights of link $e(i, j)$ before and after normalization, and $t \geq 0$ is the iteration time.

$$\begin{cases} temp\_w_i^{(t+1)} = w_i^{(t)} + \sum_{j=1}^{n} a_{ij} \omega_{e(i,j)}^{(t)} w_j^{(t)} \\ temp\_w_{e(i,j)}^{(t+1)} = temp\_w_i^{(t+1)} + temp\_w_j^{(t+1)} \end{cases}$$

The following formula normalizes the TC degrees of nodes and links.

$$\begin{cases} w_i^{(t+1)} = temp\_w_i^{(t+1)} / Max_{i=1}^{n} temp\_w_i^{(t+1)} \\ w_{e(i,j)}^{(t+1)} = temp\_w_{e(i,j)}^{(t+1)} / Max_{j=1}^{m} temp\_w_{e(i,j)}^{(t+1)} \end{cases}$$

The iterative calculation terminates if the following conditions are satisfied:

$$\begin{cases} \sum_{i=1}^{n} (w_i^{(t+1)} - w_i^{(t)})^2 < \varepsilon_N \\ \sum_{j=1}^{m} (w_{e_j}^{(t+1)} - w_{e_j}^{(t)})^2 < \varepsilon_M \end{cases}$$

The following algorithm calculates the weights of nodes and links iteratively, where *MAX* is the maximum iteration times, ε_N is the square deviation threshold of the weight difference of nodes, and ε_M is the square deviation threshold of weight difference of links to control the times of iteration. At the initializing stage, all the weights of nodes are assigned 1. If the weights of links are not given, then all the weights of links are assigned 1.

Algorithm. Calculating topological centrality of nodes and links.
Input: *number of nodes*; *number of links*; *link list*; *MAX*.
Output: TC of nodes and TC of links.

1. The new weight of each node is its original weight added by the weight of its neighbor node multiplying the link weight respectively.
2. Normalize the weights of nodes using the largest weight of nodes.
3. For each link, its new weight is the sum of the weights of its two ends (nodes).
4. Normalize the weights of links by the largest weight of links.
5. Repeat from step 1 when satisfying *iteration time < MAX* and satisfying (*deviation square of weight difference of nodes > deviation square limit of weights of nodes*) or (*deviation square of weight difference of links > deviation square limit of weights of links*).

After the first iteration, the weight of a node in the next iteration is the sum of the weights of its neighbor nodes and its own weight. The weights of the weights of the links are the sum of its two ends. The values of weights of nodes become larger comparing to the initial values. The weights of nodes and links are normalized by dividing the maximum weight of nodes and links during each time of iteration.

After the algorithm stops, the nodes with weights 1 are the topological centers. The weight of a node is the topological centrality, and the larger is the weight of node, the closer the node is to the nearest topological center.

The calculation of TC concerns the dynamic iteration process on the static networks. Each time of iteration reflects the relative authority of nodes in the network.

7.4 Discovering Research Communities

Research communities are formed by interactions among researchers, papers, projects, and research activities. The following are differences between research communities and traditional graph-based communities.

(1) Research communities are dynamically formed by research activities such as applying funding, carrying out cooperation, doing experiment, publishing, and attending conference. By comparison, the graph-based communities are viewed from connections: nodes within a community are linked more densely than the nodes cross communities.

(2) Research communities contain multiple types of nodes. Nodes can play different roles in research activities (H. Zhuge, Discovery of knowledge flow in science, *Communications of the ACM*, 49(5)(2006)101–107), and links represent diverse semantics. By comparison, there are no differences of nodes and links in graph-based communities.

Among existing centrality measures, only the PageRank considers the influences between neighbor nodes, and the authority of a node is divided by its neighbors. But PageRank does not reflect different influences through different types of links in real applications.

Generally, TC can distinguish roles of different nodes in research network.

(1) Nodes in a network elect the core nodes by the voting-like mechanism: *a node linking more nodes is more probable to be the local core nodes.* After a certain times of iterations, the local core

nodes and the global topological centers are elected. The topological centers are the nodes linking to the most core nodes with higher TC degrees.

(2) Links may play different roles in the influence between the TC degrees of nodes. This confirms some phenomena of research communities, for example, a researcher cooperating with the authority researchers will be closer to the centers of a research community. A paper, citing or is cited by authority papers, is more possibly close to the core papers on a research topic.

Nodes can play different roles according to topological positions in communities: *core node*, *margin node*, *bridge node* and *mediate node*.

(1)   The *core nodes* are usually hub or authority in the community.

(2)   The *margin nodes* belong to one community, and they have few links to other nodes in the community.

(3)   The *bridge nodes* link to two or more communities, and they usually have equal number of links to two or more communities.

(4)   Other nodes except the *core nodes*, *margin nodes* and *bridge nodes* are *mediate nodes*.

Nodes can be classified by TC degrees.

(1)   If the TC degree of a node is larger than that of the most of its neighbors, the node is a *core* node.

(2)   If the TC degree of a node is not larger than the TC degrees of all of its neighbors, the node is a *margin* node.

(3)   If the number of neighbors with lower TC degrees equals to the number of neighbors with higher TC degrees, the node is a *bridge* node.

(4)   Otherwise, the node is a *mediate* node.

Let α be the number of neighbors of n with TC degrees lower than n, and β be the number of neighbors of n with TC degrees higher than n, then the role of n is distinguished as follows:

$$role(n) = \begin{cases} core \text{ node} & \alpha>\text{threshold(core)} \\ margin \text{ node} & \alpha=0 \\ bridge \text{ node} & \alpha=\beta \\ mediate \text{ node} & \text{otherwise} \end{cases}$$

Where *threshold(core)* ∈ (0,5, 1] controls the number of core nodes.

A core node has higher TC degrees than its neighbors. However, the topological centers of a connected social network may have exceptions. So, it is significant to distinguish the roles of topological centers. If the neighbors of a topological center are all core nodes, the topological center is a bridge node. Otherwise, the topological center is a core node.

Researchers and papers may play such roles as *source*, *authority*, *bee*, *hub* and *novice* (H. Zhuge, Discovery of knowledge flow in science, *Communications of the ACM*, 49(5)(2006) 101–107). The *source*, *authority*, and *hub* may be *core* nodes. The *bee* nodes are often *bridge* nodes. The *novice* may be the *margin* nodes or *bridge* nodes.

A leader of research group usually has more publications and cooperators. Consequently, they have more *coauthor link*s to other researchers. If research group is regarded as a community, the leaders are the core nodes. The fresh students have few publications and cooperators, so, they are the margin nodes in the coauthor network. Visiting researchers and newly employed researchers are bridge nodes, because they have cooperators in different research communities. The margin nodes, bridge nodes, and mediate node can be distinguished.

In citation network, core nodes are the authority or hub papers with more citations than others. The margin nodes are the novice papers or newly published papers. The bridge nodes link two or more paper clusters. Each paper cluster may belong to a specific research topic or discipline. Funding decision and research promotion need to evaluate researchers and their papers. TC can help distinguish the roles of researchers and papers. The roles can be used to evaluate researchers and papers. TC degrees in the coauthor network help evaluate researchers, while TC degrees in the citation network help evaluate papers.

In research network, roles of nodes will change year by year. In the coauthor network, a novice researcher may become an authority, a hub, or even a bridge. With more papers published, the TC degree of a node in a coauthor network will become higher than its neighbors, and then the researcher become an *authority* or *hub*. Cooperating with researchers in different research groups or even different communities, a researcher becomes a *bridge*.

7.5   Discovering Backbone in Research Network

Given a set of research papers, the research networks such as the coauthor networks and citation networks can be constructed according to the metadata of the papers in online digital libraries.

Researchers and the *coauthor* link construct the coauthor network. Coauthors of a paper formulate the motif of research network (R. Milo, et al., Network Motifs: Simple Building Blocks of Complex Networks, Science, 298(2002)824–827). Relevant research concerns the structure of science collaboration network (A. Barab´asi, et al., Evolution of the social network of scientific collaborations, *Physica A: Statistical Mechanics and its Applications*, 311(3-4)(2002) 590–614).

In social network, after roles of nodes are distinguished by the TC degrees of node, the core nodes and links among them form a *backbone network*.

The backbone network is useful for visualization and browsing the important component of a social network, and can play the following roles in scientific research:

(1) Help display research network of different levels. A community is closely related to the core nodes in the backbone network. Focusing a core node, the detailed information of its local community can be browsed.
(2) Show important researchers in a research network. When a research community or group is often concerned, the leaders are well-known. Some core nodes often formulate the connected components, linked by the bridge nodes. This is "rich club" phenomenon (V. Colizza, A. Flammini, M. Serrano, and A. Vespignani, Detecting rich-club

ordering in complex networks, *Arxiv preprint physics/0602134*, 2006): the richer nodes more possibly link to other richer nodes.

(3) Propagate information. The core nodes are important during information propagation because they have more impact in communities. For example, if we want to invite PC members of conference, the researchers in the backbone network should take the priority.

(4) Papers formulate communities via the citation link, and papers in a community share the same or relevant research topics. The core nodes are often important papers citing or are cited by more important papers. The backbone network of citation network helps find the history of a research area or a research topic. The core nodes and its neighbors reflect the main achievements at different research stages.

(5) Study the development of scientific research by showing the evolution of research networks through times.

The backbone network in a research network has the following characteristics:

(1) New researchers in the coauthor network often cooperate with the researchers that have published papers in the same place, because the scales of the connected components in the coauthor networks become larger with time.

(2) Scientific researchers tend to cooperate with others. The evolution of network shows that the isolated nodes enter the connected components step by step.

(3) The core researchers tend to cooperate with each other. The number of researchers in the largest connected component of the backbone networks becoming larger and larger.

(4) The core researchers are active locally, and they have more cooperators than their neighbors. The roles of researchers in the coauthor network also keep changing: a new researcher may become core researchers, while core researchers may become a mediate node or a margin node.

(5) The topological centers of the largest connected component keep changing. Centers emerge through a voting-like mechanism.

The backbone network of heterogeneous research networks links important resources such as researchers, papers, conferences, journals, institutions and publishers in a research topic. This helps find and recommend information.

The PageRank algorithm can also find the local core nodes, but it does not provide the way to link the most core nodes into a backbone network, because it is hard to choose the linking nodes between the core nodes by the ranks. While TC can choose the appropriate core nodes and form a backbone network that is likely linked, because the core nodes include the central nodes of community and the nodes linking different communities.

7.6   Discussion

In semantic link networks, weights of nodes are affected by their neighbors, and different links have different effects. So, it is necessary to consider the influences of links in the TC calculation. Links can be assigned weights and participate in the iterative calculation as follows, where r is the link $e(i, j)$, and ω_r is the weight of r that affects the calculation of TC in each iteration:

$$
\begin{cases}
temp\_w_i^{(t+1)} = w_i^{(t)} + \sum_{j=1}^{n} a_{ij}\omega_r\omega_{e(i,j)}^{(t)} w_j^{(t)} \\
temp\_w_{e(i,j)}^{(t+1)} = temp\_w_i^{(t+1)} + temp\_w_j^{(t+1)}
\end{cases}
$$

The following is an important characteristic.

The original topological centers may change when two networks are merged into one by some links and recalculate the topological centers in the new network.

If the coauthor network and the citation network are merged by the *authorOf* links, the topological centers of the new network may not be simply the sum of the topological centers in the coauthor network and those in the citation network. Recalculation of topological centers can synthesize more links, so this can more accurately evaluate nodes. For example, authors can be evaluated by more factors (e.g., the number of publications, co-authors, and citations) in the new network than in previous networks.

If applications need to keep the old topological centers in the new network and avoid recalculation, the following strategy can be used:

Find the links between the old topological centers, and then compose the corresponding old topological centers to form the new topological centers.

Such integrated topological centers can provide semantic relevant information services for applications in large networks, e.g., the authority author and his/her high impact papers can be obtained at the same time.

A semantic link network concerns relational reasoning. New semantic links could be derived from existing semantic links. Therefore, TC in the network may change. On the other hand, semantic communities emerge with operations on the network (H. Zhuge, Communities and emerging semantics in semantic link network: Discovery and learning, *IEEE Transactions on Knowledge and Data Engineering*, 21(6)(2009)785–799), so, measuring the centrality in dynamic networks is a challenge (S. Lee, et al., Centrality measure of complex networks using biased random walks, *The European Physical Journal B*, 68(2)(2009)277–281).

Existing centrality measures concern either nodes or links, which cannot reflect the topological characteristic of centrality, because influences exist between nodes, between links, and, between node and link. Detailed comparison is made in (H.Zhuge and J.Zhang, Topological Centrality and Its Applications, *Journal of the American Society for Information Science and Technology*, 61(9)(2010)1824-1841).

In real social network, centrality will be limited by some constraints, as discussed in (H.Zhuge, The Future Interconnection Environment, *Computer*, 38 (4) (2005) 27-33). If a node represents human individual, he/she has limited lifetime, energy, and social resources (e.g., money). Maintaining many links, an individual needs to expend his/her time, energy and social resources.

So, the centrality of a social network will be put into a reform process when the limits of time, energy and social resources are approaching.

Chapter 8

A Peer-to-Peer SLN for Decentralized Knowledge Sharing

Recommending, querying and answering usually involve in one knowledge sharing process. A self-evolving and adaptive peer-to-peer semantic link network can support efficient decentralized knowledge sharing.

8.1 Decentralized Peer-to-Peer Recommendation and Query

Recommending, querying and answering are basic activities of knowledge sharing in a cooperative team. A recommendation process may involve in querying and answering since a recommender may need to confirm or complete the content of recommendation by querying peers and getting answers. A querying and answering process may also involve in recommendation since answering can be seen as a kind of recommendation, and the person who answers may also receive recommendations from collaborators.

Knowledge of individuals increase, new links between individuals are established, and communities emerge and evolve with continuous querying, answering and recommending between individuals of a cooperative network. As the consequence, the performance of the network continuously evolves to support knowledge sharing.

Various semantic links involve in recommending, querying and answering. Studying the intrinsic relations between various semantic links and the efficiency of query routing in a decentralized networking system is the key to realize efficient decentralized knowledge sharing.

407

Here suggests a P2P Semantic Link Networking framework to support efficient query routing over unstructured P2P network by making use of semantic links between peers, between query and peer, and between semantic links. The framework will be further featured with the combination of query and recommendation to form a cooperative network system by incorporating active peer recommendation with efficient query routing.

8.1.1 *Peer-to-peer networks*

Peer-to-Peer (P2P) systems aim at decentralization, scalability, ad-hoc connectivity, reduced cost of ownership and anonymity (S. Androutsellis-Theotokis et al., A Survey of Peer-to-Peer Content Distribution Technologies, *ACM Computing Surveys*, 36(4)(2004)335–371).

Peers in the system can join and leave casually and the cost of ownership is shared among peers. The nature of P2P determines its potential to be more scalable than centralized and client-server systems (H. Balakrishnan, et al, Looking Up Data in P2P Systems, *Communications of the ACM*, 46(2)(2003)43–48).

Structured P2P networks like CAN, Chord, Pastry and Tapestry assign each resource a unique key and build a Distributed Hash Table (DHT) to map each key onto a specific peer. The whole network is highly structured and it only supports exact matching. This structured nature brings efficiency and accuracy in locating information, but it also leads to less dynamicity and high maintenance cost (S. Ratnasamy, et al, A Scalable Content-addressable Network, *ACM SIGCOMM Symposium on Communication, Architecture, and Protocol*, pp. 161–172, 2001; A. Rowstron et al., Pastry: Scalable, Distributed Object Location and Routing for Large-scale Peer-to-Peer Systems, *International Conference on Distributed Systems Platforms*, pp. 329–350, 2001; I. Stoica, et al., Chord: A Scalable Peer-to-Peer Lookup Service for Internet Applications, *SIGCOMM* 2001, 149–160; B. Y. Zhao, et al., Tapestry: An Infrastructure for Fault-resilient Wide-area Location and Routing, Technical Report UCB/CSD-01-1141, U.C.Berkeley, 2001).

In unstructured P2P networks like Gnutella (http://rfc-gnutella.sourceforge.net) and KaZaA (www.kazaa.com), peers are self-organized and resources are randomly placed without any restriction. Such networks have low maintenance cost and are robust against accidental failures, but they are limited in ability to efficiently locate information. The commonly used routing approach is flooding, a peer forwards queries to every neighbors. An optimization to the flooding approach, called directed flooding, only sends queries to the peers of a certain part of the P2P network according to query history. Techniques for reducing communication and increasing the probability of achieving answer were proposed (B. Yang et al., Efficient Search in Peer-to-peer Networks, *ICDCS* 2002).

8.1.2 *Towards a semantic peer-to-peer network*

Traditional P2P networks are limited in ability to support semantics-rich applications. To establish a semantic overlay is a way to enhance the semantic ability of P2P networks. Efforts have been made to establish various distributed indexes over P2P networks (K. Aberer, et al., GridVine: Building Internet-Scale Semantic Overlay Networks, *ISWC*2004; E. Cohen, et al., Associative search in peer to peer networks: Harnessing latent semantics, *Computer Networks*, 51(8)(2007)1861-1881; H. Zhuge et al., Distributed Suffix Tree Overlay for Peer-to-Peer Search, *IEEE Transactions on Knowledge and Data Engineering*, 20(2)(2008)276–285; H. Zhuge et al., Peer-to-Peer in Metric Space and Semantic Space, *IEEE Transactions on Knowledge and Data Engineering*, 19(6)(2007)759–771; H. Zhuge, et al., Query Routing in a Peer-to-Peer Semantic Link Network, *Computational Intelligence*, 21(2)(2005)197–216). How to incorporate diverse semantics, especially the implicit semantic links, into P2P networks is a challenge.

The Vector Space Model was used to characterize users and resources, and the ideas of tag clouds and cloud-specific feature vectors were used in a P2P environment (O. Gorlitz, et al., PINTS: Peer-to-Peer Infrastructure for Tagging Systems, *The 7th International Workshop on Peer-to-Peer Systems*, Feb. 2008). Edutella is an open source project that builds upon JXTA framework and the aims to provide a RDF-based metadata infrastructure for P2P applications (W. Nejdl, et al, Edutella: a P2P Networking Infrastructure Based on RDF, *WWW*2002, 604-615).

Piazza is a peer data management system that enables heterogeneous data to be shared in P2P networks (I. Tatarinov, et al, The Piazza Peer Data Management Project, *SIGMOD Record*, 32(3)(2003)47-52). It assumes that users are willing to define pairwise mappings between their schemas, like ontology or RDF-schemas. Mapping languages and query reformulation algorithms are developed to assist users' access to the shared data.

The Semantic Link Networking model SLN can be seen as a self-organized semantic data model consisting of semantic nodes, semantic links and rules for relational reasoning, where a semantic node can be a concept, an instance of concept, a schema of data set, a URL, any form of resources or even a SLN (H. Zhuge, Autonomous Semantic Link Networking Model for the Knowledge Grid, *Concurrency and Computation: Practice and Experience*, 7(19)(2007)1065–1085). A semantic link reflects a kind of relational knowledge represented as a pointer with a tag describing semantic relations. The semantics of tags are usually commonsense and can be regulated by its category, relevant reasoning rules, and instances of usage. New semantic links can be reasoned out from existing ones according to the predefined reasoning rules. The distinguished feature of the SLN is its self-organization nature, dynamicity, and relational reasoning ability.

8.1.3 *Characteristic of the peer-to-peer semantic link network*

Besides explicit and concrete semantic links, there are some implicit semantic links that cannot be represented in one simple concept but they do play very important role in realizing efficient information sharing. How to automatically discover and make use of the implicit semantic links to improve the performance of P2P information sharing is an important issue.

Routing and answering to the past queries were used to guide the succeeding queries in P2P network (C. Tempich, et al., REMINDIN: Semantic Query Routing in Peer-to-Peer Networks Based on Social Metaphors, *WWW*2004, pp. 640–649). Information of resources along neighbors' path was used as routing indices to improve the routing efficiency (A. Crespo et al., Routing Indices for Peer-to-peer Systems,

*ICDCS*2002, pp. 23–32).

This chapter suggests a P2P Semantic Link Network framework P2P-SLN by incorporating the basic semantic links into unstructured P2P network. It has the following characteristics:

(1) *Semantic link directed routing.* P2P-SLN makes use of the link between query and peer as well as the implicit relation between peers such as the content of resources owned by neighboring peers as well as the routing and question-answering history. These implicit semantic links are adapted to the evolution of the network and coordinate with each other as the potential forces to form semantic communities and to significantly raise the routing efficiency in P2P network.

(2) *Adapting TTL to the dissemination of query messages.* It helps dispatch query messages further when a query is likely to be answered, and will stop sooner when the query would not be answered in nearby neighbors. This characteristic leads to reasonable network traffic.

(3) *Self-evolving communities of peers.* Peers are self-organized into communities according to common interests, and communities can self-evolve with peers' join and departure to make the P2P-SLN scalable.

(4) *Incorporating recommendation and query.* The evolution of the contents in P2P-SLN is stimulated by peer recommendation. The query process and recommendation process are fused to form an effective knowledge sharing framework.

8.2   Basic Idea and Architecture

The basic idea of P2P-SLN is to classify the basic semantic links into the following two classes:

(1) *Implicit semantic links.*
(2) *Explicit semantic links.*

This leads to the following two effects:

(1) Peers and resources are self-organized into semantic communities of different levels. The dynamicity of P2P network drives the self-evolution of communities. This helps raise the efficiency of query routing.

(2) Appropriate candidate for routing a query can be predicted. This also helps raise the efficiency of query routing.

The semantic links and operations of the P2P-SLN are abstract variables, which include concrete semantic links, domain-specific semantic links, functions for determining semantic links between peers and between peer and query, semantic link reasoning rules, and the relationship between these semantic links. These variables need to be instantiated in applications.

Fig. 8.2 depicts the architecture of P2P-SLN. Each peer manages the routing table recording the information on semantic links and neighbors' addresses. The semantic links are classified as intercommunity links and intra-community links.

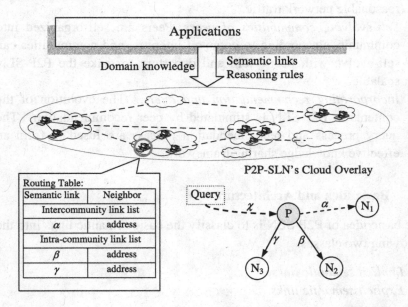

Fig.8.2 The architecture of P2P-SLN.

8.3 Semantic Links for Peer-to-Peer Networking

8.3.1 *Explicit semantic link*

The following are two types of semantic links that can be used in P2P network to support semantic search.

(1) *Resource-to-Resource Semantic Link* (in simple *RRS*). It reflects the explicit link between resources like the *coAuthor* relation between papers, which yields more search probes and supports relational queries. *RRS* can be defined by users or be automatically discovered in some application domains. Usually, a set of basic links exists in a domain, and it can compose a complex links. Reasoning rules on *RRS* may exist for deriving out more links.

(2) *Resource-to-Query Semantic Link* (in simple *RQS*). It reflects the link between query and resources, which is given by users. *RRS* and *RQS* support diverse semantic search.

The concrete definition of *RRS* depends on applications. It can be represented by different models, e.g., predicate in RDF, and commonsense between meta-data like the *sameAuthor* link.

RRS can be established when peers join the P2P network, and it can be expanded in the search process. For file sharing, peers can just create *RRS* between files of their own when they firstly join the network. When getting files from other peers, they create new *RRS* between the new files and the existing ones, and then more *RRS* can be generated automatically by using the reasoning rules introduced in section 8.3.3. Fig. 8.3.1 depicts an example of this process.

With the semantic links and reasoning rules on semantic links, a P2P network can support various relational queries, for example, it can find out all the resources linked to the given resource with the given links, and can find the links between two given resources.

8.3.2 *Implicit semantic link*

An implicit semantic link is a kind of basic relation that is hard to be represented by a simple concept but it can be judged by machine and can be used to improve the performance of systems.

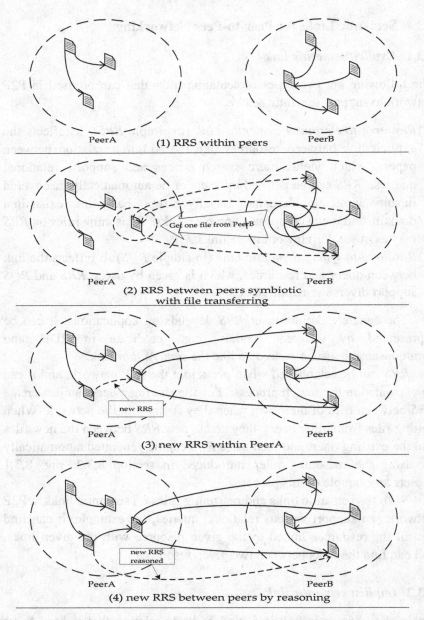

(1) RRS within peers

(2) RRS between peers symbiotic
with file transferring

Get one file from PeerB

new RRS

(3) new RRS within PeerA

new RRS
reasoned

(4) new RRS between peers by reasoning

PeerA   PeerB

Fig.8.3.1 A process of *RRS* construction between peers, where arrows represent semantic links and dotted circles represent peers.

The following are two types of implicit semantic links in P2P-SLN:

(1) *Peer-to-Neighbor Semantics* (in simple *PNS*). It reflects the interest or synthesized semantics of a neighbor from a peer's point of view. This general semantic link enables a peer to know its neighbors' interest. *PNS* can make use of query-answer histories and the local linking structure. Generally, *PNS* reflects the synthesized semantics of all *RRS* between resources in the two peers. The *RRS* and *PNS* constitute two-level semantic links shown in Fig. 8.3.2. *PNS* can be defined as *PNS(peer, neighbor)*=f_1(*content, QA-history, local-structure*), where *content*= ζ_1(*peer's content, neighbor's content*) represents the semantic link between the contents of resources managed by the peer and the contents of resources managed by the neighbor, *QA-history*=ζ_2(*peer's QA-history, neighbors' QA-history*) represents the semantic link between the question-answering history of the peer and that of the neighbor (including the successful answers and unsuccessful answers), and *local-structure*=ζ_3(*peer's local-structure, neighbor's local-structure*) represents the semantic link between the local link structures of the peer and that of the neighbor. The information of local link structure can be used to improve the performance of query routing (H. Zhuge and X. Li, Peer-to-Peer in Metric Space and Semantic Space, *IEEE Transactions on Knowledge and Data Engineering*, 19(6)(2007) 759–771). The functions ζ_1, ζ_2 and ζ_3 can be dynamically adjusted to play different roles at different stages of the evolution of the network. The structure information plays more important role at the initial stage, the content of resources plays more important role when resources become rich, and the QA history plays more important role when many queries have passed through the network. Further, the structure can be adjusted according to the status of query routing flows.

(2) *Peer-to-Query Semantics* (in simple *PQS*). It reflects the semantic relation between the content of the query and the content of resources managed by a peer. It is temporarily established when a query arrives at a peer. *PQS* reflects the synthesized semantics of *RQS*. *PQS* can also make use of QA-histories, e.g. whether the query has been answered by this peer. *PQS* can be defined as *PQS(peer, query)*=

$f_2(content, QA\text{-}history)$, where $content=\zeta_1(peer\text{'}s\ content,\ query\text{'}s\ content)$ represents the content of resources managed by the peer and the content of the query, and *QA-history* represents the question-answering history of the peer.

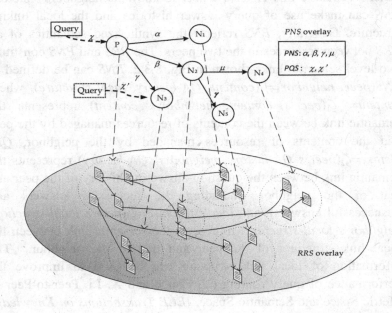

Fig.8.3.2 The two-level P2P-SLN: the high-level implicit semantic link P2P network and the low-level explicit semantic link P2P network.

After defining the semantic links in P2P network, the next key issue is how to use these semantic links to improve search efficiency. The semantic links in P2P network allow a node to evaluate the goodness of its neighbors for a query. The notion of goodness may vary with applications but in general it should reflect the number of appropriate answers the neighbor could return. The notion of the Semantic link to Semantic link Goodness (*SSG*) is to reflect the goodness of a *PNS* for a *PQS* or a *RRS* for a *RQS*.

$SSG=f_3(PNS(peer,\ neighbor),\ PQS(peer,\ query))\ |\ f_4(RRS(resource,\ resource),\ RQS(resource,\ query))$ such that *SSG* is high if a *PNS* or *RRS* can direct the query to a neighbor or a resource which can answer the query with high probability (the query has *PQS* link with the current peer or *RQS* with the current resource), otherwise *SSG* is low.

SSG is used to evaluate neighbors for guiding efficient query routing. Fig. 8.3.2 depicts these semantic variables. Suppose in an application, peer P is a student, one neighbor N_1 is a lecturer, and the semantic link α between P and N_1 reflects the semantics of '*learnFrom*' or in more detail form '*learnFrom(software engineering)*' (i.e., learn "software engineering" from). Then, if the semantic link χ reflects the semantics of '*queryOn*' or in more detail '*queryOn(software engineering)*', the goodness value between α and χ would be high. Therefore, if the query is forwarded to N_1, it will get the required answers with high probability.

The introduced semantic links *RRS*, *RQS*, *PNS*, and *PQS* can cooperate with each other to provide the semantic ability for P2P network: *PQS* and *PNS* can cooperate with each other to efficiently route queries between peers. *RQS* and *RRS* can cooperate with each other to route queries among resources.

8.3.3 Reasoning operations

The P2P-SLN framework includes the following two reasoning operations.

(1) *Reasoning on semantic links*. It can derive out new semantic links over P2P-SLN. Its abstraction form is $\alpha \cdot \beta \rightarrow \gamma$, where α and β represent existing semantic links and γ represents the new semantic link. To reflect the inexactness of *PNS* and *RRS*, a typical semantic link consists of a semantic link type and a weight reflecting its certainty degree. Suppose peer P has $PNS_1=\alpha(w_1)$ with x, and x has $PNS_2=\beta(w_2)$ with peer N, the relation between P and N can be reasoned by PNS_1 and PNS_2, i.e., $PNS_3=\gamma\,(\partial(w_1\times w_2))$, where w_1, w_2, $\partial(w_1\times w_2)\in[0, 1]$, and ∂ is determined in applications.

(2) *Calculation of SSG*. The semantic variables *SSG*, *PNS*, *PQS* and their reasoning rules reflect the basic semantics in P2P-SLN. However, giving *SSG* values for every pair of *PNS* and *PQS* is impractical. Here gives a reasoning formula to compute the value of *SSG* from existing rules. We firstly give a *SSG* calculation form $\chi \odot \alpha \rightarrow \nu$, where

v is the *SSG* value of *PNS* α for *PQS* χ. The reasoning formula of *SSG* is $\chi \odot (\alpha \cdot \beta) = (\chi \cdot \alpha) \odot \beta$. Its meaning is depicted in Fig. 8.3.3, where α, β and γ are *PNS*, χ and η are *PQS*, and the semantic link reasoning rules between them are $\alpha \cdot \beta \rightarrow \gamma$ and $\chi \cdot \alpha \rightarrow \eta$. Then, the left part of the formula $\chi \odot (\alpha \cdot \beta) = \chi \odot \gamma$ reflects the goodness for routing query to node *N*. The right part $(\chi \cdot \alpha) \odot \beta = \eta \odot \beta$ also reflects the goodness for routing query to node *N*. The difference only exists in the initial dispatching peer. From this view, the two values should be equal.

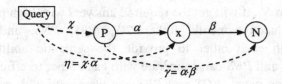

Fig.8.3.3 Calculation of *SSG* (Semantic link to Semantic link Goodness).

8.4   Communities in P2P-SLN

In a randomly connected unstructured P2P network, it is tough to efficiently route a query to appropriate peers, even navigation is based on semantics. P2P-SLN uses the semantic link to reorganize the topology of the P2P network, i.e., cluster semantically close peers into semantic communities.

A semantic community contains semantically relevant peers that share some common external (link structure) or internal (content) features. These common features are called the *guide semantics* of the community, which can produce more effective search probes, and therefore improve the query routing process. Instantiating the underlying guided semantics depends on applications.

Each community is an overlay where each peer maintains a small list of other peers within the same community. The construction of this community overlay can be initialized with peer join, and it is symbiotic with the search process and semantic link reasoning.

The semantic distance between peers in P2P-SLN means the following:

The peer that can answer a query has shorter semantic distance to the query initiator than those that cannot answer the query.

Peers belonging to multiple communities act as the bridge between communities. An example of overlapping communities is shown in Fig. 8.4. Peers within a community connect with each other by intra-community semantic links, which are denser than the intercommunity ones. The intra-community links and intercommunity links constitute peers' routing tables.

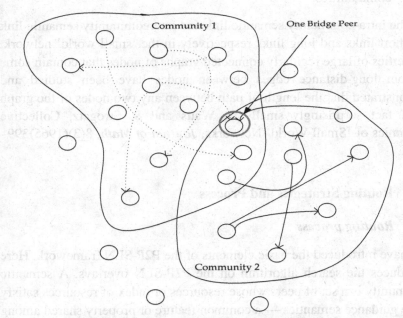

Fig.8.4 An example of overlapping communities of peers.

In P2P-SLN, peers randomly link to one another within semantic community. Each community looks like an unstructured network and exhibits similar connectivity and expansion properties. For a community of size n, its radius could be limited within the magnitude of $lg(n)$ if each peer maintains $lg(n)$ intra-community semantic links. And, this size of intra-community semantic link list is easy to be satisfied in application.

The advantage of this topology lies in the following aspects.

(1) The whole network is organized into semantic communities. A query will be sent to and then routed in appropriate community. Irrelevant communities will ignore the query. This reduces many unnecessary routing messages in the network.

(2) The intercommunity semantic links enable a query to find its community easily and quickly just as highways between communities.

The intra-community semantic link and intercommunity semantic link are short links and long links respectively in the 'small world' network. Properties of large regularly connected graphs of nodes that contain some random long-distance edges between nodes have been studied and demonstrated that the length of path between any two nodes of the graph is in fact surprisingly small (D. Watts and S. Strogatz, Collective Dynamics of 'Small World' Networks, *Journal of Math*, 8(3)(1965)399–404).

8.5 Routing Strategies and Process

8.5.1 *Routing process*

We have introduced the basic elements of the P2P-SLN framework. Here introduces the search algorithm on the P2P-SLN overlays. A semantic community is a set of peers whose resources or index of resources satisfy some guidance semantics — a common feature or property shared among these resources like written by the same author or belong to the same domain. Peers that participate in the same community form a sub-overlay that resembles a traditional unstructured network. The sub-overlays of different communities can overlap. Search is conducted between these sub-overlays via semantic links. Similar to search in traditional unstructured networks, it is propagated from peer to neighbors but propagation is restricted to peers belonging to relevant communities. It is reasonable to assume that each community sub-overlay has similar properties to a traditional unstructured overlay network: a peer in each community needs to remember a small list of peers within the same community; and, the neighbors should ensure that the guided-search can reach a large number of peers. Its specifics can vary from a Gnutella-like design (each peer has few viable neighbors, typically 2-4, through which many other peers can be reached) to a FastTrack-like design where search is facilitated through a core network of super nodes. The specifics are orthogonal to our basic approach, and we only need to ensure that our semantic model can form the underlying unstructured network.

The semantic query in P2P-SLN usually conforms to the form: *search resources having one specific semantic relation with a resource*, which usually is also the RQS between the query and the resource.

Intuitively, the query should be routed within the communities whose guide semantics are related to the query, since it not only improves the routing effect to get more relevant results quickly, but also reduces the number of irrelevant query messages.

Which communities should be selected to spread the query depends on SSG. The community-based routing process consists of the following steps:

(1) The query is given by the initiator along with the initial RQS between the query and one resource. Of course, more RQSes are preferable. The state at this step is shown in Fig. 8.5.1(a).

(2) Reasoning the RQSes between the query and other resources in the initiator. These resources having RQS with the query, either initialized or reasoned, are called as *seed resources*. The state at this step is shown in Fig. 8.5.1(b), where there are three seed resources.

(3) For each community the initiator belongs to, if its guide semantics specifies one seed resource, compute the SSG value of RRS in this community.

(4) Rank the communities according to their corresponding SSG values, and send query to communities according to their rank.

(5) As each community is also an unstructured network, routing within community can use the same query routing methods in the network.

In order to improve the routing efficiency by utilizing the P2P-SLN features, the following two sections will discuss two search strategies.

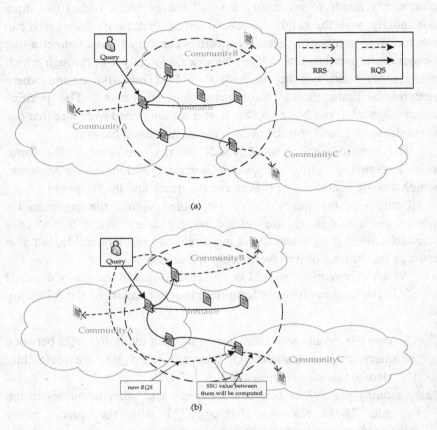

Fig.8.5.1 Community-based Routing.

The following two search strategies define the routing choice when facing a message transferring. For example, whether should the message be sent further or to which neighbors the message should be sent.

8.5.2 *Adaptive TTL*

In previous routing approaches, TTL is decreased by one per hop to avoid endless message transferring in the network. P2P-SLN enables the decrement value of TTL to vary with the routing path. Taking flooding as an example, if TTL is decreased by one per hop, the query will be routed within a circular area where the initiator is the center and TTL is the radius as shown in Fig. 8.5.2(a).

As the distribution of resources in the network generally conforms to a locality feature, previous flooding approaches send message to many irrelevant peers, therefore lead to a heavy burden of the network traffic. If TTL value is adaptive, for example, by lengthening the radius towards the prospect direction and shortening the radius toward the irrelevant directions, the number of messages can be reduced and more required resources can be located.

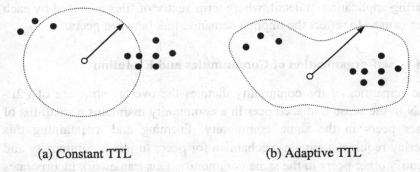

(a) Constant TTL   (b) Adaptive TTL

Fig.8.5.2 Intuitive comparison between constant TTL and adaptive TTL.

In P2P-SLN, the decrement value of TTL for one hop could be defined according to *SSG* value, for example, taking a monotonic descent function of *SSG*.

This routing strategy can find answers more reasonably as TTL decreases slowly when *SSG* value is high (i.e., the neighbors are more likely to answer the query). The TTL decreases quickly and the query message will not be sent to more peers in that direction when *SSG* value is low.

8.5.3 *Semantics-based neighbor selection*

P2P-SLN provides a general framework for implementing the semantics-based neighbor selection. A strategy of semantics-based neighbor selection is to select the next hop with the probability in proportion to the neighbors' *SSG* values about the query. Neighbors that can answer a query with higher probability are likely to be selected in the next hop.

This framework can be instantiated to reflect semantic link of various types. Neighbor selection strategy varies with these types. An example of instantiation is to enable each peer to record query-answering history from neighbors, which has positive and negative impact on the probability of neighbor selection. The routing mechanism should forward queries with high probability to the neighbors who have answered similar queries and with low probability to the neighbors who have failed to answer similar queries.

Section 8.7 presents another example of instantiation in P2P file sharing application in detail, where term vector of files managed by each peer is used to reflect the implicit semantic link between peers.

8.6   Self-organization of Communities and Evolution

The semantics of the community dictates the overlay structure of P2P-SLN in the sense that each peer in a community maintains a small list of other peers in the same community. Forming and maintaining this overlay requires a simple mechanism for peers to join a community and identify other peers in the same community. Our framework incorporates this mechanism into the search process.

8.6.1 *Peer join*

When a peer joins the P2P-SLN network, it can join one community assigned by application; otherwise, P2P-SLN will select one community for the joining peer based on the common interests between the joining peer and the existing communities. If no community is suitable, a new community will be created for the peer.

The community selection process works as follows:

The joining peer initiates a query, and sends the query to its introducer, which dispatches the query by using the strategy and process introduced in section 8.5 to get feedbacks, and selects the best matching one as the community introducer. The basic premise is that the query and answer are relevant to the resources of the joining peer.

When joining one community, a peer should link to other peers by the following two steps to inform its existence:

(1) Creating the links. The joining peer links itself to the community introducer. Then, it copies the semantic link list from the introducer. These lists form the semantic link list of the joining peer.

(2) Semantic binding of the links by semantic link reasoning. The semantic link reasoning carries out according to the copied semantic links and the semantic link between the joining peer and the introducer. This process resembles the creation of *RRS* links depicted in Fig. 8.3.1. When the semantic link list of the routing table is relatively stable, the joining peer should update its semantic links gradually. It updates its rth neighbor in the list of the routing table with the peer that has a path of r-length to the joining peer. This updating enhances the connectivity of the community and eliminates possible cut points. Eventually, the joining peer notifies all its neighbors of its existence.

8.6.2 *Peer departure*

The simplest way for a peer to leave the P2P-SLN is that it leaves silently. In this case, the maintenance of the community depends on the remaining peers. When a peer contacts its neighbor without response for a period of time, this peer will assume that the neighbor leaves the network and deletes it from the routing table for the community the neighbor belongs to. The peer will check the size of the semantic link list of the routing table for that community. If the size is too small, it will copy semantic link list of the routing table from one of its neighbors in the same community. The peer will search in the routing tables of its neighbors in the same community to find a peer p which has linked to the departing peer, then adds p to its semantic link list. This process will eliminate cut points with high probability.

8.7 Application and Experiment

Here we apply the P2P-SLN framework to a P2P scientific document sharing network. Each peer in the network holds a set of interested documents, and it is willing to share documents with other peers. The aim is to efficiently organize these document resources and to efficiently respond queries over an unstructured P2P network.

8.7.1 *Instantiation of P2P-SLN framework*

The P2P scientific document sharing network should instantiate the variables of the P2P-SLN such as the definitions of concrete semantic links and operations on semantic links. This application uses the term vector to represent the content of documents held by a peer. Typically, the value of each element of the vector is a function of the frequency that the term occurs in the peer. The instantiation uses the term vector to reflect the contents in peers as shown in Table 8.7.1.

Table 8.7.1 An instantiation of P2P-SLN framework.

Concept	Instantiation
PNS	The term vector of a peer's neighbor is regarded as the semantics of the peer to the neighbor. The weight element is assign 1 since the term vector represents the peer's documents. For example, if peer p connect to peer q via a semantic link, the link can be represented as $TermVector_q(1)$.
PQS	The term vector of the query is regarded as the peer-to-query semantics.
SSG	The similarity between *PNS*' term vector (denoted as *PNSV*) and *PQS*' term vector (denoted as *PQSV*) is regarded as the value of *SSG*, which can be calculated by $PNSV \cdot PQSV/(\|PNSV\| \cdot \|PQSV\|)$.
Reasoning operation	If peer p has a semantic link α pointing to peer x, and x has a semantic link β pointing to peer q, then p has a derived semantic link γ pointing to q, i.e., $\gamma = \alpha \cdot \beta$. In this application, we have $\gamma = \alpha \cdot \beta = \beta$.

As shown in Fig. 8.7.1, peers in the network are clustered into different communities. The dotted lines show the mapping from the views to actual peers in the network. Besides peer vectors, community vectors are used to represent classification semantics of peers in the same community. Herein, for all peers (e.g., p) in community C, the community vector C_v is the sum of peer vectors of all peers in the community. Each peer maintains the following two kinds of views:

(1) *Intra-community view* contains links to peers in the same community.
(2) *Intercommunity view* contains links to other communities.

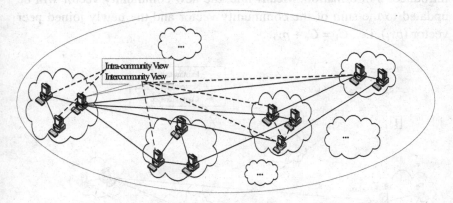

Fig.8.7.1 Maintenance of the views in P2P-SLN cloud overlay.

8.7.2 *Peer join and departure*

The community of a new peer is determined according to the matching degree of the term vector. The similarity between the term vector of the new peer (A) and the term vector of the community (B) can be measured by $A \cdot B/(\|A\| \cdot \|B\|)$ (M.W. Berry, et al, Matrices, Vector Spaces, and Information Retrieval, *Society for Industrial and Applied Mathematics Review*, 41(1999)335–362). The candidate community that the new peer belongs to depends on the maximum similarity between the community and the peer. If the maximum similarity is larger than the threshold, the peer belongs to the community. Otherwise, the peer itself will construct a new community, in this case, its view only contains intercommunity view and its community vector is the same as its peer vector.

As shown in Fig. 8.7.2.1, when one peer r joins the system, it contacts its introducer first. With the community vector information fed back from the introducer, the newly joined peer decides its community with reference to its own peer vector. If there is no community that the newly joined peer belongs to, it will establish its intercommunity view with the peers' information in different communities with the help of the introducer. Otherwise, if the peer decides the community it belongs to, it forms a join message including address and peer vector, and forwards the message to one of the peers in that community by utilizing the introducer's information. Meanwhile, the new community vector will be updated to the sum of the community vector and the newly joined peer vector (pv_r), i.e., $C_v = C_v + pv_r$.

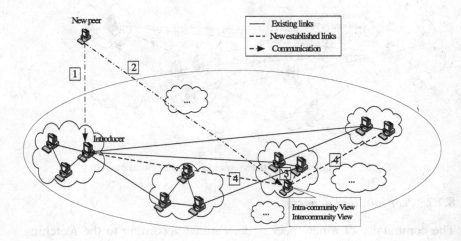

Fig.8.7.2.1 Peer join process. The dashed lines denote the links to the new peer's neighbors by establishing its views — the interest of its neighbors. Step 1: The new peer contacts the introducer. Step 2: If the new peer finds the community it belongs to, goes to step3; else the new peer establishes a new community and its intercommunity views, and terminates the process. Step 3: The new peer contacts one peer in that community with the help of the introducer. Step 4: The new peer establishes its views.

During the process, a limit *sl* restricting the whole steps of dissemination should be set. It is reduced by one at each hop during the message is transferred. When a peer in the community receives the message, it first decides whether to add the joining peer to its view with reference to its view size. If this causes the overflow of the view size, it forwards the joining message to one randomly selected neighbor in the community until the joining peer is accepted or *sl* becomes zero. If the joining peer is still not accepted by any peer when *sl* reaches zero, the community is regarded as full and a new community should be created. Meanwhile, this is the way to guarantee the routing efficiency of the network by restricting the radius of the community. The joining peer forms its views by exchanging information with the peers within the same community.

Fig. 8.7.2.2 describes the peer departure process. When a peer departs the system, other peers detect this situation by interchanging their states periodically. If no response is returned from one of its neighbors within a certain period, the peer regards it as being crashed and removes it from the corresponding view (R. V. Renesse, et al., A Gossip-style Failure Detection Service, *Middleware98: IFIP International Conference, Distributed Systems and Platforms and Open Distributed Processing*, 1998, pp. 55–70). The community vector is updated with the help of the departing peer's neighbor.

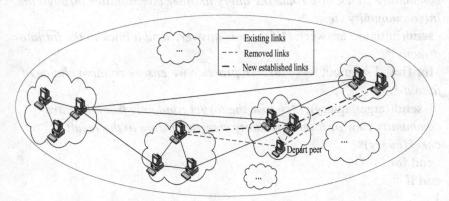

Fig.8.7.2.2 Peer departure process. The dashed lines denote the links that will be removed since the departure peer leaves the network, and the darker lines denote the new links established by the departure peer's neighbors. Step 1: The departure peer informs its neighbors. Step 2: The peer leaves the P2P network. Step 3: The neighbors establish new links.

8.7.3 *Query routing process*

When a peer receives a query, it compares the query with the peer vector, if the similarity is bigger than a threshold, the query will be routed through its intra-community view, otherwise, the query will be routed through its intercommunity view. The flooding, the gossip (M. Haridasan and R. Renesse, Gossip-based Distribution Estimation in Peer-to-Peer Networks, *The 7th International Workshop on Peer-to-Peer Systems*, 2008), and the random walk mechanisms can be adopted for query routing.

The query routing algorithm at each node of P2P-SLN is as follows.

Receive(sender, query){
if query.**getId**()$\notin$ historyIdList **then**
/*if the node has received the query, add the new query to the history and remove the oldest one*/
  historyList.**add**(query);
  check(query); /* *if the query could be answered in the community, initiate the routing process in the community through the intra-community views, else route the query to other communities through the intercommunity views.*/
  send(initiator, answer); /**if there is answer, send it back to the initiator directly* */
  for (i=0; i < fanout, i++) **do** /**In practice we ensure random choice of fanout* */
    send(target, query); /**choose the target randomly from the intra-community view or intercommunity view according to the result of check(query)*/
  end for
end if
}

8.7.4 *Performance analysis*

Suppose the number of peers in the system is n, and the system evolves into m communities dynamically. For simplicity, we assume that community members are evenly distributed, that is, the sizes of communities are equal to n/m approximately. The assumption will be relaxed in the experiments. We adopt the following notations for easier discussion.

(1) s: denotes the source peer of one message.
(2) ε: denotes the probability of message loss during the gossiping process.
(3) τ: denotes the probability of a peer crash during the gossiping process.
(4) A: denotes the event that there is a directed path from s to all nodes in the community that s belongs to.
(5) B: denotes the event that there is a directed path from s to other communities.
(6) P(C): denotes the probability that the event C happens.

Gossip style protocols are reliable in a probabilistic sense. By adopting the analysis mentioned in reference (A.M. Kermarrec, et al., Probabilistic Reliable Dissemination in Large-scale Systems, *IEEE Transactions on Parallel and Distributed Systems*, 14(3)(2003)248–258), it is shown that the probability of a given peer receiving the disseminated message will be as follows.

$$1 - \frac{1}{n^{fanout}} \cdot (1 + o(1))$$

If the message loss and peer crash are considered, the probability will be as follows.

$$1 - \frac{1}{n^{(1-\varepsilon) \cdot (1-\tau) \cdot fanout}} \cdot (1 + o(1))$$

When query routing process is initiated, the whole process consists of two phases: routing in the intercommunity views and routing in the intra-community views. Utilizing the intercommunity views, the query is routed to the appropriate community. Thereafter, a gossiping process is initiated in the community. In this precondition, we have:

P(*every peer in the community will receive the message*)
= P(A)·P(B)
=

$$(1 - \frac{1}{(n/m)^{(1-\varepsilon) \cdot (1-\tau) \cdot fanout}} \cdot (1 + o(1))) \cdot (1 - \frac{1}{m^{(1-\varepsilon) \cdot (1-\tau) \cdot fanout}} \cdot (1 + o(1)))$$

In real application, the messages communicate reliably through protocols such as TCP, and in this way, ε would approach zero. The negative influence of peer crash could be reduced by re-forwarding message and choosing different neighbors. Thus, the influence of τ would approach zero too. In addition, being a large number in P2P-SLN, n ensures the protocol to be reliable.

With reference to (B. Pittel, On Spreading a Rumor, *SIAM Journal of Applied Mathematics*, 47(1)(1987)213-223), the total rounds TTL(n, *fanout*) in the gossip style system, necessary to infect an entire community of size n obeys (c is a constant) :

$$\text{TTL}(n, fanout) = \log\, n \times (\frac{1}{fanout} + \frac{1}{\log(\ fanout\ )}) + c + o(1).$$

From the equation, there exists a tradeoff between *fanout* and TTL in the network of n peers. Therefore, in our systems, all peers self-evolve into different communities. As the sizes of communities are assumed to be equal approximately, the round of message dissemination in the community will be TTL($n\,/\,m$, *fanout*). Considering the community selection process, the round of message dissemination to find the appropriate community will be TTL(m, *fanout*). Therefore, the hop count of message dissemination in the whole system will be as follows:

TTL$_1$(n, *fanout*)
= TTL(m, *fanout*) + TTL(n/m, *fanout*)
= $(\log\, m + \log(\ n\,/\,m)) \times (\frac{1}{fanout} + \frac{1}{\log(\ fanout\ )}) + c_1 + o(1),$

where c_1 is a constant.

8.7.5 *Experiment*

8.7.5.1 *Term vector simulation results*

We generated 100 base files, each of which is represented by a 200-keyword semantic vector. The state-of-the-art of information retrieval algorithms based on VSM (Vector Space Model) and LSI (Latent Semantic Index) show that typically 200-300 keywords are capable of characterizing a file. The similarity between these base files approaches zero. Each of the remaining 500,000 files is similar to only one of these base files. The number of files similar to each base file follows a Zipf-like distribution. Namely, the number of the remaining 500,000 files sharing similarity with the ith base file is proportional to $1/i^\sigma$. In this experiments, $\sigma=0.7$, this setting is to simulate the hot topics in real document sharing system. In addition, we determine the similarity between each remaining file and its corresponding base file within (0, 0.3), [0.3, 0.6), and [0.6, 1.0) with a probability of 20%, 30% and 50% respectively (Zipf-like) (Y. W. Zhu, et al., Integrating Semantic-Based Access Mechanisms with Peer-to-Peer File System, *the 3rd International Conference on Peer-to-Peer Computing*, 2003, pp: 118–125).

After preparing these files, we simulate 100,000 peers each of which corresponds to a base file. The number of peers for each base file also follows the Zipf-like distribution similar to the distribution of the files. Each peer selects the interested files from 500,000 files that have the same corresponding base file. Then, the peers join the network gradually to form a file sharing system.

Two types of network are simulated: *P2P-SLN network* and *random network with semantic links*. The following five routing approaches are performed: flooding, gossip, flooding with semantics, gossip with semantics, and community-based routing. Here, flooding with semantics uses the adaptive TTL strategy, gossip and gossip with semantics chooses *fanout*=2, and gossip with semantics uses both adaptive TTL and semantic-based neighbor selection strategies. In the experiments, queries are generated as follows: for each base file, 100 queries are generated with the term number varying from 1 to 10.

The following two comparison criteria are used:

(1) The total number of messages transferred during query process; and,
(2) The recall rate of results returned for the query.

The experiment result is shown in Fig. 8.7.5.1. The proposed semantic routing approaches can always run on the P2P-SLN network at an efficient level. Compared with the performance on random network, the adaptive TTL is very sensitive to the locality of resources, and the community-based routing performs best because of its high usage of the community information.

The effectiveness of these routing strategies comes from the following aspects:

(1) Direction of semantic links.
(2) Adaptive TTL.
(3) Self-organized community topology.
(4) Routing strategy with high usage of above aspects.

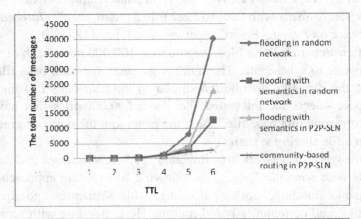

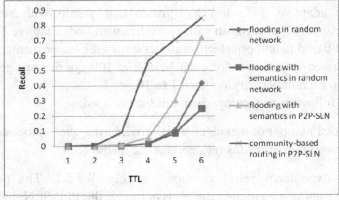

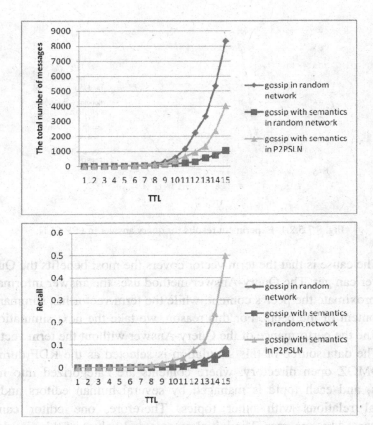

Fig.8.7.5.1 Experimental results for comparisons.

It can be anticipated that the effect will be better if QA history can be considered.

8.7.5.2 *Query-answer simulation results*

This simulation firstly examines the performance of Query-Answer along with the term vector. The experiment result is shown in Fig. 8.7.5.2.1, from which, we can see that Query-Answer could improve the recall rate in the random network. However, Query-Answer does not perform much better in P2P-SLN than the algorithm that does not use it.

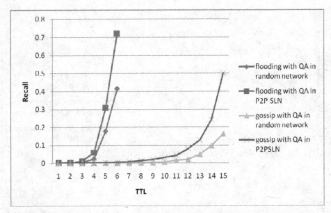

Fig. 8.7.5.2.1 Experiment results for query answer in P2P-SLN.

The cause is that the term vector covers the most benefits the Query-Answer can get. The Query-Answer method uses the answer information to approximate the peer's content, while the term vector has summarized the content of the peers. For this reason, we take the next simulation to examine the performance of the Query-Answer without the term vector.

The data source of this simulation is selected as the RDF dump of the DMOZ open directory, where contents are categorized into many topics, and each topic is managed by several human editors and has several relations with other topics. Therefore, one editor can be represented by one peer. The initial parameters' values of this simulation are shown in Table 8.7.5.2.

Table 8.7.5.2 An instantiation of P2P-SLN framework.

Parameter	Value
TTL	6
fanout	2
Number of peers	1000
Out degree per peer	5

Fig. 8.7.5.2.2 depicts the comparison between the approach of using the Query-Answer and the flat approach. This simulation uses 10,000

queries, about 10 queries per peer. We can see that the recall rate of the Query-Answering approach increases with the number of queries and reaches a stable value of 45% after a number of queries, while the flat approach gets a constant recall rate of approximately 20%.

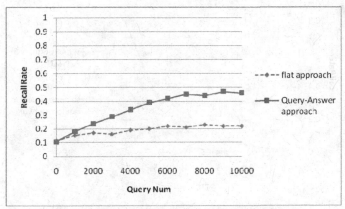

Fig.8.7.5.2.2 Experiment results for query answer.

8.7.5.3 *Semantic query experiment*

The term vectors of peers reflect an implicit semantic links between peers. But for explicit semantic links, it never provides an easy and direct representation, for example, queries like "search songs of the same artist as of a given song" or "search the web sites closely related to one given URL". Such type of semantic queries can be easily represented by explicit semantic links, while they are difficult to be represented by traditional vector space methods. Here, we concern how the explicit semantic links affect the routing efficiency.

The data used in this simulation is the same as the data used in section 8.7.5.2 except that it adds the *RRS*es between resources in peers and never records QA histories. These *RRS*es are extracted from the DMOZ RDF data source.

A random network and a P2P-SLN are both simulated, and the 1000 semantic queries are generated based on the *RRS*es. Fig. 8.7.5.3 depicts the recall rate of semantic queries randomly chosen from the *RRS*es as a function of TTL. The P2P-SLN can dramatically improve the efficiency of semantic queries. Thus, we can conclude that if the query can be associated with some semantics or itself is a semantic query, the routing can be significantly improved by using P2P-SLN.

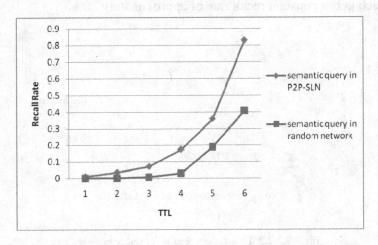

Fig.8.7.5.3 Recall rate of semantic queries as a function of TTL.

8.8   Performance of P2P-SLN

Previous P2P research mainly concerns the issue of efficiently locating the target node in the network. In real applications, each node (peer) needs time to search the answer in the node, so only a limited number of queries can be answered during a certain period of time. If every node frequently issues queries, some queries may be lost due to the limitation of TTL. So a P2P-SLN has a certain service capacity, which is an evidence for designers to select appropriate network for a particular application.

On the other hand, a certain amount of queries passing through the network makes it alive. If every peer (individual) in P2P-SLN is equipped with a knowledge base recording all the questions and answers it handles, then a certain amount of queries routing through a P2P-SLN keeps the network developing from initial status without any problem-solving knowledge to a high-level status with rich problem-solving knowledge. With the growth of individual knowledge, the capacity of the network increases.

In random walk network, if every individual only obtain knowledge within the network, knowledge increase will slow down when the knowledge bases of individuals become close. While in P2P-SLN, most queries are routed within communities, so knowledge difference between communities is clear. Individuals of one community can learn new knowledge from other communities when necessary. P2P network can overcome knowledge equilibrium because new nodes will join in.

8.9   Incorporating Recommendation

Recommendation is a process that a resource finds the peers that need it. Query is a process that a peer finds the needed resources. The two processes can be integrated to complement each other in the same knowledge sharing process.

8.9.1 *Recommendation process*

Before recommendation, each peer should have the ability to determine which resources should be recommended to which peers. In P2P-SLN, resources are linked with semantic links called *RRS*. A resource can be recommended to peers whose resources have *RRS* link to it. For example, peer P_1 has a song S_1, P_2 has a song S_2, and S_1 and S_2 link to each other by the *RRS* of *sameSinger*, then it is appropriate for P_1 to recommend S_1 to P_2. This recommendation is based on semantic link. More recommendation methods could be employed.

After the recommendation method is determined, the recommendation process works as follows:

(1) When a new resource is published on one peer, as a recommender it will actively recommend this resource to relevant peers in the P2P network. In order to avoid endless recommendation and heavy traffic overhead, there may be a limit value r such that the peer can only recommend its new resource to a range of radius r. But not all peers in the range are appropriate to receive this recommendation. The peer

will determine which peers it should recommend to according to the *RRS*.

(2) When a peer receives a recommendation, it checks if the recommendation is required. If required, it will index the recommended resource in its local repository and send a confirmation back to the recommender.

(3) The recommender records the unconfirmed peer(s) and the resources to avoid recommend similar resources to it or them.

Along with the recommendation process, the P2P-SLN network will evolve into a state that every peer knows the location of its potentially needed resources within a scope of radius r. This information can improve the routing efficiency as the routing can take each hop of length r.

8.9.2 *Query routing process*

The recommendation process enables peers to gather the information of resources within the scope of radius r in the network. Just searching in the local repository could know if the needed resource exists within the recommendation range of radius r. Therefore, the routing hop can take the length of r to improve the efficiency.

The routing process works as follows:

(1) The query initiator firstly searches in its local repository. If the termination condition is not satisfied, the initiator adds itself to the visited list for avoiding backward hops, searches the repository to find a peer at a r-distance from the initiator (the distance between peers can be recorded along the recommendation process), and forwards the query to this peer.

(2) When a peer receives a query, it firstly checks if any peer in the visited list except the last one is also in its local repository. If there is such a peer, it transfers the query to the last peer in the visited list and deletes the last peer from the visited list. This backward process is to ensure that the current peer has not been within the influencing scope of the past visited peers. Otherwise, the current peer searches its local repository and responds the matched resources to the initiator. If the

termination condition is not satisfied, the peer adds itself to the visited list, and forwards the query to a peer at r-distance.

(3) When a peer receives a backward query, it only searches its local repository to find another peer at r-distance and forwards the query to it. If no such peer exists and the termination condition is not satisfied, the peer will backward again.

8.9.3 *Experiment*

In order to know how r influences the query efficiency, we carry out the following simulation based on the same set up as that in Query-Answer Simulation section. The experimental result is depicted in Fig 8.9.3. TTL=0 means just searching in the initiator's local repository. When r=5, just searching in local repository can get a relatively high recall rate.

The peer who issues query can always get many feedbacks quickly, which provide more information for peer to avoid blindness in recommendation and query routing. With the increasing of r, the recall rate increases quickly. In return, it produces the increasing number of message transfers during the recommendation process. Balancing these two factors is important for choosing appropriate r.

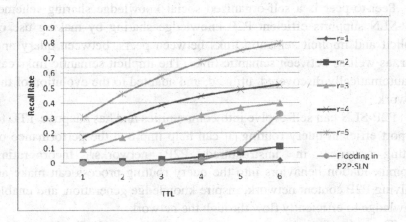

Fig.8.9.3 Recommendation and query with recommendation radius r.

In this simulation, r=5 seems a reasonable value. Compared with the simulation result without using recommendation, *the recall rate of the method without using recommendation heavily depends on the TTL.* Only when TTL value is high enough it can get a reasonably good recall rate. Therefore, it has a longer response time than the method incorporating recommendation.

8.10   Toward P2P Knowledge Flow Networking

Coordinating recommendations, queries, and answers constructs knowledge flow networks through cyber, physical, mental, and socio networks. For example, the knowledge flow through citation network plays an important role in scientific behaviors (H. Zhuge, Discovery of Knowledge Flow in Science, *Communications of the ACM*, 49(5)(2006)101-107).

Various semantic links between individuals play an important role in raising the efficiency of knowledge flows, which carry effective knowledge intensive cooperation although they are invisible.

Various semantic links involve in recommending, querying and answering. Studying the intrinsic relations between various semantic links and the efficiency of query routing in a decentralized network is the key to realize efficient decentralized knowledge sharing.

Peer-to-peer is a self-organized social knowledge sharing scheme. P2P-SLN supports efficient P2P knowledge sharing by making use of explicit and implicit semantic links between peers, between query and peer, as well as between semantic links. The implicit semantic links can be automatically discovered, utilized, and adapted to the evolution of the network.

P2P-SLN can self-evolve into communities and has adaptive TTL to support efficient query routing. It can help improve the performance of routing queries in unstructured P2P networks. Incorporating recommendation behaviors into the query routing process can make an evolving P2P content network, inspire knowledge generation, and enable knowledge to efficiently flow through the network.

The peer who issues query can always get many feedbacks quickly, which provides more information for peers to avoid blindness in recommendation and query routing. In contrast, the recall of the method without using recommendation heavily depends on the TTL. P2P-SLN can be also used in other P2P applications after instantiating the framework.

In P2P-SLN, every individual can issue recommendations, queries, answers, and forward resources, queries and answers in a decentralized network. Knowledge flows through individuals of the network with active recommending, querying, answering and forwarding behaviors. Semantic links between individuals are the basic factor that influences the efficiency of knowledge sharing. Knowing these semantic links enables individuals to communicate only the relevant ones so that decentralized knowledge sharing can be effective.

Recommending, querying and answering are basic behaviors of knowledge sharing in a cooperative network system. A recommendation process may involve in querying and answering since a recommender may need to confirm or complete the content of recommendation by querying peers and getting answers. A querying and answering process may also involve in recommendation since answering can be seen as a kind of recommendation, and the person who answers may also receive recommendations from collaborators.

With continuous querying, answering and recommending between peers, knowledge of peers increase, new links emerge, and communities form and evolve. As the consequence, the performance of the network continuously evolves to support knowledge sharing.

Fig. 8.10 depicts the interactive process consisting of querying, answering, recommending, forwarding, and linking behaviors. Receiving an answer, a peer may generate new relevant queries, which may inspire more thinking of relevant peers in the network and generate more answers and queries. Therefore, more knowledge can be generated in peers' minds and shared through this interactive process.

During the interactive process, peers link queries to answers, link queries to relevant queries, and link answers to relevant answers. A semantic link network of queries and answers are established during the interactive process. The cooperation of the up-level SLN, the low-level SLN and knowledge flow supports intelligent behaviors of peers in the network.

Building the up-level SLN can reserve the semantic image of the cooperative team. Although some peers may leave the team, their knowledge will be reserved in the up-level SLN. The semantic image can keep the knowledge standard of the team. This can also protect the knowledge property of a team.

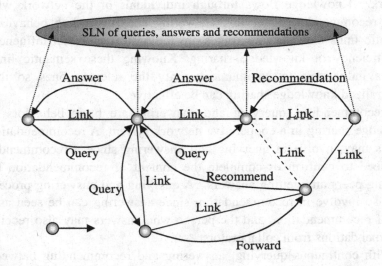

Fig.8.10 Interactive knowledge sharing through social and semantic networking. The solid lines denote the semantic links between peers and the dotted lines denote derived semantic links.

Recommending, forwarding, querying, answering and forwarding behaviors and the interaction among them develops an interactive semantic image for the self-evolving and adaptive peer-to-peer semantic link network to support decentralized knowledge sharing (H.Zhuge, Interactive Semantics, *Artificial Intelligence*, 174(2010)190-204).

During the evolution of the semantic image, various knowledge spaces are generated, linked to queries, answers and recommendation, and keep evolving.

Previous P2P research mainly concerns the issue of efficiently locating the target node in the network. In real applications, each node needs time to search the answer in the node, so only a limited number of queries can be answered during a certain period of time. If every node frequently issues queries, some queries may be lost due to the limitation of TTL. So P2P-SLN has a certain service capacity, based on which designers select appropriate network for a particular application.

If every individual only obtain knowledge within the network, knowledge increase will be slow down when knowledge and knowledge structure of peers become close. While in P2P-SLN, most queries are routed within communities, so knowledge difference between communities is clear. Individuals of one community can learn new knowledge from other communities when necessary. P2P-SLN can overcome knowledge equilibrium because new nodes will join in from time to time.

Chapter 9

P2P Semantic Overlay Networks

Building semantic overlays over P2P networks is a way to realize efficient information and knowledge services over large-scale networks. The problems are: how a P2P network can be adaptive for high-level semantic information management, and how semantic information can be efficiently managed over the network. The first problem concerns network topology and routing. The second problem concerns publishing, indexing and querying complex semantic information.

This chapter suggests a set of scalable solutions for inspiring better innovations. The structured approaches mainly use the structured topology as the underlying network infrastructure to support exact and efficient complex query. Unstructured approaches build the network topology in a loosely coupled way without too much rules and restrictions and queries are processed through random walk or broadcasting methods.

9.1 Structured Approaches

Structured P2P networks are derived from previous parallel and distributed computing platforms that are used to support highly efficient data storage and computing in a parallel way. Mainframes and clusters adopts a certain type of structured graph topology such as hypercube, butterfly or de-bruijn graph to build the underlying network platform for connecting a set of computing nodes or storage nodes high-speed communication channel. Fast communication channels can help distribute both data and computing among nodes so that the load can be evenly shared by nodes and the computing can be parallelized, which greatly improve the efficiency and the scalability of the system. With the rapid development of the cyber space, more and more end-users can access resources with higher bandwidth and availability. Large-scale data publishing and sharing need a new solution that can handle the dynamicity and high-throughput in a large-scale network with millions of users. P2P technique emerges as a promising network infrastructure that received much attention from both industries and academic communities.

To build a P2P network, a natural way is to upgrade traditional distributed computing platforms to adapt to the the dynamicity and in the Internet-scale network environment. The key is to break up the central control and management of the network construction and resource allocation in traditional distributed systems. The server-client infrastructure is not scalable in dealing with large-scale data request in dynamic environments. We need to build the network topology to a more decentralized way so as to reduce the load of the central servers and the risk of single-point failures. Hypercube (B.Y. Zhao, et al. Tapestry: A Resilient Global-Scale Overlay for Service Deployment. *IEEE Journal of Selected Areas in Communication*. 22(1)(2004)41-53), ring with regular long range links (I. Stoica, et al. Chord: A Scalable Peer-to-Peer Lookup Service for Internet Applications. ACM *SIGCOMM*, (2001)149-160), butterfly network (D. Malkhi, et al. Viceroy: A Scalable and Dynamic Emulation of the Butterfly. *ACM PODC '02* pp.183-192) and de-bruijn network (M. F. Kaashoek and D. R. Karger. Koorde: A Simple Degree-Optimal Distributed Hash Table. *IPTPS*2003, pp.98-107) are tuned to the structured P2P networks to support decentralized queries with high availability and scalability. One key advantage of structured P2P networks is that they can support exact decentralized query in logarithmical routing steps with each node having logarithmical or constant routing tables size in terms of the network size. To evenly distribute the data storage load over the network, most of structured P2P networks use consistent hashing method to map data objects to nodes according to their ID distance, named Distributed Hash Table (DHT) P2P networks (H. Balakrishnan, et al. Looking Up Data in P2P Systems. *Communications of ACM* 46(2)(2003) 43-48). Each node maintains a routing table in the ID space to process exact query in a greedy way. That is, each step in a routing process tries to approach the target node ID according to certain distance measurements over the ID space.

To build more intelligent information and knowledge services, we need to support more complex queries with semantics than exact keyword query. However, hashing method destroys original semantic relationships among data objects, making it difficult to support those queries such as range query and prefix query who are basic operators of more complex queries such as join and multi-dimensional queries. To deal with this problem, there are two ways in general: one can design a non-hashing structured P2P network to preserve the original semantics of the data objects, and the other way is to build an extra index over a structure DHT P2P network. The following introduce the two solutions in details.

9.1.1 *An order-preserve structured P2P network*

In DHT P2P networks, a structured ID space is first specified. Then, nodes are evenly mapped into the ID space using a universal hash function such as SHA1 to partition the ID space in ranges where each node holds a specific range according to their hash IDs (H. Balakrishnan, et al. Looking Up Data in P2P Systems. *Communications of ACM*, 46(2)(2003)43-48). Then, data objects are also hashed to the ID space so that they can be evenly held by the network nodes according to the ID distance to the node. Finally, each node builds a routing table by setting up a set of links to remote nodes according to a certain length distribution of links in the ID space. In general, the lengths of links in a routing table of a node are exponentially increasing in the ID space so that they can reach a remote node in a logarithmical scale and the number of links is also in logarithmical scale in terms of the network size. The efficiency of the query routing depends on the length distribution of links in routing tables which in turn depends on the even distribution of node IDs in the ID space.

When nodes join and depart dynamically, the uniformity of node IDs is hard to maintain. Moreover, preserving the order of data objects means that we cannot use hashing function for generating node IDs and data object IDs. Then, the uniformity of node IDs in the ID space is hard to ensure. Actually, any ID dependent routing table construction method will suffer this problem. To solve this problem, we need to seek other information of network to build scalable routing tables for efficient query processing. That is, we still can use an ID space that can preserve a certain order of data objects to build the base network and assign data objects to the network nodes in an order preserving way.

For example, if data objects have integer as their IDs and the increasing order of integer IDs need to be preserved. Then, we can also assign nodes with a set of integer IDs and arrange the nodes in an increasing order in a ring network. Then, a data object is placed to the node that is closest to the data object. In this way, the increasing order of data objects is preserved. Since the distribution of data objects IDs may not uniform (because we do not use hash function), we can also assign node IDs according to the data object ID distribution so that each node can have an even load. In this case, node IDs are also not evenly distributed and routing tables cannot be evenly built. Fig. 9.1.1.1 shows a simple case that uneven distributed node IDs can reduce the routing efficiency.

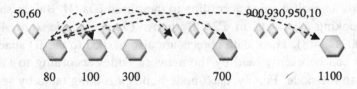

Diamond shapes represent data objects and pentagons are nodes with integer IDs. For example, objects with ID 50 and 60 are in the first node with ID 100 because they fall in the range of 0 to 100. Dotted lines are routing table links of node 100 in a uniform distribution of node IDs. But in this figure node IDs are not uniformly distributed. So, many links that previous point to different nodes will point to one node, in this case, node 700. The long links that can skip across a large set of nodes in an even distribution of IDs now can only cover a smaller set of nodes, which will reduce the greedy routing efficiency.

Fig. 9.1.1.1 Uneven distribution of network node IDs.

To overcome this issue, an ID-independent routing table construction method can be devised to ensure a highly efficient query routing processing in an one-dimensional linear ID space. HRing P2P network is a non-hashing one-dimensional ring P2P network (H. Zhuge, et al. HRing: A Structured P2P Overlay Based on Harmonic Series. *IEEE*

Transactions on Parallel Distributed Systems, 19(2)(2008)145-158). The basic idea of HRing is to build long-range links through traversing a sequence of nodes one by one along a ring network and setting up a connection according to the distance that the traversal has been made.

The Basic Structure

The base network of HRing is a ring topology. The ID space is determined by a linear order relationship such as the order of integers or the prefix order of strings over data objects. Network nodes are assigned an ID from the ID space and are sorted in the increasing order so that each node holds a continuous range between the previous node ID and its node ID in the ID space. We use v_1, v_2, ..., v_n to denote the sorted nodes. Nodes with neighboring ranges are connected and the last node connects to the first node to form a base ring topology. To find an object is equivalent to locate the node that has the range cover the object ID. Without any long range links, $O(n)$ greedy routing hops is required to locate a node in a network of size n.

To facilitate query routing, each node builds a set of long range links over the base ring network in a simple way. Assuming that the base network is already built, each node then sends a routing message along the base ring network to traverse the ring in one direction. The traversal only uses the direct neighboring nodes and visits nodes one by one along the ring. Considering a node v_i that starts its traversal. For the first visited node, that is v_{i+1}, node v_i setups a link to v_{i+1} with probability 1. Since the neighboring node already has been connected, we continue to the next node v_{i+2} and connect v_i to v_{i+2} with probability 1/2. That is, v_i has one-half chance to link to v_{i+2}. Continuing this process, node v_i connects to node v_{i+k} with probability $1/k$ until it visits all the reset nodes in the ring and loops back. Each node in the ring will execute the same scheme to build their routing tables. In this process, we do not use any ID information of nodes. So, this process of building routing tables is ID-independent. Note that, this basic approach will need $O(n)$ hops to build a routing table and we will discuss how to avoid this in the following sections. Fig. 9.1.1.2 shows a basic long links building process.

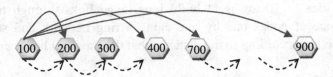

Solid links are those links that are selected during the traversal from node 100. Dotted links are the traversal process along the neighboring nodes from node 100.

Fig. 9.1.1.2 Building long range links.

Let k be the kth node v_j visited from a given node v_i, that is, $j = i + k$. and let the $d(v_j, v_i) = k$ be ring distance between node v_i and v_j. It is obvious that the expected number links that v_i builds in one round is $H_n = \sum_{k=1}^{n} \frac{1}{k}$, which is coincident with the well-known Harmonic Series that approaches to $ln(n) + e$ as n increases (J. Havil and F. Dyson. The Harmonic Series, Chapter.2 in Gamma: Exploring Euler's Constant. *Princeton, NJ: Princeton University Press*, 2003), where e is Euler number. So, the expected number of long links is approximately $ln(n)$.

The greedy query routing process is simple. For a given node v_i sending a query to a data object u_i, it just selects from its routing table the link v_r with the ID closest but less than the ID of u_j and forward the query to v_r until reaching the host node of the data object. To analyze the routing efficiency, we just need to calculate how far a long link can reach during one step of the routing process.

Theorem 9.1. *Given two nodes v_i and v_j with $d(v_i, v_j) = d$ in a HRing network of size n, the greedy routing steps is $ln(d)+1$ in expectation.*
Proof. For a node u with $d(u, v_j) = x$, then, we have

$$\frac{1}{d} + \frac{1}{d-1} + \frac{1}{d-2} + ... + \frac{1}{d-x} = 1 \Rightarrow (1-\frac{1}{e})d - 1,$$

which means that in expectation there is a long link that can reduce the distance to v_j to d/e. In another word, we can find a link to reduce the distance to v_j to d/e in one step. Then, after $ln(d) + 1$ steps, we can reduce the distance to zero, which means that we find the target node. □

Dynamic Management

In a real application, we cannot assume a perfect ring network to be built before long links are constructed for each node. In fact, P2P networks are constructed in an evolving mode. Thus, the long links also need to be dynamically constructed and maintained.

In a dynamic environment, nodes can keep joining for a long period to form a larger network. Consider a HRing network of size n that has been well constructed, another new set of nodes of size n joins the network, without updating previous long-range links. Then, in an evenly join case where new nodes are uniformly distributed in the previous ring network, the routing efficiency does not deteriorate much, increasing to $ln(2n)$. So, we do not need to frequently update the routing tables of nodes when new nodes joins or depart, as long as the join and departure are evenly distributed and the base ring network is maintained. However, traversal in the network is still a problem for the basic routing table construction of HRing. We need to design a more efficient routing table construction

Theorem 9.2. *Let* $I_i = [e^i, e^{i+1})(i = 0, 1, ..., \lceil ln(n) \rceil - 1$ *be the ith range starting from the point at the distance e^i from node v. Then, there are $ln(n)$ such ranges from v. Selecting randomly from each range one node as a long range link for node v, the routing table can still help achieve $O(ln(n))$ in expectation.*

Proof. It is obvious that jumping into ith range can reduce the distance to $1/e$ of the distance of previous routing step. After $ln(n)$ such steps, the distance is reduced to zero. □

From Theorem 9.2, we can see that there are actually a large set of candidates for each long links in a routing tables. We can use this property to build routing tables more efficiently. First, we need to estimate the current network size as the network keeps growing. To do this, a new node randomly selects an existing node v and visits the next $k = ln(n)$ continuous nodes from v. Note that each node has a chance of $ln(n)/n$ to be visited in this process. When an existing node u is visited by some new node, u can estimate a new current network size by following equation:

$$\frac{\ln(n_0)}{n_0} + \frac{\ln(n_0+1)}{n_0+1} + \frac{\ln(n_0+2)}{n_0+2} + \dots + \frac{\ln(n_0+x_1)}{n_0+x_1} = 1$$

That is, the summation of the probability of being visited at time 0, time 1 and time x is 1. Thus, u has a new network size and will update n_0 for the next update. Then, the current network size is estimated as $n_0 = n_0 + x$. In this way, each node can estimate the growing network size periodically and new node can acquire the current network size by existing network nodes.

After getting an estimated network size n, a new node v cannot build up its routing tables. Suppose that v visited an existing node u and its next $k = ln(n)$ consecutive nodes. Let u_k be the kth node in this visiting process. Considering one neighbor w of u_k that is located in the ith long link range I_i of u_k, then, we have $e^i + k \le d(v, u_k) \le e^{i+1} + k$, that is, we can use u_k as the $i+1$ long range link of node v. In this way, we can build an approximate long range link table by visiting only $O(ln(n))$ nodes. Experiments show compared with that of perfect environments. But the logarithmical scale is still perfectly maintained (H. Zhuge, et al. HRing: A Structured P2P Overlay Based on Harmonic Series. *IEEE Transactions on Parallel Distributed Systems*, 19(2)(2008)145-158).

Discussion

One of key issue in HRing is the load balancing problem. Since no hash function is used and data object distributions can be highly skewed, a portion of network can have a high load. There are many works have been proposed to address load balancing problem. One approach is to let those lightly loaded nodes join highly loaded ranges to share the load (P. Ganesan, et al. Online Balancing of Range-Partitioned Data with Applications to Peer-to-Peer Systems. *VLDB04*, pp.444-455). In HRing, leaving and re-joining network need to update routing tables to maintain the routing efficiency. This can be done in period to avoid frequent routing table updates.

HRing provides a scalable method to build routing tables independent of specific application ID space. Many attributes such as integer and real number, date, address, and strings can be published in

HRing and their orders can be explicitly retained so that range queries can be directly supported. Multi-attributes can also be published into the same HRing network with each attribute occupy a certain continuous range of the whole ID space. HRing can support more complex semantic indexing scheme.

9.1.2 *Distributed suffix tree*

This section introduces an indexing structure built over a structure P2P network to support complex string queries including prefix string query and sub-string query. As we have discussed in the beginning of the section, DHT P2P networks cannot directly support complex queries. To support string queries, a direct way is to deploy a traditional indexing structure over a structure P2P network so that complex string queries can be efficiently processed in large scale distributed networks. On one hand, we can leverage the advantages of DHT P2P networks to deal with large-scale dynamic network nodes management. On the other hand, we can deploy different indexing schemes over one structured DHT P2P network to seamless extend the functions of the system. Fig. 9.1.2.1 shows an infrastructure of indexing structures over a structured DHT P2P network.

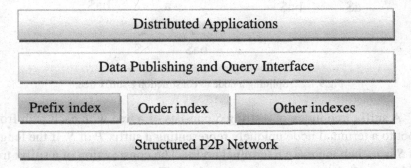

Fig. 9.1.2.1 Indexes Over DHT P2P Networks.

It can be seen that we need to tune an index structure to a DHT P2P network, which requires both a new indexing construction method over a distributed and dynamic network and a new query scheme that can leverage DHT query routing processes. To show how this can be done, we introduce a way to build a Distributed Suffix Tree (DST) over a DHT P2P network for supporting string query (H. Zhuge and L. Feng. Distributed Suffix Tree Overlay for Peer-to-Peer Search. *IEEE Transactions on Knowledge and Data Engineering*.20(2)(2008)276-285.).

Basic Suffix Index

Suffix Index is designed for supporting efficient string query on a set of strings (E.M.McCreight. A Space-Economical Suffix Tree Construction Algorithm. *Journal of ACM*, 23(2)(1976)262-272). It is designed for indexing sub-strings so that sub-string query can be efficiently processed. For a query that has a matched sub-string of length M, suffix tree index can find the matched sub-string in M steps of traversal on the index tree. Suffix tree can also be used to locate matches for sub-strings with a certain number of mistakes and for locating matches of a regular expression.

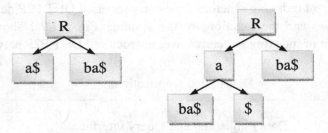

Fig.9.1.2.2 Splitting a node to construction a suffix tree.

A suffix tree index of a string S consists of a tree with each path from root to a terminal node uniquely representing a suffix P of S. If the length of S is n, then there are n terminal nodes. The construction of a suffix tree index startS from an empty root node R. Then, we start from rightmost position of S and scan S from right to left. That is, each time we got a suffix string s_i of S and add s_i to a prefix tree. See an example of *ababa*$ where $ is the ending tag of string. We have the first suffix $a$$, so just add it as the first child of THE root R. Then, moving to one character left, we have $ba$$, which shares no prefix with a$, so we just add it to the root R. Now root R has two children. Next, we have *aba*$.

This time, *aba*$ share a prefix *a* with *a*$, so we add it the node *a*$, by splitting *a*$ to two nodes, one is for $ the other is for *ba*$ and leave *a* as the sub-root of this new node. See Fig. 9.1.2.2 for such a splitting process during the suffix tree construction. This process is executed until the whole string *S* is scanned. Searching for a sub-string will start from the root and follow the child links that has matched prefix characters until the whole matched pattern is completely found.

Publishing Suffix Tree

The DST indexing builds a virtual suffix tree over a DHT P2P network to support sub-string queries. In any structured DHT P2P network, there are two basic data operators: PUBLISH(*key*, *object*) is to published an *object* with keyword *key* onto the network, where key can be a title or even the full string of the object. LOCATE(*key*) is to retrieve all the published objects with the matching *key* string. The DST indexing scheme will use this two basic functions to deploy the indexing nodes over a DHT P2P network.

To publish a suffix tree on a DHT P2P network, DST method simply publishes each edge in the tree using PUBLISH(*key*, *object*) function, where *key* is the edge label string and *object* is the edge structure that contains the adjacent nodes of the edge in the suffix tree. Considering the root node R with with child nodes *a* and *ba*$ in Fig. 9.1.2.2, two objects are published, one is ob_1 = [*key*= a, *edge* = a, *childkey* = 2, *object* = h(ababa$)], the other is ob_2 = [*key*= b, *edge* = ba$, *childkey* = 0, *object* = h(ababa$)]. Then, for a child of node *a*, we publish the object as ob_3 = [*key* = 2, *edge* = ba$, *childkey* = 0, object = h(ababa$)]. Note that ob_3 use the *key* = 2 as the hash ID for publishing. In this way, we can follow the *childkey* of ob_1 to get ob_3, which is a childe of node *a* in the suffix tree.

In an object, four attributes are recorded. Attribute *key* is used as the key for publishing the object. *edge* is used to represent the edge string. *childkey* is used to denote the child node linked by the current edge. *object* is the pointer to the resources that contain the whole string. Fig. 9.1.2.3 shows the published objects in a ring DHT network. Note that we do not store the root node, but only store the child nodes of the root node. Query routing using DST is also simple. Considering a query for finding 'aba', the first character 'a' is extracted and using LOCATE($key=a$), we can get node 1 that host the object ob_1. Then, following the *childkey* = 2 of ob_1 we issue a new query LOCATE($key = a$) and get node 10 that hosts object ob_3. In this way, we can search the DST until reaching the end tag of the string.

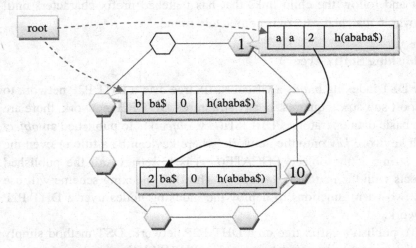

Fig. 9.1.2.3 Publishing suffix tree in a ring DHT. P2P. Network

Locating a sub-string firstly needs to find the network node that hosts the root node of the suffix tree, and then follows the suffix tree pointers to the sub-string pattern match process. If the network size is n and the matched sub-string has length L, then, the query process can be bounded in $O(\ln(n) + L)$. Thus, when $L \gg \ln(n)$ is large, the query efficiency is approaching an optimal one.

Discussion

The DST publishes a suffix tree over a DHT P2P network to support sub-string query in a large-scale distributed environment. It does not depend on any specific DHT P2P network and can be easily deployed and updated dynamically. One key advantage of DST is that it supports sub-string query in distributed environment. Sub-string queries can be extended to implement various applications such as distributed inverted index, XML path query, RDF subsumption path query, ..., etc.

9.1.3 *IMAGINE — A general index structure over structured DHT P2P networks*

Previous section introduces a distributed suffix tree index that supports sub-string query over a DHT P2P work. As we can see, more general indexing schemes can be deployed over a DHT P2P network to support various different queries that enable Knowledge Grid services over a large scale and dynamic environment. The IMAGINE platform is such a platform that enables users to deploy a traditional index structure over a Chord network to support distributed indexing query (H. Zhuge, et al. A Scalable P2P Platform for the Knowledge Grid. *IEEE Transactions on Knowledge and Data Engineering*, 17(12)(2005)1721-1736). The IMAGINE platform publishes the edge set of an index in a DHT P2P network as a semantic overlay to support different kinds of queries over one network.

Basic Structure of IMAGINE

For a tree like indexing structure such as B-tree, binary tree, trie index, etc, IMAGINE takes each edge of the index as a semantic object and publish it using the incident nodes of the edge. That is, an edge in an index can be represented as a tripe $SO(a, R, b)$. Thus, we can use either a or b, or both as the *key* of function PUBLISH(key, SO) to publish this semantic object over a DHT P2P network. A path in the index is a semantic path $sp(a_1R_1a_2R_2...a_{n-1}R_{n-1}a_n)$. A semantic path sp can be decomposed into $n-1$ semantic objects: $SO_1(a_1, R_1, a_2)$, $SO_2(a_2, R_2, a_3)$, ..., $SO_{n-1}(a_{n-1}, R_{n-1}, a_n)$. Note that an edge with the same node labels but in different paths cannot be discriminated in this way. Thus, we can use path IDs to publish the semantic path. That is, a semantic path $sp(a_1R_1a_2R_2...a_{n-1}R_{n-1}a_n)$ is decomposed into: $SO_1(a_1, R_1, a_2)$, $SO_2(a_1a_2, R_2, a_3)$, ..., $SO_{n-1}(a_1a_2...a_{n-1}, R_{n-1}, a_n)$. For two physical nodes (i.e., the nodes in the underlying DHT P2P network), if they host a set of semantic objects that belong to one or more edges of the index, a routing link is built between these two physical nodes. Fig 9.1.3.1 shows that four semantic objects are published onto two index nodes in two DHT nodes. SO_2 and SO_3

are published in the same nodes because they have the same key. SO_1 and SO_4 are located in the same node because their hash IDs are coincidently hosted by the same node, i.e., node B. The dotted links represent the edges in the index. The solid arrow represents the routing table link from node A to node B. In this case, a query along two different paths from SO_3 to SO_4 and from SO_1 to SO_2 and to SO_4 can be processed in one network routing path from node A to node B. Thus, it can be seen the routing hops can be compressed.

The query processing in a published index is simple. To located one

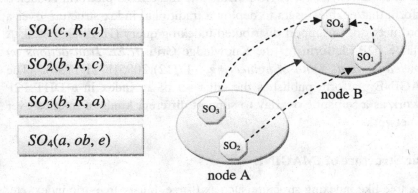

Fig. 9.1.3.1 Publishing semantic objects in two DHT network nodes A and B.

semantic object $SO(a, R, b)$, one just uses the function LOCATE(key = a) or LOCATE(key = b) to find the object in the DHT P2P network. Similarly, to locate a semantic path $sp(a_1R_1a_2R_2...a_{n-1}R_{n-1}a_n)$, a sequence of sub-queries is issued for locating semantic objects with path keys: $SO_1(a_1, R_1, a_2)$, $SO_2(a_1a_2, R_2, a_3)$, ..., $SO_{n-1}(a_1a_2...a_{n-1}, R_{n-1}, a_n)$. Note that, one can use the last semantic object to judge if the path exists, but if there are data objects attached to the internal nodes in the path, one needs to locate those semantic objects one by one. For one semantic object query, we can locate the object with $O(\log(n))$ query hops based on the DHT P2P network query process. For a semantic path query, the query process can be finished in $O(\log(n) + L)$ hops when all the indexing links are built among physical nodes, where L is the length of the semantic path.

Publishing a distributed trie index on IMAGINE

We show how to publish a trie index on IMAGINE. A trie index is a tree structure indexing strings by arranging the strings that share a certain prefix in a unique path from the root in the index. More specifically, for each

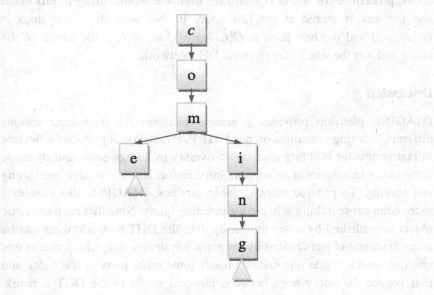

Fig. 9.1.3.2 A trie index for two strings 'come' and 'coming'.

character of a string, a path is constructed by scanning the string from the left to the right and for each character, an indexing node is built and for each adjacent pairs of character an edge is built. Fig 9.1.3.2 shows how two strings 'come' and 'coming' are organized in a trie index. The two strings share the common prefix 'com', so they share the path from 'c' to 'm'. A query over a trie index is processed by the following matched characters of the query string over the trie index until reaching the leaf node. Trie index supports efficient prefix query with less space cost than the suffix tree index.

To published a distributed trie index on IMAGINE, it simple takes the indexing edges as semantic objects to publish a key string. For example, considering a key string 'come', we decompose it into a set of semantic objects: SO_1('c', 'o'), SO_2('co', 'm'), and SO_3('com', 'e'). First semantic object query will find the node A that host key 'c', if there is already an indexing link to a physical node B that host 'co', then we just follow that indexing link to node B and proceed the next character 'm' in the same way. If there is no such an indexing link to node B, we need to issue another semantic object query to locate node B that host 'co'. After reaching node B, we continue the above procedure for the next character until the whole string is processed and the key is stored at the last node. In this way, the worst hops is $O(Llog(n))$ and the best hops is $O(L+log(n))$, where L is the length of the string and n is the size of the physical DHT network.

Discussion

IMAGINE platform provides a general platform for publishing various different indexing structures on one DHT P2P network. It provides a flexible infrastructure for building a semantic overlay in a large-scale and dynamic networking environment to support information and knowledge publishing and sharing. To provide more scalable services, IMAGINE also enables a more compact searching scheme for indexing query. Note that each semantic object is published by a key uniformly over the DHT network, there can be many semantic objects hosted by the same physical nodes, which means that one can search inside one node to reach some other parts of the index and thus reduce the query hops between physical nodes in the DHT network. Another problem is load balancing. Many traditional indexing schemes use a tree structure and queries are issued from the root node in the index, which can impose heavy load on the physical node that hosts the root indexing node. To relieve the load IMAGINE adopts a load moving method to balancing load in a heterogeneous physical network. Basically, a node with high query load will produce replica around its neighboring nodes to help relieve the query pressure. Experiments show that the basic idea works fine for various different situations.

9.1.4 *Building small-world network in multi-dimensional space*

Many data sets are multi-dimensional, for example, space data, image data, and relational data with multiple attributes. To publish multi-dimensional data on a large-scale distributed network, we need to design specific distributed indexing structure to efficiently support point query and range query. Most DHT P2P networks use linear ID space (H. Balakrishnan, et al., Looking Up Data in P2P Systems. *Communications of ACM.* 46(2)(2003)43-48), which is not suitable for multi-dimensional data. CAN is multi-dimensional P2P network that supports point and range query in distributed way (S. Ratnasamy, et al., A Scalable Content-Addressable Network. *ACM SIGCOMM.* 2001, pp161-173). It partitions the space into a set of sub ranges and builds links between neighboring sub ranges. In CAN, the routing hops is $O(dn^{1/d})$ and $O(\log n)$ for $d = O(\log n)$. This section introduces a small-world CAN network (SCAN) that can achieve a better routing hops with augmenting the base CAN network node a set of long range links (H. Zhuge and X. Sun. A Virtual Ring Method for Building Small-World Structured P2P Overlays. *IEEE Transactions on Knowledge and Data Engineering.* 20(12)(2008)1712-1725). The long range link is built in a small-world way in a multi-dimensional Cartesian ID space so that logarithmical routing efficiency can be attained in d-dimensional space.

Basic Idea of SCAN

Small-world phenomenon is an interesting network property that was first experimentally studied in social networks (S. Milgram. The Small World Problem. *Psychology Today*, 1(61)(1967)). Small-world networks extensively exist in various large-scale systems such as Internet, World Wide Web, social network, citation network, neural system, ecological systems etc. (D. Watts and S. Strogatz. Collective Dynamics of small-world networks. *Nature*, 393(6684)(1998)440-2). The small-world network has two basic properties, that is, the short diameter that is in logarithmical scale in terms of the network size and a high cluster co-efficiency that shows the links are more likely to connect near neighboring nodes than far nodes. Researchers have already proposed many models to explain the basic properties of small-world networks and discover many important features such as power-law degree distribution (R. Albert and A.-L.Barabasi, Statistical Mechanics of Complex Networks, *Reviews of Modern Physics*, 74(47)(2002)47-97). Kleinberg proposed a constructive model that to explicitly build a small-world network in a 2-D Cartesian space (J. Kleinberg, Small-World Phenomena and the Dynamics of Information, *Proceeding of Advances in Neural*

Information Processing Systems, 14, (2001)431-415). The basic idea is to use a harmonic distribution to generate one long links based on the L_2-distance in the space for each node to support efficient and deterministic greedy query routing. Manku proposed a structured P2P network Symphony that use Kleinberg's model to build long links in one-dimensional ring network in a linear ID space (G. Manku, et al. Symphony: Distributed Hashing in a Small World. *Proceeding of the 4th USENIX Symposium on Internet Technologies and Systems*, (2003)10-22). Both Kleinberg's model and Symphony require the network size as the normalized factor of the harmonic distribution to build long links. SCAN design a small-world network model named virtual ring model to build long-range links in d-dimensional Cartesian space.

First, we introduce how to build long links in a ring topology with a ring distance without using the real network size n. Assuming I is a real interval $[0, H]$ ($H \geq 1$). We randomly draw n real numbers from I as node IDs and sort them in increasing order as id_1, id_2, ..., id_n. Neighboring nodes in I (id_1 and id_n are neighbors) are connected. Data objects also have IDs from I. A node id_i holds data with IDs falling in the range (id_{i-1}, id_i]. We define the ring distance as $d_R(x, y) = (y - x + H) \mod H$. For each node id_i we generate $log(N)$ long link IDs in H, where N is a predefined integer $N \gg n$. Each long link ID r is produced as: $r = (id_i + H / e^x) \mod H$, where x is randomly drawn from interval $[0, \log N]$. In this way, the generated long links ID r follow a harmonic distribution. Then, node id_i connects those remote nodes that host long link ID r. In this process, only N and H are predefined parameters.

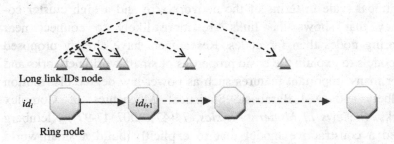

Fig. 9.1.4.1 Ring network with long links.

It can be seen that $\log(N)$ long link IDs will finally be hosted by $O(log\ (n))$ different nodes in a uniformly distributed ring network. Basically, most links near id_i will be hosted by its direct next neighbor. Fig. 9.1.4.1 shows most long links of a node id_i is hosted by its direct neighbor id_{i+1} in the ring network. Using this property we can build long links without getting the network size.

But, how can be build long links in a multi-dimensional space in the similarly way? By mapping a multi-dimensional space into a virtual ring network, we can leverage one-dimensional method to build long links in a multi-dimensional ID space with a distance metric. The basic idea is to put all the nodes that are at the distance k from a node id_i into the kth ring node and thus build a ring network of size L, where L is the network diameter. This method assumes that the network is symmetry and even distributed in its ID space. That is, the virtual ring network is similar for each real node. Fig.9.1.4.2 shows how to map a network into a virtual ring network for a real network node A. Node A is mapped into the first node in the virtual ring and the direct neighbors of A are mapped into one virtual node next to the virtual node id_1. In this way, we can get a virtual ring network for a real node.

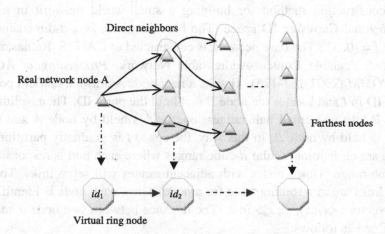

Fig. 9.1.4.2 Virtual ring method.

After mapping a network to a virtual ring network, we can design a long link construction based on the virtual ring network and then map those long links in the virtual ring back to the real network to build the real routing table links.

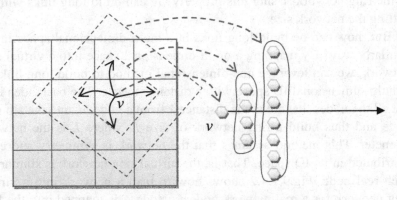

Fig. 9.1.4.3 Map a 2d CAN to a virtual ring network.

Building long links in SCAN

This section shows that how to use the virtual ring method to design long link construction method for building a small-world network in a *d*-dimensional Cartesian ID space. The base ID space is a *d*-dimensional range $I = [0, 1]^d$. The base network is constructed as CAN (S. Ratnasamy, et al. A Scalable Content-Addressable Network. *Proceeding of ACM SIGCOMM* (2001)161-173). That is, a new node *A* draws a random point as an ID in *I* and locates the node *B* that hold the point ID. Then, splitting node *B* into two equal half ranges, one half is held by node *A* and the other is held by node *B*. In this way, the space *I* is gradually partitioned into a set of disjoint regular *d*-cube ranges where each nod is responsible for one range. Those nodes with adjacent ranges will setup links. Thus, $O(d)$ links are in a routing table for a node. Then, each node is identified by a vector $v<x_1, x_2, ..., x_d>$ in *I*. The distance between two node *u* and *v* is defined as follows:

$$d(v,u) = \sum_{i=1}^{d} d_i(x_i, y_i),$$

where $d_i(x_i, y_i) = min\{abs(x_i - y_i), H - abs(x_i - y_i)\}$. Obviously, $L_{max} = dH / 2$.

Considering a node v, it can be seen that the number of nodes at the network distance l from v is $f_v(l) = O(d \cdot l^{d-1})$ and $l_{max} = O(dn^{1/d})$. Thus, for a given node v, the virtual ring size is $O(dn^{1/d})$. Fig. 9.1.4.3 shows the mapping from a 2d CAN to a virtual ring for a node v. Then, the node v is mapped to the first node of the ring network, the direct neighbors (those cube chained with inner dotted line) are mapped to the next node of v, the nodes at the two steps away from v, i.e., those nodes chained by the outer dotted line, are mapped to the third virtual node from v.

But, we do not know the real network size n. Fortunately, we have shown that long links can be built without knowing n in previous discussions. We first build long link in this virtual ring. Note that the maximum Manhattan distance L_{max} is $dH / 2$. We generate $logN$ random real numbers $r_1, r_2, ..., r_k$, as the distance from a set of remote nodes to v. Here we assume that the virtual ring ID of node v is zero, so $r_i = L_{max} / e^x$, where x is a real number randomly drawn from the real interval $[0, log N]$ and N is a predefined large integer greater than l_{max}. So, we setup $logN$ long links in the virtual ring. And then, we need to map those long links back the real network nodes. r_i is actually a distance value but not a real node ID. That is, we know that there must be some points held by a certain node at distance r_i from v. In a one-dimensional ring ID space, that point can be easily calculated as $R_i = id_i + r_i$. In a multi-dimensional ID space with Manhattan distance, we need a little more work to get the ID of a remote point that is at distance r_i from a node $v < x_1, x_2, ..., x_d >$. Just as shown in Fig. 9.1.4.3, points at distance l from node v forms a diamond shape in the ID space. What we do is to randomly select one point p_l from the border of that diamond shape. Then, we find the physical node u that hosts the point p_l and connect u as a long link of v. Similar to the one-dimensional ring network, using $logN$ points can finally generate $O(log n)$ physical nodes as long links.

SCAN uses a simple greedy routing method to locate a node. That is, each intermediate node selects from its routing tables a node that is the closest to the target in the d-dimensional space based on the Manhattan distance. It is demonstrated that the routing hops is bounded by $O(log_2(dn^{1/d}))$ in expectation (H. Zhuge and X. Sun, A Virtual Ring Method for Building Small-World Structured P2P Overlays. *IEEE Transactions on Knowledge and Data Engineering.* 20(12)(2008)1712-1725).

Discussion

SCAN uses a simple method to map a d-dimensional CAN network to a virtual ring network and builds long links using one-dimensional ring method, then maps those long links to real network to form a small-world structure network. The key is the harmonic distribution in the distance space and the uniformly distributed nodes in the ID space and in the distance space. Note that the uniformity can be in different styles. For example, SCAN method can be used in an irregular d-dimensional space where nodes form an $m_1 \times m_2 \times ... \times m_d$ grid. That is, the ID space is partitioned more times in one dimension than another. In this case, SCAN also works. One problem is the uneven partition of nodes where some nodes hold much larger links than others. This can be incurred when nodes keep join and departure or nodes have even distributed IDs. In this case, the larger node will holds more data objects and links. To relieve this unbalance, one can use neighbors to share the range so the the partition becomes more and more even. One key advantage of SCAN is that it naturally supports range query, similarity query and nearest neighbor query in a distributed way, which can be leveraged to support many large scale intelligent services.

9.2   Unstructured Approaches

9.2.1 *Explicit semantic link*

Structured P2P networks can support exact query efficiently and complex indexing structure can be deployed over a structured P2P network to support more query types. However, the dynamicity of networks makes structured P2P network hard to maintain in real networks. Unstructured networks are more suitable for those large-scale networks of huge dynamicity. In fact, most real P2P applications are based on unstructured network topologies. An unstructured P2P network allows nodes to freely setup a set of links to any node existing on the network. Data objects are located at the node that publishes them. That is, they do not explicitly map data objects to a deterministic network node according to certain mapping rules. Keyword queries are broadcasted over the network to find the desired data objects. To improve performance, cached replica of data objects are published on those nodes that have retrieved the objects. Most unstructured P2P networks are capable for handling millions of users for file or stream sharing such as KaZaa (*www.kazaa.com*), Gnutella (*www.gnutella.com*) and Bittorent (*www.bittorrent.com*).

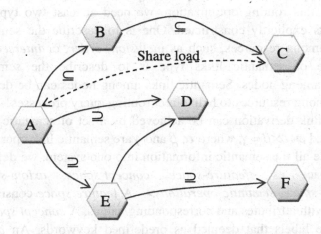

Fig. 9.2.1 Semantic links in an unstructured P2P network.

To enable data publishing and query with more semantics over large-scale dynamic network environment, we need to incorporate semantic object representation method to allow users publish more structured information. Semantic Link Network is a candidate method (H. Zhuge, Autonomous semantic link networking model for the Knowledge Grid. *Concurrency and Computation: Practice and Experience.*

19(7)(2007)1065-1085). With the semantic links and reasoning rules on semantic links, a P2P network can support various relational queries, for example, it can find all the resources linked to the given resource with the given relations, and can find the relations between two given resources. In an unstructured P2P network, a node can setup semantic links with its neighbors to guide queries with more semantic meanings (H. Zhuge, X. Li. Peer-to-Peer in Metric Space and Semantic Space. *IEEE Transactions on Knowledge and Data Engineering.* 19(6)(2007)759-771). For example, if a node A knows the resources of node B are also included in A, queries towards B may not be necessary, which can reduce the query load over the network. Or, a load balancing scheme can be adopted based on this inclusion information. Fig. 9.2.1 shows an example. Resources in node A are also in node B and node C. We can infer that resources in A is also in node C and build an extra link from A to B to speed up the query by sharing loads among node A and C.

To enable this routing optimization, we need at least two types of semantic links explicitly constructed. One is to describe the semantic relationship among resources, such as *inclusion*, *order*, or *intersection*. Another type of semantic links type is to describe the semantic relationships among nodes. Semantic links among nodes can be derived from those among resources to help direct routing query processes.

Semantic link derivation can be achieved by a set of semantic rules that are defined as $\alpha \times \beta = \gamma$, where α, β and γ are semantic link operators. To incorporate all the semantic information into one system, we define a semantic space as *<feature-space, concept-space, axiom-space, semantic-link-space, semantic-operations>*. A *feature space* consists of a set of data with attributes and corresponding values. A *concept space* is a set of node labels that deemed as predefined keywords. An *axiom space* consists of a set of semantic links taken to be true. A *semantic link space* consists of tuples like *<u, r, v>* where u and v are taken from the feature space, the concept space and the axiom space. r is the relationship defined for a semantic link. Semantic link operations are defined as the mapping from the Cartesian product of two semantic link spaces to one semantic link space. Using semantic link operations, one can derive new semantic links from existing ones.

9.2.2 *Gossip through semantic unstructured P2P network*

Gossip methods adopt the virus propagation mode to disseminate information on a network (N. T. J. Bailey. The Mathematics Theory of Infectious Diseases and Its Applications, second ed. *Hafner Press*. 1975). They are generally used for application level multi-cast. On a large-scale unstructured P2P network, we can use a gossip method to disseminate messages quickly, reliably, and fault-tolerantly (W. Vogels, et al., The Power of Epidemics: Robust Communication for Large-Scale Distributed Systems. *ACM SIGCOMM Computer Communication Review*. 33(1) (2003)131-135). The basic idea of a gossip method is to randomly select a set of neighbor nodes to forward messages. Messages are redundantly broadcasted, ensuring that most nodes can be reached even in node crashes and network changes. Gossip methods are more scalable and robust than general flooding methods.

In a general unstructured network, those nodes with high incoming link number will receive more messages than those that have few incoming degree. Moreover, traditional gossip methods did not consider high-level semantics of nodes. A gossip method that incorporates metric space into gossip method to guide message dissemination is introduced (H. Zhuge and X. Li, Peer-to-Peer in Metric Space and Semantic Space. *IEEE Transactions on Knowledge and Data Engineering*. 19(6) (2007)759-771).

The basic gossip method is as follows: when a node v receives a message, it first checks the Time-To-Live(TTL) value. If TTL >0, then the message should be forwarded to some neighbors by reducing TTL by one. For each neighbor u_i, v chooses it as the next step of the message by a probability p_i, where p_i is defined as:

$$p_i = \frac{\varphi(u_i)}{\sum_j \varphi(u_j)}$$, where $\varphi(u_i)$ is the neighbor selection function

according to certain metric defined based on the network topology information.

We can use different $\varphi(u_i)$ to guide the the neighbor selection. For example, we take the incoming link as an important factor. Then we can set:

$$\varphi(u_i) = \begin{cases} \dfrac{\alpha}{d(u_i)}, & \text{if } d(u_i) > 0 \\ 0, & \text{otherwise} \end{cases} \quad \text{, where } d(u_i) \text{ is the in-degree of } u_i.$$

If the out-degree is considered, we can set

$$\varphi(u_i) = \begin{cases} \alpha_2 - \dfrac{\alpha 2}{D(u_i)}, & \text{if } D(u_i) > 0 \\ \beta_1, & \text{if } D(u_i) = 1 \\ \beta_2, & \text{if } D(u_i) = 0 \end{cases} \quad \text{, where } D(u_i) \text{ is the out-degree of}$$

node u_i, α_2, β_1 and β_2 are control parameters.

When taking both in-degree and out-degree into consideration, we can set:

$$\varphi(u_i) = \begin{cases} \alpha_1(\alpha_2 - \dfrac{\alpha 2}{D(u_i)})\dfrac{1}{d(u_i)}, & \text{if } D(u_i) > 0 \text{ and } d(u_i) > 1 \\ \beta_1, & \text{if } D(u_i) > 0 \text{ and } d(u_i) = 1 \\ \beta_2, & \text{if } D(u_i) > 0 \text{ and } d(u_i) = 0 \\ 0, & \text{if } d(u_i) = 0 \end{cases}$$

Experiments show that above the three method of choosing neighbors can be well tuned to achieve a better multicast performance and robustness in unstructured P2P networks than flooding.

The neighbor selection function can be used to incorporate semantic link networks deployed over an unstructured P2P network to guide the gossip routing process. Let $\mu(u_i)$ be the set of node semantic links from node v to node u_i. We can use the number of semantic links for the neighbor selection, instead of using the degree. Then, we have:

$$\varphi(u_i) = \begin{cases} |\mu(ui)|, & \text{if } \mu(ui) > 0 \\ \dfrac{\alpha}{d(u_i)}, & \text{otherwise} \end{cases}$$

We can also combine both degree parameter and the semantic link parameter together to make a more synthetic selection:

$$\varphi(u_i) = \begin{cases} \alpha \dfrac{|\mu(u_i)|}{\sum\limits_j |\mu(u_j)|}, & \text{if } \mu(u_i) > 0 \\ \dfrac{\alpha}{d(u_i)}, & \text{otherwise} \end{cases}$$

We can use this neighbor selection to incorporate many such semantic parameters into the gossip process, making the whole message dissemination more intelligent and scalable.

9.3   Discussion

Structured P2P networks have many advantages such as deterministic and efficient query processing. They also have a controllable network topology and a data management scheme that can be extended to support different high-level applications. Although, structured P2P networks require network maintenance to ensure the consistency of topology and routing process, their high scalability can be leveraged to build large-scale distributed systems in a local and relatively stable networking environment. We can either build a semantic overlay on a structure P2P network for specific application or design a new structured P2P for a semantic overlay to support a real application. The former one focuses on the extensibility and flexibility while the later focuses on the performance. So designers can select a proper way to adopt certain infrastructures that can full fill the future development of an application.

Unstructured P2P networks are inherently robust against failures, node departure and join, and many other dynamic problems. Flooding method is used to broadcast queries among nodes. This feature can be used to build an extremely large network with millions of dynamic users. A semantic overlay network can be built on an unstructured P2P network to support semantic information publishing and querying. Moreover, semantic links can be leveraged to guide the information dissemination more accurately and more efficiently.

In general, P2P techniques provide a scalable network infrastructure that enables us to deploy large-scale knowledge grid services for millions of users. As the cyber physical society quickly develops, we call for such enabling techniques more eagerly than ever before. Wireless networks, sensor networks, mobile networks as well as World Wide Web platform give us many ways to connect more people, devices, and physical world together into an information world where data, service, information and knowledge are integrated to provide an intelligent, ubiquitous, and scalable platform for our daily work and life.

P2P semantic overlay will play an important role in this process by providing a scalable application-level networking infrastructure. These emerging techniques and applications require more underlying research focusing on both performance and functions. The breakthroughs in network topology maintenance, semantic data indexing, complex query processing, privacy, security, and service integration will greatly accelerate the development of the Knowledge Grid environment.

Chapter 10

The Energy-Knowledge Grid

Energy is the most basic force that drives the motion of various individuals (including machines and organisms) and the execution and evolution of various spaces. It is becoming more and more important to save and efficiently use energy for ensuring harmonious development of the complex space consisting of cyber space, physical space and social space.

10.1 The Knowledge Grid Meets the Smart Grid

The cyber space and the energy system developed separately. The development of the cyber space seldom considered the energy issue, the consumption of natural resources, and the impact on the physical space and social space. The development of energy systems seldom considered the impact on the cyber space. The limitation of natural resources requires humans to develop a green society to realize harmonious development of nature and society. So, the development of the cyber space needs to consider the energy issue, and the development of energy systems needs to consider its impact on the nature and society as well as raising the efficiency and efficacy of using energy by making use of the cyber space.

An electrical Grid refers to a vast, interconnected network for delivering electricity from suppliers to consumers supported by the following three main components: power plants; transmission networks for carrying electricity from power plants to demand centers; and, transformers for reducing voltage so that distribution networks carry power for final delivery. Users can get electricity service through simple

475

plug-in without knowing where the power plants are and how electricity is transmitted and scheduled. Grid computing borrowed this idea in realizing on-demand computing services.

The Smart Grid is to provide intelligent, economic, reliable, secure, and sustainable electricity services for all electric power users including suppliers and consumers. It employs monitoring, control, communication, self-healing and information technologies to make better connection and operations of generators; allows consumers to participate in optimizing the operations of the system; provides consumers with diverse choices of supply; and, significantly reduces environmental impact (S.M.Amin and B.F.Wollenberg, Toward a Smart Grid, *IEEE Power & Energy Magazine*, Sept/Oct, (2005)34-41; A.Ipakchi and F.Albuyeh, Grid of the Future, *IEEE Power & Energy Magazine*, March/April, (2009)52-62).

The smart Grid concerns smart management of energy demand and supply, for example, in reducing peak demand, shifting usage time, reducing total energy consumption, arranging electric car charging, and arranging diverse energy resources such as solar, wind, and new green material energy. To implement the smart Grid needs some smart mechanisms, for example, smart meters and appliances, dynamic pricing, real-time energy information feedback, and scheduling of loads.

The smart Grid can be extended to smart rooms, which are expected to detect and understand the behaviors of individuals in rooms through various sensors and pattern recognition, and to provide appropriate services through various appliances (A.P. Pentland, Smart Rooms, *Scientific American*, April, 1996).

Knowledge sharing, knowledge management and knowledge service, which play important roles in raising the efficiency of the electric power Grid by making optimization and intelligent decision in generating, scheduling and using energy, have been neglected in the development of the smart Grid.

Studying the integration of the Knowledge Grid and the Smart Grid can not only promote smart Grid research and Knowledge Grid research but also provide a typical practice for the cyber-physical society as research involves the cyber space, the physical space and the social space.

10.2 Architecture and Characteristics

The Energy-Knowledge Grid upgrades the idea of the smart grid by linking energy systems to the cyber space and the mental space so as to enhance the harmonious development of various spaces through pervasive knowledge sharing and services.

Fig.10.2.1 shows a general architecture of the Energy-Knowledge Grid, where different units (power plants, consumers, transmission and distribution networks, ..., etc.) can know real-time demands and market information through the cyber space, can make prediction, and can make intelligent decisions and operations in planning, generating, scheduling, marketing, and using energy through knowledge sharing and knowledge service.

Each unit can autonomously decide the time and amount of consuming or selling energy according to the assessment of demand and the status of market. The consumers with solar and wind energy generation equipments could get profit by supplying energy based on appropriate market analysis. With the development of renewable energy, more and more consumers will become energy suppliers. The government can make macroscopic development plan considering the statuses of nature, society and economy.

In green society, some manufacturers can sale their wastes to the renewable power plants as resources to gain profit. Farmers can not only use solar energy to support daily life but also can sell agricultural by-product like straw to biomass power plants. It is especially important for the developing countries that have large countryside region and population like China and India.

In addition to electrical services, users can book knowledge services through the Knowledge Grid facilities, which are high-level facilities of the cyber space. The facilities evolve along multiple dimensions as discussed in Chapter 1. Consumers can get knowledge to assist decision and obtain recommendation in time.

The power plants can make decision in real-time on when and how much electricity should be generated, how many resources are needed, according to the demands, market, and impact on the physical space. The transmission and distribution networks can decide in real-time on when and how much electricity should be connected to which stations or consumers, and how much profit they can get.

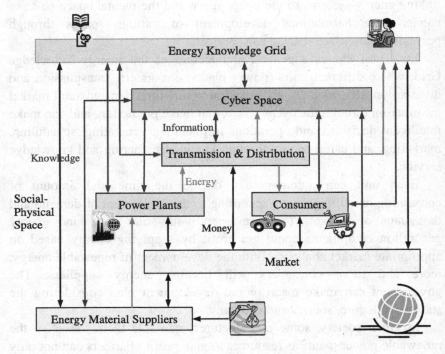

Fig.10.2.1 Architecture of Energy-Knowledge Grid.

The market mechanism is an open platform that supports optimization of energy supply and consumption by publishing real-time energy price and supporting the buy operation and sale operation of energy and resources. The price is determined according to demand, supply and market behaviors.

Different from previous information and knowledge systems, the *Energy-Knowledge Grid knows its energy consumption, economic status, and impact on the physical space and society in real-time and in its whole life cycle*, including development, execution, and maintenance, as shown in Fig.10.2.2.

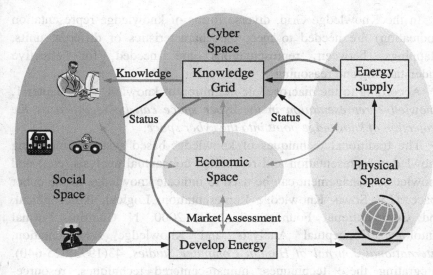

Fig. 10.2.2 Energy-Knowledge Grid.

The Energy-Knowledge Grid will be deployed onto various decentralized smart mechanisms such as smart meters and appliances in offices, homes, cars, and production workshops. It is estimated that there will be 50 billion connected devices by 2020. Users can book and buy various services including knowledge services, and can also obtain certain profit by providing knowledge services for others. The advantages of decentralization include light-weight knowledge and reasoning, rapid response, knowledge protection, collective intelligence, and robustness.

Currently, operations and decisions of the electrical Grid still rely on operators' experience in mind, on documents, and on limited information services, which is difficult to ensure appropriate operations on various situations over time.

The Knowledge Grid can evolve knowledge by interacting with various users, supporting interaction between users, extracting important contents from documents, carrying out analysis, displaying contents from multiple facets, and, linking symbol representations to appropriate points in the physical space and social space including culture and economy.

In the Knowledge Grid, diverse forms of knowledge representation (indication) are needed to meet the characteristics of different units. Mappings between representations are needed for effective understanding and reasoning.

According to the macroscopic definition of knowledge in Chapter 1, *Knowledge representation in the cyber space can be regarded as the projection of knowledge point into the cyber space.*

The traditional techniques of knowledge-based systems (including knowledge representation and reasoning, conceptual analysis, etc.) and knowledge management can be used to indicate knowledge in the cyber space. (J.F. Sowa, Knowledge Representation: Logical, Philosophical, and Computational Foundations, MIT, 2000; N Guarino, Formal Ontology, Conceptual Analysis and Knowledge Representation, *International Journal of Human Computer Studies*, 43(1995)625-640). Integrating these techniques, human-centered techniques, resource-centered techniques and the space notion of knowledge is the right way to indicating knowledge.

Knowledge representation in the cyber space is the process of codifying the projection in the knowledge space, which concerns the following levels:

(1) *Meta rules*, which includes constraints and rules for explaining and operating rules.

(2) *Rules*, which includes event→event (event to event, i.e., if event happens then another event happens) rules, event→action rules, action→action rules, relation→relation rules, relation→action rules, relation→event, concept→concept rules, and concept→action rules.

(3) *Service descriptions*, which include services of various hard devices and soft-devices.

(4) *Semantic link networks*, which can semantically link points in various spaces, or through spaces, e.g., link concepts in the mental space to the statuses in the physical space, to the texts in the symbol space, to the events and values (e.g., economic value) in the social space.

(5) *Classification*, which includes hierarchies of classes.

(6) *Ontology*, which includes commonsense concepts and relations

supporting exchange between various forms of representations and explanations of basic representations.

(7) *Language*, which uses natural language to represent meaning. Natural language is the most effective means for humans to communicate and the basic vehicle to establish consensus and convey knowledge.

Different from previous knowledge-based systems, knowledge representation in this application domain has the following features:

(1) *Relevant to time and space*, including reasoning on time and space.
(2) *Multiple sources*, including communities, homes, manufacturers, and public facilitates, as well as the construction, execution, and maintenance of the whole Grid.
(3) *Multiple spaces*, including physical space, cyber space, and social space. The social space concerns social development, life, well-being, economy, security, culture, etc.
(4) *Multiple media*, including minds, data of various forms, and artifacts, which keep evolving with interactions in various spaces.

The above features determine that knowledge acquisition cannot rely on static representation. Evolution will be the main approach to knowledge acquisition. Knowledge summarization, refinement, verification, and learning are necessary for knowledge evolution.

Fig. 10.2.3 shows the roles of various techniques such as classification, semantic link, summarization and mining in the Energy-Knowledge Grid.

The Resource Space Model helps manage various resources including knowledge by multi-dimensional classifications. Resources should be classified for effective operations (H.Zhuge and Y.Xing, Probabilistic Resource Space Model fro Managing Resources in Cyber-Physical Society, *IEEE Trans. on Service Computing*, http://doi.ieeecomputersociety.org/10.1109/TSC.2011.12).

Isolated data is meaningless, while meaning comes when data is linked to relevant texts in the symbol space, to events in the social space, and to statuses in the physical space, to values in the social space, and to classifications and reasoning in the mental space. The Semantic Link

Network connects different types of resources through spaces to form the context of explanation.

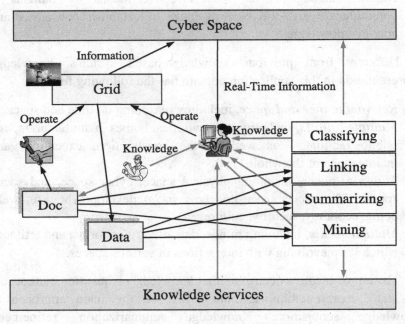

Fig.10.2.3 Techniques used in the Energy-Knowledge Grid.

The text summarization technique can help find the important contents in large-scale documents (R. Barzilay and M. Elhadad, Using Lexical Chains for Text Summarization, *ACL Workshop on Intelligent Scalable Text Summarization*, 1997; R.Barzilay, et al., Information Fusion in the Context of Multi-Document Summarization, ACL *Workshop on Intelligent Scalable Text Summarization*, 1999). The semantic lens with advanced functions will play an important role in facilitating interaction between texts, machines and humans (H.Zhuge, Interactive Semantics, *Artificial Intelligence*, 174(2010)190-204).

The link mining techniques can help find the implicit links within documents and between documents (H. Zhuge and J. Zhang: Automatically constructing semantic link network on documents.

Concurrency and Computation: Practice and Experience, 23(9)(2011) 956-971).

Techniques for discovering centralities and semantic communities can help find the important resources (documents, data, etc) and the semantic communities among resources (H.Zhuge, Communities and Emerging Semantics in Semantic Link Network: Discovery and Learning, *IEEE Transactions on Knowledge and Data Engineering*, 21(6)(2009)785-799).

10.3   Multi-Dimensional Devices and Requirements

An important issue is the representation of various devices and user requirements so that applications can find right devices and devices can cooperate with each other to provide appropriate services. The multi-dimensional classification of the Resource Space Model provides a means for representing and managing devices and requirements from multiple dimensions.

A device can have functions of multiple facets, e.g., a table can be used for holding physical objects such as papers, books, hands, cups, etc. A device can have multi-facet attributes, including physical attributes, chemical attributes, and social attributes. Intelligent devices have rules to take actions when situations are satisfied, e.g., an action of sending an alarm signal or switching on the cooling system will be taken when the distance between two devices are shorter than a safe distance, or when the working temperature is out of the design region.

The following form represents a device, where [...] means by default:

DeviceName (*Dimension₁*, ..., *Dimensionₖ*) {

Attributes:

   PhysicalAttributes: (*attributeName* (*type*): attributeValue)

   ChemicalAttributes: (*attributeName* (*type*): attributeValue)

   SocialAttributes: (*attributeName* (*type*): attributeValue)

   CyberAttributes: (*attributeName* (*type*): attributeValue)

Functions:

Function₁: (*Input, Output, Description*)

......

Function$_n$: (*Input, Output, Description*)
[*Rules:*
Rule$_1$: situation→ action
......
Rule$_n$: situation→ action]
}.

A dimension consists of a subset of attributes, functions and rules. The designer is the best person who knows the functions and rules. WSDL can be used to describe the functions. However, it is difficult to accurately define the semantics of the functions. For domain applications, service modeling is a feasible way (D. Roman, et al., Web Service Modeling Ontology, *Applied Ontology*, 1(1)(2005)), as it is important for users to find and use services. The semantic link networks of functions provide the grounds for modeling functions (H.Zhuge, Semantic linking through spaces for cyber-physical-socio intelligence: A methodology, *Artificial Intelligence*, 175(2011)988-1019).

A user can have multi-dimensional requirements. The basic requirements include daily life (cloth, food, accommodation, etc.), learning, travel, information, and knowledge. Multi-dimensional management of devices and requirements can effectively organize the functions of devices to provide services for users according to their requirements.

The Resource Space Model discussed in Chapter 3 is suitable for managing resources, functions and requirements from multiple dimensions (H.Zhuge, The Web Resource Space Model, Springer, 2008).

With multi-dimensional classifications, one device can serve multiple users, and can serve one user's multi-facet requirements. *Devices can be organized from multiple facets to provide services of multiple facets for users.*

Much work has been done in service computing area (D. Ardagna and B. Pernici, Adaptive Service Composition in Flexible Processes, *IEEE Transactions on Software Engineering*, 33 (6) (2007) 369-384). The techniques such as service description, discovery and composition can be used for references in representing functions and publishing devices on the Web.

Dimensions of devices will be updated with the change of the dimensions of user requirements. So, the management of dimensions is needed to ensure up-to-date consistency between user requirements and services. The relations between dimensions like orthogonal relation can be determined according to the semantics in domain applications. However, knowing the relations between dimensions is not the precondition of using devices.

10.4 Multi-Layer Complex Networks

A Cyber-Physical Society consists of various networks of multiple layers as shown in Fig.10.4. Different networks may follow different rules. The following are important networks, which interact with each other and influence one another:

(1) *Material flow network.* It is formed through the motion and transformation of materials. Water flow, food web and logistic flow are examples of material flow network. Material flow networks are in the physical space, while some are also in the social space, e.g., logistic flow.

(2) *Energy network.* Energy exists in the physical space of different scales, e.g., atomic scale, geological scale and universal scale. Energy transformation networks widely exist in the physical space. The electric energy networks provide energy for driving various devices of the modern society.

(3) *Relation network.* Relation networks in the physical space reflect various physical relations and geographical relations. Relation networks in the social space reflect various social relations between various individuals. Relation networks in the cyber space reflect various relations between digital objects. Relation networks in the mental space reflect various relations between concepts. Emotion and trust propagate through social relation networks to form high-level social architecture.

(4) *Information flow network.* Information reflects the characteristics and statuses of individuals in various spaces. Information flow networks are formed through passing the characteristics and statuses, and evolved with the movement of individuals.

(5) *Knowledge flow network.* Knowledge flow networks exist in the social space and pass through minds and various devices. Those in the mental space are formed through internal linking, reasoning and evolution.

The execution and development of society rely on these networks, which interact and cooperate with each other.   Humans need materials and energy to support their life, and need to communicate with each other to share information and knowledge on these networks.

Knowing these networks and their cooperation enables people to reduce material and energy consumption when making decisions on social behaviors. Changing the locations of events could change energy consumption.

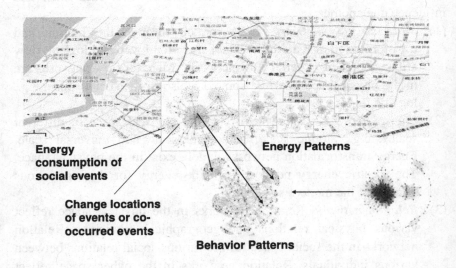

Fig.10.4 Multi-layer cooperative networks.

The motion of individuals and the evolution of networks form various patterns. Some patterns can be detected through the cyber space, for example, human motion patterns can be detected by identifying and tracing the locations of individuals' cell phones. Changing the patterns is an important way to raise social efficiency and reduce energy consumption and material consumption.

Individuals involve in various networks to hold the richness of life in the complex space. Operations like searching in the complex space needs to consider this richness, which leads to more complicated computing than in one space.

The Energy-Knowledge Grid provides new conditions and requirements for studying artificial intelligence and smart Grid as well as typical practice for realizing cyber-physical society by using not only information technology but also physical and social principles.

The following is the definition of the Energy-Knowledge Grid.

The Energy-Knowledge Grid is a set of public facilities that provides appropriate information, knowledge and energy services for devices, agents, and humans to contribute to harmonious development of the complex space consisting of the cyber space, the physical space, and the social space.

Bibliography

Aberer, K., Cudre-Mauroux, P., Hauswirth, M. and Pelt. T.V. (2004). GridVine: Building Internet-Scale Semantic Overlay Networks, *The 3rd International Semantic Web Conference*, LNCS 3298, pp.107-121.

Adamic, L. A. and Huberman, B. A. (2000). Power-law distribution of the World Wide Web, *Science*, 287, No.24, pp.2115.

Aiello, W., Chung, F. and Lu, L. (2000). A random graph model for massive graphs, *Proc. 32nd ACM Symposium on the Theory of Computing*, New York, pp.171-180.

Albert, R., Jeong, H. and Barabási, A. L. (1999). Diameter of the World-Wide Web, *Nature*, 401, pp.130-131.

Albert, R. and Barabási, A. L.(2000). Topology of evolving networks: local events and universality, *Phys. Rev. Lett.*, 85, pp.5234-5237.

Albert, R. and Barabási, A. L. (2002). Statistical mechanics of complex networks, *Rev. Mod. Phys.*, 74, pp.48-94.

Allan, J. (1997). Building hypertext using information retrieval, *Information Processing and Management*, 33, No.2, pp.145-159.

Amaral, L.A.N. et al. (2000). Classes of small-world networks, *Proc. Nat. Acad. Sci.*, 97, No.21, pp.11149-11152.

Androutsellis-Theotokis, S. and Spinellis, D. (2004). A Survey of Peer-to-Peer Content Distribution Technologies, *ACM Computing Surveys*, 36, no. 4, pp. 335-371.

Anthonisse, J. (1971). The Rush in a Graph, *Amsterdam: University of Amsterdam Mathematical Centre*.

Bachman, C. (1972). The Evolution of Storage Structures, Communications of the ACM, 15, No.7, pp.628-634.

Bachman, C. (1973) The Programmer as Navigator. *Communications of the ACM*, 16(11) 653-658.

Bailey. N. T. J. (1975) The Mathematics Theory of Infectious Diseases and Its Applications, second ed. Hafner Press.

Balakrishnan, H. et al. (2003). Looking Up Data in P2P Systems, *Communications of the ACM*, 46, no. 2, pp. 43-48.

Barabási, A. L. and Albert, R. (1999a). Emergence of scaling in random networks, *Science*, 286, pp. 509-512.

Barabási, A. L., Albert, R. and Jeong, H. (1999b). Mean-field theory for scale-free random networks, *Physica A*, 272, pp.173-187.

Barabási, A. L., Jeong, H., Neda, Z., Ravasz, E., Schubert, A. and Vicsek, T. (2002). Evolution of the social network of scientific collaborations, *Physica A*, 311, pp.590-614.

Barabási, A. L. and Bonabeau, E. (2003). Scale-free networks, *Scientific American*, May, pp.50-59.

Barrat, A. and Weigt, M. (2000). On the properties of small-world networks, *Eur. Phys. J. B*, 13, pp.547-560.

Barabasi, A., Jeong, H., Neda, Z., Ravasz, E.. Schubert A., and Vicsek T. (2002). Evolution of the social network of scientific collaborations, *Physica A: Statistical Mechanics and its Applications*, 311, no. 3-4, pp. 590–614.

Batagelj, V. and Mrvar, A. (2000). Some analyses of the erdös collaboration graph, *Social Networks*, 22, pp.173-186.

Batty, C. D. (1966) *An introduction to the Dewey decimal classification. Melbourne*, Cheshire.

Beckmann, N., Kriegel, H. P., Schneider, R. and Seeger, B. (1990) The R* tree: an efficient and robust index method for points and rectangles. In *SIGMOD*, pp322-331.

Beckwith, R., Fellbaum, C., Gross, C. and Miller, G. (1991). WordNet: a lexical database organized on psycholinguistic principles, lexical acquisition: exploiting on-line resources to build a lexicon, U.Zernik, ed., *Lawrence Erlbaum*, pp.211-231.

Berners-Lee, T., Hendler, J. and Lassila, O. (2001). Semantic Web, *Scientific American*, 284, No.5, pp.34-43.

T. Berners-Lee, et al. (2006). A Framework for Web Science, Now Publishers Inc.

Berry, M.W. et al. (1999). Matrices, Vector Spaces, and Information Retrieval, *Society for Industrial and Applied Mathematics Review*, 41, pp.335-362.

Bianconi, G. and Barabási, A. L. (2001a). Bose-Einstein condensation in complex networks, *Phys. Rev. Lett.*, 86, pp.5632-5635.

Bianconi, G. and Barabási, A. L. (2001b). Competition and multiscaling in evolving networks, *Europhys. Lett.*, 54, pp.436-442.

Bocy, R. et al. (1975). Specifying queries as relational expressions, *Communications of the ACM*, 18, No.11, pp.621-628.

Booch, G., Rumbaugh, J. and Jacobson, I. (1999). The unified modeling language: user guide. Reading, Mass. *Addison-Wesley*.

Bornholdt, S. and Ebel, H. (2001). World Wide Web scaling exponent from Simon's 1955 model, *Phys. Rev. E*, 64, 035104(R).

Bonacich, P. (1972). Factoring and weighting approaches to status scores and clique identification, *Journal of Mathematical Sociology*, 2, no. 1, pp. 113–120.

Bradshaw, J. M., Greaves, M. and Holmback, H. (1999). Agents for the masses? *IEEE Intelligent Systems*, 14, No.2, Mar./Apr., pp.53-63.

Broder, A. et al. (2000). Graph structure of the Web, *Proc. of the 9th WWW Conf.*, Amsterdam, May, pp.309-320.

Broekstra, J. et al, (2001). Enabling knowledge representation on the Web by extending RDF schema, *Proc. 10th International WWW Conf.*, Hong Kong, pp.467-478, available at http://www.cs.vu.nl/~frankh/abstracts/www01.html.

Bush, V. (1945). As we may think. *The Atlantic Monthly*, 176, No.1, pp.101-108.

Callaway, D. S. et al. (2001). Are randomly grown graphs really random? *Phys. Rev. E.*, 64, cond-mat/0104546.

Cascia, M. L., Sethi, S. and Sclaroff, S. (1998). Combining textual and visual cues for content-based image retrieval on the worldwide web. *Proc. IEEE Workshop on Content-based Access of Image and Video Libraries*, pp.24-28.

Cass, S. (2004). A fountain of knowledge. *IEEE Spectrum*, 41, No.1, pp.60-67.

Chakrabarti, S., Dom, B., Gibson, D., Kleinberg, J., Raghavan, P. and Rajagopalan, S. (1998). Automatic resource list compilation by analyzing hyperlink structure and associated text, *Proc. 7th International WWW Conf.*, pp.65-74.

Chen, P. (1976) The Entity-Relationship Model: Toward a Unified View of Data, *ACM Transactions on Database Systems*, 1, No.1, pp.9-36.

Chen, Q. et al. (2002). The origin of power laws in Internet topologies revisited, *Proc. of the IEEE INFOCOM Conf.*, pp.608-617.

Clauset, A., Newman, M., and Moore, C. (2004). Finding community structure in very large networks, *Physical Review E*, 70, no. 6, p. 66111.

Codd, E. F. (1970). A relational model of data for large shared data banks, *Communications of the ACM*, 13, No.6, pp.377-387.

Cohen, E., Fiat, A. and Kaplan, H. (2007). Associative search in peer to peer networks: Harnessing latent semantics, *Computer Networks*, 51, no. 8, pp. 1861-1881.

Colizza, V., Flammini, A., Serrano, M., and Vespignani, A. (2006). Detecting rich-club ordering in complex networks, *Arxiv preprint physics/0602134*.

Cortes, C. and Vapnik, V. (1995), Support-Vector Networks. *Machine Learning*, 20(3)(1995) 273-297.

Crespo, A. and Garcia-Molina, H. (2002). Routing Indices for Peer-to-peer Systems, *Proceedings of the 22nd International Conference on Distributed Computing Systems*, pp. 23-32.

Dachselt, R. Frisch, M. Weiland, and M. (2007) FacetZoom: a continuous multi-scale widget for navigating hierarchical metadata, CHI08, 2008, pp.1353-1356.

Dakka, W., Ipeirotis, P.G., and Wood, K.R. (2007) Faceted Browsing over Large Databases of Text-Annotated Objects, ICDE 2007, pp.1489 – 1490.

Davenport, T. H., Jarvenpaa, S. L. and Beer, M. C. (1996). Improving knowledge work process, *Sloan Management Review*, 34, No.4, pp. 53-65.

Davis, G. F. and Greve, H. R. (1997). Corporate élite networks and governance changes in the 1980s, *Am. J. Sociol.*, 103, pp.1-37.

Dean, J. and Henzinger, M. R. (1999). Finding related pages in the World Wide Web, *Proc. 8th International WWW Conf.*, pp.1467-1476.

Decker, S., et al. (2000). The Semantic Web: the roles of XML and RDF, *IEEE Internet Computing*, 4, No. 5, pp.63-74.

Desouza, K. C. (2003). Facilitating tacit knowledge exchange, *Communications of the ACM*, 46, No.6, pp.85-88.

Dieng, R. (2000). Knowledge management and the Internet, *IEEE Intelligent Systems*, 15, No.3, May/June, pp.14-17.

Dorogovtsev, S. N. and Mendes, J. F. F. (2000a). Scaling behavior of developing and decaying networks, *Europhys. Lett.*, 52, pp.33-39.

Dorogovtsev, S. N. and Mendes, J. F. F. (2000b). Evolution of reference networks with aging, *Phys. Rev. E.*, 62, pp.1842-1845.

Dorogovtsev, S. N., Mendes, J. F. F. and Samukhin, A. N. (2000c). Structure of growing networks with preferential linking, *Phys. Rev. Lett.*, 85, pp.4633-4636.

Dorogovtsev, S. N., Mendes, J. F. F. and Samukhin, A. N. (2000d). WWW and Internet models from 1955 till our days and the "popularity is attractive" principle, *Condensed Matter Archive*, cond-mat/0009090.

Dorogovtsev, S. N. and Mendes, J. F. F. (2001). Language as an evolving word Web, *Proc. Royal Soc. London B*, 268, No.2603, cond-mat/0105093.

Drucker, P. F. (1998). Harvard business review on knowledge management, Boston, *Harvard Business School Press*.

Faloutsos, M., Faloutsos, P. and Faloutsos, C. (1999). On power law relationships of the Internet topology, *Comput. Commun. Rev.*, 29, pp.251-262.

Fensel, D., et al. (2001). OIL: an ontology infrastructure for the Semantic Web, *IEEE Intelligent Systems*, 16, No.2, Mar./Apr., pp.38-45.

Ferrer, R., Janssen, C. and Sole, R. V. (2001b). The topology of technology graphs: small-world patterns in electronic circuits, *Phys. Rev.E.*, 64, No.32767.

Ferrer, R. and Sole, R. V. (2001a). The small-world of human language, *Working Papers of Santa Fe Institute*, http://www.santafe.edu/sfi/publications/Abstracts/01-03-004abs.htm.

Franz, T. et al. (2009) TripleRank: Ranking Semantic Web Data by Tensor Decomposition. In *Proceedings of the International Semantic Web Conference*, 2009, pp.213-228.

Freeman, L. (1979), Centrality in social networks: Conceptual clarification, *Social Networks*, 1, no. 3, pp. 215–239.

Freeman, L. (1977). A Set of Measures of Centrality Based on Betweenness, *Sociometry*, 40, no. 1, pp. 35–41.

Fikes, R. and Farquhar, A. (1999). Distributed repositories of highly expressive reusable ontologies, *IEEE Intelligent Systems*, 14, No. 2, Mar/April, pp.73-79.

Fortunato, S., Latora, V., and Marchiori, M. (2004). Method to find community structures based on information centrality, *Physica Review E*, 70, no. 5, p. 56104.

Foster, I. (2000). Internet computing and the emerging Grid, 408, No.6815, *Nature*, http://www.nature.com/nature/webmatters/grid/grid.html.

Foster, I., Kesselman, C., Nick, J. M. and Tuecke, S. (2002). Grid services for distributed system integration, *Computer*, 35, pp.37-46.

Ganesan, P. Bawa, M. and Garcia-Molina, H. (2004) Online Balancing of Range-Partitioned Data with Applications to Peer-to-Peer Systems. *VLDB '04*. pp.444-455.

Gevers, T. and Smeulders, A. W. M. (1999). The PicToSeek WWW image search system, *Proc. IEEE International Conf. on Multimedia Computing and Systems*, pp.264-269.

Girvan, M. and Newman, M. (2002). Community structure in social and biological networks, *Proceedings of the National Academy of Sciences*, 99, no. 12, p. 7821.

Goldberg, A. (1984). SMALLTALK-80: the interactive programming environment, Addison-Wesley Longman Publishing Co., Inc. Boston, MA, USA.

Gong, L. (2001). JXTA: a network programming environment, *IEEE Internet Computing*, 5, no.3, pp.88-95.

Gorlitz, O., Sizov, S. and Staab, S. (2008). PINTS: Peer-to-Peer Infrastructure for Tagging Systems, *The 7th International Workshop on Peer-to-Peer Systems*.

Govindan, R. and Tangmunarunkit, H. (2000). Heuristics for Internet map discovery, *Proc. of the IEEE INFOCOM Conf.*, Tel Aviv, Israel, March, pp.1371-1380.

Gray, J. (2003). What next? A dozen information-technology research goals, *Journal of the ACM*, 50, No.1, pp.41-57.

Green, S. J. (1999). Building hypertext links by computing semantic similarity, *IEEE Trans. On Knowledge and Data Engineering*, 11, No.5, pp.713-730.

Grosz, B. J. and Kraus, S. (1996). Collaborative plans for complex group action, *Artificial Intelligence*, 86, pp.269-357.

Gupta, A. and Jain, R. (1997). Visual information retrieval, *Communications of the ACM*, 40, No.5, pp.71-79.

Gyssens, M .et al., (1994). A graph-oriented object database model, *IEEE Transactions on Knowledge and Data Engineering*, 6, No.4, pp.572-586.

Han, J. and Kambr, M. (2000). Data mining: concepts and techniques, *Morgan Kaufmann Publishers*.

Haridasan, M. and Renesse, R. (2008). Gossip-based Distribution Estimation in Peer-to-Peer Networks, *the 7th International Workshop on Peer-to-Peer Systems*.

Harmandas, V., Sanderson, M. and Dunlop, M. D. (1997). Image retrieval by hypertext links. *Proc. 20th Annual International ACM SIGIR Conf. on Research and Development in Information Retrieval*, pp.296-303.

Hammer, M. and McLeod, D. (1978) The Semantic Data Model: A Modeling Mechanism for Database Applications, *SIGMOD78*, pp.26-36.

Havil, J. and Dyson, F. (2003). The Harmonic Series, Chapter.2 in Gamma: Exploring Euler's Constant. *Princeton, NJ: Princeton University Press*.

Heflin, J. and Hendler, J. (2001). A portrait of the Semantic Web in action, *IEEE Intelligent Systems*, 16, No.2, Mar./Apr., pp.54-59.

Hendler, J and McGuinness, D. (2000). The DARPA agent markup language, *IEEE Intelligent Systems*, 15, No.6, Nov./Dec., pp.72-73.

Hendler, J. (2001). Agents and the Semantic Web, *IEEE Intelligent Systems*, 16, No.2, Mar./Apr., pp.30-37.

Henzinger, M. R. (2001). Hyperlink analysis for the Web, *IEEE Internet Computing*, 5, No.1, Jan./Feb., pp.45-50.

Heylighen, F. (1992). A Cognitive-systemic reconstruction of maslow's theory of self-actualization, *Behavioral Science*, 37, pp.39-58.

Huberman, B. A. and Adamic, L. A. (1999). Growth dynamics of the World-Wide Web, *Nature*, 401, 131p.

Huynh D.F. and Karger D.R. (2009). Parallax and companion: Set-based browsing for the data web, WWW09, pp.145-156.

Jeong, H., Tombor, B., Albert, R., Oltvai, Z. N., Barabási, A. L. (2000). The large-scale organization of metabolic networks, *Nature*, 407, pp.651-654.

Jeong, H. Neda, Z. and Barabási, A. L. (2003). Measuring preferential attachment for evolving networks, *Europhysics letters*, 61, pp.567-572.

Kanth, K., Agrawal, D. and Singh, A. (1998). Dimensionality reduction for similarity searching in dynamic databases, *Proc. ACM SIGMOD International Conf. on Management of Data*, 75, pp.166-176.

Kaashoek, M. F. and Karger and Koorde, D. R. (2003). A Simple Degree-Optimal Distributed Hash Table. *Proceeding of International Workshop on Peer-to-Peer Systems (IPTPS)*. (2003)98-107.

Kee, K.-P., Swearingen, K., Li, K. and Hearst, M. (2003). Faceted metadata for image search and browsing, CHI03' *Proceedings of the SIGCHI Conference on Human Factors in Computing Systems*, 2003, April 5-10, 2003, Florida, USA.

Kermarrec, A.M., Massoulié, L. and Ganesh, A.J. (2003). Probabilistic Reliable Dissemination in Large-scale Systems, *IEEE Transactions on Parallel and Distributed Systems*, 14, no. 3, pp. 248-258.

Klein, M. (2001). XML, RDF, and relatives, *IEEE Internet Computing*, 16, No.2, Mar./Apr., pp.26-28.

Kleinberg, J. M. (1999). Authoritative sources in a hyperlinked environment. *Journal of the ACM*, 46, No.5, pp.604-632.

Kleinberg, J and Lawrence, S. (2001). The structure of the Web, *Science*, 294, No.5548, pp.1849-1850.

Kleinberg, J. (2001) Small-World Phenomena and the Dynamics of Information, *Proceeding of Advances in Neural Information Processing Systems* (NIPS) 14, pp.431-415.

Krapivsky, P. L. Redner, S. and Leyvraz, F. (2000). Connectivity of growing random networks, *Phys. Rev. Lett.*, 1.85, pp.4629-4632.

Krapivsky, P. L. and Redner, S. (2001a). Organization of growing random networks, *Phys. Rev. E.*, 63, cond-mat/0011094.

Krapivsky, P. L., Rodgers, G. J. and Redner, S. (2001b). Degree distributions of growing networks, *Phys. Rev. Lett.*, 86, pp.5401-5404.

Krapivsky, P. L. and Redner, S. (2002). A statistical physics perspective on Web growth, *Computer Networks*, 39, pp.261-276.

Kumar, R. et al. (1999). Extracting large-scale knowledge bases from the Web, *Proc. 25th VLDB Conf.*, Edinburgh, Scotland, September, pp.639-650.

Larry, P., Sergey, B., Motwani, R. *et al.* (1998). The PageRank citation ranking: Bringing order to the web, *Online: http://citeseer. nj.Nec com/page98pagerank. html [04.06. 2003]*.

Latora, V. and Marchiori, M. (2004). A measure of centrality based on the network efficiency, *Arxiv preprint cond-mat/0402050*.

Lawrence, S. and Giles, C. L. (1998). Searching the World Wide Web, *Science*, 280, No.5360, pp.98-100.

Lawrence, S. and Giles, C. L. (1999). Accessibility of information on the Web, *Nature*, 400, No.8, pp.107-109.

Lazer, D. et al. (2009), Computational social science, *Science*, 323, no.5915, pp.721-723.

Lee, S., Yook, S., and Kim, Y. (2009). Centrality measure of complex networks using biased random walks, *The European Physical Journal B*, 68, no. 2, pp. 277–281.

Leland, W. E. et al. (1994). On the self-similar nature of Ethernet traffic, *IEEE/ACM Transactions on Networking*, 2, no.1, pp.1-15.

Lempel, R. and Moran, S. (2000). The stochastic approach for link-structure analysis (SALSA) and the TKC effect. *Proc. 9th International WWW Conf.*, pp.387-401.

Lempel, R. and Soffer, A. (2001). PicASHOW: pictorial authority search by hyperlinks on the Web, *Proc. 10th International WWW Conf.*, pp.438-448.

Levene, M., Fenner, T., Loizou, G. and Wheeldon, R. (2002). A stochastic model for the evolution of the Web, *Computer Networks*, 39, pp.277-287.

Leymann, F. and Roller, D. (1997). Workflow-based applications, *IBM Systems Journal*, 36, No.1, pp.102-122.

Licklider, J.C.R. (1960). Man-Computer Symbiosis, Transactions on Human Factors in Electronics, vol. HFE-1, pp.4–11, March.

Lieberman, H. (2008). A Creative Programming Environment, in HCI Remixed, T.Erickson and D.W.McDonald (Ed).

B. Libet, Mind Time, Harvard University Press, 2005.

Liu, Z. Q. and Satur, R. (1999). Contextual fuzzy cognitive maps for decision support in geographic information systems, *IEEE Transactions on Fuzzy Systems*, 7, No.10, pp.495-502.

Mack, R., Ravin, Y. and Byrd, R. J. (2001). Knowledge portals and the emerging knowledge workplace, *IBM Systems Journal*, 40, No. 4, pp. 925-955.

Maedche, A. and Staab, S. (2001). Ontology learning for the Semantic Web, *IEEE Intelligent Systems*, 16, No.2, Mar./Apr., pp.72-79.

Malkhi, D., Naor, M. and Ratajczak, D. (2002). Viceroy: A Scalable and Dynamic Emulation of the Butterfly. *Proceeding of the 21st ACM SIGACT-SIGOPS Symposium on Principles of Distributed Computing* (PODC '02), pp.183-192.

Manku, G. Bawa, M. and Raghavan, P. Symphony, (2003), Distributed Hashing in a Small World. *Proceeding of the 4th USENIX Symposium on Internet Technologies and Systems*, pp.10-22.

Marchionini, G., Dwiggins, S., Katz, A. and Lin, X. (1990). Information roles of domain and search expertise, *Library and Information Science Research*, 15, no.1, pp.391-407.

Martin, P. and Eklund, P. W. (2000). Knowledge retrieval and the World Wide Web, *IEEE Intelligent Systems*, 15, no.3, May/June, pp. 18-25.

Martinez, N. D. (1991). Artifacts or attributes? Effects of resolution on the Little Rock Lake food web, *Ecological Monographs*, 61, pp.367-392.

Maybury, M. (2001). Collaborative virtual environments for analysis and decision support, *Communication of the ACM*, 14, no.12, pp. 51-54.

McCreight, E. M. (1976) A Space-Economical Suffix Tree Construction Algorithm. *Journal of ACM*, 23, no.2, pp. 262-272.

McHraith, S. A., Son, T. C. and Zeng, H. (2001). Semantic Web services, *IEEE Intelligent Systems*, 16, No.2, Mar./Apr., pp. 46-53.

Miao, Y., et al. (2001). Dynamic cognitive network, *IEEE Transactions on Fuzzy System*, 9, no.5, pp. 760-770.

Milgram, S. (1967) The Small World Problem. *Psychology Today*, 1, no.61.

Milo, R., Shen-Orr, S., Itzkovitz, S., Kashtan, N., Chklovskii, D., and Alon, U. (2002). Network Motifs: Simple Building Blocks of Complex Networks, pp. 824–827.

Mitri, M. (2003). Applying tacit knowledge management techniques for performance assessment, *Computers & Education*, 4, pp.173-189.

Mok, W.Y. (2002). A comparative study of various nested normal forms, *IEEE Trans. on Knowledge and Data Engineering*, 14, no.2, pp. 369-385.

Nasukawa, T. and Nagano, T. (2001). Text analysis and knowledge mining system, *IBM Systems Journal*, 40, no. 4, pp. 967-984.

Nejdl, W. et al. (2002). Edutella: a P2P Networking Infrastructure Based on RDF, *Proceedings of the 11th International Conference on World Wide Web*, pp. 604-615.

Newman, M. E. J. et al.(2001a). Random graphs with arbitrary degree distribution and their applications", *Phys. Rev. E*, 64, no.026118, cond-mat/0007235.

Newman, M. E. J. (2001b). The structure of scientific collaboration networks, *Proc. Nat. Acad. Sci. U.S.A.*, 98, pp.404-409.

Newman, M. E. J. (2001c). Scientific collaboration networks: I. Network construction and fundamental results, *Phys. Rev. E*, 64, No.016131.

Newman, M. E. J. (2001d). Scientific collaboration networks: II. Shortest paths, weighted networks, and centrality, *Phys. Rev. E*, 64, No.016132.

Newman, M. E. J. (2001e). Who is the best connected scientist? A study of scientific coauthorship networks, *Phys. Rev. E,* 64, No.016131.

Newman, M.(2004). Analysis of weighted networks, *Physical Review E,* 70, no. 5.

Ng, W.S. et al. (2003). PeerDB: A P2P-Based system for distributed data sharing, *Proc. of International Conf. on Data Engineering,* ICDE2003, Bangalore, India.

Nieminen, J. (1974). On the centrality in a graph, *Scandinavian Journal of Psychology,* 15, no. 1, pp. 332–336, 1974.

Nissen, M. E. (2002). An extended model for knowledge-flow dynamics, *Communications of the Associations for Information Systems,* 8, pp. 251-266.

Nonaka, I. (1994). A dynamic theory of organizational knowledge creation, *Organization Science,* 5, No.1, pp. 14-37.

Nowak, M. A. Komarova, N. L., and Niyogi, P., Computational and Evolutionary Aspects of Language, *Nature,* 417(2002)611-617.

Oida, K. (2002). The birth and death process of hypercycle spirals, in: R.K. Standish, M.A. Bedau, H.A. Abbass, edd., Artificial Life VIII, *MIT Press.*

Oren, E., Delbru R. and Decker, S. (2006). Extending Faceted Navigation for RDF Data, ISWC2006, pp.559-572.

O'Leary, D. E. (1998). Enterprise knowledge management, *Computer,* 31, no.3, pp.54-61.

O'Neil, P. O'Neil, E. Pal, S. Cseri, E. and Schaller, G. (2004), ORDPATHs: Insert-Friendly XML Node Labels, *SIGMOD,* pp. 903-908.

Ozsoyoglu, Z. M. and Yuan, L. Y. (1987). A new normal form for nested relations, *ACM Trans. Database Systems,* 12, no.1, pp.111-136.

Pansiot, J. J. and Grad, D. (1998). On routes and multicast trees in the Internet, *Computer Communications Review,* 28, pp.41-50.

Parise, S. and Henderson, J. C. (2001). Knowledge resource exchange in strategic alliances, *IBM Systems Journal,* 40, no. 4, pp.908-924.

Peltz, C. (2003). Web Services Orchestration and Choreography, *Computer,* 36, no.10, pp. 46-52

Perra, N. and Fortunato, S. (2008). Spectral centrality measures in complex networks, *Physical Review E,* vol. 78, no. 3, pp. 036107.

Pittel, B. On Spreading a Rumor, (1987). *SIAM Journal of Applied Mathematics,* 47, no. 1, pp. 213-223.

Raman, V. and Hellerstein (2001), J. M. Potter's wheel: An interactive data cleaning system, *VLDB2001,* Roma, Italy.

Ratnasamy, S. et al. (2001). A Scalable Content-addressable Network, *ACM SIGCOMM Symposium on Communication, Architecture, and Protocol,* pp.161-172.

Redner, S. (1998). How popular is your paper? An empirical study of the citation distribution, *European Physics Journal B,* 4, pp.131-134.

Renesse, R. V., Minsky, Y. and Hayden, M. (1998). A Gossip-style Failure Detection Service, *Middleware98: IFIP International Conference, Distributed Systems and Platforms and Open Distributed Processing,* pp. 55-70.

Ritter, F. E., Baxter, G. E., Jones, G and Young, R.M. (2000). Supporting cognitive models as users, *ACM Trans. on Computer-Human Interaction*, 7, no.2, pp.141-173.

Robertson, S., Walker, S., and Beaulieu, M. (1998). Okapi at TREC-7: Automatic ad hoc, filtering, VLC and interactive. *Proceedings of the 7th text retrieval conference (TREC-7)*, NIST special publication, pages 500–242.

Rowstron, A. and Druschel, P. (2001). Pastry: Scalable, Distributed Object Location and Routing for Large-scale Peer-to-Peer Systems, *International Conference on Distributed Systems Platforms*, pp. 329-350.

Sabidussi, G.(1966). The centrality index of a graph, *Psychometrika*, 31, no. 4, pp. 581–603, 1966.

Simon, H. A. (1955). On a class of skew distribution functions, *Biometrika*, 42, pp.425-440.

Simon, H. A. and Van Wormer, T. (1963). Some Monte Carlo estimates of the Yule distribution, *Behavioral Sci.*, 8, pp.203-210.

Srihari, R. K., Zhang, Z. and Rao, A. (2000). Intelligent indexing and semantic retrieval of multimodel documents, *Information Retrieval*, 2, no.2, pp. 245-275.

Stoica, I. et al., (2003). Chord: A scalable Peer-to-Peer lookup protocol for Internet applications, *IEEE/ACM Transactions on Networking*, 11, pp. 17–32.

Sun, X. (2010), OSLN: An Object-Oriented Semantic Link Network language for complex object description and operation. *Future Generation Computer Systems*, 26, no.3, pp.389-399

Tari, Z., Stokes, J. and Spaccapietra, S. (1997). Object normal forms and dependency constraints for object-oriented schemata, *ACM Trans. Database Systems*, 22, no.4, pp.513-569.

Tatarinov, I. et al. (2003). The Piazza Peer Data Management Project, *SIGMOD Record*, 32, no. 3, pp. 47-52.

Tempich, C., Staab, S. and Wranik. A. (2004). REMINDIN': Semantic Query Routing in Peer-to-Peer Networks Based on Social Metaphors, *Proceedings of the 13th international conference on World Wide Web*, pp. 640-649.

Thistlewaite, P. (1997). Automatic construction and management of large open Webs, *Information Processing and Management*, 33, no.2, pp. 145-159.

Thomas, J. C., Kellogg, W. A. and Erickson, T. (2001). The knowledge management puzzle: Human and social factors in knowledge management, *IBM Systems Journal*, 40, no. 4, pp.863-884.

Tudhope, D. and Taylor, C. (1997). Navigation via similarity: automatic linking based on semantic closeness, *Information Processing and Management*, 33, no.2, pp.233-242.

Turing, A.M. (1950). Computing machinery and intelligence, *Mind*, vol.59, no.236, pp.433-460.

Ullman, J. D. (1988). Principles of database and knowledge-base systems, *Computer Science Press, Inc.*,

Valverde, S., Cancho, R. F. and Sole, R. V. (2002). Scale-free networks from optimal design, *Europhysics Letters*, 60, pp.512-517.

W. Vogels, R. V. Renesse, and K. Birman. (2003) The Power of Epidemics: Robust Communication for Large-Scale Distributed Systems. *ACM SIGCOMM Computer Communication Review*. 33, no.1, pp.131-135.

Warshall, S.(1962). A theorem on boolean matrices, *J. ACM*, 9, no. 1, pp. 11–12.

Wasserman, S. and Faust, K. (1994). *Social Network Analysis: Methods and Applications*. Cambridge University Press.

Watts, D. J. and Strogatz, S. H. (1998). Collective dynamics of "Small-world" networks, *Nature*, 393, pp.440-442.

Watts, D. J. (1999). Networks, dynamics, and the small-world phenomenon, *Am. J. Sociol.*, 105, pp.493-592.

Wilks, Y. Is There Progress on Talking Sensibly to Machines? *Science*, 5852(318)927-928.

Yang, B. and Garcia-Molina, H. (2002). Efficient Search in Peer-to-peer Networks, *International Conference on Distributed Computing Systems*, pp.5-14.

Yook, S. H. et al. (2002). Modeling the Internet's large-scale topology, *Proc. the National Academy of Sciences*, pp. 13382-13386, cond-mat/0107417.

Zeng Q., Jiang X. and Zhuge, H. (2012). Adding logical operators to tree pattern queries on graph-structured data, *VLDB* 2012.

Zhao, B. Y., Kubiatowicz, J.D. and Joseph, A.D. (2001). Tapestry: An Infrastructure for Fault-resilient Wide-area Location and Routing, Technical Report UCB/CSD-01-1141, U.C.Berkeley.

Zhu, Y. W., Wang, H. and Hu, Y. M. (2003). Integrating Semantic-Based Access Mechanisms with Peer-to-Peer File System, *Proceedings of the 3rd International Conference on Peer-to-Peer Computing*, pp. 118-125.

Zhuge, H. (1998). Inheritance rules for flexible model retrieval, *Decision Support Systems*, 22, no.4, pp. 383-394.

Zhuge, H. (2000a). Conflict decision training through multi-space co-operation, *Decision Support Systems*, 29, no. 5, pp.111-123.

Zhuge, H., Cheung, T. Y. and Pung, H. K. (2000b). A timed workflow process model, *Journal of Systems and Software*, 55, no.3, pp.231-243.

Zhuge, H. (2002a). A Knowledge Grid model and platform for global knowledge sharing, *Expert Systems with Applications*, 22, no.4, pp.313-320.

Zhuge, H. (2002b). A knowledge flow model for peer-to-peer team knowledge sharing and management, *Expert Systems with Applications*, 23, no.1, pp.23-30.

Zhuge, H. (2002c). Clustering soft-device in the Semantic Grid, *IEEE Computing in Science and Engineering*, 4, no.6, Nov./Dec., pp.60-62.

Zhuge, H. (2003b). China e-science Knowledge Grid Environment, *IEEE Intelligent Systems*, 19, No.1, Sep./Oct., pp. 13-17.

Zhuge, H. (2003c). Workflow-based cognitive flow management for distributed team cooperation, *Information and Management*, 40, no.5, pp.419-429.

Zhuge, H. (2003d). Active e-Document Framework ADF: model and tool, *Information and Management*, 41, no.1, pp. 87-97.

Zhuge, H. and Shi, X. (2003e). Fighting epistemology in knowledge and information age, *Computer*, 36, no.10, pp.114-116.

Zhuge, H. (2004a). Resource Space Model, its design method and applications, *Journal of Systems and Software*, 72, no.1, pp. 71-81.

Zhuge, H. (2004b). Semantics, resources and Grid, *Future Generation Computer Systems*, Special issue on *Semantic Grid and Knowledge Grid: the Next-generation Web*, editorial, 20, no.1, pp.1-5.

Zhuge, H. (2004c). Fuzzy resource space model and platform, *Journal of Systems and Software*, 73, no.3, pp.389-396.

Zhuge, H. (2004d). Resource Space Grid: model, method and platform, *Concurrency and Computation: Practice and Experience*, 16, no.13.

Zhuge, H. (2004e). Retrieve images by understanding semantic links and clustering image fragments, *Journal of Systems and Software*, 73, no.3, pp.455-466.

Zhuge, H. (2004f). Toward the eco-grid: a harmoniously evolved interconnection environment, *Communications of the ACM*, 47, no.9, pp.78-83.

Zhuge, H. (2004g). Semantics, Resource and Grid, *Future Generation Computer Systems*, 20, no.1, pp.1-5.

Zhuge, H. (2005a). The Future Interconnection Environment, *IEEE Computer*, 38, no.4, pp.27-33.

Zhuge, H. (2005b). Exploring an Epidemic in an E-Science Environment, *Communications of the ACM*, 48, no.9, pp.109-114.

Zhuge, H. et al. (2005c), Query Routing in a Peer-to-Peer Semantic Link Network *Computational Intelligence*, 21, no. 2, pp. 197–216.

Zhuge, H. (2005d). Semantic Grid: Scientific Issues, Infrastructure, and Methodology. *Communications of the ACM*, 48, no.4, pp.117-119.

Zhuge, H., Sun, X., Liu, J., Yao, E. and Chen, X., (2005). A Scalable P2P Platform for the Knowledge Grid, *IEEE Transactions on Knowledge and Data Engineering*, 17, no.12, pp.1721-1736.

Zhuge, H. (2006). Discovery of Knowledge Flow in Science, *Communications of the ACM*, 49, no. 5, pp. 101-107.

Zhuge, H. (2007). Autonomous Semantic Link Networking Model for the Knowledge Grid, *Concurrency and Computation: Practice and Experience*, no.19, pp.1065–1085.

Zhuge H. and Li, X. (2007), Peer-to-Peer in Metric Space and Semantic Space, *IEEE Transactions on Knowledge and Data Engineering*, 19, no. 6, pp. 759–771.

Zhuge H. and Feng, L. (2008), Distributed Suffix Tree Overlay for Peer-to-Peer Search, *IEEE Transactions on Knowledge and Data Engineering*, 20, no.2, pp.276–285.

Zhuge, H. (2008). The Knowledge Grid Environment, *IEEE Intelligent Systems*, 23, no. 6, pp.63-71.

Zhuge, H. and Sun, X. (2008). A Virtual Ring Method for Building Small-World Structured P2P Overlays, *IEEE Transactions on Knowledge and Data Engineering*, 20, no.12, pp.1712-1725.

Zhuge, H. Xing, Y.and Shi, P. (2008). Resource Space Model, OWL and Database: Mapping and Integration, *ACM Transactions on Internet Technology*, 8, no.4.

Zhuge, H., Chen, X., Sun, X. and Yao, E. (2008), HRing: A Structured P2P Overlay Based on Harmonic Series, *IEEE Transactions on Parallel and Distributed Systems*, 19, no.2, pp.145-158.

Zhuge, H. and Feng, L. (2008). Distributed Suffix Tree Overlay for Peer-to-Peer Search, *IEEE Transactions on Knowledge and Data Engineering*, 20, no.2, pp.276-285.

Zhuge, H. (2009), Communities and Emerging Semantics in Semantic Link Network: Discovery and Learning, *IEEE Transactions on Knowledge and Data Engineering*, 21, no.6, pp.785-799.

Zhuge, H. and Sun, Y. (2010) The schema theory for semantic link network. *Future Generation Computer Systems*, 26, no.3, pp. 408-420.

Zhuge, H. (2010) Interactive Semantics, *Artificial Intelligence*, 174, no.2, pp.190-204.

Zhuge, H. (2011) Semantic linking through spaces for cyber-physical-socio intelligence: A methodology, *Artificial Intelligence*, 175, pp.988-1019.

Index